lonely

D0454151

# Jamaica

**Negril & West Coast**
p137

**Montego Bay & Northwest Coast**
p108

**Ocho Rios, Port Antonio & North Coast**
p75

**South Coast & Central Highlands**
p156

**Kingston, Blue Mountains & Southeast Coast**
p40

Paul Clammer, Anna Kaminski

# Contents

WESTEND61 / GETTY IMAGES ©

GREG DAVID / 500PX ©

MONTEGO BAY P109

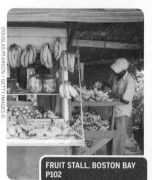
DOUGLAS PEARSON / GETTY IMAGES ©

FRUIT STALL, BOSTON BAY P102

BLUE LAGOON, PORT ANTONIO P98

# Contents

# Welcome to Jamaica

*Jamaica is the Caribbean country that comes with its own soundtrack. Groove to its singular rhythm as you explore beyond the beaches and all-inclusives.*

## Jah's Garden

Even in a region as crammed with jewels as the Caribbean, Jamaica is a powerfully beautiful island. Jamaica begins with crystalline waters flowing over gardens of coral, lapping onto soft sandy beaches, then rises past red soil and lush banana groves into sheer mountains. Rushing waterfalls seem to erupt out of nowhere. Jamaican culture can be a daunting subject for foreigners to understand, but ultimately it's a matter of appreciating this great green garden of a land and how its cyclical rhythms set the pace of so much island life.

## Adventure Playground

While Jamaica's beaches are certainly alluring, this is a country to dive into, literally and figuratively. Beneath the waves there's great scuba diving and snorkeling, and you can float on the water too with lazy bamboo-raft trips (let someone else pole). The adventurous can go caving, or get their hiking boots on to explore the remote crags and forests of this crumpled landscape. You don't even need to be as fit as Usain Bolt to enjoy the hike through lush mountains to the top of Blue Mountain Peak.

## Island Riddims

With Bob Marley, Jamaica gifted us the first global superstar from the developing world. But he didn't spring from nowhere – this tiny island has musical roots that reach back to the folk songs of West Africa and forward to the electronic beats of contemporary dancehall. Simply put, Jamaica is a musical powerhouse, a fact reflected not just in the bass of the omnipresent sound systems, but in the lyricism of the patois language and the gospel sounds from the island's many churches. Music is life in Jamaica, and you'll soon find yourself swaying along with it.

## Caribbean Flavors

Like many aspects of Jamaican culture, the food is a creole, born somewhere between the Old and New Worlds. African spice rubs have evolved into delicious jerk, while yam, rice and plantain form the basis of rich stews, and fish abound in local waters. Throw in the astounding array of tropical fruits that seem to drip from the trees, washed down with a shot of rum, and you can see (and taste) how the Jamaican cultural story retains its original voice while adapting to the setting – and of course, rhythms – of the Caribbean.

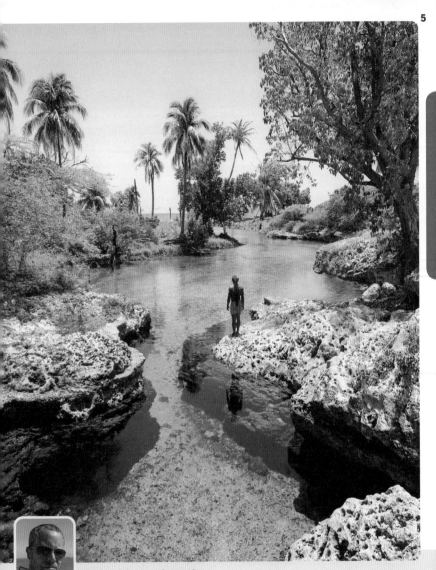

## Why I Love Jamaica

By Paul Clammer, Writer

It's the spicy plate of jerk washed down with a cold Red Stripe beer. No, it's the giant speakers of a sound system blasting out dub reggae after dark, while the DJ cues up the next track on his decks stationed under a mango tree. No, the Rastafari street art in a downtown Kingston neighborhood. It's the cheeky tour guide at the waterfalls getting the tour group to strike Usain Bolt's lightning pose. It's getting lost in Maroon country and sunsets over the sea. What, you wanted only *one* thing I love about Jamaica? Wait, let me try again...

**For more about our writers, see p224**

Above: Black River (p166)

# Jamaica

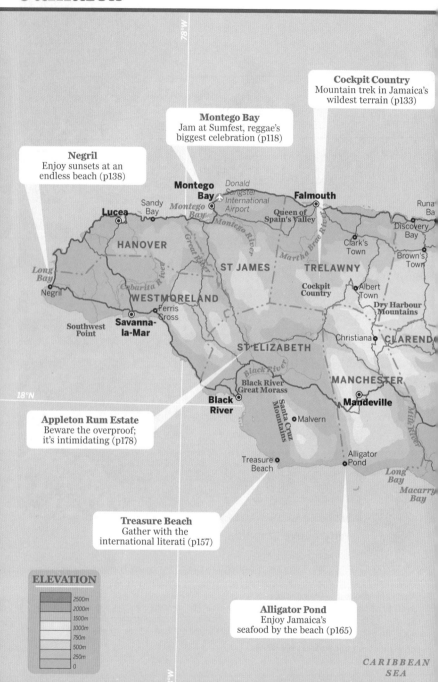

**Cockpit Country**
Mountain trek in Jamaica's
wildest terrain (p133)

**Montego Bay**
Jam at Sumfest, reggae's
biggest celebration (p118)

**Negril**
Enjoy sunsets at an
endless beach (p138)

**Appleton Rum Estate**
Beware the overproof;
it's intimidating (p178)

**Treasure Beach**
Gather with the
international literati (p157)

**Alligator Pond**
Enjoy Jamaica's
seafood by the beach (p165)

**ELEVATION**

| | |
|---|---|
| | 2500m |
| | 2000m |
| | 1500m |
| | 1000m |
| | 750m |
| | 500m |
| | 250m |
| | 0 |

*CARIBBEAN
SEA*

Montego
Bay

*Donald
Sangster
International
Airport*

Falmouth

Lucea

Sandy
Bay

*Montego
Bay*

Queen of
Spain's Valley

Runa
Ba

Discovery
Bay

*Great River*

*Montego River*

*Martha Brae River*

Clark's
Town

Brown's
Town

HANOVER

ST JAMES

TRELAWNY

*Long
Bay*

*Cabarita River*

WESTMORELAND

**Cockpit
Country**

Albert
Town

**Dry Harbour
Mountains**

Negril

Ferris
Cross

Christiana

CLAREND

**Southwest
Point**

**Savanna-
la-Mar**

ST ELIZABETH

MANCHESTER

18°N

*Black River*

**Black River
Great Morass**

**Mandeville**

**Black
River**

*Santa
Cruz
Mountains*

Malvern

Treasure
Beach

Alligator
Pond

*Long
Bay*

*Macarry
Bay*

78°W

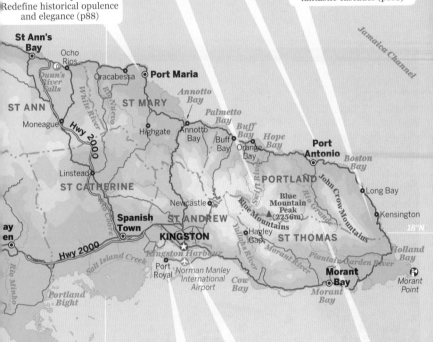

**N** 0 ___ 50 km
0 ___ 25 miles

**Blue Lagoon**
Dive through the
famous Blue Hole (p98)

**Blue Mountain Peak**
Feel exhilarated at Jamaica's
best sunrise (p72)

**Reach Falls**
Slide down these
fantastic cascades (p103)

**Firefly**
Redefine historical opulence
and elegance (p88)

St Ann's
Bay
Ocho
Rios
Dunn's
River
Falls
Oracabessa
**Port Maria**

ST ANN
Moneague
*White River*
*Rio Nuevo*
**ST MARY**
*Annotto Bay*
*Palmetto Bay*
Highgate
Annotto Bay
Buff Bay
*Buff Bay*
Orange Bay
*Hope Bay*
**Port Antonio**
*Boston Bay*
*Jamaica Channel*

Hwy 2000
Linstead
**ST CATHERINE**
Newcastle
*Swift River*
**PORTLAND**
Blue Mountain Peak (2256m)
*Rio Grande*
*John Crow Mountains*
Long Bay
Kensington
18°N

Spanish Town
**ST ANDREW**
**KINGSTON**
*Blue Mountains*
Hagley Gap
*Yallahs River*
**ST THOMAS**
*Morant River*
*Plantain Garden River*
Holland Bay

ay en
*Rio Minho*
Hwy 2000
*Salt Island Creek*
Kingston Harbour
Port Royal
Norman Manley International Airport
*Cow Bay*
**Morant Bay**
*Morant Bay*
Morant Point

*Portland Bight*

*Portland Point*

**Port Royal**
Follow in pirate Henry
Morgan's footsteps (p61)

**Kingston**
Dance till dawn at a
pumping street jam (p41)

**Rio Grande**
Pole through tranquil
riverine jungle (p106)

# Jamaica's
# Top 15

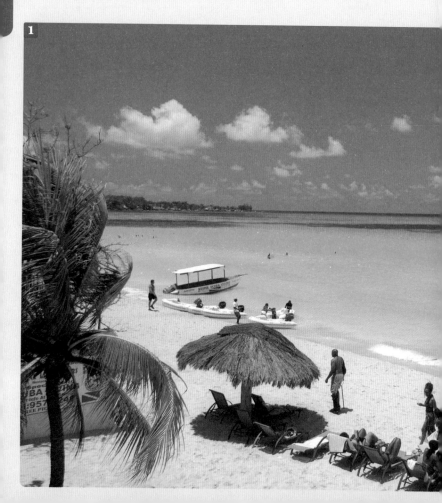

1

## Best Beaches

**1** Jamaica's beach experiences are as varied as the island's topography. The tiny, delicate Lime Cay, only reachable by boat from Port Royal, is perfect for snorkeling and picnics. Hellshire Beach heaves with Kingstonians and reverberates with loud music, its wooden shacks doing a roaring trade in fried fish. The north coast's Winnifred Beach (p99) draws the locals with its azure waters and weekend parties, while Negril's Seven Mile Beach is crisscrossed by Jet Ski riders, and its long crescent of white sand lined with the bodies of sun worshippers. Seven Mile Beach, Negril

## Reggae Grooves

**2** If there's any cultural trend that defines Jamaica to the rest of the world, it's reggae music – quite literally the soundtrack of the island. The reggae calendar is dominated by two huge events that celebrate the country's love of 'riddims,' both worth planning your trip around – Rebel Salute, held every January in St Ann, and then Reggae Sumfest (p118), held in Montego Bay in the middle of the broiling Jamaican summer. Break out a sweat amid the throbbing mass of bodies and the nonstop dancing. Red Stripe Reggae Sumfest, Montego Bay

RICHARD BROADWELL / ALAMY STOCK PHOTO ©

SHELBY SOBLICK / GETTY IMAGES ©

## Rafting the Rio Grande

**3** No less a celebrity than Errol Flynn started the habit of sending discerning tourists on romantic, moonlit rafting trips through the Rio Grande Valley (p106), from Berridale to Rafter's Rest at St Margaret's Bay. These days the experience isn't quite as exclusive as it was when Mr Flynn was running the show – the Rio Grande rafting trips are actually quite affordable as Jamaican tourism activities go – but if the moon is full, you can still pole onto the waters, which turn silver and unspeakably romantic.

## Kingston Nightlife

**4** Whether you're attending a nightclub (p57) or a street dance, expect a sweaty, lively, no-holds-barred event. Dress up to the nines and follow the locals' lead. At a street dance, two giant speakers are placed facing each other, the street pounding with the bass, while nightclubs provide a similar experience indoors. Expect to be pulled into the melee as the locals will want to see how well you can dance, and bump and grind to some dancehall riddims or slowy skank to the deepest dub.

## Negril

**5** So you've walked on the snowy sands of Negril's (p138) Seven Mile Beach, wandered past the nude sunbathers, seen the sun sink behind the horizon in a fiery ball, plunged into the ocean to scrub your soul and fended off all the hustlers. How about topping off all of those experiences by snorkeling or scuba diving in the cerulean waters that lap against the cliffs, and then rocking out to reggae or dancehall at one of Negril's many music nights?

## Climbing Blue Mountain Peak

**6** A night hike to reach Jamaica's highest point (p72) by sunrise, your path lit by the sparks of myriad fireflies, is an experience unlike any other. As you climb, the vegetation becomes less and less tropical, until you're hiking amid stunted trees draped with lichen, and giant ferns. In the predawn cold at the summit, you wait in rapt silence as the first rays of the sun wash over the densely forested mountain peaks all around you, illuminating the distant coffee plantations and Cuba beyond.

## Escape to Brighton

**7** With its empty, quiet beaches and somnolent pace of life, the fishing community of Brighton exudes a certain timelessness that has long disappeared from Jamaica's other coastal areas. Here you can plunge into the Blue Hole (p155) *cenote* (sinkhole), chill with the fishers or simply switch off and let yourself be hypnotized by the lapping waves.

## Perfect Retreats in Treasure Beach

**8** The most interesting varieties of accommodations (p161) in Jamaica are found in Treasure Beach, on the south coast. Here, instead of huge all-inclusive resorts, you'll find quiet, friendly guesthouses; artsy enclaves dreamed up by theater set designers; Rasta retreats favored by budget backpackers; and private villas that are some of the classiest, luxury residences in the country. Some places offer extras such as cooking classes, rooftop yoga, farm-to-table banquets and movie nights.

SEAPHOTOART / ALAMY STOCK PHOTO ©

STUART DEE / GETTY IMAGES ©

## Swimming in the Blue Lagoon

**9** From the forested cliffs that surround it, the Blue Lagoon (p98), named after the film starring the teenage Brooke Shields, is a seemingly bottomless pool of turquoise water, nestled in a protected cove – intensely picturesque and perfect for a dip. Fed by several underground streams coming down from the mountains, its waters are a refreshing mixture of warm tidal waves and cool freshwater currents. If you're a diver, you can plumb the lagoon's depths, which reach 55m at its deepest point.

## Diving Montego Bay

**10** You might find the resorts of Montego Bay to be crowded with people, but wait till you dive (p115) in the surrounding waters. They're crowded, yes, although not with human beings – just multicolored fish and swaying sponges. For all the tropical pastels and cool blue hues, this is a subdued seascape, a silent and delicate marine ecosystem that is one of the island's unique natural resources. The best sea walls are to be found at the Point, while more advanced divers should explore the ominous (and gorgeous) Widowmakers Cave.

## Crocodile-spotting in the Black River Great Morass

**11** This is one of our favorite ways of exploring wild Jamaica: setting off by boat in the Black River Great Morass (p168), gliding past spidery mangroves and trees bearded with Spanish moss, while white egrets flap overhead. Your tour guide may tell you about the local women who sell bags of spicy 'swimp' (shrimp) on the riverside, and point to a beautiful, grinning American crocodile cruising by.

## Cockpit Country

**12** The Cockpit Country (p133) of the island's interior is some of the most rugged terrain throughout the Caribbean, a series of jungle-clad round hills intersected by powerfully deep and sheer valleys. The rains gather in these mountains and the water percolates through the rocks, creating a Swiss cheese of sinkholes and caves. Since most of the trails within the Cockpit Country are badly overgrown, the best way to appreciate the place is to hike the old Barbecue Bottom road along its eastern edge or go caving in the Painted Circuit Cave.

## Bob Marley Museum, Kingston

**13** Marley's creaky home (p47) is crammed with memorabilia, but the visitor is drawn to his untouched bedroom, adorned with objects of spiritual significance to the artist, the small kitchen where he cooked I-tal food, the hammock in which he lay to seek inspiration from the distant mountains, and the room riddled with bullet holes, where he and his wife almost died in an assassination attempt. The intimate surrounds speak eloquently of Marley's turbulent life. Statue of Bob Marley by Jah Bobby

## Rum Tours on the Appleton Estate

**14** Red Stripe is the alcohol everyone associates with Jamaica, but you may find that rum, the local spirit, provides a more diverse boozing experience. We're not saying Appleton produces the best rum on the island, but it is the most commonly available, bottled as several different varieties, and you can sample all these examples of the firewater at the Appleton Rum Estate (p178) in the Central Highlands. A lot of rum is served, so don't expect to accomplish much else on one of these day trips!

## Playing Pirates at Port Royal

**15** The sleepy fishing village of Port Royal (p61) only hints at past glories that made it the pirate capital of the Caribbean and 'the wickedest city on Earth.' Stroll in the footsteps of pirate Sir Henry Morgan along the battlements of Fort Charles, still lined with cannons to repel the invaders; become disorientated inside the Giddy House artillery store, tipped at a jaunty angle; or admire the treasures in the Maritime Museum, rescued from the deep after two-thirds of the town sank beneath the waves in the monstrous 1692 earthquake.

# Need to Know

**For more information, see Survival Guide (p205)**

## Currency
Jamaican dollar (J$), US dollar (US$)

## Language
English, Patois (pa-*twa*)

## Visas
Most nationals require no visa to visit Jamaica. Most of those who do can obtain one on arrival.

## Money
ATMs are widely available. Credit cards are accepted in most medium-size and larger businesses, particularly in tourist areas.

## Cell Phones
You can bring your own cellular phone into Jamaica (GSM or CDMA). Be aware of hefty roaming charges or buy a local SIM card.

## Time
Eastern Standard Time (GMT/UTC minus five hours)

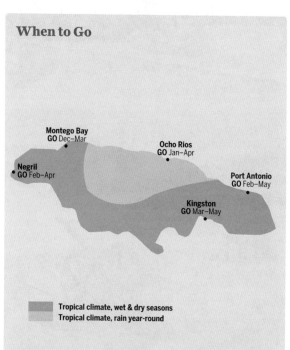

### When to Go

Montego Bay
**GO** Dec–Mar

Ocho Rios
**GO** Jan–Apr

Negril
**GO** Feb–Apr

Port Antonio
**GO** Feb–May

Kingston
**GO** Mar–May

Tropical climate, wet & dry seasons
Tropical climate, rain year-round

## High Season
(Dec–Mar)

➡ Expect sunny, warm days, especially on the coast. Little rainfall, except in Port Antonio and the northeast.

➡ At night it can become chilly, particularly in the mountains.

## Shoulder Season
(Apr & May)

➡ Good time to visit; weather is still pretty dry (again, except in Port Antonio).

➡ Rates drop for accommodations.

➡ Far fewer tourists, especially in the big resorts/cruise ports.

## Low Season
(Jun–Nov)

➡ Sporadic heavy rainfall across the island, except the south coast.

➡ Heavy storms, including hurricanes, gear up August to October.

➡ Many of Jamaica's best festivals happen in midsummer.

# Useful Websites

**Lonely Planet** (www.lonely planet.com/jamaica) Destination information, hotel bookings, traveler forum and more.

**Jamaica National Heritage Trust** (www.jnht.com) Excellent guide to Jamaica's history and heritage buildings.

**Jamaica Gleaner** (www.jamaica-gleaner.com) The island's most reliable newspaper.

**Visit Jamaica** (www.visit jamaica.com) The tourist board's version of Jamaica. Listing information may be outdated.

**Jamaicans** (www.jamaicans.com) Jamaican lifestyle and culture website.

# Important Numbers

Jamaica's country code is ☑876, which is dropped if dialing in the country.

| | |
|---|---|
| Ambulance | ☑110 |
| Directory assistance | ☑114 |
| International operator | ☑113 |
| Police | ☑119 |
| Tourism board | ☑929-9200 |

# Exchange Rates

| | | |
|---|---|---|
| Australia | A$1 | J$97 |
| Canada | C$1 | J$95 |
| Euro zone | €1 | J$136 |
| Japan | ¥100 | J$111 |
| New Zealand | NZ$1 | J$89 |
| UK | UK£1 | J$156 |
| US | US$1 | J$128 |

For current exchange rates see www.xe.com.

# Daily Costs

## Budget:
## Less than US$100

➡ Plate of jerk: US$3.50

➡ Route taxi fare: US$1–2

➡ Double room: US$50–60

➡ Red Stripe beer: US$1.20

## Midrange:
## US$100–200

➡ Admission to major attractions: US$20

➡ Short taxi ride: US$10

➡ Meal at midrange restaurant: $20

➡ Single-tank scuba dive: US$50

## Top End:
## More than US$300

➡ Fine dining: from US$30

➡ Luxury accommodations: from US$200

➡ Private taxi hire per day: US$100

# Opening Hours

The following are standard hours for Jamaica; exceptions are noted in reviews. Note that the country virtually shuts down on Sunday.

**Banks** 9:30am to 4pm Monday to Friday.

**Bars** Usually open around noon, with many staying open until the last customer stumbles out.

**Businesses** 8:30am to 4:30pm Monday to Friday.

**Restaurants** Breakfast dawn to 11am; lunch noon to 2pm; dinner 5:30pm to 11pm.

**Shops** 8am or 9am to 5pm Monday to Friday, to noon or 5pm Saturday, late-night shopping to 9pm Thursday and Friday.

# Arriving in Jamaica

With the exception of those passing through by cruise ship, all visitors to Jamaica arrive by air. There are two international airports, which are modern and efficient, although there are frequently not enough immigration officers on duty if several planes arrive at once, so queues are possible.

**Norman Manley International Airport** (p211) Taxis to New Kingston cost US$30 to US$35; bus 98 runs to Parade, downtown Kingston (J$100).

**Donald Sangster International Airport** (p211) Taxis cost US$15 to US$20 to downtown Montego Bay, US$100 to Negril.

# Getting Around

Public transportation in Jamaica consists of buses, minibuses and route taxis; they run between Kingston and every point on the island.

**Bus** Cheap travel between towns, but often overcrowded and dangerously driven. More expensive and reliable scheduled coaches are also available.

**Car** Useful for traveling at your own pace, or for visiting regions with minimal public transportation. Cars can be hired in every town or city. Drive on the left.

**Route taxi** Run set routes within and between nearby towns and cities. Cheap and convenient.

For much more on **getting around**, see p212

# If You Like...

## Diving & Snorkeling

Major dive centers are concentrated on the northwest coast; snorkeling opportunities can be found almost anywhere. Dive or snorkel and you'll soon discover a plethora of vibrant small fish and good visibility.

**Montego Bay** Gets green points due to protected waters at Montego Bay Marine Park & Bogue Lagoon. (p115)

**Ironshore** Shares operators with Montego Bay. Sights such as the Point and the underwater tunnel at Widowmakers Cave are highlights. (p127)

**Negril** The calm waters that characterize Negril make it a good place for newbies seeking scuba certification. (p139)

**Ocho Rios** A reef stretches from Ocho Rios to Galina Point, making for fine diving and snorkeling expeditions. (p81)

## Music

Jamaica is, per capita, one of the most musically influential nations in the world. From local sound-system parties to international festivals, beats and bass are always happening here.

**Kingston parties** Downtown Kingston's sound-system parties are the stuff of legend, with the brashest dancehall on the streets. (p57)

**Red Stripe Reggae Sumfest** The world's definitive reggae experience features the best of old sweet sounds and dancehall's raucous 'riddims.' (p118)

**Rebel Salute** Held on the north coast in January, this is the biggest roots reggae festival in Jamaica. (p90)

**Negril** There's something going on in Negril most nights, from reggae and dancehall beach parties to January's Jazz Festival. (p150)

## History

Jamaica's complex story can be explored in a variety of ways, from its beautiful colonial architecture to community tourism projects recounting history from the bottom up.

**Falmouth** This friendly town on the north coast boasts the greatest concentration of historic buildings in all Jamaica. (p128)

**Port Royal** Just a skip away from Kingston is this old haven of pirates and streets of Georgian architecture. (p61)

**Black River** Nicely preserved colonial houses and other remnants of a once-powerful boomtown. (p166)

**Accompong** The isolated outpost of the living Maroons, descendants of escaped slaves who have retained deep African cultural roots. (p176)

## Food & Drink

When home is a garden island populated by a cultural mélange of Africans, Chinese, Indians, Spanish and English, you should probably expect food to evolve in some interesting ways.

**Boston Bay** The supposed birthplace of jerk, Jamaica's most famous spice rub, is the best place to sample it. (p102)

**Appleton Rum Estate** Sip the strong stuff in the Central Highlands and realize how much flavor rocket fuel can have. (p178)

**Fine Kingston dining** The nation's capital is the place to sample haute Caribbean cuisine. (p54)

**Alligator Pond** It's hard to imagine a better seafood feast in Jamaica than in the beachside shacks at Little Ochie. (p165)

## Waterfalls & Rivers

Jamaica's rivers have historically been the country's

most important arterials. Today, they're also a playground for tourists visiting the Caribbean's most dramatic waterfalls.

**YS Falls** Deeply secluded in St Elizabeth parish, you'd be forgiven for thinking YS Falls emerged out of Eden. (p179)

**Martha Brae River** Be gently poled down this emerald-green tunnel, a silent riverine paradise close to MoBay. (p129)

**Reach Falls** These tall falls, which cascade through pools into lush jungle, may be the most beautiful in Jamaica. (p103)

**Dunn's River Falls** They may be slightly overcrowded, but it's still tons of fun to clamber up these slippery falls. (p79)

## Romantic Getaways

Jamaica is an island where it's pretty easy to fall in love, or fall back into love, or, as the case may be, lust (hey, all those dirty dancehall lyrics start getting to you after a while, what can we say). When you've got a country that zigs between powder beaches and misty mountains, and zags from clear waterfalls to molten sunsets, there are lots of perfect-kiss moments.

**Treasure Beach** A proliferation of small guesthouses, opulent villas and friendly locals – and yes, of course, a gorgeous beach. (p157)

**Oracabessa** Hideaways don't come much more elegant than Goldeneye in Oracabessa, the spiritual birthplace of James Bond. (p86)

**Negril** OK, Negril is over-touristed, but watch that sunset off the west coast and try not to be lovestruck. (p138)

**Top:** Cliff diving at Rick's Cafe (p150)
**Bottom:** YS Falls (p179)

# Month by Month

## January

January is prime tourist season, when the rains are few and the weather is pleasantly sunny and warm.

### ☆ Rebel Salute

The biggest Roots Reggae concert in Jamaica goes down on the second Saturday in January at Plantation Cove in St Ann's Bay on the north coast. Details at www.rebelsaluteja.com. (p90)

## February

The weather is dry and the sun continues to shine as some of the important cultural festivals on the island occur in the east.

### ☆ Reggae Month

A month of concerts and sound-system parties across the island celebrate Jamaica's iconic music, centered on Bob Marley's birthday on February 6.

### ☆ Jamaica Carnival

This carnival draws thousands of costumed revelers to the streets of Kingston, MoBay and Ochi. Sometimes spills over into March. (p52)

## March

You may find Jamaica less crowded, yet still blessed with good weather, as the high tourism season comes to an end. In the capital, thoughts turn to getting fit.

### ☆ Boys & Girls Championships

Held during the last week before Easter, this century-old, four-day event is a crown jewel of Jamaican athletics. Around 30,000 spectators (and talent scouts) crowd the national stadium to try to spot the next Usain Bolt. Details at www.issasports.com.

## April

While this is the beginning of the Jamaican shoulder season, the weather stays largely dry even as the crowds, and accommodations rates, start to plummet.

### ☆ Trelawny Jam Festival

In ruggedly beautiful Albert Town: yam-balancing races, best-dressed goat and donkey, the crowning of the Yam King and Queen – how can you resist? Perhaps the most idiosyncratic, unique festival on an island full of 'em. Details at www.stea.net.

## May

The rainy season really gears up in May, although things stay dry in the south for the nation's top literary festival.

### ☆ Calabash International Literary Festival

This innovative literary festival held in even-numbered years draws some of the best creative voices from Jamaica, plus highly touted international intelligentsia, to Treasure Beach. Details at www.calabashfestival.org. (p161)

## June

A soupy combination of heat and humidity from the

Top: Local musicians performing in Kingston

Bottom: Red Stripe Reggae Sumfest (p118)

rains begins to take hold, but sea breezes on the coast and mountain chill in the interior keep things fresh.

## Caribbean Fashion Week

You may not be able to access some of the most exclusive tents here, but the vibe of Caribbean Fashion Week can be felt all across Uptown and the posher suburbs of Kingston.

## July

Phew. It's hot. And not just the weather: one of the island's best music festivals heats up the events calendar. The rainy season continues.

## Reggae Sumfest

The big mama of all reggae festivals, held in late July in Montego Bay, this event brings top acts together for an unforgettable party. Even if you're not attending, you're attending – the festivities tend to take over MoBay. (p118)

## August

It's as hot as Jamaica gets, and about as humid too. In fact, the rains may be coalescing into ominous storm clouds. Yet the celebrations on the island aren't slowing down.

## Independence Day

August 6 marks Jamaica's independence from the British Empire, and occurs with no small fanfare

and delivery of dramatic speeches, especially in the Kingston area. Celebrations mark the event island-wide.

## October

Now the rains are coming in hard, and there may be hurricanes gathering off the coast. On the plus side, accommodations run dirt cheap.

## Jamaica Coffee Festival

Thousands of coffee-lovers converge on the spacious lawns of Devon House in Kingston during the first week of October to slurp up Jamaica's world-famous coffee in an orgy of beverages, liqueurs, ice cream, cigars and classic Jamaican chow.

## November

The rains are beginning to slacken off, although the northeast is still getting drenched. This is the end of low-season rates.

## Restaurant Week

Jamaican restaurant week has been building over the years, and organizers clearly hope it will grow in international cachet. It shows off the dishes of participating restaurants from Kingston, Ocho Rios and Montego Bay. Details at http://go-jamaica.com/rw.

## One World Ska & Rocksteady Music Festival

Held in Kingston, this one-day festival flies the

flag for some of Jamaica's pioneering yet sometimes overlooked musical genres, ska and rocksteady. Expect national and international acts. More details at www. facebook.com/oneworldska.

## December

The weather becomes refreshingly dry again, and resorts start raising their prices accordingly. During Christmas, thousands of Jamaicans fly in from the US, Canada and the UK to spend time with family.

## LTM Pantomime

The Jamaican take on social satire is raw, irreverent and amusing, and presented at this annual song-and-dance revue in Kingston from December through January. This is some of the best theater in the Caribbean. Details at www.ltmpantomine.com.

## Jamaica Biennial

Kingston's National Gallery shows works by Jamaica's newcomers and old hands at this biennial display – one of the most anticipated cultural events in the Caribbean. The current cycle hits on even-numbered years. Details at www. natgalja.org.jm.

## Rastafari Rootz Fest

Three-day celebration of Rastafari culture near Negril with excellent live music, I-tal food and a lot of ganja – including the Ganjamaica Cup for best in show. More details at www. rastafarirootzfest.com.

# Itineraries

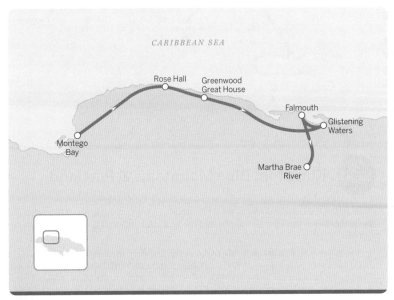

CARIBBEAN SEA

Rose Hall
Greenwood Great House
Falmouth
Glistening Waters
Montego Bay
Martha Brae River

## 1 WEEK Montego Bay & Around

Montego Bay is the entry point to Jamaica for most travelers, and this one-week itinerary helps you see the most of the surrounding area while still allowing plenty of time for the beach.

Start in **Montego Bay**, the gateway to Jamaica for about 80% of international travelers. Hit Doctor's Cave Beach for water sports and head downtown to Sam Sharpe Sq, taking in the historic architecture and the hustle of a real Jamaican city. Finish up with a fine meal on the Hip Strip.

Spend the next morning relaxing on Montego Bay's beaches and maybe enjoy a cold Red Stripe and plate of jerk for lunch, but don't linger too long. Heading east from MoBay you'll find two great houses: the more (in)famous **Rose Hall** and the more authentic **Greenwood Great House**; we recommend the latter. Grab lunch on the north coast and relax on the beach before taking a nighttime boating expedition at **Glistening Waters**.

The next day give yourself a crash course in Jamaican history with a walking tour of **Falmouth** and its faded Georgian buildings. Finish this itinerary with a rafting trip down the **Martha Brae River**.

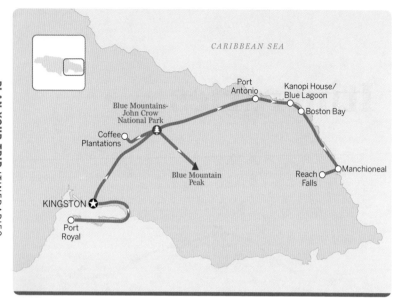

## 3 WEEKS Kingston, Blue Mountains & Portland

Take in the wild side of Jamaica with this itinerary, with the nightlife of Kingston, the rugged peaks of the Blue Mountains and the beautiful untamed greenery of Portland parish.

Touch down in **Kingston** for three days of sightseeing, excellent food and rip-roaring nightlife. Don't miss the art at National Gallery and Life Yard. Take in historic Devon House, enjoying Jamaica's best patties and ice cream while you're there. Afterwards head up to Bob Marley Museum. After hours, enjoy dinner at an upscale restaurant, seguing into some of the liveliest nightlife in the Caribbean, such as the famous Dub Club. For a captivating day trip, visit **Port Royal**, the earthquake-shattered former haunt of pirates and privateers.

Those hills looming over the city are calling, so slip into the Blue Mountains. Enjoy the breathtaking scenery and crisp mountain air from hiking trails in **Blue Mountains-John Crow National Park**. The main event here is making an early-morning ascent of **Blue Mountain Peak**, Jamaica's highest mountain. If you are truly adventurous, whiz down from the highlands on a bicycle tour; if such a trip seems like a bit too much, enjoy a pleasant day seeing how the Caribbean's most prized coffee rises from bean to brewery at the one of several **coffee plantations**.

Descend from the Blue Mountains to Portland parish, on the prettiest stretch of the north coast. Walk the atmospheric streets of **Port Antonio**, taking lodging in one of the many intimate spots to the east of town or within the port's atmospheric historic district. East of Port Antonio, you'll find appealing communities with stellar beaches and attractive places to stay.

You can explore this terrific stretch of coast quickly or slowly, but it lends itself to some lingering. In the course of, say, five days you could go diving in the **Blue Lagoon** and stay at gorgeous **Kanopi House**, take a visit to **Boston Bay**, the home of jerk cooking, and stop in **Manchioneal**, a terrific base for visiting the sublime **Reach Falls**, one of the best waterfalls on the island.

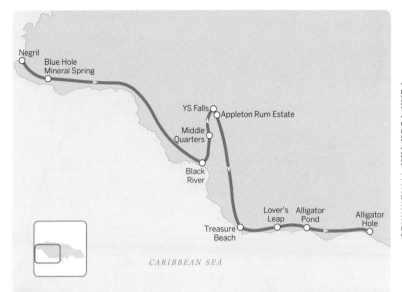

## The Sunny South

Take three weeks to enjoy a leisurely tour of Jamaica's south, taking in trendy Negril, laid-back Treasure Beach and the waterways of the Black River Great Morass and Alligator Hole.

Start your trip in **Negril** and head to the little-traveled back road that passes through the fishing village of Brighton, where you'll find deserted beaches and a slow pace of life, along with the local hot spot of **Blue Hole** – a perfect sinkhole for jumping into.

Linger at this quiet fishing beach for a day or three, then continue on to **Black River**, a sleepy port town with lovely historic buildings and vintage hotels. This is the gateway for boats into the mangrove swamps of the Black River Great Morass, a gorgeous wetlands where crocodile sightings are common. A trip up the river will take up a day of your time; afterwards visit the Ashton Great House.

In the morning head north to **Middle Quarters** for an unforgettable lunch of pepper shrimp at a crossroads eatery and an afternoon at the lovely **YS Falls**. Wet your whistle at the **Appleton Rum Estate**, then head south to **Treasure Beach**. Stay awhile in the welcoming embrace of this tight-knit community (folks seem to easily lose a month here). Be sure to take a boat trip to one of the planet's coolest watering holes, the Pelican Bar, perched on stilts on a sandbar 1km out to sea.

From Treasure Beach, visit **Lovers' Leap** for an astonishing view of the coastland. You could spend a day here walking around the sweet pastureland of Back Seaside. Continue along the coast to the fishing village of **Alligator Pond**. Far from packaged tourism, here you can enjoy traditional village life and unspoiled scenery at its best. You'll also enjoy a seafood feast at a truly extraordinary beachside restaurant, Little Ochie.

If you have your own car, preferably a 4WD, and are a confident driver, head east from Alligator Pond on the 'lonely road.' This really is an isolated stretch of road, but you'll find wild, empty beaches here and, after many potholes, **Alligator Hole**, a small preserve where manatees can be spotted.

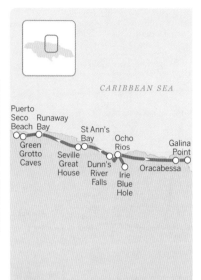

 **Ocho Rios & the Central Coast**

One week around Ocho Rios reveals far more than just another cruise port, with stunning waterfalls and caves to explore, charming beaches and exclusive villas.

Start this trip in the tourist town of **Ocho Rios**. Give yourself two days to chill out around Ocho Rios, taking full advantage of the tourist menu of activities, especially the amazing **Dunn's River Falls** and **Irie Blue Hole**.

Drive along the coast towards **Oracabessa** to see sights associated with James Bond author Ian Fleming, such as the lovely hotel of Goldeneye; and **Galina Point** for Noël Coward, whose former estate Firefly is now an excellent museum.

Turning back, head past Ocho Rios before stopping in at **St Ann's Bay** to see the Columbus and Marcus Garvey monuments, then on to the **Seville Great House** to learn about the region's history.

Now head to **Runaway Bay**, where you can eat well, sleep well and base yourself for an exploration of the awesome **Green Grotto Caves** before continuing on to Discovery Bay and the simple charms of **Puerto Seco Beach**.

 **A Taste of Cockpit Country**

This weeklong itinerary really gets you off the beaten track, trekking deep into the hills and gorges of Cockpit Country. It's possible to get around via route taxi, but you'll get the most out of it by renting a 4WD.

From Montego Bay, head out to the **Good Hope Estate**, a beautiful great house and working plantation. Enjoy horseback riding, lunch on the terrace and tremendous views.

On narrow roads, travel to the hamlet of **Windsor**. Stay at the former Windsor Great House and explore Windsor Cave with the Rastafari guide or, better yet, go birding with the resident biologist and watch a vortex of bats stream out of the cave at sunset.

Prepare for some challenging but rewarding hiking. While the trails through the interior of Cockpit Country are overgrown, a half-day hike with a guide from STEA along the disused road from Kinloss to Spring Garden, offers a wonderful overview of Jamaica's wilderness.

At Rock Spring, near Spring Garden, you can explore the watery **Painted Circuit Cave** with a local guide before pressing on southwest to **Accompong**, where you can meet Jamaica's remaining Maroons.

Top: Devon House
(p47), Kingston

Bottom: Green Grotto
Caves (p92), Discovery
Bay

## Plan Your Trip
# Eat & Drink Like a Local

One of the best ways to learn about Jamaica is through its food, so why not eat your way around the island? Ackee and saltfish for breakfast, curried goat for lunch and an I-tal vegetarian dinner will teach you more about Jamaica than a month at any all-inclusive resort.

## The Year in Food

### July
Portland Jerk Festival, a celebration of everything smoked and spicy, is held across Portland parish, the spiritual home of Jamaican jerk.

### October
Farmers, roasters and baristas alike gather together in Kingston to celebrate everything coffee, from Blue Mountain bean to cup, at the Jamaica Coffee Festival. A stone's throw from Kingston, Port Royal Seafood Festival celebrates a fisherman's haul of splendid seafood (and music) in Jamaica's old pirate capital.

### November
Held across Kingston, Montego Bay and Ocho Rios, Jamaica Restaurant Week is Jamaica's biggest festival of the island's culinary arts.

## Eating in Jamaica
### Jamaican Favourites

**Ackee & saltfish** The Jamaican breakfast of champions. Ackee fruit bears an uncanny resemblance to scrambled eggs when cooked, while the salty, flaky fish adds a savory depth to the pleasing blandness of the ackee. Usually served with johnny cakes and *callaloo* (a spinach-like vegetable).

**Bread-kind** A sort of catch-all term for starch accompaniments, which can include yams, breadfruit, *bammy* (cassava flatbread), *festival* (sweet fried cornbread), johnny cakes (dumplings) and steamed bananas (plantain), among others. While not technically bread-kinds, rice and peas (rice and beans) is also a major addition.

**Brown stew** Often more of a sauce than a stew, brown stew dishes are a nice combination of savory and sweet (and slightly tangy); it's a good choice for those who don't like spicy food.

**Curry** All kinds of curry are popular in Jamaica, but goat curry is king, chopped into small bits with meat on the bone. While the curry has Indian roots, it's not as hot as its motherland cuisine.

**Escoveitch** Imported from Spain by Spanish Jews, escoveitch is a marinade – most commonly used on fish – made of vinegar, onions, carrots and Scotch bonnet peppers.

Top: Spicy grilled jerk chicken (p30)

Bottom: Appleton Rum (p178)

## JAMAICAN FRUIT A-Z

| | |
|---|---|
| ACKEE | Its yellow flesh is a tasty and popular breakfast food, invariably served with saltfish |
| CHO CHO | Also known as christophine or chayote; a pulpy squashlike gourd served in soups and as an accompaniment to meats. Also used for making hot pickles. |
| GUAVA | A small ovoid or rounded fruit with a musky sweet aroma. It has a pinkish granular flesh studded with regular rows of tiny seeds. It is most commonly used in nectars and punches, syrups, jams, chutney and even ice cream. |
| GUINEP | A small green fruit (pronounced 'gi-nep') that grows in clusters, like grapes, and can be bought from July through November. Each 'grape' bears pink flesh that you plop into your mouth whole. It's kind of rubbery and juicy, and tastes like a cross between a fig and a strawberry. Watch for the big pip in the middle. |
| JACKFRUIT | A yellow fruit from the large pods of the jackfruit tree. Jackfruit seeds can be roasted or boiled. |
| MANGO | A lush fruit that comes in an assortment of sizes and colors, from yellow to black. Massage the glove-leather skin to soften the pulp, which can be sucked or spooned like custard. Select your mango by its perfume. |
| NASEBERRY | A sweet, yellow and brown fruit that tastes a bit like peach and comes from an evergreen tree. Also known as sapodilla. |
| PAPAYA | Cloaks of many colors (from yellow to rose) hide a melon-smooth flesh that likewise runs from citron to vermilion. The central cavity is a trove of edible black seeds. Tenderness and sweet scent are key to buying papayas. |
| SCOTCH BONNET PEPPER | Celebrated for its delicious citrus sparkle just before your entire mouth and head go up in flames, Scotch bonnets are small hot peppers that come in yellow, orange and red. |
| SOURSOP | An ungainly, irregularly shaped fruit with cottony pulp that is invitingly fragrant yet acidic. Its taste hints at guava and pineapple. |
| STAR APPLE | A leathery, dark-purple, tennis-ball-sized gelatinous fruit of banded colors (white, pink, lavender, purple). Its glistening seeds form a star in the center. The fruit is mildly sweet and understated. |
| SWEETSOP | A heart-shaped, lumpy fruit packed with pits and a sweet, custardlike flesh. |
| UGLI | A fruit that is well named. It is ugly on the vine – like a deformed grapefruit with warty, mottled green or orange skin. But the golden pulp is delicious: acid-sweet and gushingly juicy. |

**Jerk** The island's signature dish, jerk is the name for a tongue-searing marinade and spice rub for meats and fish, and for the method of smoking them slowly in an outdoor pit over a fire of pimento wood for its unique flavor. Every chef has a secret ingredient, but allspice, a dark berry that tastes like a mixture of cinnamon, clove and nutmeg, is essential.

**Oxtail** Simmered with butter beans and served with rice, stewed oxtail is a national obsession.

**Patties** Delicious meat pies; fillings can include spicy beef, vegetables, fish and shrimp. A Jamaican favorite is a patty sandwich – a patty squeezed between two thick slices of coco bread (a sweet bread baked with coconut milk). Juici Patties and Tastee Patty are reliable, national fast-food chains selling patties and other Jamaican takeout dishes.

**Rundown chicken** Cooked in spicy coconut milk, and usually enjoyed for breakfast with johnny cakes. Some say the dish is named for the method by which the chicken is caught.

**Fish tea** 'Warm up yuh belly' with this favorite local cure-all. Essentially, fish broth.

## I-Tal Cuisine

Thanks to the Rastafari, Jamaica is vegetarian-friendly. The I-tal diet (derived from 'vital') has evolved an endless index of no-nos. For instance: no salt, no chemicals, no meat or dairy (the latter is 'white blood'), no alcohol, cigarettes or drugs (ganja doesn't count). Fruits, vegetables, soy, wheat gluten and herbs prevail. Because of the popularity of the I-tal diet, many restaurants offer I-tal options on their menus. Popular dishes include eggplant curry, whipped sweet potatoes and steamed vegetables.

**'All fruits ripe'** A Jamaican expression meaning 'all is well,' which is also the state of Jamaican fruit. This island is a tropical-fruit heaven. Sampling them all and finding your favorites is a noble, healthy and rewarding task. Don't just taste the obvious, like coconut, banana, papaya and mango. Savor your first star apple, soursop, ortanique, naseberry, ugli or tinkin' toe.

# Drinks
## Non-alcoholic Drinks

**Coffee** Jamaican Blue Mountain coffee is considered one of the most exotic and expensive coffees in the world. It's relatively mild and light-bodied with a musty, almost woody flavor and its own unmistakable aroma. Most upscale hotels and restaurants serve it as a matter of course. The majority of lesser hotels serve lesser coffees from other parts of the country or – sacrilege! – powdered instant coffee. Be careful if you ask for white coffee (with milk), which Jamaicans interpret to mean 50% hot milk and 50% coffee.

**Tea** 'Tea' is a generic Jamaican term for any (usually) hot, nonalcoholic drink, and Jamaicans will make teas of anything. Irish moss is often mixed with rum, milk and spices. Ginger, mint, ganja and even fish are brewed into teas (though the latter is really a thin soup).

**Cold drinks** A Jamaican favorite for cooling off is 'skyjuice,' a shaved-ice cone flavored with sugary fruit syrup and lime juice, sold at streetside stalls. You may also notice 'bellywash,' the local name for limeade.

**Ting** A bottled grapefruit soda, Ting is Jamaica's own soft drink, although Pepsi is pretty popular too (Coca-Cola is surprisingly difficult to find).

**Coconut water** Sold straight from the nut from streetside vendors, along with its white 'jelly.'

**Roots tonics** Made from the roots of plants such as raw moon bush, cola bark, sarsaparilla and dandelion, roots tonics are widely available in small shops, and are sold roadside in handmade batches. They taste like dirt...but in a good way.

## Alcoholic Drinks

**Rum** Jamaica is proud of its rum – the smooth and dark Appleton rum is the most celebrated brand and is great sipped or mixed. You can even visit the estate (p178) where it's made. Wray & Nephew's white overproof rum carries a knockout blow – it may come in a shot glass, but if you down it in one go you're heading home early. Mix it with ginger beer, or even milk ('cow and cane').

**Beer** Red Stripe is Jamaica's famous beer, a crisp and sweet antidote to spicy jerk creations. Real Rock is a slightly heavier, local lager, while Dragon Stout is also popular. Heineken and Guinness are brewed locally under license.

# Self-Catering

Food at grocery stores is usually expensive, as many canned and packaged goods are imported. Dirt-cheap fresh fruits, vegetables and spices are sold at markets and roadside stalls island-wide. You can always buy fish (and lobster, in season) from local fishers.

# Foodie Tours

To travel and taste at the same time, join a specialist culinary tour. Those offered by Jamaica Cultural Enterprises (p49) in Kingston and Falmouth Heritage Walks (p129) in Falmouth are particularly recommended. Stush in the Bush (p91) near Ochi Rios offers tours of their farm followed by sumptuous meals. Don't forget coffee tasting in the Blue Mountains (p65), and the tours offered by the Appleton Rum Estate (p178).

# Plan Your Trip

# Outdoor Activities

Jamaica might be in the Caribbean, but it offers a lot more than just sunbathing on a beach, from mountain biking and rafting to horseback riding and birdwatching. Get a natural high hiking in the mountains, or dive below the waves to explore shipwrecks and coral.

## Best of the Best

### Best Wall Dive

**The Point** (p115) Swimming amid sharks and shoals along this coral-clad seawall.

### Best Wreck Dive

**The Kathryn** (p81) Diving alongside the wreck of a minesweeper on a reef near Ocho Rios.

### Best Long Hike

**Blue Mountain Peak** (p72) Getting to the top just in time for the best sunrise in Jamaica.

### Best River-Rafting

**Rio Grande** (p106) Heading up into the jungle-clad, rain-soaked green tunnels of the eastern parishes.

### Best Wildlife-Viewing

**Black River Great Morass** (p168) A boat trek from Treasure Beach, past jumping dolphins, up the river by sunning, grinning crocodiles.

## Birdwatching

All you need in the field are a good pair of binoculars and a guide to the birds of the island. Expect to pay anywhere from US$25 for an hour's jaunt to US$75 for a good half-day of birdwatching in the bush.

### Where to Go

Good spots include the following:

➡ **Blue Mountains** (p65)
➡ **Cockpit Country** (p133)
➡ **Black River Great Morass** (p168)
➡ **Negril Great Morass** (p145)
➡ **Rio Grande Valley** (p105)
➡ **Marshall's Pen, Mandeville** (p173)

### When to Go

The best time for birdwatching in Jamaica runs from December to June; at this time of year birds can be expected to show off their best plumage. This is also the dry season, so you're less likely to be drenched in your binoculars. A good online resource is the Caribbean Birding Trail (www.caribbeanbirdingtrail.org), a conservation and ecotourism organization that covers the Caribbean Basin.

## Operators

Suggested operators include the following:

➡ **Ann Sutton** (📞904-5454; asutton@cwjamaica.com) Based in Marshall's Pen (p173) in Mandeville; has been leading major bird tours in Jamaica for more than 30 years.

➡ **Arrowhead Birding Tours** (www.arrowheadbirding.com; full-day tours for 2 people US$130) Tours of one to seven days from Kingston, plus custom itineraries.

➡ **Hotel Mocking Bird Hill** (p100) Hotel outside Port Antonio, known for its highly regarded custom birding tours.

➡ **Hope Gardens** (p49) Birdwatching tours on the first Saturday of every month.

## Caving

Jamaica is honeycombed with limestone caves and caverns, most of which boast fine stalagmites and stalactites, underground streams and even waterfalls. Expect to pay a guide at least US$50 per person for a short, half-day exploration of a cave; if you want to go deeper and longer into spelunking territory, rates for guides start at US$70 to US$85 for full-day treks.

### Where to Go

You can find guided tours at these caves:

➡ **Painted Circuit Cave** (p134), Rock Spring

➡ **Winsor Caves** (p135), Cockpit Country

The following are for advanced cavers:

➡ **Peterkin-Rota Caves**, St James

➡ **Gourie Caves** (p180), Christiana

➡ **Coffee River Caves**, Troy

## Cycling

You can hire basic road bicycles at most major resorts and many smaller guesthouses. For anything more serious, you should consider bringing your own mountain or multipurpose bike. You will need sturdy wheels to handle the potholed roads. Check requirements with the airline well in advance. Remember to always have, at a minimum, a flashlight for the front of your bike and reflectors for the rear. If you're in the fixed-gear bicycle camp, note that Jamaica's many hills and unpredictable traffic make riding a 'fixie' extremely difficult.

Good online resources include the Jamaican Cycling Federation (www.jamaicacycling.com).

## Diving & Snorkeling

Diving has been a part of the Jamaican tourist landscape since the late 1960s, when the first facilities opened in Montego Bay, even then the tourism capital of the island. Thanks to nearby reefs and the MoBay marine park, the northwest coast from Negril to Ocho Rios remains the epicenter of Jamaican diving culture. By law, all dives in Jamaican waters must be guided, and dives are restricted to a depth of 30m.

### Where to Go

Dive sites:

➡ **Airport Reef** (p115), Montego Bay

➡ **Rose Hall Reef** (p115), Montego Bay

➡ **The Throne** (p139), Negril

Snorkeling sites:

➡ **West End** (p139), Negril

➡ **Belmont Beach** (p170)

### When to Go

It's best to go from January to April, when the weather is driest and least prone to storms.

---

### DIVING COSTS

Exact prices vary from operator to operator, but expect to pay around:

**One-tank dive** US$65

**Two-tank dive** US$95

**Snorkeling excursion** around US$35

**PADI or NAUI certification course** around US$450

**Rental** of masks, fins, snorkels, buoyancy control devices and regulators usually adds an extra $15

## Operators

**Montego Bay:**

→ **Resort Divers** (☑881-5760; www.resort divers.com; Runaway Bay; 1-/2-tank dive US$50/95)

→ **Jamaica Scuba Divers** (☑957-3039; www. scuba-jamaica.com; 1-/2-tank dives US$68/110) Based out of Falmouth, Negril and Runaway Bay, but does excursions to MoBay.

→ **Dressel Divers** (p115)

**Negril:**

→ **Sundivers Negril** (p139)

→ **Marine Life Divers** (☑957-3245; www. mldiversnegril.com; Samsara Hotel, West End Rd; 1-/2-tank dives US$55/90)

**Ocho Rios:**

→ **Garfield Diving Station** (p81)

→ **Resort Divers** (p91)

**Port Antonio:**

→ **Lady G'Diver** (p96)

# Fishing

Deepwater game fish run year-round through the Cayman Trench, which begins just over 3km from shore on the western side of the island. The waters off Jamaica's north coast are also particularly good for game fishing; an abyss known as 'Marlin Alley' teems with game fish. Charters can be arranged for US$550 to US$650 per half-day or US$900 to US$1200 for a full day through hotels or directly through operators in Montego Bay, Negril, Ocho Rios and Port Antonio. A charter includes captain, tackle, bait and crew. Most charter boats require a 50% deposit.

## When to Go

Summer is good for game fishing, but major tournaments go off in Montego Bay in late September and October.

## Operators

→ **Errol Flynn Marina** (p211), Port Antonio

→ **Montego Bay Yacht Club** (p212)

→ **Garfield Diving Station** (p81), Ocho Rios

# Hiking

Hiking is a great way of seeing the Jamaican interior, but keep in mind it's always best to head into the jungles and the mountains with a guide. It's easy to get lost out here, and it's good to have a contact who can vouch for you with locals. Expect to pay at least US$50 a day for local expertise, and possibly a good deal more to head into particularly difficult terrain.

## Where to Go

The most developed area for hiking is in Blue Mountains-John Crow National Park (p67), followed by the Rio Grande Valley (p106) in Portland parish, where some of the hikes venture into the Blue and John Crow Mountains. The remote Cockpit Country, with its jungle-clad limestone hills, is perhaps the most dramatic landscape on the island; small community-tourism outfits are growing in that region.

→ **Best short trek** The one to the summit of Blue Mountain Peak (p72). Reaching it at sunrise is one of the Caribbean's most exhilarating experiences. The view out over the entire island (and as far as Cuba if the day's clear) more than compensates for having to get up at an inhuman hour.

---

### DON'T WANDER OFF THE TRACK

Wherever your walk carries you, be sure to stay on the established trails: the mountainous terrain in Jamaica is too treacherous to go wandering off the track as thick vegetation hides sinkholes and crevasses. You should seek local advice about trail conditions before setting out, and take a good guide even if you know the route.

If you're heading into the backcountry, don't forget the following:

→ hiking boots

→ mosquito netting

→ bug spray

→ drinking water

→ sunblock

Top: Diver, Negril (p139)

Bottom: Horse riding near Montego Bay (p127)

→ **Best medium trek** A trek along the disused road from Kinloss to Spring Garden (p133) traverses some of the most beautiful yet roughest terrain in the country. You'll need a guide.

→ **Best bird-walking** Head out in the area around Windsor, in North Cockpit Country, with the guides of STEA (p133). It's a fun walk (although you need to be fit) and the accompanying scientific expertise is priceless.

## When to Go

It's best to go from January to April, when the weather is driest and least prone to storms.

# Horse Riding

Horseback riding is a popular attraction, particularly along the coast, where you can ride your horses into the sea, or to explore some of the larger plantations. Expect to pay around US$70 for a two-hour excursion. Reliable operators include the following:

→ **Hooves** (p90), St Ann's Bay

→ **Chukka Cove Farm** (p90), near Ocho Rios

→ **Braco Stables** (☑954-0185; www.braco stables.com; per person US$70; ☉rides 10:30am & 2:30pm), near Falmouth

→ **Rhodes Hall Plantation** (p153), Negril

# Rafting

Errol Flynn first saw the fun of coasting down the river on a raft of bamboo poles lashed together. Today, you sit on a raised seat with padded cushions, while a 'captain' poles you through the washboard shallows and small cataracts.

## Where to Go

The best river-rafting in Jamaica is in the mountainous interior of the northwest, near the Great River (p132) and Martha

Brae River (p129). Both of these are within easy day-tripping distance of Montego Bay and Ironshore. On the other side of Jamaica, head to the Rio Grande Valley (p106), which sits within day-trip distance of Kingston and Port Antonio in the east.

## When to Go

The best time to go rafting is in the dry season (December to April), when the waters aren't too swollen. If you want a white-water experience, head here in summer.

## Operators

Rio Grande Experience (p106) offers rafting trips down the green Rio Grande river. The craft are made from long bamboos, and your rafter gently poles you down the river, acting as a tour guide through the stunning scenery and providing stops for swimming. There's a small restaurant en route where lunch is provided. A couple of other operators, **Rafters Village** (☑940-6398; www.jamaicarafting.com; per raft 1-2 people US$60) and Martha Brae Rafting (p129), offer rafting on the Martha Brae near Falmouth, within easy distance of Montego Bay.

# Surfing & Kiteboarding

The easterly trade winds bless Jamaica with good summer surfing.

→ **Jamnesia Surf Camp** (p63) Undoubtedly the sport's home on the island; operates a surf camp at Bull Bay, 13km east of Kingston.

→ **Longboarder** (p73) Further east, near Morant Bay; also has boards and lessons.

→ **Boston Bay Surfing** (p102) Fourteen kilometers east of Port Antonio, Boston Bay has consistent good waves and this small surfing outfit, which offers lessons and rents out boards cheaply.

→ **Kiteboarding Jamaica** (p127) At Ironshore near Falmouth, home to Jamaica's nascent kiteboarding scene.

# Regions at a Glance

## Kingston, Blue Mountains & Southeast Coast

Nightlife
History
Hiking

### Sound-System Culture
Kingston never sleeps and you can join a party on any night of the week. Its nightlife ranges from formal nightclubs to sound-system parties consisting of giant speakers set up at either end of a street.

### Pirates & Colonists
Visit Port Royal in search of past pirate glory, stroll amid the ruined buildings of Spanish Town, the island's former capital, or take a walking tour through the streets of downtown Kingston to trace the capital's development.

### Blue Mountains
As well as the island's most popular hike – the nighttime climb up to Blue Mountain Peak, the island's highest point – the Blue Mountains offer numerous other trails to suit all abilities. The mountains in the morning afford some of the best wildlife-spotting in Jamaica.

p40

## Ocho Rios, Port Antonio & North Coast

Activities
Landscape
History

### Adventure Sports
The Ocho Rios area has arguably the most activities packed into a relatively small space in Jamaica. There are good diving spots, horseback-riding adventures, ATV safaris and zip-line tours, which attract active travelers.

### Coastal Retreats
Compared to the crowded northwest coast, tourists are much thinner on the ground when exploring the outdoors in Portland parish. Relax on quiet Winnifred Beach or wade up through the forest river to Reach Falls.

### Sugar Plantations & Banana Ports
Explore early colonial settlements at the old sugar plantation of Seville Great House in St Ann's Bay, the Windward Maroon stronghold of Moore Town, and the quaint old banana port of Port Antonio.

p75

## Montego Bay & Northwest Coast

Activities
History
Hiking

### Water Sports

The beaches in Montego Bay are OK, but there's better sand elsewhere; we really recommend swimming in the Glistening Waters and rafting up the Martha Brae. The infrastructure for guided activities is more developed here than elsewhere on the island.

### Colonial Architecture

Falmouth is the most historically preserved town in Jamaica, with excellent walking tours on offer, while near Ironshore there are protected great houses.

### Cockpit Country

Head deep into Cockpit Country, south of Montego Bay, to find fascinating caves and some of the best birding in Jamaica near Windsor and Albert Town. For an easier challenge, you can go on light hill walks in the area near Lethe.

**p108**

## Negril & West Coast

Activities
Eating
Nightlife

### Water Sports

Sure, you can go waterskiing and parasailing and cliff-diving and all that, but a lot of the joy of Negril is at the end of an active day, watching that perfect sunset every evening, and doing nothing at all.

### Negril Restaurants

Negril has a plethora of eating options, from simple, satisfying beach fare on Long Bay to the classier confines of the fusion and high-end restaurants of the West End. Sunsets off the island's west coast make for some of the most romantic dining experiences in Jamaica.

### Beach Parties

If you're looking for a beach party in Jamaica, you can't really do much better than Negril. Alternatively, head east to Brighton to leap into Blue Hole cenote and dance to pounding speakers.

**p137**

## South Coast & Central Highlands

Landscape
Culture
Relaxing

### Caves & Waterfalls

From the extensive cave networks of the Central Highlands to the glorious cascades of YS Falls, and even gentler options such as the rolling pastureland near Lovers' Leap, there's a lot to keep you outdoors.

### Jamaican Stories

Accompong, in dramatic South Cockpit Country, is the best place in Jamaica to interact with the Maroons. For intellectual pursuits, hit Treasure Beach during the Calabash International Literary Festival. Many members of the island intelligentsia are attracted to the laid-back resorts in and around Treasure Beach.

### Boat Trips & Beaches

You know what? Crocodiles are relaxing. Look how laid-back they are, chilling as you glide past by boat on Black River. Even more relaxing? Picking the perfect Treasure Beach accommodations and losing yourself for days, weeks, months...

**p156**

# On the Road

# Kingston, Blue Mountains & Southeast Coast

## Best Places to Eat

➡ Mi Hungry (p54)
➡ Andy's (p54)
➡ Moby Dick (p57)
➡ Gloria's (p63)
➡ Longboarder (p73)

## Best Places to Sleep

➡ Reggae Hostel (p53)
➡ Neita's Nest (p53)
➡ Jamnesia Surf Camp (p64)
➡ Strawberry Hill (p69)
➡ Lime Tree Farm (p71)

## Why Go?

Kingston is Jamaica's beating heart, its raw energy contrasting sharply with the languor of resorts and villages elsewhere on the island. This is a city on the up and up, with a positive, go-ahead vibe. It's the launchpad for some of the world's most electrifying music, and sound systems still provide its essential soundtrack. The perfect mix of the undeniably local and refreshingly cosmopolitan, Kingston isn't to be missed.

Kingston is also the ideal base for exploring Jamaica's southeast corner. There are beaches within easy striking distance of the capital, but the island's story is really thrown into relief by the faded pirate glory of Port Royal and the grit of Spanish Town, while the majestic, forest-covered Blue Mountains allow you to escape into nature and hike old Maroon trails or taste a gourmet cup at a working coffee plantation.

## When to Go

### Kingston

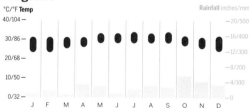

**Feb** Carnival and Reggae Month offer plenty of chances for music and partying.

**Nov–Apr** Best for sightseeing; in December the island's choice lineup of stars appears at Sting.

**Dec–Mar & Jul–Sep** Best time for surfing (there are few waves outside these seasons).

# KINGSTON

POP 670,323

Squeezed between the Blue Mountains and the world's seventh-largest natural harbor, Kingston simultaneously impresses you with its setting and overwhelms you with its noise and hustle. This is the island's cultural and economic heart, and a place named a Creative City of Music by Unesco in 2015. Like a plate of spicy jerk washed down with a cold Red Stripe beer, a visit to Kingston is essential to taste the rich excitement of modern Jamaica.

Kingston is a city of two halves. Downtown is home to historic buildings, the courts, banks, street markets and one of the Caribbean's greatest art museums. By contrast, Uptown holds the city's best hotels and restaurants, largely confined to New Kingston, with its cluster of tall buildings around Emancipation Park.

Uptown and Downtown seldom mix, but taken together they form a compelling and sometimes chaotic whole. Kingston is certainly never boring – we encourage you to jump right in.

## History

When the English captured Jamaica in 1655, Kingston was known as Hog Crawle, little more than a site for raising pigs. It took an earthquake that leveled nearby Port Royal in 1692 to spur the town planners into action and turn Kingston into a going concern.

In the 18th century Kingston became one of the busiest ports in the western hemisphere, and a key trans-shipment point for the slave trade. By 1872 it became the colony's official capital.

In 1907 an earthquake leveled much of the city, sending Kingston's wealthier elements uptown. Downtown became a breeding ground both for the new Rastafarian movement, and labor unions and political parties alike.

In the 1960s the port was expanded and attempts were made to spruce up the waterfront. But as cruise ships docked in Kingston Harbour, the boom also drew in the rural poor, swelling the shantytowns.

Unemployment soared, and with it came crime. The fractious 1970s spawned politically sponsored criminal enterprises whose trigger-happy networks still trouble the city. Commerce began to leave Downtown for New Kingston, and the middle class edged away as well.

Modernization in the 1990s, the ongoing expansion of the port and other signs of cultural rejuvenation – not least the city's music scene – suggest that Kingston's prospects are finally on the up again.

## ⊙ Sights

### Downtown

⭐ **National Gallery of Jamaica**     GALLERY

(Map p48; ☑ guided tours 922-1561; www.natgalja.org.jm; 12 Ocean Blvd; admission J$400, 45min guided tours J$3000; ⊙10am-4:30pm Tue-Thu, to 4pm Fri, to 3pm Sat) The superlative collection of Jamaican art housed by the National Gallery is the finest on the island and should on no account be missed. As well as offering a distinctly Jamaican take on international artistic trends, the collection attests to the vitality of the country's artistic heritage as well as its present talent.

The collection is organized chronologically, introduced by Taíno carvings and traditional 18th-century British landscapes, whose initial beauty belies the fact that their subjects include many slave plantations. Ten galleries represent the Jamaican school, from 1922 to the present. Highlights include the boldly modernist sculptures of Edna Manley, the vibrant 'intuitive' paintings of artists John Dunkley and David Pottinger, and revivalist bishop Mallica 'Kapo' Reynolds. Later galleries chart the course of 'Jamaican art for Jamaicans' up to the recent past, including abstract religious works by Carl Abrahams, Colin Garland's surrealist exercises, ethereal assemblages by David Boxer, and the work of realist Barrington Watson.

Temporary exhibition spaces frequently offer up the best of contemporary Jamaican art, as seen during the superb biennial temporary exhibition (www.natgalja.org.jm; ⊙Dec-Mar) that takes place on alternate, even-numbered years between mid-December and March.

⭐ **Liberty Hall**     MUSEUM

(Map p48; ☑948-8639; http://libertyhall-ioj.org.jm; 76 King St; adult/child J$400/200; ⊙9am-5pm Mon-Fri) At the end of a tree-lined courtyard, decorated with cheerful mosaics and a mural depicting Marcus Garvey, stands Liberty Hall, the headquarters of Garvey's UNIA (United Negro Improvement Association) in the 1930s. The building now contains a quite excellent multimedia museum about the man and his work, which allows

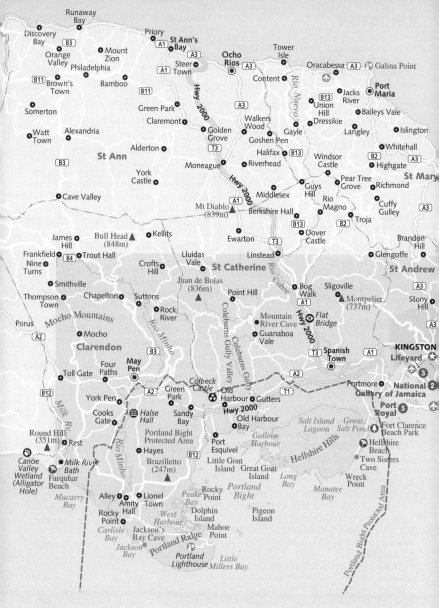

# Kingston, Blue Mountains & Southeast Coast Highlights

① **Bob Marley Museum** (p47) Delving into the life of Jamaica's most revered contemporary hero at his former home and studio.

② **National Gallery of Jamaica** (p41) Appreciating the vision of Jamaican artists at this internationally acclaimed gallery.

③ **Lifeyard** (p46) Exploring the renaissance of a downtown neighborhood through an innovative art and permaculture project.

④ **Dub Club** (p58) Grooving at Kingston's coolest sound-system night.

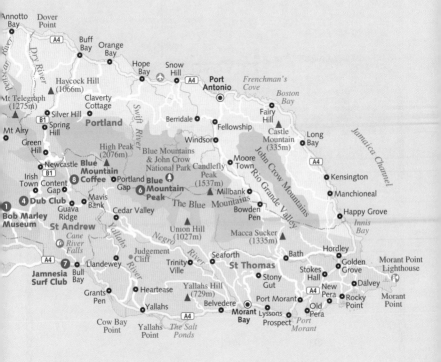

**5** **Port Royal** (p61)
Retracing the steps of
Blackbeard and Henry Morgan
at the former pirate capital of
the world.

**6** **Blue Mountain Peak**
(p72) Setting out before dawn
to experience the greatest
high in Jamaica.

**7** **Jamnesia Surf Camp**
(p63) Catching breaks in Bull

Bay at Jamaica's first surf
camp.

**8** **Blue Mountain coffee**
(p65) Seeing a red berry
transformed into the world's
best coffee bean.

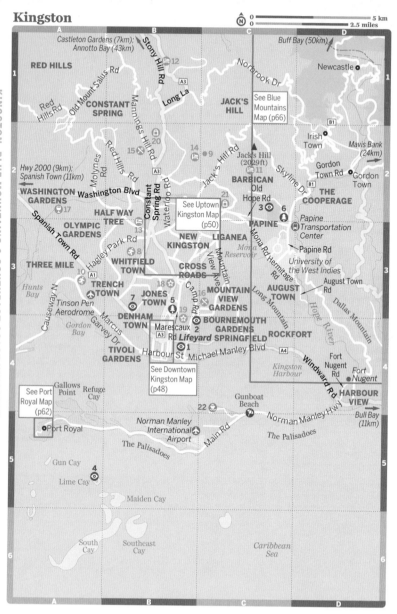

the visitor to appreciate Garvey's impact as a founder of pan-Africanism.

As in Garvey's day, Liberty Hall has a community outreach program, holding after-school programs for neighborhood children and computer literacy classes. There's also a superb reference library with a focus on Garvey, African history and the diaspora.

Parade                              SQUARE
(William Grant Park; Map p48) William Grant Park, more commonly known as 'Parade,'

# Kingston

is the bustling heart of Downtown, and originally hosted a fortress erected in 1694 with guns pointing toward the harbor. The fort was replaced in 1870 by Victoria Park, renamed a century later to honor Black Nationalist and labor leader Sir William Grant. The north and south entrances are watched over by cousins and political rivals Norman Manley (Map p48) and Alexander Bustamante (Map p48), respectively. A large fountain stands at its center.

At North Parade, the distinguished Ward Theatre (Map p48; www.wardtheatrefoundation.com), built in 1911, once hosted the annual Boxing Day pantomime – a riotous, irreverent social satire. Sadly, the building has fallen into disrepair over the years, although there are plans to restore it to its former glory. For now, you can admire the cracked sky-blue facade with white trim.

The gleaming white edifice facing the park's southeast corner is Kingston Parish Church (Map p48), which replaced an older church destroyed in the 1907 earthquake. Note the tomb dating to 1699, the year the original was built. The tomb of Admiral Benbow, commander of the Royal Navy in the West Indies at the turn of the 18th century, is near the high altar, while plaques commemorate soldiers of the colonial West Indian regiments.

The crenelated redbrick building facing East Parade is the 1840 Coke Memorial Hall (Map p48), named after the founder of the Methodist churches in the Caribbean, Thomas Coke.

South Parade, packed with street vendor stalls and the blast of reggae, is known as 'Ben Dung Plaza' because passersby have to bend down to buy from hawkers whose goods are displayed on the ground. King St leads from here to the waterfront, and to a replica of Edna Manley's Negro Aroused statue (Map p48; King St), depicting a crouched black man breaking free from bondage; the original is in the National Gallery of Jamaica (p41).

**Coronation Market**                    MARKET
(Map p48; ⊙Mon-Sat) This huge cast-iron-framed hall hosts the biggest market in the English-speaking Caribbean. It holds a special place in Jamaican culture as both 'stomach' of the country and the old heart of Kingston's commerce; indeed half the country appears to be shopping here, especially on a Saturday. It's a brilliant and lively show of noise, produce and commerce, but leave your valuables at home and watch out for pickpockets.

**Institute of Jamaica**                  MUSEUM
(JCDT; Map p48; ☑922-0620; www.instituteof jamaica.org.jm; 10-16 East St; adult/child J$400/200; ⊙10am-6pm Tue-Sun) The Institute of Jamaica is the nation's small-scale equivalent of the British Museum or Smithsonian, housed in three separate buildings. The institute hosts permanent and visiting exhibitions. Buy your ticket at the Natural History Museum, accessed by a separate entrance around the corner on Tower St.

## LIFEYARD – PAINT JAMAICA

The innovative art and permaculture scheme Lifeyard (Paint Jamaica; Map p44; 📞 298-4313, 809-3198; www.facebook.com/lifeteam360; Fleet St; donation requested) is regenerating an area of downtown Kingston once beset with gang problems. Lifeyard is centered on an urban farming project, and its Rastafari organizers have also worked with the community and visiting artists to cover the whole street with beautiful and uplifting murals. It's not just pretty pictures though – the art is backed up by youth projects including breakfast and homework clubs, workshops, educational support and media training so the community can tell their own stories.

There's a cafe selling I-tal food, with much of the produce coming from the permaculture garden. Several of the residents are registered tour guides – contact them in advance to set up a tour. It's essential to introduce yourself when you arrive – this is a residential area, so don't just snap photos of the walls without asking permission (which is readily given). Inquiries from long-term volunteers with transferable skills are welcomed.

When we visited, the institute was undergoing a multimillion-dollar refit, so expect the layout to change and improve.

Downstairs there is small exhibition on natural history and agriculture, while upstairs holds a temporary exhibition space. The small but informative Museum of Music on the top floor displays traditional musical instruments and traces the history and development of Jamaica's music, from Kumina, mento and ska to reggae and dancehall. Next door, the Africa Collection features weapons, carvings and some exquisite craftwork from various African countries.

**National Library**                    LIBRARY
(Map p48; www.nlj.org.jm; ⊙ 9am-5pm Mon-Fri, 10am-3pm Sat) Adjacent to the Institute of Jamaica (p45), the National Library incorporates the Caribbean's largest repository of books, maps, charts and archival documents on West Indian history.

**Trench Town Culture Yard**    CULTURAL CENTER
(Map p44; 📞 859-6741; 6-8 Lower First St; tours J$1000; ⊙ 6am-6pm daily) Trench Town, which began life as a much-prized housing project erected by the British in the 1930s, is widely credited as the birthplace of ska, rocksteady and reggae music. It has been immortalized in numerous reggae songs, not least Bob Marley's 'No Woman No Cry,' the poignant anthem penned by Marley's mentor, Vincent 'Tata' Ford, which was written here.

The yard's museum is stocked with Wailers memorabilia, along with the rusted-out carcass of a VW bus that belonged to the Wailers in the 1960s and the small bedroom that was Bob and Rita Marley's home before superstardom. As with many things

Marley-related, tours can be rather brisk, with visitors steered towards the gift shop.

Also on-site is the Trench Town Development Association, responsible for transforming the home into a community-based heritage site, and dedicated to promoting social justice and self-reliance.

Visits are best arranged in advance – it's safe to visit, but we don't advise wandering elsewhere around Trench Town on your own.

**National Heroes Park**                    PARK
(Map p44) The 30-hectare, oval-shaped National Heroes Park hosts National Heroes Circle, dedicated to Jamaica's seven national heroes. Sir Alexander Bustamante, Norman Manley and Marcus Garvey are all buried here, and there are symbolic memorials to Queen Nanny and Sam Sharpe, as well as Paul Bogle and George William Gordon of the 1865 Morant Bay Rebellion.

Other celebrated Jamaicans buried here include Michael Manley, 'Crown Prince of Reggae' Dennis Brown, and 'Miss Lou,' the revered patois poet Louise Bennett.

**Shaare Shalom Synagogue**        SYNAGOGUE
(Map p48; 📞 922-5931; www.ucija.org; cnr Duke & Charles Sts; ⊙ services 10am Sat) Jamaica's only synagogue is an attractive white building dating from 1912. It's usually locked, though on weekdays there is often someone in the little office around the back who will open it up for a small donation. The hall adjacent to the synagogue houses a well-presented exhibition on the history of Jamaica's Jewish community.

Sand muffles your footsteps – the practice dates from the time of the Inquisition when Jews had to worship in secret, and is a gesture of solidarity by local Jews, who were never subject to religious restrictions in Jamaica.

### Ba Beta Kristian
### Church of Haile Selassie I    CHURCH

(Map p48; Oxford St) The line between Rastafari and the Ethiopian Orthodox Church can sometimes be a fluid one. A Sunday afternoon service here is a colorful affair, but to attend, women must sit on the right-hand side, wear dresses and keep their hair covered.

---

## ⊙ Uptown

### ★ Bob Marley Museum    MUSEUM

(Map p50; ☑ 927-9152; www.bobmarleymuseum .com; 56 Hope Rd; adult/child J$3000/1500; ⊙9:30am-4pm Mon-Sat) The large, creaky, colonial-era wooden house on Hope Rd, where Bob Marley lived and recorded from 1975 until his death in 1981, is the city's most visited site. Today the house functions as a tourist attraction, museum and shrine, and much remains as it was in Marley's day.

The hour-long tour provides fascinating insights into the reggae superstar's life after moving uptown. His gold and platinum records are there on the walls, alongside Rastafarian religious cloaks, Marley's favorite denim stage shirt, and the Order of Merit presented by the Jamaican government. One room is entirely wallpapered with media clippings from Marley's final tour; another contains a replica of Marley's original record shop, Wail'n Soul'm. Marley's simple bedroom has been left as it was, with his favorite star-shaped guitar by the bed. At the rear of the house you'll see the spot where gunmen attempted to kill him in 1976.

The former recording studio out back is now an exhibition hall with some wonderful photos of Bob, and a theater, where the tour closes with a 20-minute film. Photography isn't allowed inside the house, but you'll almost certainly be instructed to sign 'One Love' at some point.

### ★ Devon House    MUSEUM

(Map p50; ☑ 929-6602; www.devonhousejamaica. com; 26 Hope Rd; adult/child J$1000/500; ⊙9.30-5pm Mon-Sat) This beautiful colonial house was built in 1881 by George Stiebel, the first black millionaire in Jamaica. Antique-lovers will enjoy the visit, highlights of which include some very ornate porcelain chandeliers. Note the trompe l'oeil of palms in the entrance foyer and the roundabout chairs, designed to accommodate a man wearing a sword. Amid the grand surroundings, Stiebel even managed to discreetly tuck a gambling room away in the attic. Admission includes a mandatory guided tour.

The tree-shaded lawns of Devon House attract Kingstonians who come here to canoodle and read. The popular former carriage house and courtyard are home to several shops – tours include a scoop from Devon House I-Scream (p55), Jamaica's best.

---

## MARLEY'S GHOST

Although Bob Marley (1945–81) was born and buried in Nine Mile in St Ann parish, it was from Kingston that Jamaica's most famous son made his mark on the global music scene.

Bob and his mother moved to Trench Town in 1955, at the time a desirable neighborhood and fertile spot for the emerging music scene, where he met Bunny Wailer and Peter Tosh. In 1963 they formed the Wailin' Wailers, scoring a number-one hit with their first single, 'Simmer Down'. On signing to Island Records in the early '70s (and becoming Bob Marley and the Wailers) they began to receive international acclaim with albums *Burnin'* and *Catch a Fire*, though Peter Tosh and Bunny Wailer quit soon after. In 1975 Marley moved into the house at 56 Hope Rd, now a museum.

During the 1970s, Bob, his wife, Rita, and his manager were shot at Hope Rd by a gang, just before a major concert. Remarkably, everyone survived (and Marley even played at the concert), but afterwards Bob and Rita went into exile in Britain for two years. In 1978 Marley made his legendary homecoming when messages of peace and unity were being all but drowned out by open street warfare. On April 22 he played the 'One Love' peace concert, attended by 100,000 people.

During his world tour in 1980, Marley was diagnosed with cancer and died in a Miami hospital eight months later. While some argue that Marley was not the greatest-ever reggae musician, he was the developing world's first global superstar, and there's no denying that his music has touched more people worldwide than many other artists.

# Downtown Kingston

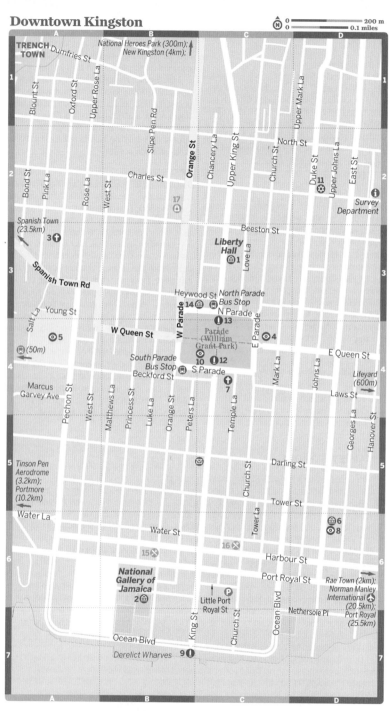

0    200 m
0    0.1 miles

TRENCH TOWN

National Heroes Park (300m);
New Kingston (4km);

Dumfries St
Blount St
Oxford St
Upper Rose La
Bond St
Pink La
Rose La
West St
Slipe Pen Rd
Orange St
Chancery La
Upper King St
Church St
North St
Upper Mark La
Duke St
Upper Johns La
East St

Survey Department

Charles St
17

Spanish Town (23.5km)
3
Spanish Town Rd
Young St
Salt La

Beeston St

Liberty Hall
1
Love La

Heywood St
North Parade
Bus Stop
W Parade
14
N Parade
13
Parade
(William Grant Park)
E Parade
4

W Queen St
5

South Parade
Bus Stop
Beckford St
10
12
S Parade
7
E Queen St
Mark La
Johns La

Lifeyard (600m)

Marcus Garvey Ave
Pechon St
West St
Matthews La
Princess St
Luke La
Orange St
Peters La
Temple La
Church St
Laws St
Georges La
Hanover St

Tinson Pen Aerodrome (3.2km);
Portmore (10.2km)
Water La

Darling St

Tower St

Water St
15
16
Water St
Tower La
6
8

Harbour St
Port Royal St

National Gallery of Jamaica
2
Little Port Royal St
Ocean Blvd
Nethersole Pl

Rae Town (2km);
Norman Manley International (20.5km);
Port Royal (25.5km)

Ocean Blvd
Derelict Wharves
9

# Downtown Kingston

**Emancipation Park** PARK
(Map p50; Knutsford Blvd) This grand open space at the center of New Kingston is a fine place for a stroll or a spot of people-watching over a takeout patty under a shady tree. Check out the controversial statue *Redemption Song,* by Laura Facey Cooper. It depicts a couple of nude, 3m-tall slaves gazing to the heavens – play art critic and pass approving or prurient comments as you see fit.

**Alpha Boys School** ARTS CENTER
(Map p44; ☑928-1345; www.alphaboysschool.org; 26 South Camp Rd; donation requested; ☺4-5pm Mon-Fri) Few have had an impact on modern Jamaican music like Alpha Boys School and its students. A nonprofit vocational school serving young men from the inner city, Alpha has been administered by the Religious Sisters of Mercy since 1890. The school is where many of Jamaica's musical pioneers in jazz, ska and reggae (from Skatalites members to Yellowman) got their start. Alpha students are still a primary source of local talent and can be heard Monday to Friday afternoons during the Alpha Live! visitor tour.

**Peter Tosh Museum** MUSEUM
(Map p50; www.petertosh.com/museum; Pulse Centre, 38a Trafalgar Rd; adult/child J$2000/1000; ☺10am-6pm Mon-Sat) Reggae legend Peter Tosh finally gets his due in this tiny museum, opened in 2016. A co-founder of The Wailers (he co-wrote 'Get up, Stand up'), the radical Tosh was an early campaigner against apartheid, a pan-Africanist and an advocate for ganja – most notably on his album *Legalize It*. The museum tells his story with respect and makes the most of its small collection of memorabilia, including a pair of Mick Jagger's gold microphones from when Tosh toured with the Stones.

The most notable item is his famous guitar shaped like an M16 rifle, while the most unexpected is Tosh's beloved unicycle, bringing a touch of levity into the life of this militant musician.

**Hope Gardens** GARDENS
(Map p44; Old Hope Rd; ☺6am-7pm) **FREE** These 18-hectare gardens, replete with manicured grounds, exotic plants and beautiful flowers, date back to 1881, when the government established an experimental garden on the site of the former Hope Estate. The spacious lawns, towering palms and flower-scented walkways provide a lovely respite from the urban jungle. Other attractions include an orchid house, greenhouses, ornamental ponds and a privet-hedge maze.

**St Andrew Parish Church** CHURCH
(Half Way Tree Church; Map p50; cnr Hagley Park & Eastwood Park Rds) This brick church is more popularly known as the 'Half Way Tree Church.' The foundations of the existing church were laid in 1692. The exterior is austere and unremarkable, but the stained-glass windows and organ are definitely worth a peek, and it's a serene escape from the busy streets beyond. Outside, there's a very atmospheric graveyard.

## ☞ Tours

**Jamaica Cultural Enterprises** CULTURAL
(☑540-8570; www.jaculture.com; Kingston tours half-/full day US$65/90) Highly recommended cultural tours in and around Kingston, including to the Blue Mountains. Excellent themed tours include history, food, music and art – there's even a boozy Kingston rum tour – either as a group or tailor-made. Every Thursday they offer a free Kingston walking tour, starting at 9am at Emancipation Park.

**Sun Venture Tours** TOURS
(Map p44; ☑924-4515; www.sunventuretours.com; 32 Russell Heights) Offers a city tour of Kingston, incorporating a walking tour of Port Royal and a visit to Devon House (US$85 per person, minimum four people, including

KINGSTON, BLUE MOUNTAINS & SOUTHEAST COAST KINGSTON

# Uptown Kingston

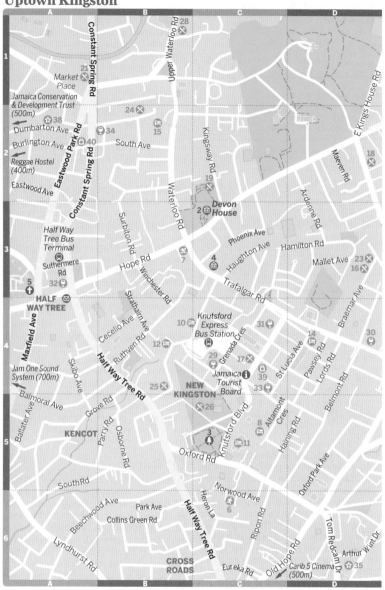

entrance fees), as well as longer day tours including Kingston's musical heritage. Sun Venture also offers hiking tours of the Blue Mountains and Maroon country, excursions to coffee plantations and more.

**Our Story Tours**                                    HISTORY
(☎377-5693; ourstorytours@gmail.com) Historical tours of Kingston, Port Royal and Spanish Town. Itineraries can be tailor-made to suit your needs.

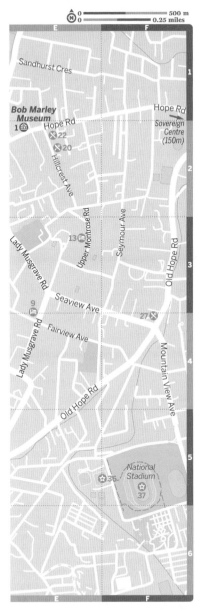

will give you the lowdown. Watch the huge speakers being assembled and tweaked, learn about the music culture and even have a go at the mic, toasting a few tracks at full volume. If you're into music, it's a fascinating exploration of one of the linchpins of Jamaican working-class culture.

Tours are scheduled on request for a minimum of two people, and the workshop needs 24-hours' notice to set things up. There's a bar on-site with a small restaurant selling stews and the like.

**Tuff Gong Recording Studios**    MUSIC
(Map p44; ☑ 923-9380; www.tuffgong.com; 220 Marcus Garvey Dr; tours J$1000) Tuff Gong is one of the Caribbean's largest and most influential studios. Bob Marley's favorite place to record, it's run by his son Ziggy. Visitors are welcome to take a 45-minute tour with the entire music production process explained, provided you call in advance – but if someone's recording, you may not be allowed to see all sections of the studio.

Excitingly, the studio started pressing vinyl again in 2017 for the first time in years, and it's hoped that future tours will encompass this.

## 🏃 Activities

**YMCA**    SWIMMING
(Map p50; ☑ 754-9034; 21 Hope Rd; J$400) Kingston YMCA is a well-run sports facility with a 25m pool.

**Rockfort Mineral Baths**    HEALTH & FITNESS
(Windward Rd; adult/child J$450/200; ⊘ 8am-4pm Mon-Fri, 7am-5pm Sat & Sun) Providing respite from the urban environment, these baths on the outskirts of Kingston, on the road to the airport, are fed by a cold spring that made its first appearance following the earthquake of 1907. There's a large public pool and 11 private pools of varying sizes, all with whirlpools and wheelchair access. The slightly saline and radioactive water is said to have therapeutic properties.

One hour is the maximum allowed in a bath. There's a cafeteria and juice bar, plus changing rooms and lockers. Massage (J$2963 per hour) is offered.

Adjacent to the baths is Fort Rock, an English fort with rusty cannons. It was built in 1694 amid rumors of an imminent invasion by the French.

To get here, take bus 99, 98 or 97 from Parade (J$100).

**Jam One Sound System**    MUSIC
(Map p44; ☑ 422-9925, 906-6743; 13 Minott Tce, off Chisholm Ave; US$20) Ever wondered how a traditional Jamaican sound system is put together? A tour at Jam One, one of Kingston's few remaining sound-system workshops,

# Uptown Kingston

### ◎ Top Sights
| | | |
|---|---|---|
| 1 | Bob Marley Museum | E2 |
| 2 | Devon House | C3 |

### ◎ Sights
| | | |
|---|---|---|
| 3 | Emancipation Park | C5 |
| 4 | Peter Tosh Museum | C3 |
| 5 | St Andrew Parish Church | A3 |

### ◉ Activities, Courses & Tours
| | | |
|---|---|---|
| 6 | Environmental Foundation of Jamaica | C6 |
| 7 | YMCA | B3 |

### ◉ Sleeping
| | | |
|---|---|---|
| 8 | Altamont Court | C5 |
| 9 | Eden Gardens | E3 |
| 10 | Indies Hotel | B4 |
| 11 | Jamaica Pegasus | C5 |
| 12 | Knutsford Court Hotel | B4 |
| 13 | Mikuzi Cottages | E3 |
| 14 | Spanish Court Hotel | D4 |
| 15 | Terra Nova All-Suite Hotel | B2 |

### ◉ Eating
| | | |
|---|---|---|
| 16 | Ashanti Oasis | D3 |
| 17 | Cannonball Café | C4 |
| 18 | Chez Maria | D2 |
| 19 | Devon House Bakery | C2 |
| | Devon House I-Scream | (see 19) |
| 20 | Fromage | E2 |

| | | |
|---|---|---|
| | Grog Shoppe | (see 19) |
| 21 | Mi Hungry | A1 |
| 22 | Opa | E2 |
| 23 | Red Bones Blues Café | D3 |
| 24 | Sonya's Homestyle Cooking | B2 |
| 25 | So-So Seafood Bar & Grill | B4 |
| 26 | Sweetwood Jerk | C5 |
| | Terra Nova All-Suite Hotel | (see 15) |
| 27 | Toyota Coffee House | F4 |
| 28 | Triple T's | B1 |

### ◉ Drinking & Nightlife
| | | |
|---|---|---|
| 29 | Cuddy'z | C4 |
| 30 | Deck | D4 |
| 31 | Escape 24/7 | C4 |
| | Fiction | (see 21) |
| 32 | Limelight | A3 |
| 33 | Privilege | C4 |
| 34 | Savannah Plaza | B2 |
| | Tracks & Records | (see 21) |

### ◉ Entertainment
| | | |
|---|---|---|
| 35 | Little Theatre | D6 |
| 36 | National Arena | F5 |
| 37 | National Stadium | F5 |
| 38 | Stone Love HQ | A2 |

### ◉ Shopping
| | | |
|---|---|---|
| 39 | Bookland | C4 |
| 40 | Carbys | A2 |

## ★ Festivals & Events

Befitting a Caribbean capital city, Kingston is the site of engaging festivals and events all year round.

**Carnival**  CARNIVAL
(www.bacchanaljamaica.com; ⊙ Feb) A week of costumed revelers taking to the streets, two carnival camps (Jamaica Carnival and Bacchanal Jamaica), paint- and rum-throwing, parades, all-night parties and live reggae, calypso, and particularly soca. Highlights include J'Ouvert, an epic night-long party, and the Road March, when the two camps parade through the streets of New Kingston in carnival costume.

**Boys & Girls Championships**  SPORTS
(www.issasports.com; National Stadium; ⊙ week prior to Easter) Jamaica's biggest annual sporting event is a highly charged youth athletics contest, as scouts from around the world arrive to get a glimpse of future champions. A great atmosphere, as locals fill the stands to overflowing.

**Kingston on the Edge**  ART
(www.kingstonontheedge.org; ⊙ Jun) Week-long urban art festival featuring the best of new painting, photography and sculpture, as well as gallery shows, concerts and readings.

**One World Ska & Rocksteady Music Festival**  MUSIC
(www.facebook.com/oneworldska; ⊙ Nov) This new one-day festival praises all that's best in some of Jamaica's earliest, yet sometimes overlooked, musical genres: ska and rocksteady. It attracts nationally and internationally famous acts, and the music runs from midafternoon to sun-up. Get your skank on.

**LTM National Pantomime**  THEATER
(www.ltmpantomime.com; ⊙ Dec) Annual event at the Little Theatre (p58), with traditional Jamaican song and dance, saucy humor and fabulous costumes.

# 🛌 Sleeping

Many lodging options cater more to business travelers than tourists, and rates don't vary much year-round. Most hotels are in Uptown, with some of the more luxurious retreats further up in the hills.

### ★ Uptown Guesthouse
GUESTHOUSE $

(Map p44; ☑ 290-1984; nicolas_gauthier_6@icloud.com; 20 Earls Ct; r from US$50) A relaxed guesthouse in a quiet part of Kingston, with access to city amenities. Rooms are spacious, and the garden is enormous, plus there are a couple of soppy hounds that make the place feel like a real home away from home. One tip: beware the rum-laced Jamaican breakfast coffee.

Your hosts have good access to Kingston's social scene and pride themselves on their ability to get VIP for top events.

### ★ Reggae Hostel
HOSTEL $

(Map p44; ☑ 920-1596; www.reggaehostel.com; 8 Burlington Ave; dm/d US$25/70; 🅿 ❄ @ 🛜) Close to Half Way Tree, this excellent hostel has a relaxed, friendly vibe. Dorms are simple, with fans, while private rooms (one with its own bathroom) are spacious and have air-con. There's a communal kitchen, patio bar and helpful staff. Highly sociable – helpful if you're looking for people to hook up with to go to a dancehall street party or on a weekend beach trip.

### Indies Hotel
HOTEL $

(Map p50; ☑ 926-2952; www.indieshotel.com; 5 Holborn Rd; s with fan/air-con US$50/80, d US$90; 🅿 ❄ @) This family-friendly 'home away from home' remains great value for its cheerful ambience and accommodating atmosphere. Rooms cluster around a green courtyard, but try to take an upstairs room for brighter sunlight. A small restaurant serves good, simple food, and the attractive patio is a good spot for alfresco dining. All doubles have air-con.

### Mikuzi Cottages
GUESTHOUSE $

(Map p50; ☑ 856-7863; tomlinsonjohn44@gmail.com; 5 Upper Montrose Rd; r US$70-90, ste US$110; 🅿 ❄ 🛜) Friendly, yellow, colonial-era guesthouse with comfortable rooms – all bright colors and funky furnishings – most with kitchenettes. There's a cushion-strewn gazebo in the lush garden for relaxing in. It's in a quiet area but well located for transport connections on both Hope Rd and Old Hope Rd.

### ★ Neita's Nest
GUESTHOUSE $$

(Map p44; ☑ 469-3005; www.neitasnest.com; Stony Hill, Bridgemount; s/d US$90/120; 🛜) A truly delightful art-filled B&B tucked up high in Stony Hill, with great views from the terrace of Kingston and the mountains. Cozy rooms and a gracious host who welcomes you into the family make this feel like a perfect retreat away from the city. Dinner is available on request (and is highly recommended).

The excellent value is compounded by the discount offered for stays of more than two nights.

### Altamont Court
HOTEL $$

(Map p50; ☑ 929-4497; www.altamontcourt.com; 1 Altamont Cres; s/d US$110/120, ste US$155-184; 🅿 ❄ @ 🛜 🏊) A rather nondescript-looking business hotel from the outside, livened up somewhat by all the greenery in the

## THE YARDS

Much of Kingston's growth in recent decades has been in the 'yards' – acres of cheap and substandard housing west of Parade, originally conceived as 'model communities' when built in the 1960s. Most famous among them are Trench Town and Tivoli Gardens.

During the 1970s the middle classes decamped to the suburbs, and the JLP (Jamaica Labour Party) and PNP (People's National Party) curried favor among the ghetto constituencies by patronizing area leaders who, in turn, encouraged their gangs to recruit voters and intimidate political opponents at election time. Today, a large percentage of the gangs' incomes come from drug- and gun-running. The most famous leader of recent years was Christopher 'Dudus' Coke, who ran Tivoli Gardens and brought a perverse sense of security to the area until the government controversially stormed the area in 2010 using military tactics, with great loss of life.

It's easy to tell which party rules an area: no-nonsense wall murals act as territorial markers. While people from neighboring areas can freely enter the turf of the 'opposition' most of the time, tempers easily flare and it's best to visit with a trusted local. (Ironically, local security for street parties is usually excellent.)

grounds. The clean one-bedroom studios and suites have standard furnishings, and Jamaican breakfasts are served in the attractive Mango Tree restaurant. It has an excellent central location, within easy walking distance of New Kingston's attractions.

### Knutsford Court Hotel
HOTEL $$

(Map p50; ☑929-1000; www.knutsfordcourt. com; 16 Chelsea Ave; r/ste US$147/205; P ☺ ✻ @ 🤶 🖭) Fine hotel with a garden setting, popular with Jamaican families and businesspeople. The rooms – some with private balconies and work desks – are modern and well appointed. Rates include continental breakfast, served in the Melting Pot restaurant, which also offers exemplary Jamaican fare and room service at other times.

### Moon Hill
BOUTIQUE HOTEL $$

(Map p44; ☑620-8259; www.moonhilljamaica. com; 5 Roedeen Cl, Jack's Hill; s US$90-105, d US$160-190; P 🤶 🖭) A great combination of seclusion and reasonable proximity to the capital's attractions, this luxurious villa located in the Blue Mountain foothills is ideal for romantic or small-group getaways. The airy bedrooms feature firm queen- and king-size beds, all freshened by a cool breeze from the mountains. The Jamaican and international menu uses fresh produce from the organic garden.

### Eden Gardens
HOTEL $$

(Map p50; ☑946-9981; www.edengardenswellness. com; 39 Lady Musgrave Rd; r US$180; P ✻ 🤶 🖭) Set amid lush vegetation – a nod to its name – this gingerbread condo and wellness resort attracts those who like to mix business with pleasure. Each of the spacious, modern rooms comes with fully equipped kitchenette and large desk, while the Therapeutic Spa has a full range of massages and other treatments. Dress smartly to eat in the Black Orchid restaurant.

### ★ Spanish Court Hotel
BOUTIQUE HOTEL $$$

(Map p50; ☑926-0000; www.spanishcourthotel. com; 1 St Lucia Ave; r US$199-209, ste US$245-319; P ✻ @ 🤶 🖭) A favorite with Jamaica's business elite, this hotel is big enough to offer everything you need but small enough to remain intimate. Thoroughly modern rooms have Jamaican-designed furniture. Relaxation options include the rooftop pool, a gym and a spa. The Gallery Café is open throughout the day, while the restaurant has beautifully presented international and Jamaican dishes.

### Jamaica Pegasus
HOTEL $$$

(Map p50; ☑926-3691; www.jamaicapegasus.com; 81 Knutsford Blvd; r US$205, ste from US$265; P ☺ ✻ 🤶 🖭) This glitzy 17-story property overlooking Emancipation Park is a long-established feature of the business travel scene, and it seems they are constantly improving the rooms. As well as a restaurant, there's a pool bar and 24-hour cafe. For an unparalleled view, ask for a room facing the mountains.

### Terra Nova All-Suite Hotel
HOTEL $$$

(Map p50; ☑926-2211; www.terranovajamaica. com; 17 Waterloo Rd; ste incl breakfast US$265-505; P ✻ @ 🖭) Kingston's grandest hotel, this colonial mansion dates from 1924, though rooms themselves have a surprisingly contemporary feel. The suites vary from regular to ultra-luxe, but king-size beds are standard – and thumbs up for the grand marble bathrooms. The restaurant is the venue for one of the city's top Sunday brunches, favored by the movers and shakers.

## ✗ Eating

As in other matters, Kingston is Jamaica's capital of food; it is here that the national cuisine was born and it is here that it continues to thrive and evolve. Let your taste buds run free!

Most of the notable eateries, which include international and fusion cuisine, are found in uptown Kingston, where the culinary adventurer is spoiled for choice.

### ✗ Uptown

### ★ Mi Hungry
VEGETARIAN $

(Map p50; Shop 24a, Marketplace; pizza half/whole J$500/1000, salads J$500-700; ⊙8:30am-11pm Mon-Sat, noon-10pm Sun) Mi Hungry serves up 'sun cooked' I-tal food that you wouldn't believe. Their 'pleaza' comes with a base of seeds and grains, topped with sun-dried tomatoes and crunchy veg (we recommend ackee with a few chilis) and is delicious in a way that the words 'raw vegan pizza' can't convey – you'll definitely want to come back for more.

The salads are equally hearty, and there's a fabulous array of fresh juices on offer. Made with love.

### ★ Andy's
JERK $

(Map p44; 49 Mannings Hill Rd; meals J$700; ⊙8am-11pm Mon-Sat) If you're after the best authentically prepared jerk chicken and pork in Kingston, then Andy's is well worth the travel. This nondescript corner stop gets particularly busy in the evenings, when locals line up for their meats accompanied by fried breadfruit, *festival*, sweet potato or plantain. There's good soup in the morning.

★**Sweetwood Jerk** JERK **$**
(Map p50; Knutsford Blvd; jerk from J$450; ☺11:30am-9pm Mon-Thu, 11:30am-midnight Fri & Sat, 1pm-9pm Sun) Our favorite New Kingston jerk joint, this place is popular with Uptown office workers and gets particularly busy once they knock off. Spicy, meaty offerings can be enjoyed in the outdoor sitting area facing Emancipation Park. Accompaniments include *festival*, sweet potato and particularly good fried breadfruit. This is one of the few jerk joints in Jamaica to feature jerk lamb.

★**Devon House Bakery** BAKERY **$**
(Map p50; Devon House; patties from J$200-450; ☺10am-10pm) Those in the know swear by patties served up in this small bakery located at Devon House. We're inclined to agree that they're some of the best in Jamaica (albeit at a slightly premium price). Lobster patty, anyone? An array of tempting cakes and juices is also available at this excellent option for a picnic on the grounds.

**Triple T's** JAMAICAN **$**
(Map p50; Annette Cres, off Upper Waterloo Rd; mains around J$1400; ☺7am-9pm Mon-Fri, 8am-9pm Sat, 8:30am-9pm Sun) An open-sided garden restaurant with trees growing through the dining room and funky art hanging everywhere, Triple T's is a great relaxed place for generous servings of traditional Jamaican dishes, both delicious and well presented. There's a bar and a host of fresh juices if you want to linger for a drink.

Kitchen service can sometimes be a bit relaxed – if you're in a rush, ask what's ready to go and you'll be eating in a trice. If you have trouble finding it, look for it opposite the giant Megamart supermarket.

**Toyota Coffee House** CAFE **$**
(Map p50; Old Hope Rd; sandwiches from J$450; ☺8am-5pm Mon-Fri, 9am-2pm Sat) 'Wait,' you think as you walk through the door, 'this is just a car showroom.' True enough, but upstairs is a lovely relaxed cafe with good service, excellent coffee and tea, sandwiches, cakes and a huge window looking up to the mountains. It's the perfect spacious spot to chill or bring your laptop. A hidden gem.

## PATTY, GLORIOUS PATTY

Patties – pastries with spicy beef, chicken, cheese or vegetable filling – are a Jamaican institution. They're cheap (from J$140), filling and delicious, and sold by the Juici Patties, Tastee Patties and Mother's franchises: who has the superior offering is a subject for endless, friendly debate. The larger branches serve ultra-filling hominy and peanut porridge for breakfast, and lunch mains such as saltfish with callaloo or cabbage. If you want to go posh, try the lobster patties at Devon House Bakery in uptown Kingston.

**Devon House I-Scream** ICE CREAM **$**
(Map p50; Devon House, 26 Hope Rd; scoops J$250; ☺10am-10pm) Some of the island's best ice cream in more than 20 flavors – check out their signature Devon Stout. Eat one while strolling in the grounds of Devon House.

**Cafe Blue/Deli Works** CAFE **$**
(Map p44; Sovereign Centre, Hope Rd; meals J$700-900; ☺8am-8pm Mon-Sat, 9am-3pm Sun; 🖥) Always full of Uptowners with laptops, this bright, air-conditioned cafe serves an array of delicious, though not cheap, Blue Mountain coffees, as well as cakes, filled bagels and sandwiches. Seating is limited in the coffee shop proper, but in the side canteen you can choose from a number of Jamaican specials (J$500 to J$650).

**Cannonball Café** CAFE **$**
(Map p50; www.facebook.com/CannonballCafe; 20 Barbados Ave; meals J$500-700; ☺7am-7pm Mon-Fri, 9am-5pm Sat & Sun; 🖥) Popular and busy cafe with wireless internet, serving excellent Blue Mountain coffee and cakes amid icy air-con. Light dishes – quiches, sandwiches and salads – are also on offer here. There's also a branch at Sovereign North Plaza on Barbican Rd.

**Fromage** FRENCH **$$**
(Map p50; 🖥622-9856; 8 Hillcrest Ave; salads J$1000, mains J$1900-3700; ☺8am-10pm Mon-Sat, to 4pm Sun) Charming French-/international-style restaurant, with a small gourmet market in reception. Lunch is about sandwiches, burgers and pasta (the crab 'burger' is tasty), while dinner is about meat – well-cooked steak, stuffed chicken and rich sauces. There's an extensive wine menu.

### M10 Bar & Grill
JAMAICAN $$

(Map p44; ☑930-2112; www.facebook.com/M10BarAndGrill; 6 Vineyard Rd, Vineyard Town; 3-course menu J$2500; ⊙11am-midnight) Where else but Kingston would you find a daytime truck stop that transforms into a slick open-air restaurant, with crisp white tablecloths and waiters in black ties? M10 is one of the city's best-kept secrets. The menu leans toward Jamaican and international – good stews, fish ribs and the like, with divine saltfish fritters to start and sticky desserts to finish.

### Chez Maria
LEBANESE $$

(Map p50; 80 Lady Musgrave Rd; meals J$750-1800; ⊙11:30am-10pm Mon-Sat, noon-9pm Sun; ☑) Whether you sit in the garden beneath the mango tree or grab a table on the terrace, you'll be treated to fine food at this Lebanese-Italian restaurant. The mezes are excellent and are complemented by home-made pita bread. A host of shawarmas and kebabs awaits if you still have an appetite, or go for one of their great pizzas.

### Sonya's Homestyle Cooking
JAMAICAN $$

(Map p50; ☑968-6267; 17 Central Ave; mains around J$1300; ⊙6:30am-6pm Mon-Fri, 7:30am-6pm Sat, 8:30am-7pm Sun) A place that's famous for big traditional Jamaican breakfasts, washed down with fresh juices; the Sunday buffet (8:30am to midday) is particularly popular. For lunches and early dinner, there's good pepperpot soup, curry goat, oxtail and beans, stew pork and fried chicken.

### Jade Garden
CHINESE $$

(☑978-3476; Sovereign Centre, 106 Hope Rd; dim-sum brunch J$2000; ⊙noon-10pm Mon-Sat, 11am-9pm Sun) Highlights of the à la carte menu at this elegant spot are the Dragon & Phoenix (chicken wings stuffed with minced pork and shrimp; J$1660) and a variety of excellent seafood dishes. If you feel like splurging, the two-course Peking duck (J$7200), traditionally prepared and carved at the table, is a delight, but the Sunday dim sum brunch is still the big draw here.

### So-So Seafood Bar & Grill
SEAFOOD $$

(Map p50; http://phoenixatsososeafood.com/; 4 Chelsea Ave; meals J$1200-2800; ⊙11am-midnight Mon-Thurs, 11am-1am Fri-Sat, 2pm-11pm Sun) A casual place with a hint of sports bar, known for its mellow after-work scene (the bar is good for chilling before your meal); its modest name belies the quality of the menu. The garlic shrimp and stew fish are particularly good, as is the weekly conch soup (Thursday and Friday), and delicious mannish water (miscellaneous goat-part soup) on Sunday.

### Grog Shoppe
JAMAICAN $$

(Map p50; Devon House; meals J$1500-3250; ⊙11am-10pm Mon-Sat) Housed in the old servants' quarters of Devon House, this atmospheric choice has the look and feel of a colonial pub. A separate dining room serves good Jamaican specialties, while the pub menu features burgers, crab cakes and other finger food.

### Opa
GREEK $$$

(Map p50; 75 Hope Rd; mains J$2000-3500; ⊙4pm-midnight) Jamaica's only Greek restaurant, this is the place to go if you're craving good lamb, sharp feta and fresh seafood. The Greek classics hold true, but other things get an inventive twist, such as the lamb burger that comes in a phyllo wrapper rather than a bun. The ackee burger is an unexpected hit too.

We could eat the grilled octopus all day and into the night, when the outside bar becomes a chilled Mediterranean-Caribbean lounge.

### Red Bones Blues Café
FUSION $$$

(Map p50; ☑978-8262; www.facebook.com/RedbonesBluesCafe; 1 Argyle Rd; mains J$3000-6000; ⊙11am-11pm Mon-Fri, 6-11pm Sat) This restaurant, bar and live-music venue has long been a beehive of cultural and culinary activity. Inside, the walls are beguilingly bedecked with photographs of jazz and blues legends. The menu offers Jamaican twists on European tastes (callaloo strudel, anyone?) with good fish, pasta and salads. The 'Nyam & Scram' lunch menu (J$1200) is excellent value.

There are quality live bands throughout the week, including blues, jazz and reggae, showcasing well-chosen local and international talent, as well as regular poetry slams.

### Terra Nova All-Suite Hotel
INTERNATIONAL $$$

(Map p50; ☑926-2211; 17 Waterloo Rd; Sun brunch J$3000; ⊙noon-3pm, 6.30-10pm Mon-Sat, 11am-4pm & 6.30-10pm Sun; ☑) The European menu has hints of the Caribbean as well as Jamaican favorites such as pepperpot soup and grilled snapper. However, the bigger draw for well-heeled Kingstonians (note: always dress up) is its famous Sunday brunch, comprising an all-you-can-eat buffet. Gorge yourself on curry goat, jerk chicken, pasta salads, ribs and more.

## ✕ Downtown

**Swiss Stores** CAFE **$**
(F&B Downtown; Map p48; cnr Church & Harbour
Sts; meals from J$800; ⊘8am-4:30pm Mon-Fri;
🛜) Pasta, pepperpot soup, sandwiches, roti
wraps and a glass of wine inside a welcome
bubble of air-con – what more could you
ask of a jewelry store! The setting seems in-
congruous, but Swiss Stores is an essential
downtown lunch and meeting spot. All the
items on the small menu are fresh and tasty,
and the coffee and cake are delicious.

★**Moby Dick** JAMAICAN **$$**
(Map p48; 3 Orange St; meals J$1100-2000;
⊘9am-7pm Mon-Sat) Don't let the plastic ta-
blecloths fool you, this unassuming hangout
has been popular with besuited lawyers and
judges for nearly a century. The curried goat
(J$1100) is outstanding, as is the conch ver-
sion (J$1700) when available, served with
roti, rice and salad, and washed down with
one of the excellent fresh fruit juices.

## 🍷 Drinking & Nightlife

Kingston is the best town in Jamaica for
bar-hopping and clubbing, and you'll never
want for after-hours action.

Many bars, nightclubs and sound sys-
tems feature regularly scheduled events and
theme nights, making it possible to get a
groove going every night of the week. Clubs
come and go – Kingston crowds are fickle
when it comes to the hippest scene.

What Kingston is really famous for is its
sound systems: giant speaker stacks with
a 'selector' (DJ) playing the tunes and a
'toaster' acting as MC to the proceedings.
Part block party, part fashion show and
all-out stereo war, sound-system parties
are an essential Jamaican experience. They
start late in the night and go into the early
morning, so you'll need to pace yourself –
don't even think of turning up much before
midnight.

KINGSTON, BLUE MOUNTAINS & SOUTHEAST COAST KINGSTON

### KINGSTON PARTY PLANNER

| | |
|---|---|
| Monday | **Hot Mondays** at Limelight (Map p57; ☏908-0841; Half Way Tree Entertainment Complex, 5-7 Hagley Park Rd; ⊘midnight-5am) |
| | **Uptown Mondays** at Savannah Plaza (Map p57; Half Way Tree); dancehall sound system |
| | Inner City Dub (The Ark; www.facebook.com/innercitydub; 6 Cargill Ave; ⊘8pm-late Mon) FREE |
| Tuesday | **Sankofa Sessions** at Ashanti Oasis (Map p57; 12 Braemar Ave) |
| | **Nipples Tuesday** at King Jammys Studio (Map p57; 30 St Lucia Rd, Waterhouse) |
| Wednesday | **Weddy Weddy Wednesdays** at Stone Love HQ (Map p57; Half Way Tree); one of the best Uptown sound systems |
| Thursday | **Vinyl Thursdays** street dance at Regal Plaza, Cross Roads |
| Friday | **After Work Jam** at the Deck (Map p57; 14 Trafalgar Rd; ⊘5pm-late) |
| | **Friday Night Party** at Privilege (Map p57; ☏622-6532; www.clubprivilegejm.com; 14-16 Trinidad Tce; J$1000; ⊘10pm-4am Fri & Sat) |
| | **Club Night** at Fiction (Map p57; ☏631-8038; Unit 6, Market Pl, 67 Constant Spring Rd; J$1000; ⊘6pm-4am Mon-Sat) |
| Saturday | **Privilege Saturday** at Privilege (Map p57; ☏622-6532; www.clubprivilegejm.com; 14-16 Trinidad Tce; J$1000; ⊘10pm-4am Fri & Sat) |
| | **Club Night** at Fiction (Map p57; ☏631-8038; Unit 6, Market Pl, 67 Constant Spring Rd; J$1000; ⊘6pm-4am Mon-Sat) |
| Sunday | **Old Hits Night**; sound system playing the best of reggae outside the Capricorn bar (14 Rae St) in Rae Town |
| | **Kingston Dub Club** at Dub Club (p58) |

It's perfectly safe to attend street parties, as the neighborhoods are responsible for security and people don't take kindly to violence spoiling the event, but it's best to come with a local and to leave obvious valuables behind.

### Tracks & Records     BAR
(Map p50; 906-3903; www.facebook.com/UBTracks; Market Pl, 67 Constant Spring Rd; 11:30am-11:30pm) Music meets athletics at this doubly punning sports bar owned by Usain Bolt. The atmosphere is lively, with plenty of drinks and bar food, plus some surprisingly good karaoke, and live music on 'Behind the Screens' Tuesday.

### Cuddy'z     SPORTS BAR
(Map p50; www.facebook.com/cuddyzsportsbar; 25 Dominica Dr; 11:30am-1am Mon-Thu, 11:30am-2am Fri & Sat, 1-11pm Sun) This hip establishment is the creation of the 'Big Man Inna Cricket,' Courtney Walsh. TVs in each booth and a lively bleachers section with an oversized screen make this a great place to catch the latest football, cricket and baseball games.

### Escape 24/7     BAR
(Map p50; 24 Knutsford Blvd; 24hr) A typical night here starts with a dominoes tournament among older clientele, fueled by the inexpensive drinks, followed by a loud music mix of hip-hop, dancehall and reggae that attracts a younger crowd. It claims to never close.

## ☆ Entertainment

Streetside billboards advertise upcoming live concerts and sound-system parties. Sports-lovers should make their way to Sabina Park (Map p44; 967-0322; South Camp Rd) or the National Stadium (Map p50; 929-4970; Arthur Wint Dr) for big events.

### Caymanas Park     SPECTATOR SPORT
( 988-2523; www.caymanaspark.com; Caymanas Dr, Portmore; J$250-500; Wed & Sat) The horse races at Caymanas Park in Portmore, one of the best racetracks in the Caribbean (and immortalized in several classic ska songs), make for a lively outing and a real slice of traditional Jamaican life; get a local to explain the complicated betting system. Take buses 17A, 18A, 20A from Half Way Tree (J$100).

### Little Theatre     THEATER
(Map p50; 926-6129; www.ltpantomime.com; 4 Tom Redcam Dr) Puts on plays, folk concerts and modern dance throughout the year. The National Dance Theatre Company performs July to August. Pantomime from late December through April.

### Carib 5 Cinema     CINEMA
(Map p44; 906-4017; www.palaceamusement.com; cnr Slipe & Half Way Tree Rds) Five screens, showing mainly Hollywood films. Tickets can be booked online.

### Palace Cineplex     CINEMA
( 978-3522; www.palaceamusement.com; Sovereign Centre, 106 Hope Rd) Two screens; tickets can be booked online.

### National Arena     STADIUM
(Map p50; 929-4970; Arthur Wint Dr) Indoor arena hosting live music, sports and other cultural events.

## 🛍 Shopping

Kingston has it all, from modern shopping malls to street craft stalls. Good crafts are found Downtown, whereas Devon House is your port of call for specialty shops. Art galleries and souvenir shops are scattered around Uptown, though many are to be found in shopping malls off and along Hope Rd.

### DUB CLUB

Dub Club (www.facebook.com/officialkingstondubclub; Skyline Dr, Jack's Hill; J$500; 8pm-2am Sun) is a house party that's become a Jamaican brand. And what a house! Set high on Jack's Hill, it looks down over the lights of Kingston, twinkling in the night. The huge sound system treats you to the deepest dub and rootsiest reggae you can imagine, with the selector standing at a pair of decks under a huge mango tree.

There's a laid-back bar and I-tal food, and the doors open from 8pm, so you can treat it as a fine early drinking spot, though things don't get going until way after 10pm. Every reggae artist and DJ worth their salt rotates through the Dub Club at some time – if there's a cooler night out in Kingston, we'd like to know about it.

## USEFUL BUS ROUTES IN KINGSTON

All bus fares within Kingston are J$100.

| DESTINATION | BUS | FREQUENCY | DEPARTURE POINT |
|---|---|---|---|
| Hellshire Beach | 1/1A | hourly | Parade/Half Way Tree |
| Spanish Town | 21B/22, 22A | hourly | Half Way Tree/Parade |
| Constant Spring | 42/42A | hourly | Parade/Half Way Tree |
| Papine | 60, 68 | hourly | Parade/Half Way Tree |
| Gordon Town | 61 | several daily | Parade |
| Barbican | 74/76 | hourly | Parade/Half Way Tree |
| Bull Bay | 97 | hourly | Parade |
| Airport, Port Royal | 98 | every 30min | Parade |
| Harbour View | 99 | hourly | Parade |
| Parade | 500/600/700 | every 30min | Half Way Tree |

One of the largest shopping centers is Sovereign Centre (Map p44; 106 Hope Rd; ⊙9am-9pm).

Rockers International MUSIC
(Map p48; ✆922-8015; 135 Orange St) Orange St was once home to a host of fabulous music shops, but Rockers International is one of the few remaining. Still, it has the best pick of reggae, dub and ska music in Kingston, all lovingly pressed on vinyl, in a shop with a great old-school vibe. You can can buy a few CDs here too.

Bookland BOOKS
(Map p50; 53 Knutsford Blvd; ⊙9am-6pm Mon-Fri, 10am-6pm Sat) Excellent New Kingston book-shop. Stock includes a strong selection of titles on Jamaica and the Caribbean, includ-ing guidebooks and a fiction section dedicat-ed to Caribbean writers. Also carries a good range of international magazines.

Carbys GIFTS & SOUVENIRS
(Map p50; Twin Gate Plaza, Constant Spring Rd; ⊙9:30am-6:30pm Mon-Sat) Tourist souvenir shop that has it all, from jerk sauce and Blue Mountain coffee to every green, gold and black item of Jamaica-branded clothing you could ever hope for.

Grosvenor Galleries ART
(Map p44; ✆924-6684; www.facebook.com/GrosvenorGalleries; 1 Grosvenor Tce; ⊙10am-5pm Tue-Sat) Excellent contemporary art and crafts by local artists.

## ⓘ Information

### DANGERS & ANNOYANCES

Kingston carries a fearful reputation before it, but in practice visitors can safely enjoy the city as long as a few commonsense guidelines are followed.

New Kingston and upscale residential areas such as Liguanea and Mona are generally safe for walking, as are most main roads and Down-town. At night, always take taxis. Watch out for pickpockets in market areas.

Trench Town, Jones Town, Denham Town, Tivoli Gardens and west of Parade, Downtown, are areas best explored with a local guide.

### INTERNET ACCESS

➡ Most hotels and plenty of coffee shops provide free wi-fi access.

➡ 4G data is available in most parts of the city.

➡ **Kingston and St Andrew Parish Library** (✆926-3315; 2 Tom Redcam Dr; per 30min J$100; ⊙9am-6pm Mon-Fri, to 5pm Sat) has internet access amid the books.

### MEDICAL SERVICES

**Ambucare** (✆978-2327; www.ambucareja.com; ⊙24hr)

**Andrews Memorial Hospital** (✆926-7401; www.amhosp.org; 27 Hope Rd)

**Kingston Public Hospital** (✆922-0210; North St)

**Liganea Drugs & Garden** (134 Old Hope Rd)

**Monarch Pharmacy** (Sovereign Centre; ⊙9am-10pm Mon-Sat, to 8pm Sun)

**St John Ambulance** (✆926-7656)

**University Hospital** (✆927-1620; http://uhwi.gov.jm; University of the West Indies campus, Mona)

## MINIBUS SERVICES FROM KINGSTON

| DESTINATION | COST (J$) | DURATION (HR) | FREQUENCY |
| --- | --- | --- | --- |
| Mandeville | 300 | 1½ | 5-6 daily |
| May Pen | 200 | 1 | 6-8 daily |
| Montego Bay | 650 | 4½-5 | 6-8 daily |
| Morant Bay | 200 | 1 | 10+ daily |
| Ocho Rios | 400 | 2 | 8-10 daily |
| Port Antonio | 500 | 2 | 6-8 daily |
| Santa Cruz | 400 | 2 | 6-8 daily |

### MONEY

Uptown, there are half a dozen banks along Knutsford Blvd and around Half Way Tree. Most banks have foreign-exchange counters as well as 24-hour ATMs. There are also ATMs along Hope Rd, particularly by the shopping malls.

### POST

**DHL** (www.dhl.com.jm; 19 Haining Rd)
**Downtown Post Office** (Map p48; ☑ 922-2120; 13 King St; ⊙ 8am-5pm Mon-Thu, 9am-4pm Fri, 8am-1pm Sat)
**FedEx** (☑ 800-463-3339; www.fedex.com/jm; 40 Half Way Tree Rd; ⊙ 8:30am-5pm Mon-Fri)
**Half Way Tree Post Office** (Map p50; Half Way Tree Rd; ⊙ 8am-5pm Mon-Thu, 9am-4pm Fri, 8am-1pm Sat)

### POLICE

**Downtown Police Station** (☑ 922-9321; 11 East Queen St) Downtown police headquarters.
**Half Way Tree Police Station** (142 Maxfield Ave, Half Way Tree)

### TOURIST INFORMATION

**Jamaica Conservation & Development Trust** (☑ 960-2848; www.jcdt.org.jm; 29 Dumbarton Ave, Kingston 10) Responsible for the management and supervision of the Blue Mountains-John Crow National Park. Can advise on guides and routes.
**Jamaica Tourist Board** (Map p50; ☑ hotline 929-9200; www.visitjamaica.com; 64 Knutsford Blvd) This Uptown office offers maps, brochures and advice for accommodations, tours and transport.

## ⓘ Getting There & Away

### AIR

**Norman Manley International Airport** (KIN; Map p44; ☑ 924-8452; www.nmia.aero), 27km southeast of Downtown, handles international flights. There's a tourist information desk in the arrivals hall, and a money-exchange bureau before customs. As you exit there's a bank, car rental booths and a booking station for official taxis. Outside, you'll find phone shops to buy local SIM cards. Bus 98 operates between arrivals hall and Parade, Downtown (J$100, 35 minutes, every 30 minutes). A taxi to New Kingston costs about US$35.
**Tinson Pen Aerodrome** (Map p44; Marcus Garvey Dr) is serviced by bus 22 or 22A from Parade (J$100, 20 minutes, hourly).

### CAR

#### From the North Coast

The new toll highway runs you quickly from Kingston to the north coast, joining the northern highway near St Ann's Bay. Tolls are around J$1000, depending on your car. The old A3 leads to Kingston via Stony Hill and Constant Springs. The more scenic but difficult B3 takes you to Papine from Buff Bay via the Blue Mountains, but is sometimes closed due to landslides.

#### From the West

Spanish Town Rd enters Kingston at the Six Miles junction. For uptown Kingston, veer left on Washington Blvd, later changing its name to Dunrobin Ave and joining Constant Springs Rd.

#### From the East

Windward Rd passes the turnoff for Port Royal and the airport. For New Kingston turn right on Mountain View Ave or South Camp Rd (the latter has helpful 'follow the hummingbird' signs directing the way).

### PUBLIC TRANSPORTATION

Buses, minibuses and route taxis run between Kingston and every point on the island. They arrive and depart primarily from Downtown **long-distance bus terminal** (Beckford St). Buses depart when full and are often packed beyond capacity; there are fewer departures on Sunday.

Comfortable **Knutsford Express** (☑ 971-1822; www.knutsfordexpress.com) buses run from their own terminal (p212) in New Kingston to the following destinations:

**Falmouth** J$2200, three hours, nine daily
**Mandeville** J$2000, two hours, three daily
**Montego Bay** J$2450, four hours, nine daily
**Negril** J$2700, five hours, two daily

**Ocho Rios** J$1600, two hours, seven daily
**Port Antonio** J$2200, four hours, two daily, via Ocho Rios
**Savannah-la-Mar** J$1500, two hours, three daily

Buying tickets more than 24 hours in advance gets a J$200 discount. Be at the bus station no later than 15 minutes before departure to register your ticket.

Minibuses to Port Antonio (J$450, two hours) arrive and depart from outside **Half Way Tree Bus Terminal** (Map p50).

If you're traveling to Kingston, find out where you will be dropped before boarding a bus.

## ℹ Getting Around

PUBLIC TRANSPORTATION

Buses, minibuses and route taxis arrive and depart from **North** (Map p48) and **South Parade** (Map p48) in Downtown; Half Way Tree bus station (p61) in Uptown; Cross Roads, between Uptown and Downtown; and **Papine** (Map p44; Main St), at the eastern edge of town off Old Hope Rd.

**Jamaica Urban Transport Co Ltd** (JUTC; www.jutc.com; city fares J$100) operates a fleet of yellow Mercedes-Benz and Volvo buses. Most are air-conditioned. JUTC buses stop only at official stops.

Minibuses and route taxis (look for their red license plates) ply all the popular routes (J$100), stopping on request.

TAXI

Taxis are numerous in Kingston, except when it rains and demand skyrockets. Use licensed cabs only, which have red PP or PPV license plates. Taxis have no meters, so confirm the fare in advance

Reputable 24-hour, radio taxi firms:

**Apollo Taxis** (☑ 969-9993)
**El Shaddai** (☑ 925-1363)
**Express** (☑ 923-2868)
**On Time** (☑ 926-3866)

CAR

Driving in Kingston isn't for the fainthearted. Be prepared for erratic and aggressive driving. All hotels and shopping centers offer parking, but secure car parking is nonexistent Downtown.

Most car-rental companies offer free airport shuttles. Some reputable companies with offices at Norman Manley International Airport:

**Avis** (☑ 924-8293; www.avis.com.jm; Norman Manley International Airport)
**Budget** (☑ 924-8762; www.budgetjamaica.com; Norman Manley International Airport)
**Hertz** (☑ 924-8028; www.hertz.com; Norman Manley International Airport)

Local car-rental companies with offices in Kingston include:

**Beaumont Car Rentals** (☑ 926-0311; 56c Studio One Blvd)
**Caribbean Car Rentals** (☑ 974-2513; www.caribbeancarrentals.net; 31 Hope Rd)
**Island Car Rentals** (☑ 926-8012; www.island-carrentals.com; 17 Antigua Ave)

# AROUND KINGSTON

There's so much more to the Kingston area than just the city itself, and it's easy to make day trips to explore the nearby coast.

Most popular among day trips is a visit to Port Royal, a former pirates' den of iniquity, easily combined with a visit to Lime Cay, the best (and closest) swimming spot in the area. Other good seaside options include Hellshire Beach – a quintessential Kingstonian seaside experience – and Bull Bay, with its small surfing community.

## Port Royal

Once the wealthiest (and 'wickedest') cities in the New World, the pirate capital of the Caribbean – and for more than 200 years the hub of British naval power in the West Indies – Port Royal today is a sleepy fishing village, yet one replete with historic buildings.

There are few hints of the town's former glory, though landmarks such as Fort Charles give a tantalizing glimpse. Restaurants serving the freshest fish in the Kingston area, and doubling as party spots after hours, along with the white-sand beach of Lime Cay make this one of the best-loved spots near Kingston.

Port Royal sits at the end of a narrow 16km-long spit called the Palisadoes that forms a natural breakwater protecting Kingston Harbour. The spit earned its name for the defensive palisade that was built across the spit to defend Port Royal from a land-based attack. The Palisadoes is fringed on its harbor side by mangroves that shelter crocodiles and colonies of pelicans and frigate birds.

### History

The English settled the cay in 1655 and built five forts here to defend Kingston Harbour. Buccaneers – organized as the Confederacy of the Brethren of the Coast – established their base at Port Royal, using it for government-sponsored raids against the Spanish.

The lawless buccaneers were big spenders. The wealth flowing into Port Royal attracted merchants, rum traders, prostitutes and others seeking a share of the profits. Townsfolk invested in the expeditions in exchange for a share of the booty and by 1682 Port Royal was a prosperous town of 8000 people.

At noon on June 7, 1692, a great earthquake shook the island, followed by a huge tsunami, and two-thirds of the town disappeared underwater. Around 2000 people died instantly, and numerous survivors were claimed by the pestilence that followed. Many claimed the destruction was God's vengeance for the town's lax morals.

Port Royal never truly recovered. Piracy was outlawed, and the town was overshadowed by the growing city of Kingston. In the 18th century, Port Royal instead began a 250-year tenure as headquarters of the Royal Navy in the West Indies; Admiral Lord Nelson was quartered here for a spell. In 1838 Jamaica ceased to be a separate naval command and, with the development of steam warships in the early 20th century, Port Royal's demise was sealed.

## ◉ Sights

★**Fort Charles**                        FORT

(☑967-8438; adult/child J$1000/500; ☺9am-5pm) Jamaica's latitude and longitude are measured from the flagstaff of Fort Charles, a weathered redoubt originally laid in 1655, and the only one of the town's forts to survive the 1692 earthquake. Originally washed by the sea on three sides, the fort is now firmly landlocked due to the gradual silt build-up.

At its peak, 104 guns protected the fort. Many cannons still point out from their embrasures along the restored battlements. In the center of the courtyard stands the small, well-presented Maritime Museum, containing a miscellany of objects – from glassware and pottery to weaponry – retrieved from the sunken city. Horatio Nelson, who later became Britain's greatest naval hero, lived in the small 'cockpit' while stationed here for 30 months.

Behind the museum is the raised platform known as Nelson's Quarterdeck, where the young Nelson kept watch for enemy ships amid fears of a French invasion. A plaque on the wall of the King's Battery commemorates his time here.

A small redbrick artillery store, the 1888 Giddy House, sits alone just behind the fort. The 1907 earthquake briefly turned the spit to quicksand and one end of the building sank, leaving the store at a lopsided angle. Next to the Giddy House is a gun emplacement with a massive cannon – which also keeled over in 1907.

**St Peter's Church**                    CHURCH

(Main Rd) Built in 1725 of red brick, this church is handsome within, despite its faux brick facade of cement. Note the floor paved with original black-and-white tiles, and the beautifully decorated wooden organ loft built in 1743. The place is replete with memorial plaques. Come dressed up for a Sunday service.

**Old Gaol House**              HISTORIC BUILDING

(Gaol Alley) The only fully restored historical structure in town is the sturdy Old Gaol House, made of cut stone on Gaol Alley. It predates the 1692 earthquake, when it

## Port Royal

served as a women's jail, and has since survived a host of disasters, including 14 hurricanes and two major fires.

**Old Naval Hospital**                    HISTORIC BUILDING
Behind the old garrison wall off New St stands the dilapidated two-story Old Naval Hospital, built by Bowling Ironworks in Bradford, UK, shipped to Port Royal and reconstructed at this site in 1818. It's in a poor state and still awaits restoration after it was damaged in Hurricane Gilbert in 1988.

## ★ Festivals & Events

**Port Royal Seafood Festival**         FOOD & DRINK
(☉Oct) The Port Royal Seafood Festival, held each year on National Heroes Day, the third Monday in October, is a rollicking good time with plenty of food (the celebrity cook-off is always popular) and live music from big-name artists.

## 🛏 Sleeping

**Admiral's Inn**                       GUESTHOUSE **$**
(☏353-4202; Henry Morgan Blvd; r US$60; ❄) Rooms inside this cheerful and friendly, yellow, family-run guesthouse have fridges and microwaves, and you can chill in the garden while the owners cook your fish supper. Trips to Lime Cay can be organized. Follow the road round past Gloria's Top Spot and past the park on your right-hand side. The guesthouse is on the left.

**Grand Port Royal Hotel Marina & Spa**                      HOTEL **$$$**
(☏967-8494; www.grandportroyalhotel.com; 1 Port Royal; r US$150-350; P❄🅿❄) This hotel, which famously featured in the Bond film *Dr No*, sits in the grounds of the old naval dockyard. Rooms with balconies are extremely comfortable, and there's a top restaurant (popular for Sunday brunch) and waterside bar overlooking Kingston's largest marina, as well as spa facilities.

## 🍴 Eating

**★Gloria's**                           SEAFOOD **$**
(5 Queen St; fish J$1300, lobster J$1750; ☉10:30am-11pm Mon-Thu & Sun, to 1am Fri & Sat) This fish restaurant fills daily with locals who drive here from miles around. Get here early, particularly on Friday night and Sunday lunchtime. Gloria's fish is nothing short of glorious – a large plate of melt-in-your-mouth perfection, accompanied by *bammy*, *festival* or rice.

## LIME CAY

The idyllic Lime Cay (Map p44) is one of half a dozen or so uninhabited, white sand–rimmed coral cays about 3km offshore from Port Royal. Immortalized in the final showdown of the movie *The Harder They Come*, it's ideal for sunbathing and snorkeling. Shacks sell food and drinks.

Arrange a trip from Morgan's Harbour Yacht Marina (Wednesday to Sunday only, J$1500, minimum four people).

You might talk the local fishers into taking you for a reduced rate on their motorized boats ('canoes'); agree a round-trip rate first and only pay half until they come to pick you up, or risk getting stranded.

Shellfish lovers, go for the curried or honey jerk shrimp or the grilled lobster.

**Y-Knot**                              SEAFOOD **$**
(meals J$1000-1500; ☉9am-7pm Mon-Sat) On a large deck over the water, this spot serves particularly good conch soup, as well as sumptuous jerk and grilled chicken, fish, shrimp and lobster. As well as a restaurant it's also the main place to catch boats to Lime Cay.

## ❶ Getting There & Away

From Kingston's north Parade take bus 98 (J$100, every 30 minutes, less frequently on Sunday).

## Bull Bay

You might easily drive through the small town of Bull Bay without really noticing it, but it's the birthplace of Jamaica's surfing scene and a great place to base yourself if you're looking to catch some waves.

Bull Bay is 14km east of Downtown Kingston – take bus 97 from Parade (J$100, 30 minutes). Minibuses between Kingston and Morant Bay pass through the town all day.

## 🏃 Activities

**★Jamnesia Surf Camp**                 SURFING
(☏750-0103; www.jamnesiasurf.com; 8 Miles, Bull Bay; lessons US$30, board rental per day US$20) Jamaica's longest-running surf school, established by the indomitable Billy Wilmot,

Jamnesia offers lessons and board rental from its Bull Bay surf camp. To catch the best breaks, there's a daily surf shuttle to the best spots along the coast (US$5). The camp also offers lessons to local youth, including the #SurfLikeAGirl summer camp. Board rental is half-price if you stay at the camp (p64).

## 🛏 Sleeping

⭐ **Jamnesia Surf Camp**     HOSTEL $
(📞750-0103; www.jamnesia.com; 8 Miles, Bull Bay; bungalow s/d US$45/55, dm US$35) This surf club (p63) with accommodation and a chilled vibe is a great place to catch the swell. There are plenty of boards to rent, decent basic rooms with shared kitchen facilities and a rustic outdoor bar that has live music on alternate Saturdays. Multinight lodging packages are also offered, including meals and surf shuttle.

# Hellshire Beach Recreation Area

White-sand beaches fringe the Hellshire Hills southwest of Kingston, making it a popular weekend destination. There are two beach options, one private, one public,

Bus 1 (J$100, 30 minutes), minibuses and route taxis (J$200) run from Kingston's Parade; bus 1A (J$00, 35 minutes) runs from Half Way Tree.

## 🏃 Activities

**Hellshire Beach**     BEACH
Hellshire Beach is a funky fishing and Rasta 'village' with dozens of brightly painted huts and stalls selling beer, jerk and fish. It's a lively place on weekends, with sound systems on Sunday nights. In the morning, fishing pirogues come in with their catch. On any day of the week, though, it's a fascinating visit, a slice of the 'real' Jamaica up close.

**Fort Clarence Beach Park**     BEACH
(adult/child J$500/250; ⊙10am-5pm Mon-Fri, 8am-7pm Sat & Sun) Fort Clarence Beach Park has clean sand, showers, toilets and secure parking. A restaurant and bar are open weekends only, and there are regular dancehall events.

# May Pen & Around

Clarendon parish is relatively little-visited. It's worth making a detour, though, to take a dip in the mineral waters of Milk River,

while keeping decidedly out of the water at Alligator Hole.

The capital of Clarendon parish, May Pen, is a teeming market and agricultural town. It's liveliest on Friday and Saturday when the market is held south of the main square.

## ⊙ Sights & Activities

**Alligator Hole Wildlife Reserve**     WILDLIFE RESERVE
(📞377-8264; canoe tours J$1000; ⊙Mon-Sat) **FREE** This lovely government-owned wildlife reserve is notable for its family of manatees that inhabit the clear water, and its crocodiles. They live amid dense reeds in jade-blue pools fed by waters that emerge at the base of limestone cliffs, and are not always easy to see. Waterfowl are abundant.

There's a small visitor center with displays on local wildlife. You can take an hour-long trip by canoe with a guide (tip expected).

**Milk River Bath**     SPA
(📞610-7745; per 15min J$600; ⊙7am-10pm) This well-known spa, operating since 1794, is fed from a saline mineral hot spring that bubbles up at the foot of Round Hill, 3km from the sea. The waters are a near-constant 33°C (92°F). The spa, which is attached to the Milk River Hotel, is owned by the government. Public and private baths are available.

Many recommend drinking the waters as a tonic, but they're the most radioactive spa waters in the world; bathers are limited to only 15 minutes, though you are allowed three baths a day. About 200m north of the spa is the open-air Milk River Mineral Spa Swimming Pool.

## 🛏 Sleeping

**Milk River Mineral Bath Hotel**     HOTEL $$
(📞449-6502; hotelmilkriver@yahoo.com; Clarendon; r half-board US$120) Milk River Hotel is a rambling white-porched hotel with shady verandas and 20 modestly furnished, pleasant rooms. Jamaican favorites are served in a cozy dining room; full board is available. If you stay here, access to the attached mineral spa is included in your tariff.

## ❶ Getting There & Away

This is a rural area best explored with your own vehicle, though minibuses do run around the May Pen area. The rural road west from Alligator Hole toward Treasure Beach is particularly bad, and a good way to mash up your car.

The transportation center in May Pen is 200m southeast of the main square, and it has frequent buses, minibuses and route taxis to and from Kingston (J$200, one hour), Ocho Rios, Mandeville, Negril and Milk River.

# BLUE MOUNTAINS

Deriving its name from the azure haze that settles lazily around its peaks, this 45km-long mountain range looms high above the eastern parishes of St Andrew, St Thomas, Portland and St Mary. The Blue Mountains were formed during the Cretaceous Period (somewhere between 144 and 65 million years ago) and are the island's oldest feature. Highest of the highlights, Blue Mountain Peak reaches 2256m above sea level, and no visit to the area should neglect a predawn hike to its summit for a sunrise view.

Unsurprisingly, the Blue Mountains' largely unspoiled character owes much to the difficulty of navigating around the area. Roads are narrow and winding, and some are dirt tracks that are utterly impossible to pass without 4WD, especially after heavy rains. If you are spending time in the area, it is highly advisable to rent a hardy vehicle, contact a tour guide or make arrangements with your hotel.

## History

With dense primary forests and forbidding topography, the Blue Mountains have discouraged all but the most determined settlers. During the 17th and 18th centuries, these same formidable qualities made the territory the perfect hideout for the Windward Maroons, who, from their remote stronghold at Nanny Town, resisted enslavement and British colonialism for more than

### A SEED-TO-CUP TASTE OF BLUE MOUNTAIN COFFEE

Coffee grows best on well-watered, well-drained slopes in cooler, tropical climates, such as Jamaica's Blue Mountains region. Its distinctly flavored coffee, with its lack of bitterness, is acclaimed by connoisseurs as among the world's best. To be designated 'Blue Mountain,' it must be grown – and roasted – at a certain altitude in a prescribed area.

In 1728, at Temple Hall Estate, north of Kingston, governor Sir Nicholas Lawes introduced arabica coffee to Jamaica from neighboring St Domingue (modern Haiti) and other planters followed suit, prompted by the growing demand in Europe. After the Haitian Revolution, many French planters settled in Jamaica, bringing their expertise with them, expanding and refining the industry. During the peak years of 1800–1840, production rose to 17,000 tons a year and Jamaica became the world's largest exporter.

Emancipation in 1838 brought an end to many of the plantations. Many ex-slaves left the estates and planted their own coffee. As steeper slopes were planted, coffee quality began to decline. The end of Britain's preferential tariffs for Jamaican coffee further damaged the industry at a time when high-quality coffee from Brazil was beginning to sap Jamaica's market share. By the close of WWII, Jamaica's coffee industry was on its last legs, prompting the Jamaican government to establish quality guidelines for coffee cultivation, thus saving the plantations.

There has been a resurgence in the popularity of Blue Mountain coffee in the last decade, largely thanks to interest from Japan, where it is a treasured commodity and sells for US$140 or more per kilogram. More than 80% of Blue Mountain coffee is sold to Japan at a preferential rate.

Sadly, this profitability only encouraged deforestation at home. Tearing down trees brought coffee farmers more valuable land, but also chased away migratory bird populations and has made Blue Mountain coffee especially vulnerable to hurricane damage. Over the past few years the industry's small farmers have been particularly hard hit by natural disasters, highlighting the need for both greater regulation and greater investment.

Currently 26 large and small estates are certified to produce Blue Mountain coffee, with quality guaranteed by the Jamaica coffee industry board. Several estates offer plantation and factory tours, allowing you to learn about this most treasured drink from seed to cup, and come away with your own beans to enjoy at home – food miles don't come much shorter than this. Estates worth checking out are the Mavis Bank Coffee Factory (p71), Craighton Coffee Estate (p69) in Newcastle, and Old Tavern Coffee Estate (p71) in Section.

# Blue Mountains

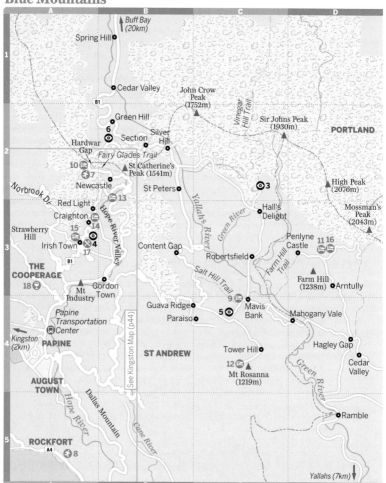

100 years. But this region's primary claim to fame has always been coffee cultivation; it has been a mainstay since the very first coffee factories were erected around Clydesdale in the mid-18th century. Meanwhile, back down at sea level, the southeast coast of St Thomas parish is notable for its long history of protest and rebellion, and the independent spirit of the region has kept it at odds with the government even to this day.

The Blue Mountains-John Crow National Park was gazetted in 1993 in recognition of the region's ecological and cultural importance.

## Hiking

The Blue Mountains are a hiker's dream, and 30 recognized trails lace the hills. Many are overgrown due to lack of funding and ecological protection programs, but others remain the mainstay of communication for locals.

The most popular route is the steep, well-maintained trail to 'The Peak,' which in Jamaica means Blue Mountain Peak (p72).

These trails (called 'tracks' locally) are rarely marked. Get up-to-date information on trail conditions from the main ranger station at Holywell. If a trail is difficult to follow, turn back. Mountain rescue is slow and you

Guides can be hired at the guesthouses in Hagley Gap and Penlyne Castle, or through most local accommodations for J$5000/7000 per half-/full day, while guided hikes in the Blue Mountains are also offered by the following:

➡ Forres Park Guest House & Farm (p71)

➡ Jamaica Conservation & Development Trust (p60) manages trails in the national park and can recommend hiking guides.

➡ Mount Edge B&B (p70)

The Blue Mountains-John Crow National Park protects 782 sq km and is managed by the Jamaica Conservation & Development Trust. The park includes the forest reserves of the Blue and John Crow Mountain Ranges and spans the parishes of St Andrew, St Thomas, Portland and St Mary. Ecotourism is being promoted and locals are being trained as guides. Camping is only permitted at designated sites – camping 'wild' is not advised.

could be lost for days. When asking for directions from locals, remember that 'jus a likkle way' may in fact be a few hours of hiking.

If you're hiking alone, normal precautions apply:

➡ Wear sturdy hiking shoes.

➡ Bring snacks, plenty of water and a flashlight (torch).

➡ Let people know where you're headed.

➡ Buy the 1:50,000 or 1:12,500 Ordnance Survey topographic maps, available from the Survey Department (Map p48; ☎ 750-5263; www.nla.gov.jm; 23½ Charles St, Kingston).

## ℹ️ GETTING AROUND IN THE BLUE MOUNTAINS

Traveling by your own vehicle is the best way to enjoy the Blue Mountains as public transportation between villages is infrequent and it's difficult to reach many points of interest. Many mountain guesthouses will arrange transfers.

### By Car

The roads in the Blue Mountains consist of endless switchbacks; they are narrow, sometimes overgrown with foliage, and can be badly rutted. Many corners are blind. Honk your horn frequently and watch out for reckless local drivers. There are no gas stations; fill up in Papine.

The main routes are usually fine for most vehicles, but the further you get from the beaten track, piste quality can deteriorate quickly (especially after heavy rains), making a sturdy 4WD with a low-gear option a better choice. Where relevant, road conditions are noted in the text.

From Kingston, Hope Rd leads to Papine, from where Gordon Town Rd (B1) leads into the mountains. Papine is your last opportunity to fill up with gas, so make sure you have a full tank. At the Cooperage, the road splits in two. Mammee River Rd forks left steeply uphill for Strawberry Hill resort (near Irish Town) and Newcastle. Alternatively Gordon Town Rd continues straight from the Cooperage and winds east up the Hope River Valley to Gordon Town, then steeply to Mavis Bank and Hagley Gap (for Blue Mountain Peak). The B1 continues across the mountains all the way to Buff Bay. A 4WD is recommended; this road is sometimes closed by landslides, so check before setting out.

### By Public Transportation

Buses 60 and 68 run hourly from Half Way Tree in Kingston up Hope Rd to Papine (J$100, 20 minutes), from where you connect to the Blue Mountains. Minibuses and route taxis depart from near the Park View Supermarket on the main square in Papine. There are two main routes: to Mavis Bank and Hagley Gap via Gordon Town (for Blue Mountain Peak), and to Newcastle and Section via Irish Town. Frequency of service depends on demand, but there's at least one morning run and one in the afternoon for the two main routes.

Sample fares include Mavis Bank (J$250, 1½ hours), Irish Town (J$200, 45 minutes) and Newcastle (J$250, 1¼ hours). Be prepared to haggle if you want to charter a route taxi. There is no regular bus service up the B1 to Buff Bay.

### By Mountain Bike

An exhilarating way to see the Blue Mountains is by mountain bike – the sturdier the better, as the going can be steep and arduous. Mount Edge B&B (p70) offers bike tours with small groups. Always check the bike's condition before setting out.

There is a national park entrance fee of US$5, which is payable at the ranger stations (open 9am to 5pm) at Holywell Recreation Area and Portland Gap (for Blue Mountain Peak), and at the Kingston office of the Jamaica Conservation & Development Trust (p60). Although it's quite possible to enter without a ticket, we do urge you to pay as funds go directly to supporting trail maintenance, ranger salaries and conservation work. The JCDT can also advise on guides and hiking routes, and sells copies of the excellent Guide to the Blue and John Crow Mountains.

## Irish Town

Mammee River Rd climbs through the Cooperage to Irish Town, a small village where the coopers lived during the 19th century. Potatoes are still an important crop, reflecting the Irish influence. Largely famous for one of the Caribbean's most luxurious resorts, it also contains St Mark's Chapel, an attractive white clapboard church restored after damage from Hurricane Gilbert.

From Irish Town, a dirt road runs up to the fundamentalist Rastafarian commune called Mount Zion Hill, consisting of just over 50 adults and children who rely on subsistence farming for a living. Though fierce in their rejection of Babylon, the residents can be seen on Papine Sq every Saturday when they come down to hold a Nyabinghi Sabbath Service consisting of drumming and dancing.

## 🛏 Sleeping

### ★ Strawberry Hill                HOTEL $$$
(☑946-1958; www.strawberryhillhotel.com; ste US$375, 1-/2-bed cottages US$ $475/530, villas US$620-695; P ❄ 🛜 🛎) Record mogul Chris Blackwell's pet, Strawberry Hill is a luxury retreat just north of Irish Town. Gaze at Kingston and the harbor 950m below from a deck chair by the infinity-edge pool, roam the bougainvillea-draped grounds or relax at the ayurvedic spa. The Caribbean-style cottages range from well-appointed mahogany-accented studio suites to a four-bedroom, two-story house built into the hillside.

Breakfast is included in the rates, as are transfers (full board is available on request). Birdwatching, hiking and other tours are available and Strawberry Hill also hosts a calendar of special events throughout the year.

Many Kingstonians make the tortuous drive to Strawberry Hill for some of the finest nouvelle Jamaican cuisine on the island (dinners US$35 to US$75). Reservations advised.

## 🍴 Eating

### Cafe Blue                CAFE $
(meals J$400-1200; ☉9am-6:30pm Mon-Thu, 8am-8:30pm Fri-Sun) Just above Irish Town, Cafe Blue, an offshoot of the popular Kingston institution (p55), serves sumptuous gourmet sandwiches, cakes and Blue Mountain coffee.

### Crystal Edge                JAMAICAN $
(meals around J$600; ☉8:30am-7pm Tue-Sun) Crystal Edge specializes in Jamaican favorites, such as curry goat, stews and filling soups. It's also popular for Sunday brunch.

# Newcastle

Newcastle was founded in 1841 as a training site and convalescent center for British soldiers. Nowadays it's a great getaway for hiking.

The road from Irish Town climbs to 1220m where you suddenly emerge on a

wide parade ground guarded by a small cannon. Since 1962 the camp has been used by the Jamaica Defense Force. Note the insignia (which dates back to 1884) on the white-washed stone wall, commemorating those regiments stationed at Newcastle. Visitors are allowed only around the canteen, shop, roadways and parade ground.

## ⊙ Sights

### Craighton Coffee Estate                FARM
(1hr tours per person J$2000; ☉9am-4pm) Just north of Newcastle, you can take a one-hour tour of the attractive 200-year-old Craighton Estate Great House and coffee plantation. During the tour, your knowledgeable guide explains to you the basics of coffee cultivation and a mildly steep walk leads you up to a gazebo surrounded by coffee bushes, with wonderful views of the mountains and the villages below. Tasting is included.

## 🏃 Activities

### Holywell Recreation Area                OUTDOORS
(☑960-2848; www.greenjamaica.org.jm; US$5; ☉9am-5pm) Spanning Hardwar Gap, this area protects 120 hectares of remnant woodland, lush with dozens of fern species, epiphytes, impatiens, violets, nasturtiums, wild strawberries and raspberries. The mist-shrouded, uppermost slopes are densely forested with rare primary montane forest, dominated by pine trees. The birdwatching is fabulous.

The staffed ranger station is a short distance beyond the entrance. The orientation center hosts occasional live entertainment such as traditional music and dance, plus outdoor games, storytelling and a treasure hunt for the kids; contact the Jamaica Conservation & Development Trust (p60) for information.

Well-maintained, easy hiking trails lead off in all directions through the ferny dells, cloud forest and elfin woodland. The 2.4km Oatley Mountain Trail, best seen with a guide (US$20) who can point out the different flora, leads to a river good for bathing. The 2km Waterfall Trail leads down along a stream to the Cascade Waterfalls – more trickle than cascade, due to recent landslides.

## 🛏 Sleeping

Newcastle has one of the wider selections of sleeping accommodations in the Blue Mountains.

★**Rafjam**
**Bed & Breakfast** GUESTHOUSE $
(☑944-8094; www.facebook.com/rafjams; Red Light; r US$70, 2-bedroom cottages US$150) This popular guesthouse sits next to the hamlet of Red Light, surrounded by nature and with lovely views. Rooms are charming if simple, but the welcome is a warm one. Birdwatching and guides for hiking can be arranged, or chill out in a hammock or in the terrace tiki bar that hangs over a burbling river.

★**Mount Edge B&B** GUESTHOUSE $
(☑351-5083, 944-8151; www.17milepost.com; r without bathroom J$3000-4000, with bathroom J$4000-6000; Ⓟ@🛜) 🍴 This quirky mountainside maze of brightly painted rooms and rustic bathrooms is a great budget option. Some rooms (as well as the chill-out lounge) have great views over the valley below and the gardens that produce organic veggies for the EITS Café. Birding and cycling tours are on offer. Meal packages can be arranged and weekly and monthly rates are negotiable.

The B&B rents out bikes (US$15 per day), as well as offering four-hour guided bike tours of the area (US$80).

**Gap Café Bed &**
**Breakfast** B&B $
(☑319-2406; cottages US$60) Just below the entrance to Holywell Recreation Area, here's a cozy, yellow, one-bedroom, self-catering cottage with a veranda.

The cafe (open for breakfast and lunch Thursday to Sunday; dinner by reservation only) is a fabulous place to take in the vistas. Dine alfresco on a wooden terrace, sampling the succulent curry goat and smoked pork chops, as well as lighter fare in the form of fancy sandwiches.

**Eating**

**EITS Café** FUSION $$
(☑944-8151; breakfasts J$800, salads J$500, mains from J$1400; ⊘9am-10pm) The acronym in the name of the restaurant at the Mount Edge B&B stands for Europe In The Summer – a reasonable summation of what the menu is attempting, with fresh organic vegetables and a 'farm to table' attitude. The food is good, but service can be a little relaxed at times – luckily the views of the valley compensate.

# Section & Clydesdale

At Section and Clydesdale you'll find one of the best Blue Mountain coffee-estate tours, and the remote botanic gardens at Cinchona.

Heading northeast from Holywell, the road drops steeply toward the hamlet of Section and then curls its way down to Buff Bay, 29km north (sometimes impassible due to landslips. A turnoff to the right at Section leads 1.5km to the ridge crest, where the main road loops south and drops to Content Gap, eventually linking up with the road from Gordon Town to Mavis Bank.

From Section take the horrendously pot-holed road south towards Guava Ridge; the turnoff for Clydesdale is about 1km above the hamlet of St Peters. Then you will cross over the Chestervale Bridge above the Brook's River and take the left, steeply uphill road at the Y-fork. It's a terribly rocky drive, suitable for a 4WD only.

## ◎ Sights

**Cinchona Gardens** GARDENS
(tip to caretaker expected) A dilapidated old house sits atop these 2.5-hectare gardens, fronted by lawns and exquisite floral beds. It's a little rundown, but the views are fabulous: to the north stand the peaks, but you can also peer down into the valleys of the Clyde, Green and Yallahs Rivers. The Panorama Walk begins to the east of the gardens, leading through a glade of towering bamboo and taking in the juniper cedar, camphor and eucalyptus trees, as well as a striking display of orchids.

It was the cultivation of Assam tea and cinchona (whose quinine – extracted from the bark – was used to fight malaria) that led to the founding of Cinchona Gardens in 1868. The grounds were later turned into a garden to supply Kingston with flowers. In 1903 the Jamaican government leased Cinchona to the New York Botanical Gardens and, later, to the Smithsonian Institute.

Finding Cinchona can be difficult without a guide. From Clydesdale you can either hike (1½ hours) or drive uphill along the muddy dirt track for about 3km. There are several unmarked junctions; ask for directions at every opportunity. Don't underestimate the awful road conditions; a 4WD with low-gear option is absolutely essential. Alternatively, you can drive up the more populated route via Mavis Bank, though the road conditions can be as atrocious.

Most of the trails that snake off into the nether reaches of the mountains are overgrown, but the 16km Vinegar Hill Trail, an old Maroon trail leading down to Buff Bay, can be negotiated with an experienced guide.

### Old Tavern Coffee Estate PLANTATION
(☏ 924-2785; tours around J$3000) Old Tavern Coffee Estate lies about 1.5km southwest of Section. Dorothy Twyman and her son David produce the superb Blue Mountain coffee. The Twymans welcome visitors by prior arrangement. You're treated to a lesson on coffee growing and production as well as a tasting session of two of the three arabica-bean roasts: dark, medium-dark and medium. Additionally, they produce the rare peaberry variety with a mild, subtle flavor.

The late Alex Twyman emigrated to Jamaica from England in 1958 and started growing coffee a decade later, his son now keeping up the tradition. Dorothy oversees the roasting, meticulously performing quality control by taste. The environmentally conscious Twymans keep their use of chemical pesticides and fertilizers to a minimum and compost all by-products before returning them to the soil

### 🛏 Sleeping

**Starlight Chalet & Health Spa** HOTEL $$
(☏ 969-3070; www.starlightchalet.com; Silver Hill Gap; r US$110-120; ℗) This plantation-style retreat is set amid a flower-filled hillside garden with dramatic alpine vistas. A great base for birding and hiking, it also offers massages at the no-frills spa, nature walks and yoga; book ahead of arrival. Off-season, you'll mostly have the place to yourself, though it's popular at weekend for weddings. Pickups are available – the road is atrocious.

## Mavis Bank
Mavis Bank, around a one-hour drive from Kingston, is a tidy little village in the midst of coffee country.

### ◎ Sights

**Mavis Bank Coffee Factory** FARM
(☏ 977-8015; tours J$1000; ◷10am-2pm Mon-Fri) Established in 1923 and located 1km southwest of Mavis Bank is the largest coffee factory in Jamaica, producing Blue Mountain coffee sold under the 'Jablum' label. Ask

the chief 'cupper' to demonstrate 'cupping' (tasting), the technique to identify quality coffee. You can tour the factory to see the coffee beans drying (in season) and being processed; call in advance. At the end of the 'from the berry to the cup' tour you can purchase roasted beans at bargain prices.

### 🏃 Activities

**Farm Hill Trail** HIKING
This trail begins beside the Anglican church, crossing Yallahs River and Green River and leading uphill for 8km (1½ to two hours) to Penlyne Castle and on to Blue Mountain Peak.

### 🛏 Sleeping
Mavis Bank has a couple of good sleeping options, offering a base from which to explore the local area.

**Forres Park Guest House & Farm** GUESTHOUSE $$
(☏ 927-8275; www.forrespark.com; cabins US$75, r US$90-220; ℗) This guesthouse is a top choice for birdwatchers. All rooms have balconies and the plushest sports a whirlpool tub. Excellent meals are cooked on request and available to nonguests. You can rent mountain bikes and enjoy the on-site spa treatments after tackling the steep, rewarding hiking trail. Excellent tours and guided hikes offered.

**★Lime Tree Farm** BOUTIQUE HOTEL $$$
(☏ 446-0230; www.limetreefarm.com; d cottage incl full board US$285; ℗) This combination of a small working coffee farm with exclusive all-inclusive lodging is hugely appealing. It offers three large, luxurious cottages with jaw-dropping mountain views as well as fine meals consumed in the attractive open-air lounge. All-inclusive packages comprise wine with dinner, transportation to and from Kingston and a variety of birdwatching and hiking tours.

## Hagley Gap & Penlyne Castle
The ramshackle village of Hagley Gap sits abreast a hill east of Mavis Bank and is the gateway to Blue Mountain Peak. The road forks in the village, where a horrendously denuded dirt road to Penlyne Castle begins a precipitous ascent.

**Penlyne Castle** is the starting point for the 12km hikes to and from Blue Mountain Peak. Many hikers stay overnight at one of several simple lodges near Penlyne Castle before tackling the hike in the wee hours.

Bring warm, waterproof clothing. One minute you're in sun-kissed mountains; the next, clouds swirl in and the temperature plunges.

## 🛏 Sleeping

Lots of people use Hagley Gap as a base from where to start the hike up to Blue Mountain Peak.

**Jah B's Guest House**                    GUESTHOUSE **$**
(☑ 377-5206; www.jahbguesthouse.com; Abbet Green; dm/r J$20/30; **P**) This friendly place, run by a family of Bobo Rastas and particu-larly popular with shoestring travelers, has a basic but cozy guesthouse with bunks and simple rooms. I-tal meals are prepared amid a cloud of ganja smoke and a nonstop volley of friendly banter; the manager can help ar-range transfers from Kingston.

Guides are available for hiking up Blue Mountain Peak.

**Whitfield Hall**                         GUESTHOUSE **$**
(☑ 878-0514; www.whitfieldhall.com; camping per tent US$5, dm/s/d US$20/30/55; **P**) Nes-tled amid pine trees, this former planta-tion dating from 1776 is an atmospheric but basic option (it's electricity-free), with shared bathrooms and kitchen. The dark, cavernous lounge has a huge fireplace and smoke-stained ceiling. Camping is allowed on the lawn beneath the trees. Order meals in advance.

---

### DON'T MISS

### BLUE MOUNTAIN PEAK

Most hikers set off from Penlyne Castle around 2am to reach Blue Mountain Peak for sunrise. Fortified with a breakfast of coffee and cereal, you set out single file in the pitch black along the 12km round-trip trail (you'll need a flashlight and a spare set of batteries, just in case). The first part of the trail – a series of steep scree-covered switchbacks named Jacob's Ladder – is the toughest. Midway, at Portland Gap (4km above Abbey Green), there's a ranger station where you pay the US$5 park fee. Also here are two ba-sic wooden cabins maintained by the Jamaica Conservation & Development Trust (p60). You can camp outside, where there's a cooking area and water from a pipe. Bring your own tent, or sleep on a bunk bed (BYO sleeping bag) or on the floor (foam mats available for rent; J$200). Reserve in advance.

As you hike, reggae music can be heard far, far below, competing with the chirps of crickets and katydids. Myriad peeny-wallies flit before you, signaling with their phospho-rescent semaphore.

You should arrive at the peak around 5:30am, while it is still dark. Your stage is gradu-ally revealed: a flat-topped hump, marked by a scaffolding pyramid and trig point (in the cloud it is easy to mistake a smaller hump to the left of the hut near the summit – Lazy Man's Peak – for the real thing). If the weather's clear, Cuba, 144km away, can be seen from the peak, which casts a distinct shadow over the land below. After a brief celebra-tory drink and snacks, you'll set off back down the mountain, passing through several distinct ecosystems – stunted dwarf or elfin forest, with trees like hirsute soapwood and rodwood no more than 2.5m high, an adaptation to the cold, followed by cloud forest, dripping with filaments of hanging lichens, festooned with epiphytes and moss, and dotted with wild strawberries, while further down you encounter bamboo and primordial giant tree ferns. Your guide points out Blue Mountain coffee growing and you arrive at your accommodations in time for brunch.

Don't hike without a guide at night. Numerous spur trails lead off the main trails and it is easy to get lost. Although hiking boots or tough walking shoes are best, sneakers will suffice, though your feet will likely get wet. At the top, temperatures can approach freez-ing before sunrise, so wear plenty of layers. Rain gear is also essential, as the weather can change rapidly.

# SOUTHEAST COAST

Jamaica's southeast corner, the parish of St Thomas, is one of the least-developed parts of the island, which is part of its charm. Don't be surprised if you come across Obeah circles in isolated villages – this parish is strongly associated with the practice.

## Morant Bay

Morant Bay, the town that played a pivotal role in Jamaica's history, squats on a hill behind the coast road. These days, it's a busy little town with a lively central market, its sugar-producing heyday long behind it. Most of the town's early colonial-era buildings were burned in the Morant Bay Rebellion of 1865, led by the town's national hero, Paul Bogle, but a couple of gems remain.

October 11 is Paul Bogle Day, when a party is held in the town square and a 10km road race sets out from Stony Gut.

### ◉ Sights

**Reggae Falls**　　　　　　　　　　　　WATERFALL
(Hillside Dam) `FREE` These falls, created by the Hillside Dam, make an attractive swimming hole. Drive from Morant Bay through Seaforth to get here, then walk along the river by the Morant River bridge to get here. It's great with a group of friends, but better not to visit alone as it's a long way from anywhere.

**Courthouse**　　　　　　　　　　HISTORIC BUILDING
Port Morant's courthouse was rebuilt in limestone and red brick after being destroyed in the 1865 rebellion and burned down again in early 2007, its ruins standing defiant behind an empty plinth that once bore the Edna Manley statue of Paul Bogle, his hands clasped over the hilt of a machete. Bogle is buried beside the courthouse alongside a mass grave holding the remains of many slaves who lost their lives in the rebellion.

Diagonally across from the courthouse is a handsome, ochre-colored Anglican church dating to 1881.

**Stony Gut Monument**　　　　　　　MONUMENT
This marker, commemorating Bogle's birthplace, stands opposite the Methodist church, 8km inland at the tiny hamlet of Stony Gut. His great-grandson Phillip Bogle is buried behind the marker. A second marker was erected in 2016 by the BBC, to commemorate Bogle's role in black British history.

### ⌨ Sleeping

**Whispering Bamboo Cove**　　　　　HOTEL $$
(☑982-1788; 105 Crystal Dr, Retreat; r US$80; P ❄) This is a comfortable villa-style hotel facing the beach in Retreat, 5km east of Morant Bay. It has spacious airy rooms tricked out with tropical decor. Those nearest the sea have the best views. Call in advance if you want to arrange full board.

### ✖ Eating

★**Longboarder**　　　　　　　　　JAMAICAN $$
(☑427-0408; www.facebook.com/thelongboarder bar; Coast Rd, Rozelle; mains from J$800; ⊙kitchen 12am-8pm) A super-relaxed beach bar, restaurant and surf spot, the Longboarder has a small bar area and a series of tables spread out under a wide tree, plus vistas down the rolling surf on the beach below. It claims to be open all hours for drinks, though the kitchen runs to a schedule. It has great fish, lobster, jerk, burgers and salads.

There's live music on Saturday, while Sunday is deemed a chill-out lounge day.

Longboarder Bar also rents surfboards for US$25 per day, and offers lessons at J$3000 a day.

### ❶ Information

**Police station** (7 South St) Next to the old courthouse.
**Scotiabank** (23 Queen St) Bank with ATM.

### ❶ Getting There & Away

Buses serve Kingston (J$160 to J$250, 90 minutes, multiple daily) and Port Antonio (J$250 to J$300, 2½ hours, three daily).

Minibuses and route taxis arrive at and depart from beside the Shell gas station on the A4 at the west end of town.

## Bath

This village, 10km north of Port Morant by a very attractive road, lies on the bank of the Plantain Garden River, amid sugarcane and banana plantations. The town owes its existence to the discovery of hot mineral springs in the hills behind the present town in the late 17th century, which attracted socialites for a time.

# ◉ Sights

## Bath Botanical Garden                    GARDENS
(☉ dawn-dusk) **FREE** At the east end of town is an old limestone church marking the entrance to a somewhat rundown horticultural garden established in 1779. Many exotics introduced to Jamaica were first planted here, including the famous breadfruit brought from the South Pacific by Captain Bligh in 1793. Every September, Bath's Breadfruit Festival commemorates what's now a firm Jamaican staple.

# ★ Activities

## Bath Fountain                    HOT SPRINGS
(Bath House 20min bath for 1/2 people J$400/600; ☉ Bath House 8am-9:30pm) Local legend says that a runaway slave discovered hot springs here that cured the leg ulcers he'd had for years. In 1699 the government bought the spring, and formed a corporation to administer mineral baths for the sick and infirm. The water's high sulfur and lime content, and slight radioactivity, have therapeutic value for skin and rheumatic problems.

You can walk to the hot springs near the Bath Hotel & Spa, though you'll sadly have to fend off the attentions of 'guides' offering massages. Alternatively have a peaceful soak in the spa at the Bath Fountain Hotel & Spa.

The homey spa also offers a variety of massages. Arrive early on weekends. To get here, turn up the road opposite the church in Bath and follow the road 3km uphill.

## Bath Fountain–Bowden Pen Trek    HIKING
This one-day trek, a former Maroon trading route – for experienced hikers only – leads from Bath Fountain up over Cuna Cuna Gap to Bowden Pen. Obtain Sheets 19 (St Thomas parish) and 14 (Portland parish) of the Ordnance Survey 1:12,500 map series from the Survey Department (p67) for more detailed information or hire a guide from the JCDT.

# ⌂ Sleeping

## Bath Fountain Hotel & Spa    HOTEL $
(☎ 308-5736; bathmineralspahotelja@yahoo. com; r US$60; P) Your only option is this 18th-century pink colonial hotel, which contains the spa baths on the ground floor. The clinically white bedrooms are modestly furnished. There's a small restaurant serving generous portions of Jamaican dishes as well as breakfast.

# ❶ Getting There & Away

Minibuses and route taxis run daily from the downtown bus terminal in Kingston (J$250, 90 minutes).

# Ocho Rios, Port Antonio & North Coast

## Why Go?

Ocho Rios, Jamaica's third-largest town, dominates the north coast's tourist scene. Cruise ships call in several times a week, and although tourist numbers are large, they never seem overwhelming. Perhaps this is because there's so much to distract, from adventure activities to working plantations to sights unveiling the breadth of Jamaican history. It's a great place to base yourself.

Further east, sleepy Portland parish is the least developed resort area in Jamaica, and the most rugged and beautiful. Forested mountains with deep gorges and rushing rivers spread their fingers toward fringes of white sand and cool-blue surf that rolls into beach-lined coves. There's a relaxed vibe with zero hustle – its the favorite part of Jamaica for many Jamaicans. From Port Antonio, you can explore gorgeous, untouristed beaches, or head into the mountains and rainforest for hiking and birdwatching.

## Best Places to Eat

➡ Toscanini (p86)
➡ Wilkes Seafood (p97)
➡ The Italian Job (p97)

## Best Places to Sleep

➡ Reggae Hostel (p81)
➡ Great Huts (p102)
➡ Cottage at Te Moana (p82)
➡ Germaican Hostel (p96)

## When to Go
### Ocho Rios

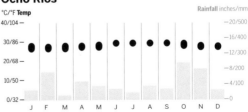

**Aug–Oct** While rain may be persistent, you're likely to get good wind for serious adventure surfing.

**Dec–Mar** Even in the high season this region doesn't see nearly as many crowds as the rest of Jamaica.

**Apr–Jul** In the low season, temperatures reach their peak, but accommodation prices can be lower.

# Ocho Rios, Port Antonio & North Coast Highlights

**1 Irie Blue Hole** (p80) Swimming and climbing one of Jamaica's most exhilarating sets of waterfalls.

**2 Firefly** (p88) Savoring the jaw-dropping view from author

Noël Coward's well-preserved former home.

**3 Seville Great House** (p89) Exploring Jamaican history from the Taínos to the sugar slave plantations.

**4 Mystic Mountain** (p80) Admiring panoramic views of the coast from the chairlift and zipping down Jamaica's longest canopy line.

**5 Port Antonio** (p93)

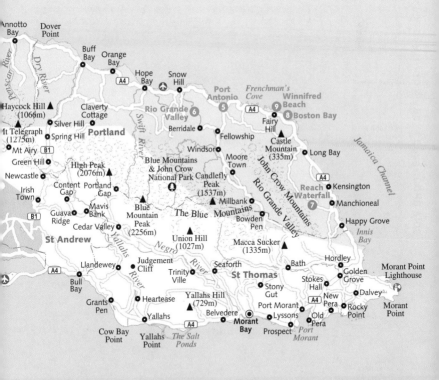

CARIBBEAN
SEA

Wandering the streets of a
pretty, crumbling banana port.

**6 Rio Grande Valley** (p105)
Drifting merrily on a raft down
the Rio Grande past former
banana plantations.

**7 Reach Falls** (p103)
Contemplating wonderful
nature from the pools of this
Portland beauty spot.

**8 Boston Bay** (p102)
Shredding some waves then

enjoying a plate of jerk at the
dish's spiritual home.

**9 Winnifred Beach** (p99)
Lazing on this white-sand
beach hugging a pretty cove.

# OCHO RIOS

POP 16,700

Ocho Rios is a former fishing village on a wide bay that was developed for tourism in the mid-1980s. The frequent docking of cruise ships (sometimes three in a day) at the central pier that commands the town's focus gives 'Ochi' a slightly 'packaged' feel, spiced up by the entreaties of 'guides' and souvenir sellers. The hassle quotient is relatively minor, however, and the town has a relaxed vibe when there's no ship in dock.

Tourism has endowed the town with a great eating scene, lively nightlife, and a plethora of guiding companies offering everything from scuba diving to zip-line tours. Throw in some of Jamaica's best waterfalls on its doorstep, and Ocho Rios makes an excellent base for exploring the north coast.

## History

The name Ocho Rios is a corruption of the Spanish term *chorreros* (swift water), for the area's rivers. Not only was the area west of Ocho Rios the site of Columbus' first landing in Jamaica and of the first Spanish settlement, it also saw Spain's last stand in Jamaica at nearby Rio Nuevo. It was here that the British instituted huge slave-run sugar and

## Ocho Rios

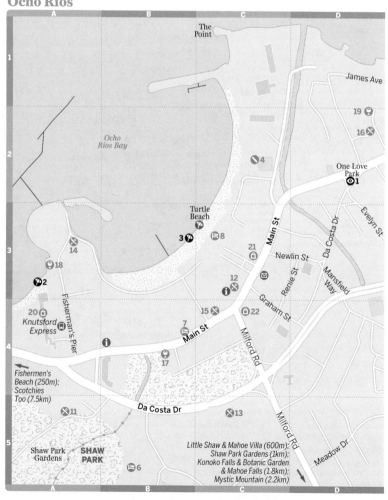

pimento (allspice) plantations, crops that defined the region until the mid-20th century, when bauxite mining and tourism took over.

## ◉ Sights

**Dunn's River Falls**                  WATERFALL

(☏974-2857; www.dunnsriverfallsja.com; adult/child US$20/12; ⊙8:30am-4pm Sat-Tue, 7am-4pm Wed-Fri) These famous falls, 3km west of town, are Jamaica's top-grossing tourist attraction. Great throngs of people can sometimes make it can seem more like a theme park than a natural wonder, but this doesn't make the climb up the falls any less exhilarating. You clamber up great tiers of limestone that step down 180m in a series of beautiful cascades and pools. The water is refreshingly cool, with everything shaded by tall rainforest.

Guides can help with the climb (tip expected), but aren't strictly necessary; although the current is strong in places, the ascent is easily achieved by most able-bodied people. Swimwear is essential. There are changing rooms, and you can rent lockers (J$500) and buy jelly shoes from vendors.

The park also includes food stalls and a restaurant, a kids' playground, and a hard-selling craft market.

Try to visit when the cruise ships aren't in dock, and ideally when the gates open in the morning. Route taxis (J$100) from Ocho Rios to St Ann's Bay can drop you at the entrance.

OCHO RIOS, PORT ANTONIO & NORTH COAST OCHO RIOS

★ **Irie Blue Hole** WATERFALL
(Thatch Hill; US$10) High on the White River, the heavenly Irie Blue Hole is a vision of what Dunn's River Falls was 20 years ago, and an undisputed highlight of the north coast. You make your way up a series of magical falls and blue pools surrounded by forest, with ample opportunity to swim, dive and swing off ropes into the water. Guides accompany you through the cascades on a well-marked trail (with steps and ropes where necessary for safety).

The tiny cave climb under one of the falls is safe but isn't for claustrophobes. The guides are excellent, know the best places to take photos of you (and show off their diving skills), and are very attentive to both kids and more senior visitors who might be uncertain on some of the climbs. Vendors sell jelly shoes at the entrance, and life jackets are also available for those who want to enjoy the falls but aren't strong swimmers. There are food and drink stands at the entrance to the falls. Take nothing you aren't happy to get wet.

★ **Mystic Mountain** AMUSEMENT PARK
(www.rainforestbobsledjamaica.com; adult/child US$47/23; ◷9am-4pm) Mystic Mountain is one of Ochi's biggest attractions, featuring a series of zip lines crisscrossing the forest in a superb canopy tour, as well as the signature 'bobsled' ride through the dense foliage.

The park begins with the Sky Explorer chairlift through the forest, with views of the coastline along the way. As well as the adrenaline rushes of the bobsled and zip line, there's also an exhibition on Jamaican sport, a contemporary Caribbean restaurant and an infinity pool with waterslide.

Costs add up quickly: a Sky Explorer and Bobsled combo is US$69; a Sky Explorer and Zipline combo is US$115; a combination of all three is US$137. Avoid the park on cruise-ship days.

Mystic Mountain is 3km west of Ocho Rios; to get here, catch a route taxi heading toward St Ann's Bay (J$100).

**Konoko Falls & Botanic Garden** GARDENS
(www.konokofalls.com; Shaw Park Rd; adult/child J$2500/1250; ◷8am-6pm) This beautiful botanic garden has walkways and trails leading past pools and streams, and feeders buzzing with hummingbirds – a lovely quiet escape from the cruise-ship buzz of town. The small museum traces Jamaica's history, and there's

an aviary with parrot feedings (and an enormous crocodile). Past the aviary, the paths lead down to an attractive series of waterfalls, surrounded by trees, ferns and flowers, all beautifully maintained. There's a cafe onsite for refreshments.

It was formerly called Coyaba Gardens & Mahoe Falls, a name still more familiar to some Ochi taxi drivers.

**Shaw Park Gardens** GARDENS
(www.shawparkgardens.com; J$1000; ◷8am-5pm) This is a tropical fantasia of ferns and bromeliads, palms and exotic shrubs, spread out over 11 hectares centered on an old great house (once a hotel). Trails and wooden steps lead past waterfalls that tumble in terraces down the hillside. A viewing platform offers a bird's-eye vantage over Ocho Rios. The gardens are signed from opposite the public library on the A3.

## 🏖 Beaches

**Ocho Rios Beach** BEACH
(Turtle Beach; J$200; ◷8am-5pm; 🅿) The main beach of Ocho Rios, popular with tourists, is the long fenced-off crescent known variously as Turtle Beach and Ocho Rios Bay, stretching east from the Turtle Towers condominiums to the Renaissance Jamaica Grande Resort. There are changing rooms and palms for shade. It's a pleasant scene but can be a bit overshadowed by cruise ships when they're in port.

**Mahogany Beach** BEACH
**FREE** The small and charming Mahogany Beach is particularly popular with locals; it comes to life on weekends with loud music, smells of jerk cooking and impromptu football matches. There is plenty of parking plus showers, and a small shop selling beach goods. The beach is about 1km east of the town center – it's quickest to jump in a taxi to get here.

**Island Village Beach** BEACH
(J$250; ◷6am-6pm) The compact Island Village Beach, located at the west end of Main St, is a peaceful, smaller beach with lockers, towels, beach chairs and umbrellas for hire. Also on offer is a complete range of water sports.

**Fishermen's Beach** BEACH
**FREE** Immediately west of Island Village Beach is the tiny public Fishermen's Beach, with colorful fishing boats and several eater-

ies serving fresh fish and more. The area was closed for redevelopment when we visited – we hope it will have the same public access when finished.

# 🏃 Activities

Virtually the entire shoreline east of Ocho Rios to Galina Point is fringed by a reef, and it's great for snorkeling and scuba diving. One of the best sections is Devil's Reef, a pinnacle that drops more than 60m. Nurse sharks are abundant at Caverns, a shallow reef about 1km east of the White River estuary; it has many tunnels plus an ex-minesweeper, the *Kathryn*. Most resorts have their own scuba facilities. As well as independent operators, upscale hotels also offer water sports.

**Garfield Diving Station**                        DIVING
(📱395-7023;      www.garfielddiving.com;      Turtle Beach) Ocho Rios' longest-running water-sports operator with more than 30 years' experience. Dive packages include one-tank dives (US$50), PADI certification courses (UD$475) and wreck dives. Other activities offered include snorkeling excursions (US$35), glass-bottom boat rides (US$30), and Jet Ski rental (prices on request). Boat charter is available for deep-sea fishing (half-day for up to four people US$650).

**Calypso Rafting**                        WATER SPORTS
(📱974-2527; www.calypsorafting.com; Epping Rd) Reliable operator offering bamboo rafting and inner tubing on the White River (from US$80), as well as half-day deep-sea fishing trips on fully equipped yachts (half-/full day US$600/$1000).

# 👉 Tours

The Ocho Rios area offers more organized outdoor adventure tours than any other Jamaican resort area. All operators offer transportation from hotels. As well as operators in Ocho Rios, others to the west of town, including Chukka (p90) and Hooves (p90), will pick you up from your hotel.

**Wilderness Tours**                        TOURS
(📱382-4029; www.wildernessatvtours.com; tours per person US$75/105; ⊙9am & 1pm Mon-Sat) Two all-terrain-vehicle tours into the mountains and through the forest, the more expensive one including Dunn's River Falls.

**Cool Runnings**                        CRUISE
(📱974-2446; www.coolrunningscatamarans.com; 1 Marvins Park, Ocho Rios) Specializes in catama-

ran cruises, including: the Dunn's River Falls Cruise (US$86), which includes an hour's snorkeling and entry to the falls; the charming Sunset Dinner Cruise (US$75), with drinks and buffet dinner; and the adults-only Wet & Wild Cruise. Prices include pick-up from your hotel.

# 🎊 Festivals & Events

**Ocho Rios Jazz Festival**                        MUSIC
(www.ochoriosjazz.com) This five-day event at the end of May/start of June draws some big names in jazz and stages concerts under the stars, showing that Jamaican music is more than just reggae and dancehall.

**Fat Tyre Festival**                        SPORTS
(⊙Feb) This rip-roaring mountain-bike race and festival is the nation's premier mountain-biking festival, and definitely not for the weak of heart (or calves). It spreads over St Ann, St Mary and up into the Blue Mountains.

# 🛏 Sleeping

Ocho Rios is one of the main tourist centres on the north coast and has accommodation for all tastes and budgets, from backpacker hostels to opulent resorts. If you can't find what you're looking for in town, it's a short hop to further sleeping options in Oracabessa to the east or along the coast to Discovery Bay to the west.

**★Reggae Hostel**                        GUESTHOUSE $
(📱974-2607; www.reggaehostel.com; 19 Main St; dm/r US$20/60; P ❄ 🛜) An ever-popular hostel, this relaxed guesthouse is perfectly located in the center of Ocho Rios. There's a good mix of simple, air-con, private rooms, some with mini-verandas, and dorms (some with fan, others with over-icy air-con). There's a kitchen for self-caterers and a rooftop bar that's made for socializing. The staff are fonts of local knowledge for backpacker-friendly excursions.

**Rooms**                        RESORT $
(📱467-8737; www.roomsresorts.com; Main St; r US$127-149, studios US$172; P ❄ @ 🏊) This family-friendly resort has all the trappings of an all-inclusive without being one. Everything – from meals (apart from breakfast) to water sports – costs extra, but the location is superb, the beachfront pool and gym are bonuses, and the spacious rooms boast sea or pool views.

**Mahoe Villa** GUESTHOUSE **$**

(📞 974-6613; 11 Shaw Park Rd; r without/with bathroom US$50/80; P 🛜) This large guesthouse on the hill up to Shaw Park Gardens, run by the effusive hosts, is great value for money. The spick-and-span, fan-cooled rooms with dark wood floors share a communal kitchen, and a chilled vibe prevails. One room (for cozy couples?) has a double bathtub. The owner also runs a reggae sound system in London.

**★Cottage at Te Moana** COTTAGE **$$**

(📞 974-2870; www.harmonyhall.com; cottages US$150-180; P ❄) With its small clifftop garden overhanging a reef, this exquisite reclusive property with two delightful cottages offers a wonderful alternative to Ochi's resorts. Think wicker furniture and a host of art collected from across the Caribbean. Both cottages have fully equipped kitchens, separate living areas, plus verandas with hammocks. Steps lead down to a coral cove good for snorkeling.

Sea kayaks and paddleboards are also available. There's a three-night minimum stay (five nights in high season).

**Hibiscus Lodge** HOTEL **$$**

(📞 974-2676; www.hibiscusjamaica.com; 83 Main St; r US$150-192; P ♨ ❄ @ ≋) A stairway descends alongside a cliff overhang, past flowering gardens overflowing with bougainvillea, and down to a private sunning deck, perfect for a spontaneous jump in the sea. A small gallery of contemporary Jamaican art complements the main building nicely. Rooms are modestly furnished, though a refit to freshen things up was taking place when we visited. Deluxe rooms are worth the extra expense for the large private balconies. There's also a breezy bar and the Almond Tree Restaurant (p84).

**Mystic Ridge** RESORT **$$**

(📞 974-8050; www.mysticridgejamaica.com; 17 Da Costa Dr; r/ste/apt US$124/145/260; P ❄ 🛜 ≋) This modern hilltop resort (formerly Crane Ridge) features spacious and cheery loft suites and two-bedroom apartments, plus some regular double rooms – all decorated in a breezy modern style. The airy June Plum restaurant serves Jamaican dishes with an emphasis on fresh fruit. There's a poolside bar and the very relaxing Samambaia spa, plus a tennis court for a knockabout.

Guest discounts to Mystic Mountain (p80) are available.

**Silver Seas** HOTEL **$$**

(📞 974-2755; www.silverseashotel.com; 66 James Ave; r J$6900; P ❄ ≋) Ocho Rios' first-ever resort is somewhat worn and creaky, but atmospheric nevertheless and welcoming to families. Inside the colonial-style building with a cavernous hall and wooden floors, each well-kept room has a large, private patio with a stellar ocean view. Dining takes place on the waterfront patio and there's good snorkeling to be had off the jetty.

**★Jamaica Inn** GUESTHOUSE **$$$**

(📞 974-2514; www.jamaicainn.com; ste US$569-879, cottages US$989-2389; P ♨ ❄ 🛜 ≋) Winston Churchill loved this place (and is echoed in the colonial-era prints and furnishings), an exquisite family-run 'inn,' tucked in a private cove, that exudes patrician refinement. There's a library and a bar with a warm clubby feel, and on-site spa. Dining requires a collared shirt and trousers for men. Water sports include scuba diving, snorkeling and fishing.

Half- and full-board are available on request. There's a minimum three-night stay.

**Blue House** GUESTHOUSE **$$$**

(📞 994-1367; www.thebluehousejamaica.com; White River Bay; r US$200-260; P ❄ @ 🛜 ≋) This gem offers luxurious bedrooms in cool blue hues – a real home from home. The separate two-bedroom Cozy Cottage provides even greater seclusion, with its private patio and hammock hidden behind a curtain of flowers. The resident Barefoot Chef cooks up superb fusion cuisine, drawing on Chinese and Indian influences, and the lavish three-course dinners are worth every penny.

**Couples Sans Souci**
**Resort & Spa** RESORT **$$$**

(📞 994-1206; www.couples.com; A3; d US$750-780, ste US$780-1341, cottages US$1391; P ♨ ❄ @ ≋) East of town, this all-inclusive resort has a sublime setting in a secluded cove. The top-end suites have Jacuzzis and one of the two beaches is for nude bathing. Rates include gourmet dining (there are three restaurants and six bars), while Charlie's Spa is set on mineral springs rumored to have rejuvenating powers.

The huge range of water sports on offer includes scuba lessons.

## 🍴 Eating

Ocho Rios has a good range of international cuisine and several economical Jamaican restaurants; many places are open late. Af-

## BACKROADS TO KINGSTON

The A3 winds through sweeping pastoral country on its way south. At Moneague, the road meets up with the A1 from St Ann's Bay, and continues up the pine-forested slopes of Mt Diablo (839m). At 686m the A1 crests the mountain chain and begins its steep, winding descent to Ewarton and the lush Rosser Valley, beautiful when seen from these heights.

Until the opening of the toll highway from Kingston, this road was the main route from the capital to the north coast. It's much quieter now, though some minibuses and trucks still tear around the mountain bends to avoid the tolls.

Just beyond Moneague, 27km south of Ocho Rios, is Faith's Pen, famous for it's road-side dining. **Faith's Pen Rest Stop** (Faith's Pen; meals from J$100; ⊙10am-9pm) has around 30 food stalls. It's all here – jerk, soups and stews, curry goat, porridge and roast corn. Business has undoubtedly dropped off since the opening of the new highway diverted traffic away from the village, but we reckon it's still worth making a detour for.

ter dark, you'll find many smoking oil-drum barbecues along the roadside, particularly in the area surrounding the clock tower.

★ **Live Food** VEGAN $
(19 Main St; mains from J$800; ⊙9am-10pm) This Rastafari-run joint – a cute thatched shack enlivening an otherwise boring strip of shops – is a great way to get an injection of I-tal food. The big salads are filling and delicious, and the raw take on a pizza a definite surprise. If you're in a rush, go for the fabulous and healthy smoothies. Opening hours can be somewhat relaxed.

**Ocho Rios Jerk Centre** JERK $
(☑974-2549; 16 Da Costa Dr; meals J$550-1000; ⊙11am-midnight) The liveliest jerk joint in town serves excellent jerk pork, chicken and conch, as well as barbeque ribs. There are daily specials, the best being curry goat (J$550) and goat-head soup. Grab a Red Stripe and watch sports on the big-screen TV while you're waiting for your food. There are DJs on Friday nights.

**Mongoose Restaurant and Lounge** JAMAICAN $
(Main St; mains J$900-2500; ⊙9am-1am) Lively restaurant and bar that quickly serves up big plates of hearty food. If you want Jamaican, go for the stews (particularly the oxtail), otherwise you can get really good burgers, grilled fish, pizzas and the like. It's pretty empty during the day unless there's a cruise ship in town, when it heaves.

Evenings are more relaxed, and there's live reggae on Saturdays.

**Mom's** JAMAICAN $
(7 Evelyn St; mains around J$1000; ⊙8am-10pm Mon-Sat) This home-style restaurant has

few frills but is a gem nonetheless. Eat in or takeout generous servings of oxtail stew, chicken, pork and fish, and all the Jamaica classics. If you had a Jamaican auntie, this is how she'd cook for you.

**Boardwalk Bistro** INTERNATIONAL $
(☑398-2582; Island Village; meals J$700-2000; ⊙7am-8.30pm) The setting seals the deal here – this cafe-restaurant is on the boardwalk facing the beach, and serves up good Jamaican and American breakfasts, filling sandwiches and a mix of international and Jamaican standards for lunch and dinner. Sit outside if you can to enjoy the air. Friendly service.

**Tropical Kitchen** BAKERY $
(Main St; ⊙8am-5pm Mon-Sat; ☑) Cakes, pastries and damn fine sweet-potato pudding. And, whisper it, but we reckon that the flaky pastry on their patties beats the big chains hands down.

**World of Fish** SEAFOOD $
(3 James Ave; meals J$650; ⊙11am-8pm Mon-Sat) Popular with locals, this casual and economical eatery has been serving fried fish, stew fish and steamed fish for years. Get it with *bammy* (cassava flatbread), rice and peas or *festival* (deep fried dough dumpling).

**Healthy Way** VEGETARIAN $
(☑974-9229; Ocean Village Plaza; meals from J$450; ⊙8am-5pm; ☑) A vegetarian kitchen and health-food store selling herbs, teas, I-tal juices and supplements, plus hearty chow such as a delicious tofu cheeseburger, stew peas and large fruit plates to go.

**Caffe Da Vinci** ITALIAN $$
(☑630-7025; Island Village; starters J$750, mains J$1100-2600; ⊙11am-10pm) An excellent addition to Island Village, the Italian food here is

top notch, with some good wines and service to match. Eat in an open restaurant spilling into a series of gazebos surrounded by trees and ferns by the village 'pond'. Look out for the lobster ravioli, though the chicken parmigiana is also very good as are the salads.

Leave space for the tiramisu.

**Almond Tree Restaurant**  INTERNATIONAL **$$**
(✑ 974-2813; Hibiscus Lodge, 83 Main St; meals J$1200-4000; ◷ 11am-10pm) Providing a splendid perch for a sunset dinner, this clifftop spot at the Hibiscus Hotel features a dining pavilion that steps down the cliffside. Candlelit dinners are served alfresco. Seafood and steaks are their highlight offerings, though you can get good pasta and a few steadfast Jamaican dishes. Dress smartly.

**Evita's**  ITALIAN **$$**
(✑ 974-2333; Eden Bower Rd; meals J$1400-2500; ◷ noon-4pm & 6pm-midnight; ✑) This charming restaurant sits high above Ochi in a romantically decorated 1860s house – an airy setting with exquisite views. The Italian-Jamaican menu includes jerk spaghetti, the ackee and callaloo 'Lasagna Rastafari' and the seafood-filled 'Lasagna Capitano'. Lighter dishes include a selection of salads; half-portions of the pasta dishes are also available. Good but overpriced.

**Passage to India**  INDIAN **$$$**
(✑ 795-3182; Fisherman's Point; meals J$1800-3200; ◷ 11am-1pm Tue-Sun, to 3pm Mon; ✑) Passage to India offers very good northern Indian fare, with a few local seafood twists thrown in for good measure. The naan is crisp, the lassis flavorful, the curries sharp, and the menu divided into extensive chicken, mutton, seafood and vegetarian sections. Tandoori options are also on offer.

The restaurant only opens on Mondays if there's a cruise ship docked.

## 🍷 Drinking & Nightlife

There's a healthy bar scene and a decent choice of nightspots, though Ochi lacks the after-hours verve of Negril or the authenticity of Kingston. Nonetheless, it's not hard to find a good party atmosphere *somewhere* on any night of the week.

Some all-inclusive resorts sell night passes permitting full access to meals, drinks and entertainment.

**Island Coffees**  COFFEE
(Island Village; ◷ 9am-9pm; 🕿) Small but cheery modern coffee shop, serving excel-

lent coffee (Blue Mountain, of course) and other hot drinks, smoothies and a host of sandwiches and wraps (from J$500), plus suitably sweet and sticky cakes (J$250).

**John Crow's Tavern**  SPORTS BAR
(10 Main St; ◷ 10am-1am) The big TV above the bar screens the latest football games and the outdoor terrace is perfect for a beer, a burger and a spot of people-watching on the main street. The beer is cold and there's a wide selection of rum.

**Ocean's 11 Watering Hole**  BAR
(Fisherman's Point; ◷ 4pm-midnight) With its prime spot on the pier, it's little surprise that Ocean's 11 is popular with cruise-ship passengers, who knock back the potent cocktails and cheer each other on during Tuesday-night karaoke. The upstairs space doubles as a small art gallery and coffee shop. There's dancehall on Friday and oldies ska and reggae on Sunday.

**Reggae Inferno**  CLUB
(7 James Ave; men J$500, women free; ◷ 9pm-late Wed-Sun) The gritty Reggae Inferno sends earth-shattering music across the roofs of town; it's the place to get down and dirty with the latest dancehall moves (despite the name, there's not a lot of reggae played here).

**Jimmy Buffett's Margaritaville**  BAR
(✑ 675-8800; Island Village; ◷ 11am-4am) This corporate franchise has turned getting drunk into big business. The music is loud and the signature margaritas don't come cheap, but many tourists find the orchestrated good-time vibe to be irresistible, and it's popular with middle-class Jamaica visitors too. Admission is charged for special events, such as their Wet'n'Wild Pool Party.

Although Margaritaville 'goes until you say when,' things wind up earlier when there's no ship in town.

## ⭐ Entertainment

**Cove Theatre**  CINEMA
(✑ 675-8886; Island Village) Cinema in the Island Village that carries all the Hollywood releases.

## 🔒 Shopping

Souvenirs here are aimed at the cruise ships, and are generally of fairly poor quality. For art, head out of town to Harmony Hall (p86).

**Wassi Art**  ARTS & CRAFTS
(✑ 974-5044; Bougainvillea Dr; ◷ 9am-5pm Mon-Sat, 10am-4pm Sun) Family-owned Wassi Art

employs more than 50 artists to make its colorful, richly decorated terra-cotta pottery. Free tours are offered, detailing the entire process including clay processing, painting and firing. Pots start from US$5 and go all the way up to hundreds of dollars.

Wassi Art is in the Great Pond District, signed from Milford Rd (the A3), from where it's a convoluted (but signed) drive.

The pottery is named for the 'wassi' wasp, or potter wasp, which makes a mud pot for each of its eggs and stuffs it with a caterpillar for food for the hatchlings. The owners can ship your purchases abroad.

### Olde Craft Market                    ARTS & CRAFTS

(Main St; ☉9am-5pm) This market features fair quality ceramics and art, as well as the usual T-shirts with chirpy Jamaican slogans and Rasta tams with fake dreadlocks attached.

### Island Village                              MALL

(☎974-8353; village free, beach J$200; ☉9am-midnight) Since its 2002 opening, this self-contained entertainment park has changed the face of Ocho Rios. The 2-hectare development claims to resemble a 'Jamaican coastal village.' It doesn't remotely, but you'll still find a peaceful beach, upscale craft shops, a cinema (p84), Jimmy Buffett's Margaritaville bar (p84), several cafes, and an amphitheater for live performances.

### Ocho Rios Craft Park        GIFTS & SOUVENIRS

(Main St; ☉9am-5pm) For all your tacky T-shirt, batik, wooden sculpture and crafts-made-of-coconut-shells needs.

## ⓘ Information

### DANGERS & ANNOYANCES

Good humor and a firm 'no' should be enough to deal with Ochi's hustlers and would-be tour guides. Use caution at night anywhere, particularly in some of the streets around the clock tower.

### EMERGENCY

**Police Station** (☎974-2533; Da Costa Dr)

### INTERNET

**Computer Whizz** (Shop 11, Island Plaza; per 30min/1hr J$150/250; ☉8:30am-7:30pm Mon-Sat)

**Ez Access Internet Café** (☎974-7038; 67b Ocean Village Plaza; per 30min/1hr J$150/200; ☉9am-8pm Mon-Sat)

### MEDICAL SERVICES

The nearest hospital is in St Ann's Bay (p90).

**Kulkarni Medical Clinic** (☎974-3357; 16 Rennie Rd)

**Ocho Rios Pharmacy** (☎974-2398; Main St, Ocean Village Plaza)

### MONEY

There are numerous banks along Main St. All have foreign-exchange facilities and ATMs.

### POST

**FedEx** (☎795-3723; 17 Main St; ☉9am-5pm Mon-Sat)

**Post Office** (Main St; ☉8am-5pm Mon-Sat)

### TOURIST INFORMATION

**Tourist Information** (☎974-7705; Shop 3, Ocean Village Plaza, Main St; ☉9am-5pm Mon-Thu, to 4pm Fri) Represents the Jamaica Tourist Board, with helpful, knowledgeable staff. It also operates an **information booth** on Main St, but it's open only when cruise ships are in port.

## ⓘ Getting There & Away

### CAR

If you have your own vehicle and are driving between Ocho Rios and Kingston, note that the fast new toll highway costs around J$1000.

Shopping malls along Main St have car parks, though not secure ones. Most hotels offer parking; all upmarket hotels offer secure parking. Main St during rush hour is one long traffic jam.

Some car-rental outlets:

**Avis** (☎974-8047; avis.com.jm; 15 Milford Rd)

**Bargain Rent-a-Car** (☎974-8047; Shop 1a Pineapple Place Shopping Centre, Main St)

**Salem Car Rental** (☎974-0786; www.salemcarrentals.com; Shop 7, Sandcastles Resort)

### PUBLIC TRANSPORTATION

Buses, minibuses and route taxis arrive at and depart from Ocho Rios' **transportation center** (Evelyn St). During daylight hours there are frequent departures (fewer on Sundays) for Kingston and destinations along the north coast. There is no set schedule: they depart when full.

Sample destinations:

**Discovery Bay** J$180, 30 minutes

**Kingston** J$350, 2½ hours

**Montego Bay** J$500, 90 minutes

**Port Maria** J$180, 50 minutes

**Runaway Bay** J$150, 30 minutes

**St Ann's Bay** J$100, 10 minutes

**Knutsford Express** (www.knutsfordexpress. com; Island Village) has scheduled departures to Kingston and Montego Bay from its depot at Island Village. Arrive 15 minutes prior to departure to register your ticket. Sample fares include Kingston (J$1950), Montego Bay (J$1950), Negril (J$2700) and Port Antonio (J$2050).

## ℹ Getting Around

Chartered taxis are in great abundance along Main St. Negotiate the fare before setting off, as the drivers will quote any figure that comes to mind.

Minibuses and route taxis ply Main St and the coast road, costing J$100 for short hauls.

# EAST OF OCHO RIOS

The seaside resorts of Ocho Rios quickly give way to isolated villas and fishing villages like Port Maria as the coastal road winds its way east along cliffs and bluffs. The sense of leaving tourist Jamaica behind is enhanced by the drop in road quality.

Drawn by its coastal beauty and unspoiled character, two of Jamaica's most famous visitors, author Noël Coward and James Bond-creator Ian Fleming, made their homes in the area. While Coward settled in Firefly, with its spectacular view down on the coastline, Fleming found refuge at Goldeneye, now an exclusive resort.

## Reggae Beach to Boscobel Beach

East of Ocho Rios, habitations begin thinning out along the A3 past White River. Several beaches lie hidden below the cliffs; notable among them is Tower Isle, 9km east of Ocho Rios, with its cluster of resorts. The Rio Nuevo meets the ocean about 1km west of Tower Isle.

### ◉ Sights & Activities

**Harmony Hall**                                    GALLERY
(☑974-2870; www.harmonyhall.com; ⊙10am-5:30pm Tue-Sun) A lovely gingerbread house easily spotted on the main road, Harmony Hall dates to 1886, when it was a Methodist manse that adjoined a pimento estate. The restored structure is made of cut stone, with a wooden upper story trimmed with fretwork and a shingled roof with a spire. Reborn as an arts-and-crafts showcase, it offers the best in contemporary and traditional Jamaican art, aimed at both casual art lovers and the serious collector.

The acclaimed Toscanini restaurant is on the ground floor.

**Rio Nuevo Battle Site**                     HISTORIC SITE
(J$500; ⊙10am-5pm Mon-Fri, to 2pm Sat & Sun) On the bluff west of the Rio Nuevo river mouth is this little-visited site where, in 1658, the English forces fought their decisive battle against the Spanish, sending them fleeing to Cuba. A plaque here records the events and there's a small exhibition on the area's historical heritage.

It's on the main road, behind gates that make it look like you're entering a private housing estate.

**Yaaman Adventure Park**                      PLANTATION
(☑994-1058; www.yaamanadventure.com; full-day package adult/child US$149/79; ⊙Mon-Sat) Formerly the more sedately named Prospect Plantation, this beautiful old hilltop great house and 405-hectare property has rebranded as an active adventure park. Get off-road in the 'wet & dirty' buggy ride. More relaxing are tours through scenic grounds among banana, cassava, cocoa, coconut, coffee, pineapple and pimento by Segway (adult/child US$76/54), horse (US$54/43) or tractor-powered jitney (US$39/22).

**Bamboo Beach Club**                               BEACH
(J$1000; ⊙9am-5pm) This clean yellow-sand beach is hustler-free and popular with tourists only, due to the high admission rate. Locals still call it by its old name, Reggae Beach. Kayaks are available for rent, and jerk chicken and fish are readily available. On a hot day with a cruise ship in Ocho Rios, the place gets absolutely packed.

### ✕ Eating

**★Toscanini**                                ITALIAN $$$
(☑975-4785; Harmony Hall; mains US$18-45; ⊙noon-2pm & 6.30-10pm Tue-Sun; ☑) In a gingerbread house, this is one of the finest restaurants in Jamaica. It's run by two gracious Italians who use the freshest local ingredients in the recipes – the manager greets guests and explains the use of local herbs in the cooking. The daily menu ranges widely, from prosciutto with papaya to rich rabbit ragù with tagliatelle.

There's plenty of excellent local seafood and a good wine list, but leave room for sumptuous desserts. Check out the collection of Rolling Stones record covers by the bathrooms – Keith Richards has a house nearby.

## Oracabessa

Taking its name from the Spanish *oro cabeza* (golden head), Oracabessa, 21km east of Ocho Rios, is a small, one-street, one-story village with a vague aura of a Wild West town. The street itself is lined with Caribbean vernacular architecture, with wooden houses trimmed with fretwork. This was a major port for shipping bananas in the 19th century. While the boom era has passed, the town itself still keeps much of its charm.

## ⊙ Sights

**Sun Valley Plantation**                    PLANTATION
(📞 995-3075; tours incl snack J$2500; ⊙ 9am-4pm) This working plantation and botanical farm is at Crescent on the B13, some 5km south of Oracabessa. Owners Lorna and Nolly Binns offer enjoyable garden tours in a plantation setting, which teach visitors about banana and sugarcane – two staple crops that have played an important part in the development of the area. You can opt to visit the groves of coconuts (the current main crop) and other tropical fruits and medicinal herbs, and sample the produce and fresh juices.

**James Bond Beach**                          BEACH
(adult J$700; ⊙ 9am-6pm Tue-Sun) This attractive strip of white sand is pretty quiet during the week but livens up on weekends. If you want to enjoy more than just the beach, hire jet skis or take a boat out to a nearby spot to snorkel with the resident stingrays. A small bar and restaurant provides refreshment. The beach also hosts large-scale music events – check the flyers in Ocho Rios for what's coming up.

## ✯✯ Festivals & Events

**Beach J'ouvert**                             MUSIC
(⊙ Apr) A taste of Trinidad in Jamaica, Beach J'ouvert is a wildly popular soca music festival held at James Bond Beach during the carnival season, with all-night revelry and paint throwing.

**Follow Di Arrow**                            MUSIC
(⊙ Feb) Annual dancehall music event featuring big local artists, held at James Bond Beach on the last weekend in February.

## 🛏 Sleeping

**Villa Sake**                             GUESTHOUSE $
(📞 368-1036; www.villasake.com; opposite Ian Fleming Airport; r US$30-50) A small but charming hostel-style guesthouse near Ian Fleming Airport (look for the red and yellow sign). Villa Sake has just a handful of rooms and a communal kitchen, and a lounge area that virtually hangs over the waves of its own tiny private cove (there's a ladder running down the cliff to get to the sea).

**Tamarind Great House**               GUESTHOUSE $
(📞 995-3252; www.tamarind.hostel.com; Crescent Estate; d US$75-120; 🅿 ☒) The hilltop setting for this 'plantation guesthouse' near Sun Valley Plantation (p87) is sublime, with lush valleys and mountains all around (there's a lovely walk to a local waterfall). The large bedrooms with four-poster beds open to a vast veranda. The excellent restaurant serves stick-to-your-ribs breakfasts and dinners.

From Oracabessa, take Jack's River Rd; it's a rough 6km drive, but worth it.

**★ Goldeneye**                             HOTEL $$$
(📞 622-9007; www.goldeneye.com; beach huts US$725-980, cottages US$1220, villas US$1960-3975; 🅿 ☒ 🛜 ☒) One of Jamaica's most exclusive properties, Ian Fleming's old villa has been expanded into a stylish resort, with a selection of gorgeous beach huts and villas sprinkled across expansive grounds on a quaint cove. Staff are pampering yet discreet. The restaurants serve gourmet meals, the beach bar is a chilled-out delight, and there's plenty of access to water sports.

You can even kayak gently across the lagoon to a charming wellness center. Fleming's old residence, where he wrote the Bond novels, is now a private resort-within-a-resort, with its own beach, butler and cook.

### FLEMING... IAN FLEMING

Ian Fleming, inventor of James Bond, first came to Jamaica in 1942 while serving with British Naval Intelligence. In 1946 he bought a house on the shore at Oracabessa and named it Goldeneye, and he wintered here every year until his death in 1964. It was here that Fleming conceived agent 007, the creation of whom the author attributes to living in Jamaica.

All 14 of Fleming's Bond novels were written here, and five were set in Jamaica. Even his hero's name was locally inspired – looking for a deliberately dull name, he chanced upon the ornithological classic, *Birds of the West Indies*, written by a certain James Bond. Throw in a typewriter, sea dips to keep invigorated, and endless evening cocktails with a host of fabulous guests, and you have the makings of literary history.

For the definitive account of Fleming's time in the last decades of British Jamaica, check out Matthew Parker's *Goldeneye: Where Bond Was Born*.

Up to 10 guests can stay here for a cool US$8000 per night. We understand that Beyoncé is a fan, but if you can't run to that, console yourself with the entertainment room for Bond movies and a Goldeneye cocktail from the Bizot Bar.

## ℹ Getting There & Away

Minibuses and route taxis pass through, en route between Ocho Rios (J$150, 25 minutes) and Annotto Bay (for Port Antonio). Route taxis leave from the junction at the bottom of the hill on the western edge of town.

# Galina Point & Little Bay

Five kilometers east of Oracabessa, the A3 winds around the promontory of Galina Point. A 12m-high concrete lighthouse marks the headland. South of Galina you'll pass Noël Coward's first house, Blue Harbour, squatting atop 'the double bend,' where the road and shoreline take a 90-degree turn and open to a marvelous view of Cabarita Island. The road drops steeply from Blue Harbour to Kokomo Beach in Little Bay.

## ◉ Sights

★ **Firefly**      HISTORIC BUILDING
(☏994-0920, 997-7201; J$1000; ⊙9am-5pm Mon-Thu & Sat) Set amid wide lawns high atop a hill 5km east of Oracabessa and 5km west of Port Maria, Firefly was the home of Sir Noël Coward, the English playwright, songwriter,

actor and wit, who was preceded at this site by the notorious pirate Sir Henry Morgan. When he died in 1973, Coward left the estate to his partner Graham Payn, who donated it to the nation. Its hilltop location offers what might be the finest coastal view in Jamaica.

Your guide will lead you to Coward's art studio, where he was schooled in oil painting by Winston Churchill. The studio displays Coward's original paintings and photographs of himself and a coterie of famous friends. The drawing room, with the table still laid, was used to entertain such guests as the Queen Mother, Sophia Loren and Audrey Hepburn. The upper lounge features a glassless window that offers one of the most stunning coastal vistas in all Jamaica. The view takes in Port Maria Bay and the coastline further west. Contrary to popular opinion, Coward didn't write his famous song 'A Room with a View' here (it was written in Hawaii in 1928).

Coward lies buried beneath a plain white marble slab on the wide lawns where he entertained many illustrious stars of stage and screen. A dance floor nearby covers his old pool – the house is now used as an exclusive venue for society weddings.

## ⌂ Sleeping

**Blue Harbour**      HOTEL $
(☏725-0289; www.blueharb.com; r per person US$70, full board US$120; [P][⊛][✉]) Once owned by Noël Coward, this is a slightly ramshackle retreat with a laid-back atmosphere, consist-

---

### NOËL COWARD'S PEENY-WALLY

The multitalented Sir Noël Coward first visited Jamaica in 1944 on a two-week holiday. He found peace of mind here and dubbed his dream island 'Dr Jamaica.' Four years later he rented Ian Fleming's estate, Goldeneye, at Oracabessa, while he hunted for a site on which to build a home.

In 1948 Coward bought a 3-hectare estate overlooking Little Bay near Galina and set to work building Coward's Folly, a three-story villa with two guest cottages, and a swimming pool at the sea's edge. He named his home Blue Harbour and invited his many notable friends, a virtual 'Who's Who' of the rich and famous. The swarm of visitors, however, eventually drove Coward to find another retreat.

While painting with his lover Graham Payn at a place called Lookout (so-named because the pirate Henry Morgan had a stone hut built atop the hill to keep an eye out for Spanish galleons), Coward was struck by the impressive solitude and incredible view. The duo lingered until nightfall, when fireflies ('peeny-wallies' in the Jamaican dialect) appeared. Within two weeks Coward had bought the land, and eight years later he had a house built. He named it Firefly.

Coward spent 30 years in Jamaica, recording his love of the island and islanders on canvas in bright, splashy colors. When he suffered a heart attack at the age of 73, he was buried on the lawns of Firefly beneath a marble slab. A pensive statue of the man also graces the lawn, sitting in his chair and ever looking out to that inspiring view.

## SEVILLE GREAT HOUSE

The historical park Seville Great House (J$500; ⊘9am-4pm Sat & Sun), overlooking the sea and less than 1km west of present-day St Ann's, marks the site of the first Spanish capital on the island – Sevilla la Nueva – and one of the first Spanish settlements in the New World. It houses a fascinating great house, plantation remains and reconstructions of Taíno houses, African slave houses and a slave kitchen garden.

When the English captured Jamaica from the Spanish, the land on which Sevilla la Nueva had been built was granted to army officer Richard Hemming. The estate was developed for sugar, and was dominated by the Seville Great House, built in 1745 by Hemming's grandson. The family tombs are outside, and next to them is a memorial to the slaves whose remains were discovered on the site and reburied here in 1997.

The restored house contains an excellent museum depicting the history of the site from Taíno times through the era of slavery and the colonial period.

Traces of the original Spanish buildings, including a church and the castle-house of the first Spanish governor, are visible, along with the ruins of the English sugar mills and the overseer's house. This was also the site of the Taíno village of Maima; the inhabitants were forced to work as serfs under the Spanish *encomienda* (forced labor) system, and quickly died out through a combination of disease, overwork and suicide.

ing of three separate villas by a tiny rocky beach and saltwater pool. Spacious rooms feature some original furniture from Coward's day. Meals are served on a thatched veranda with bay views, and full board is worth it for the delicious home-cooked Jamaican specials.

The property is poorly signed – after turning off the main road onto the overgrown lane, look for the inauspicious beaten-up white metal fencing – the perimeter of the property.

**Galina Breeze**   HOTEL $$
(☑994-0537; www.galinabreeze.com; r US$100-120, ste US$140; P❋🅴🅿) This small, cheery hotel with superb views of the coast has just 14 light, spacious rooms, all equipped with firm king-size beds and cable TV. There's a restaurant (with good Jamaican breakfasts), a bar, and just outside the main gate, a decent jerk stand. The pool (salt water) makes up for the lack of beach.

### ❶ Getting There & Away

Minibuses and route taxis pass through, en route between Ocho Rios (J$180, 25 minutes) and Annotto Bay (for Port Antonio).

## WEST OF OCHO RIOS

The smooth coast road runs west from Ocho Rios all the way to Falmouth and Montego Bay. St Ann's Bay and Runaway Bay are the only towns of any size here. Inland, the Dry Harbour Mountains rise above the coast.

Here, you'll find the small village of Nine Mile, birthplace of Bob Marley.

## St Ann's Bay

This is a small town with a big history. In 1509 the Spaniards built the first Spanish settlement on the island about 700m west of St Ann's Bay, at Sevilla la Nueva. The site was abandoned within four decades and it was later developed as a British sugar estate. As the plantations grew, the town prospered as a bustling seaport with forts on opposite sides of the bay.

Marcus Garvey, founder of the Black Nationalist movement, was born here and is honored each August 17 with a parade.

### ⊙ Sights

Up the hill from the Columbus Monument is the exquisite Catholic church of Our Lady of Perpetual Help, built in contemporary Spanish design by an Irish priest in 1939 with stones recovered from the ruins of Sevilla la Nueva.

At the corner of Market St is the courthouse, erected in elegant cut limestone and red brick in 1866, with a pedimented porch bearing the scales of justice. Across the way is the market (⊘Tue-Sat), which gets busy on Friday and Saturday. Further west lies quaint St Ann's Bay Baptist Church. Statues at either end of St Ann's Bay provide neat bookends to the town's history: Columbus stands at one end, Garvey at the other.

## 🏃 Activities

**Hooves**　　　　　　　　　　HORSE RIDING
(☑972-0905; www.hooves-jamaica.com; 61 Windsor Rd; half-day horseback tours incl refreshments adult/child US$70/50) Offers guided horseback tours along the beach, with a bareback ride into the sea (beginners welcome), and the 'honeymoon ride,' which includes a beach meal with fizz. Reservations required.

## 🎊 Festivals & Events

**★ Rebel Salute**　　　　　　　　　MUSIC
(www.rebelsaluteja.com; ⊘Jan) The biggest roots reggae concert in Jamaica goes down on the second Saturday in January at Plantation Cove outside St Ann's Bay. The two-day festival is a must for any reggae fan.

**Emancipation Jubilee**　　　　　CULTURAL
Held annually at the grounds of Seville Great House (p89) from July 31 to August 1, to celebrate the emancipation of Jamaica's slaves on August 1, 1834. Celebrations consist of dancing and traditional folk music, such as Kumina and mento.

## 🛏 Sleeping

**★ High Hope Estate**　　　　　B&B $$
(☑972-2277; www.highhopeestate.com; r US$195; P✿@☀) This beautiful Venetian-style villa is set in large woodland grounds high in the hills above St Ann's Bay. Each of its five rooms is decorated with antiques, and three have wonderful ocean views and verandas. There's a well-stocked library for browsing and fabulous meals on request (Jamaican and Italian dishes are a specialty; cooking courses also available).

Discounts are available for stays of more than three nights.

## 🍴 Eating

There are street food stalls along Main St dishing up fish tea and jerk, and the usual Jamaican patty chains (and international fast-food brands).

**Scotchies Too**　　　　　　　JERK $
(☑794-9457; Jack's Hall Fair Ground; meals J$500-700; ⊘24hr) This roadside offshoot of the famous jerk center in Montego Bay lies adjacent to an Epping Gas station just west of Dunn's River Falls. Its pork and chicken, smoked over pimento wood, water the mouths of locals and visitors alike; the jerk sausage is also worth investigating. Accompaniments include roast breadfruit, *bammy* and *festival.*

## ℹ Information

**Police Station** (cnr Main & Braco Sts)
**Scotiabank** (18 Braco St) Has a 24-hour ATM.
**St Ann's Bay Public General Hospital** (☑972-2272) At the far west end of Main St, with an emergency clinic.

## ℹ Getting There & Away

Route taxis run throughout the day for Ocho Rios (J$100, 10 minutes) and Montego Bay (J$350, 90 minutes), via Falmouth. Transport leaves from the St Ann's Bay Bus Park.

# Priory & Around

Priory, about 1.5km west of St Ann's Bay, has a small beach with water sports and several hotels. You can turn inland and head into the hills for views down the coast. Here you'll find Lilyfield Great House, about 8km east of Brown's Town, but the area is most visited for its many activities and adventure sports.

Near the village of Bamboo in the hills above Priory, you'll find Stush in the Bush, one of the gems of Jamaica's foodie scene.

## ◉ Sights & Activities

**Cranbrook Rainforest Gardens**　　GARDENS
(☑770-8071; adult/child, US$25/12.50, canopy zip line US$79; ⊘9am-5pm) This vast botanical garden run by Chukka Cove Farm is a treat, crafted in the lush valley that carves up into the hills south of Laughlands, about 5km west of Priory. The garden is built around a colonial-era building and includes theme gardens, a hothouse orchid display, pools, and lush lawns (with croquet) fringed by banks of anthuriums and other tropical flowers.

Nature walks lead to the river, reflecting giant tree ferns, spectacular torch ginger, heliconia and other exotic species, and there are perfect spots for picnicking. If you need more adrenaline, get above the flowers with a zip-line tour.

**Chukka Cove Farm**　　　ADVENTURE SPORTS
(☑619-1382; www.chukkacaribbean.com) This former polo field west of Priory is home to the Caribbean-dominating adventure group Chukka, which offers an ever-growing list of guided excursions and activities. Popular excursions include the three-hour Horseback Ride 'n Swim (US$79), which culminates in an exciting bareback trot into the sea; ATV driving (US$115); zip-line tours (US$79); and the Zion Bus to Bob Marley's Mausoleum in Nine Mile (US$104).

**DON'T MISS**

## STUSH IN THE BUSH

Stush in the Bush (☑562-9760; www.stushinthebush.com; Bamboo; meals US$55-75; ☑) is an organic farm-to-table Rasta dining experience, and home to some of the best food you'll eat in your entire trip to Jamaica. Your experience here starts with a walking tour of the farm, learning about what you'll eat, and then proceeds to a gorgeous rustic cabin with tremendous views for your meal.

There are two options, the gourmet pizza (US$55) and the full spread (US$75), of four and five courses respectively, with sides of delicious salads, crunchy plantain chips with zingy dips, rich soups and lively juices. It's vegan-friendly too. Advance booking essential.

Rates include transfer from your hotel on the north coast. The trips are sometimes crowded, but the quality of service and guides is high.

### H'Evans Scent    ADVENTURE SPORTS

(☑427-4866; www.hevansscent.com; Bamboo; ⊙9am-5pm Mon-Fri, 10am-4pm Sat & Sun) Near the tiny hill town of Bamboo, 10km south of Priory, this adventure-sports destination is the site of several adrenaline-charged but family-friendly experiences: paintballing, ATV rides and a zip-line tour. Activity package combos are available, starting at J$3750 with discounts for groups of 10 or more; if you want to sample everything on the menu, J$6750 gives you access to all areas.

Meals are available in the bright-yellow main house.

### ❶ Getting There & Away

Minibuses that run between St Ann's Bay and Runaway Bay can drop you off at the bus stop right in front of Chukka Cove Farm. To reach H'Evans Scent and Cranbrook Rainforest Gardens, you'll need your own vehicle.

## Runaway Bay

Runaway Bay (16km west of St Ann's) is a center for sun worshippers, snorkelers and divers. This one-street village, lined with all-inclusive resorts and nondescript local shops, stretches along the A1 for 3km, merging with the small community of Salem to the east.

### 🏃 Activities

Runaway Bay has excellent diving. There's a wreck in shallow water in front of Club Ambiance, plus two cars and a plane offshore from Club Caribbean. A reef complex called Ricky's Reef is renowned for its sponges. More experienced divers might try the eponymous Canyon. Here, too, is the *Reggae Queen*, a 30m-long sunken tugboat.

Resort Divers (☑881-5760; www.resortdivers.com; Salem; 1-/2-tank dives US$50/95) is the longest-running dive operator along this stretch of coast, followed by Jamaica Scuba Divers (☑381-1113; www.scuba-jamaica.com; Franklyn D Resort, Runaway Bay).

Several small beaches are supposedly public, although most are the backyards of a few all-inclusive resorts. If you're hankering for a dip in the big blue, head to the white-sand Cardiff Hall Public Beach, opposite the Shell gas station. There is a livelier (but littered) fishers' beach in Salem, where the occasional sound-system party is staged on the weekend.

### 🛏 Sleeping

#### House Erabo    GUESTHOUSE $

(☑973-4813; www.house-erabo.com; r J$4800; P🛜) A small, yellow, German-run guesthouse hiding behind flowering shrubbery, House Erabo offers three spick-and-span rooms on the western edge of Runaway Bay with access to a small secluded beach.

#### Club Ambiance    RESORT $$

(☑973-6167; www.clubambiance.com; s/d US$180/260; P❄🛜🏊) This lively alternative to the grander all-inclusives is popular with 20- and 30-somethings and features two small private beaches, a pool with a bar, cafe and restaurant, plus a massage hut and access to water sports. All bright colors and kitschy art, the spacious rooms feature firm king-size beds and tiled floors. It's an adults-only resort, no families.

#### Franklyn D Resort    RESORT $$$

(☑973-4124; www.fdrholidays.com; Main St; all-incl 1/2/3 bedrooms US$395/495/550; P❄@🛜🏊) At this Spanish hacienda-style, all-inclusive family resort, there are kid-friendly facilities and a personal nanny assigned to each child. The resort has three restaurants and a bar, plus an oceanfront spa and waterslide. Three-night minimum stay.

# ✕ Eating

Discovery Bay has a reasonable number of eating options for a place of its size, including one of the best beachside fish restaurants in the region.

### Sharkie's
SEAFOOD $

(Fisherman's Beach, Salem; meals around J$1000; ⊘11am-10pm) Even if you're staying in Ocho Rios, you should follow the lead of locals and head for this informal seafood restaurant on Fisherman's Beach for steamed, grilled and fried fish, conch (curried, soup or fritters) and nonfishy standards.

### Jerkie's
JERK $

(Salem; jerk from J$350; ⊘10am-8pm) Mainstreet jerk joint serving jerk chicken and pork, along with *bammy* and *festival*.

### Tek It Easy
JAMAICAN $

(A1; meals J$500-700; ⊘lunch & dinner) At this economical rooftop haunt, Jamaican fare – primarily chicken and fish – competes for attention alongside the freely flowing overproof rum. There's music most nights.

# ℹ Information

**Police** (cnr Main St & B3)
**Post Office** (Main St)
**Scotiabank** (Main St) Bank with ATM.

# ℹ Getting There & Away

Minibuses and route taxis ply the A1 between Montego Bay (J$200, one hour) and Ocho Rios (J$150, 30 minutes). They can be flagged down anywhere in Runaway Bay.

# Discovery Bay

This wide flask-shaped bay, 8km west of Runaway Bay and 8km east of Rio Bueno, is a popular resort spot for locals drawn to Puerto Seco Beach, and many of Jamaica's wealthiest families have holiday villas up in the hills here. The town itself has only marginal appeal.

A giant bauxite-loading facility dominates the town. Large freighters are fed by conveyor belts from a huge storage dome that looks like a rusty pumpkin – it was used as the villain's headquarters in the James Bond movie, *Dr No*. You can follow the road signed 'Port Rhoades' uphill 1km to a lookout point offering fantastic views over the bay.

Locals believe this to be the location where Christopher Columbus first landed on Jamaican soil in 1494, though others say it was at Rio Bueno.

Accommodation in Discovery Bay is confined to privately rented villas. The area is easily accessible as a day trip from either Ocho Rios or Falmouth.

# ◉ Sights

### Green Grotto Caves
CAVE

(www.greengrottocavesja.com; adult/child U$20/10; ⊘9am-4pm) This impressive system of caves and tunnels, 3km east of Discovery Bay, extends for about 45km. The steps lead down into the impressive chambers, where statuesque dripstone formations are illuminated by floodlights. The Taíno people left petroglyphs carved into the walls; the caves have frequently been used as hideouts – by the Spanish during the English takeover of the island in 1655, by runaway slaves in the 18th century, and between the two world wars by smugglers running arms to Cuba.

The highlight is Green Grotto, a glistening subterranean lake 36m down. The entrance fee includes a guided one-hour tour, which is particularly family-friendly. The guides conduct their tours with humor and attempt to amaze you by tapping stalactites to produce hollow drumlike sounds, as well as pointing out the different species of bat that live in the cave, and maybe even their imported predator, the Jamaican yellow boa.

### Puerto Seco Beach
BEACH

(J$500; ⊘9am-5pm) The eastern side of Discovery Bay is rimmed with white-sand beaches. With its soft sand and limpid waters, Puerto Seco Beach, in the center of town, is a real charmer. Open to the public, it sports rustic eateries and bars and a fun park with a waterslide for kids not interested in suntanning. On weekends and holidays the beach is teeming, but during the week the place is often deserted. You can rent fishing boats, sea bikes and Jet Skis.

### Columbus Park
MUSEUM

(⊘9am-5pm) FREE An open-air roadside museum atop the bluff on the west side of the bay, this park features anchors, cannons, nautical bells, sugar-boiling coppers and an old waterwheel, as well as a diminutive locomotive once used to haul sugar at Innswood Estate. Nearby are remains of Quadrant Wharf, built in 1777 by the British, with a mural commemorating Columbus' landing. There's a branch of Scotchies selling jerk here, making a popular stop for tour coaches running between Mobay and Ochi.

 **Eating**

**Ultimate Jerk Centre** JERK **$**
(meals J$400-800; ⊙10am-9pm) This popular rest stop and bar opposite Green Grotto Caves (p92) caters to a captive audience. The curry goat is decent, as is the soup, *bammy* and *festival*, but you can find far better jerk elsewhere.

### ❶ Getting There & Away

Minibuses and route taxis ply the A1 between Montego Bay and Ocho Rios (J$150, 30 minutes). They depart from the Texaco gas station, opposite the entrance to Puerto Seco Beach.

## Brown's Town

Brown's Town is a lively market town 11km south of Runaway Bay in the Dry Harbour Mountains. Many noble houses on the hillsides hint at its relative prosperity.

Route taxis run several times a day to Brown's Town from Ocho Rios (J$150, one hour), via Discovery Bay. Minibuses and route taxis also run to St Ann's Bay, Kingston and Nine Mile. All transportation leaves from the east end of Top Rd, a block off Main St.

Market days – Wednesday, Friday and Saturday – have the most transport.

## Nine Mile

The small community in the Dry Harbour Mountains where Bob Marley was born and is now buried is set dramatically in the midst of the Cockpits. Despite its isolated location, the village is decidedly on the beaten path for tour groups making pilgrimages to Marley's tomb, so be prepared for plenty of hustle from people who claim to have known the great man, despite not looking old enough to have been born when he died. You'll also be offered ganja by the bucketload, including plantation tours, though you should note that while ganja's status is in flux, these are currently illegal.The drive to Nine Mile is particularly lush and scenic.

### ◉ Sights & Activities

**Bob Marley**
**Mausoleum & Museum** MUSEUM
(☑999-7003; J$2000; ⊙9.30am-4.30pm) In theory, the Bob Marley Mausoleum & Museum could be such a great attraction. The plain two-room house where the singer spent his early years is touching, as is his marble mausoleum, with its candles, Bible and stained-glass windows. Unfortunately, the site's relentless plastic commercialization, and the hoary tales from guides relentlessly grubbing for tips, may quickly depress the casual visitor, and upset those who ever got a spiritual lift from the man's music. Adjust your expectations accordingly.

**Chukka Caribbean Adventures** TOURS
(☑972-2506; www.chukkacaribbean.com; tours US$110) Chukka Caribbean Adventures runs the 'Zion Bus Line' tour to Nine Mile, picking you up from your north coast hotel.

### ❶ Getting There & Away

Nine Mile is linked by infrequent minibuses and route taxis from Brown's Town (which is in turn served by connections to Discovery Bay, St Ann's Bay and beyond). By car, follow signs from Claremont on the A1. The mountain road is beautiful but in shockingly bad condition.

## PORT ANTONIO

We're hesitant to describe anywhere as the 'real' Jamaica, but Port Antonio, with its charming mess of markets, higglers (street vendors) and Georgian architecture in various states of disrepair, its greenery and nearby beaches, does a pretty good approximation. There are definitely no Margaritavilles here; just a capillary-like tangle of backstreets, browsing goats and friendly locals. Wandering past the old houses lining the Titchfield Peninsula, it's very easy to think you've roamed into some quaint colonial ghost town.

Ironic, then, that the tentacles of Jamaican tourism first found purchase in Port Antonio. The island's major banana port, its prosperity began luring visitors at the turn of the 20th century. Celebrity visitors, led by cinematic swashbuckler Errol Flynn, descended on the town in the 1940s. When the tourist attentions moved on to the west of the island, Port Antonio reverted to bananas. As a gateway to lush Portland parish, its laidback attitude makes it a perfect destination for travelers seeking to get away from it all.

### History

Port Antonio had a slow start in life. Spanish 'Puerto Anton' never thrived, while the

# Port Antonio

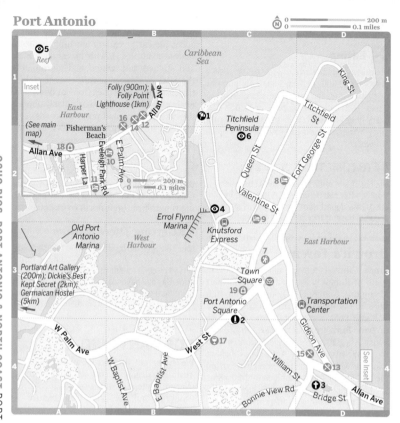

British town of Titchfield on the peninsula suffered throughout the 18th century from coastal fevers and raids by the local Maroons. It wasn't until 1871 that the town came into its own, when fruit-shipping magnate Captain Lorenzo Dow Baker settled here. Baker established the banana trade here, turning Port Antonio into a true boomtown as the 'banana capital of the world.'

In the 1890s Baker began shipping in tourists from the US in his empty banana boats. Although Portland's banana bonanza was doomed in the 1930s by the onset of Panama disease, the arrival of movie star Errol Flynn and, later, numerous blue bloods and Hollywood stars, gave new cachet to Port Antonio as a tourist resort. The jet set continued to visit through the 1960s, when hip new resorts were built.

Sadly, Port Antonio has been in quiet decline ever since. Tourist dollars migrated to Negril and Montego Bay, and Jamaica's ba-

nana trade has been outdone in the world market by Latin America.

## ◎ Sights

Port Antonio's heart is the Town Sq, at the corner of West St and Harbour St. It's centered on a clock tower and backed by a handsome redbrick Georgian courthouse from 1895; the building is surrounded by a veranda supported by Scottish iron columns and topped by a handsome cupola, and is now a branch of National Commercial Bank. About 50m down West St is the junction of William St, where the smaller Port Antonio Sq has a cenotaph honoring Jamaicans who gave their lives in the two world wars.

On the west side of Port Antonio Sq is **Musgrave Market** (West St; ⊘ Mon-Sat), decked out in yellows and blues, a quintessential chaotic developing-world market supported by thick limestone columns. Following William St south to Harbour St, you

# Port Antonio

### ◎ Sights
| | |
|---|---|
| 1 Bikini Beach | C1 |
| 2 Cenotaph | C3 |
| 3 Christ Church | D4 |
| 4 Errol Flynn Marina | C2 |
| 5 Navy Island | A1 |
| 6 Titchfield Peninsula | C2 |

### ◎ Activities, Courses & Tours
| | |
|---|---|
| Lady G'Diver | (see 4) |
| 7 Valley Hikes | C3 |

### ◎ Sleeping
| | |
|---|---|
| 8 DeMontevin Lodge | C2 |
| 9 Finjam Cottage | C2 |
| 10 Hotel Timbamboo | B2 |
| 11 Porty Hostel | A2 |

### ◎ Eating
| | |
|---|---|
| 12 Anna Banana's Restaurant & Sports Bar | B1 |
| 13 Piggy's Jerk | D4 |
| 14 Survival Beach Restaurant | B1 |
| 15 The Italian Job | D4 |
| 16 Wilkes Seafood | B2 |
| Yosch Café | (see 18) |

### ◎ Drinking & Nightlife
| | |
|---|---|
| C&S Smoothies | (see 18) |
| Marybell's Pub on the Pier | (see 4) |
| 17 Roof Club | C4 |

### ◎ Shopping
| | |
|---|---|
| 18 Craft Village | A2 |
| 19 Musgrave Market | C3 |

can turn left to peek inside Christ Church, a redbrick Anglican building constructed in neo-Romanesque style around 1840 (much of the structure dates from 1903). Look for the brass lectern donated by banana-magnate Captain Lorenzo Dow Baker.

On the north side of the Town Sq is the marvelously baroque facade of the Royal Mall, a three-story complex painted a striking red, now more or less a covered shopping parade decorated and designed in a plethora of styles, including Tudor and Renaissance.

### Titchfield Peninsula                    AREA
Along this hilly peninsula – known locally as 'the Hill' – are several dozen Victorian-style gingerbread houses, most notably DeMontevin Lodge (p96), an ornate rust-red mansion, now a hotel. Many of the finest homes line King St, which runs down the center of the peninsula (parallel to Queen and Fort George Sts). This is a relatively well-off area,

but one with a romantically sad sense of glamour gone by.

Further north at the tip of the peninsula are the ruins of Fort George, dating from 1729. The parade ground and former barracks today house the prestigious Titchfield School. Beyond the school, several George III–era cannons can still be seen mounted in their embrasures in 3m-thick walls.

### Folly                    RUINS
This rather appropriately named two-story, 60-room mansion on the peninsula east of East Harbour was built entirely of concrete in pseudo-Grecian style in 1903 by Olivia Tiffany Mitchell, heiress to the Tiffany fortune. It was only lived in for 35 years before being abandoned and given to the government in lieu of unpaid taxes, after which it fell into disrepair.

The story that it was abandoned due to the use of sea water in the concrete, causing the iron reinforcing rods to rust and the roof to collapse in 1936, is apocryphal. The shell of the structure remains, held aloft by limestone columns, and makes a perfectly peculiar locale for a picnic. The orange candy-striped Folly Point Lighthouse, built in 1888, overlooks Monkey Island – so named for the primates once kept there by Mitchell's son-in-law Hiram Bingham, the discoverer of Machu Picchu.

### Navy Island                    ISLAND
In colonial days the Royal Navy used this now-lush island to careen ships for repair. In the mid-20th century Errol Flynn bought the island and built a home that became a hotel, which later fell into decay. It's not possible to land on the island, but you might find an enterprising fisher to take you on a cruise around it.

### Bikini Beach                    BEACH
(J$500; ☉ noon-10pm) A small private beach with a pretty lick of sand near the marina on the Titchfield Peninsula. Hopefully the shuttered beach restaurant will reopen soon.

### Errol Flynn Marina                    MARINA
(☑ 715-6044, 993-3209; www.errolflynnmarina.com; Port Antonio, GPS N 18.168889°, W -76.450556°) Port Antonio has, undoubtedly, one of the finest natural harbors in Jamaica, which has been converted into a posh yachting dock where sailboats moor and the well-to-do wander. At night it's a popular place for young couples to stroll along the paths that snake around a few upmarket

restaurants and shopping centers – a quiet retreat from the bustle of town.

## 🏃 Activities

### Lady G'Diver
DIVING

(☑ 995-0246, 715-5957; www.ladygdiver.com; Errol Flynn Marina; 2-/4-dive packages US$90/160, PADI courses US$400) A full-service dive shop at the marina, with daily dives, retail store, PADI instruction and equipment rentals. The folks here are pioneering the largely undiscovered dive sites in the area, including Courtney's Reef and Fisherman's Reef, a series of drops, canyons and outcrops of coral.

## ☞ Tours

Port Antonio makes an excellent base from which to take excursions into the forests of the Rio Grande Valley and into the Maroon country towns of Moore Town and Nanny Town.

### Port Antonio Tours
CULTURAL

(☑ 859-3758; www.toursinportantonio.com) Portland enthusiast and all-round local character Joanna Hart offers excellent custom tours of the area. *Se habla español.*

### Tours & Trips
TOURS

(☑ 781-9261; alessandropastres2@gmail.com) Offers backpacker-friendly tours to local beaches and waterfalls.

### Valley Hikes
HIKING

(☑ 993-3881; Unit 41, Royal Mall, Port Antonio) Local hiking tour company, which offers trips up the Rio Grande Valley, including to Scatter Falls and up to Ambassabeth.

### Hotel Mocking Bird Hill
BIRDWATCHING

(☑ 993-7134, 993-7267; www.hotelmockingbirdhill.com) Offers bespoke birdwatching tours in Portland.

## 🎆 Festivals & Events

### Port Antonio International Marlin Tournament
FISHING

(☑ 927-0145; www.errolflynnmarina.com; ⊙ early Oct) A week-long fishing extravaganza.

## 🛏 Sleeping

Port Antonio has a good selection of accommodations, particularly in the budget category. There are glitzier options east along the coast toward Fairy Hill.

### ★ Germaican Hostel
HOSTEL $

(dm US$25-27, d US$62, cottages US$80; 🛜) Superb hilltop German-run hostel outside Port Antonio, with astounding views over the coast. The dorm is spacious and the doubles well presented, plus there's a cottage, 'hammock house' and new annex that was being built when we visited. The kitchen is well set up but the real gem is the veranda with views, and the peace of getting away from it all.

It's some distance from town, but the managers will pick you and do a run into Port Antonio a couple of times a day (a route taxi from Port Antonio to Stony Hill will take you most of the way).

### Finjam Cottage
GUESTHOUSE $

(☑ 293-2265; www.finjamcottage.com; r US$45, with sea view & balcony US$55; 🛜) On the highest point of Titchfield Hill, Finjam is a very homely and laid-back place, with simple rooms, a pleasant veranda to chill out on, use of the kitchen and a great location close to town. The friendly hosts are Finnish-Jamaican, hence the name.

### DeMontevin Lodge
GUESTHOUSE $

(☑ 993-2604; www.demontevinlodgehotel.com; 21 Fort George St; d US$70-100, without bathroom US$45) This venerable Victorian guesthouse – built in 1881 – has a homey ambience that blends modern kitsch and antiques reminiscent of granny's parlor – the place could almost be the setting of a tropical Sherlock Holmes novel. The simple bedrooms (six with private bathrooms) are timeworn, but clean as a whistle.

### Irie Vibez
HOSTEL $

(☑ 781-9261; alessandropastres2@gmail.com; 247 Anchovy Land Settlement, Anchovy Gardens; dm/d J$2000/5000) A tiny new hostel, Irie Vibez is a little out of town but popular with the ultra-budget backpackers. There's just one roomy six-bed dorm and a double; most people hang out on the terrace. The owner offers tours and good vibes. Meals – including a good ackee and saltfish breakfast – are available on request. Easy to reach by route taxi.

### Porty Hostel
HOSTEL $

(☑ 578-0198; www.portyhostel.com; 33 East Palm Ave; dm/s/d US$20/35/45) This new Italian guesthouse in a quiet residential area is close to the bay and has a selection of decent dorms, a well-run kitchen and friendly management. It's a steal for the price.

### Hotel Timbamboo
HOTEL **$$**

(☎ 993-2049; www.hoteltimbamboo.com; 5 Everleigh Park Rd; r US$75-95; P❄🛜🛝) The Timbamboo has spacious, sunny rooms with modern furniture, carpeted floors and cable TV. Some rooms have balconies with views of the Blue Mountains, though it's set a little too far back for a proper sea breeze. The hotel's sun deck is a great place to unwind.

## 🍴 Eating

For a town with few tourists compared to further west along the coast, Port Antonio has a good selection of eating options.

### ⭐ The Italian Job
ITALIAN **$**

(29 Harbour St; pasta J$1000-2000, pizza J$740-1400, salads J$500-1000; ⊙ noon-10pm Mon-Sat) This is a jolly, Italian-run, checked-tablecloth sort of a place, with great pasta dishes, pizza and salads, plus crepes for dessert. Keep an eye on the specials board too, as the chef puts a great twist on local offerings, such as lobster ravioli dressed with avocado. The wine is pretty good too.

### Yosch Café
INTERNATIONAL **$**

(Allen Ave; sandwiches J$350-500, mains J$550-1200; ⊙ 9am-9pm Sun-Thu, to 10pm Fri & Sat) This cafe on the edge of the craft village complex is all decking, driftwood and bamboo, open to the sea breeze and looking back onto Titchfield and the bay. The breakfasts and sandwiches are winners, as is the fish if you come here for dinner. Very refreshing.

### Piggy's Jerk
JERK **$**

(jerk chicken J$400, half-chicken J$800, soup J$100; ⊙ 10am-10pm Mon-Sat) A very simple jerk shack offering tasty chicken with *festival*, hearty soup and cold drinks (and despite the name, no jerk pork). It's take-out only – eat on the seafront, or grab a half-chicken for a picnic elsewhere.

### Survival Beach Restaurant
JAMAICAN **$**

(24 Allan Ave; mains US$6-12; ⊙ 10am-10pm Mon-Sat; 🖉) In addition to the usual local fare, natural juices and the best jelly coconut in town, this choice shack serves a tasty dish made with coconut milk, pumpkin, Irish potato, garlic, scallion, thyme, okra, string beans and three kinds of peas, served with sides of cabbage and callaloo. Just ask for the vital I-tal stew.

### ⭐ Wilkes Seafood
SEAFOOD **$$**

(Allen Ave; salads J$500-1000, catch of the day J$2500; ⊙ 7.30-10.30am, 11.30am-4pm & 5.30-9pm) This place looks like an unassuming beach bar from the front, but is a delightful small restaurant inside, overlooking the sea and with a semiopen kitchen that lets the cooking aromas make you hungry. Nothing you get will disappoint, though we found the coconut curried fish to be a particular winner. Dining here is a real Port Antonio highlight.

### Dickie's Best Kept Secret
FUSION **$$**

(☎ 809-6276; dinner US$20-40; ⊙ 6-10pm) Dickie's – a tiny pointy-roofed seaside hut on the western outskirts of Port Antonio – offers enormous five-course meals in rooms best described as Bob Marley meets Alice in Wonderland. There's not always a menu, but trust their suggestion that anything will be delicious. Reservations essential.

### Anna Banana's Restaurant & Sports Bar
JAMAICAN **$$**

(☎ 715-6533; Allan Ave; breakfast J$300, seafood dinners J$800-1500; ⊙ 10am-10pm) Need seafood? Jerk? An open-air bar? Head to this perennially popular breezy restaurant-bar, overlooking the beach on the southern lip of the bay, which specializes in jerk or barbecued chicken and pork, and groaning plates of conch and lobster.

This is also the place to go for darts, pool and a rum punch. Friday heats up with the help of local DJs.

## 🍸 Drinking & Nightlife

There are plenty of cheap beach bars along the bay that are good for a shot of rum and a cold Red Stripe. A popular night out near Port Antonio is Vinyl Sundays (p102) at Drapers.

### C&S Smoothies
JUICE BAR

(Allan Ave; ⊙ 8am-9pm) A great place for fresh juice and smoothies in the craft village. If you're up earlier in the morning, it's worth swinging by for traditional Jamaican breakfasts – porridge, saltfish, plantain and dumplings.

### Marybell's Pub on the Pier
BAR

(Errol Flynn Marina, Ken Wright Dr; ⊙ noon-midnight; 🛜) Inside Errol Flynn Marina, this is a good place to while away an afternoon (or evening) away from the pace of the town, at the cabana bar or one of the tables overlooking the bay. Light meals are available.

### Roof Club
CLUB

(11 West St; ⊙ 8pm-late Thu-Sun) This is Port Antonio's infamous hang-loose,

rough-around-the-edges reggae bar. Young men and women move from partner to partner. You're fair game for any stranger who wants to try to extract a drink from you. It's relatively dead midweek when entry is free, but on weekends it hops.

## 🛍 Shopping

**Craft Village**  ARTS & CRAFTS
(Allen Ave; ⊘9am-6pm) A wooden complex with a series of small huts, each with craftspeople selling carved wood, jewellery, T-shirts and other tourist paraphernalia.

## ℹ Information

### EMERGENCY
**Police Station** (☑ 993-2546, 993-2527)

### INTERNET
**Portland Parish Library** (☑ 993-2793; 1 Fort George St; per 30min J$200; ⊘9am-6pm Mon-Fri, to 1pm Sat)

### MEDICAL SERVICES
**City Plaza Pharmacy** (☑ 993-2620; City Centre Plaza, Harbour St)
**Port Antonio Hospital** (☑ 993-2646; Nuttall Rd; ⊘24hr) Above the town on Naylor's Hill, south of West Harbour.
**Square Gift Centre and Pharmacy** (☑ 993-3629; 11 West St)

### MONEY
**CIBC Jamaica Banking Centre** (☑ 993-2708; 3 West St)
**FX Trader Cambio** (☑ 993 3617; City Centre Plaza, Harbour St)
**National Commercial Bank** (☑ 993-9822; 5 West St)
**Scotiabank** (☑ 993-2523; 3 Harbour St)

### POST
**Post Office** (Harbour St)

## ℹ Getting There & Around
The town center lies at the base of the Titchfield Peninsula, where the two main drags meet at a right angle in front of the main plaza and courthouse.

### BOAT
**Errol Flynn Marina** (p95) Customs clearance and mooring for private vessels.

### CAR
There are gas stations on West Palm Ave, Fort George St and Harbour St.

Car rentals are available at **Eastern Rent-a-Car.** (☑ 993-3624; www.portantoniocarrentals.com; 16 West St)

### PUBLIC TRANSPORTATION
There's a **transportation center** (Gideon Ave) that extends along the waterfront, with minibuses leaving regularly for Kingston (to Half Way Tree bus station; J$500, two hours) via Buff Bay and Port Maria (where you change for Ocho Rios). Route taxis depart constantly for Fairy Hill (J$100, 10 minutes), Boston Bay (J$150, 20 minutes) and Manchioneal (J$250, 40 minutes).
**Knutsford Express** have two buses a day to Kingston (J$2200, four hours) via Ocho Rios.

### TAXI
For licensed taxis, call **JUTA/Port Antonio Cab Drivers' Co-op** (☑ 993-2684). They can also be found pretty easily in town, notably along by the transportation center.

# EAST OF PORT ANTONIO
The road east of Port Antonio has some of the prettiest landscape in Jamaica – gorgeous beaches and lush green hills. Reach Falls, a particularly beautiful waterfall in a country that abounds in them, is a highlight.

## Port Antonio to Fairy Hill
The A4 meanders east of Port Antonio through thick forest, jagged-tooth bays, pocket coves and the coastal villages of Drapers, Frenchman's Cove and Fairy Hill. This is where most visitors to Port Antonio, and indeed to Portland, will find accommodations and explore the nearby Rio Grande Valley and Blue Lagoon as well as the luxuriant sands of Winnifred Beach, Frenchman's Cove and San San Beach. Back in the 1950s and '60s, vacationing A-listers nicknamed this beautiful area the 'Jamaican Riviera,' and today many Jamaicans still name Portland as their favorite part of the country.

## ⊙ Sights
★**Blue Lagoon**  LAGOON
The waters that launched Brooke Shields' movie career are by any measure one of the most beautiful spots in Jamaica. The 55m-deep 'Blue Hole' (as it is known locally) opens to the sea through a narrow funnel, but is fed by freshwater springs that come in at about a depth of 40m. As a result the water changes color through every shade

of jade and emerald during the day, thanks to cold freshwater that blankets the warm mass of seawater lurking below.

You may encounter boat operators eager to take you on a short boat ride (US$20) to nearby Cocktail Beach (where parts of the Tom Cruise movie *Cocktail* was filmed) and rustic Monkey Island, a short distance away.

The lagoon is accessible from the road and is public property, but the area is under development so an entrance fee may soon be on the cards. Note that if it's been raining heavily, run-off water from the hills turns the lagoon a disappointing murky green.

**Trident Castle**                               LANDMARK

(www.castleportantonio.com) A strange slice of Ruritania in the Caribbean, this folly on a headland 3km from Port Antonio was built in the 1970s by the (in)famously eccentric Baroness Elisabeth Siglindy Stephan von Stephanie Thyssen, also know as Zigi Fami. Resembling a rather magnificent wedding cake, it is a popular backdrop for society weddings and music video shoots. Sadly, the castle is closed to the public, but it makes one hell of a landmark from the road.

## 🏖 Beaches

⭐**Winnifred Beach**                              BEACH

FREE Perched on a cliff 13km east of Port Antonio is the little hamlet of Fairy Hill and a rugged dirt track. Follow that road steeply downhill and you'll reach Winnifred Beach, yet another totally gorgeous beach that puts a lot of the sand in more famous places to shame. It's the only truly public beach on this stretch of the coast, and has a great vibe, with food and drink stands, weekend sound systems and Jamaicans from all walks of life.

**Frenchman's Cove**                              BEACH

(J$1000; ⊙9am-5pm) This beautiful little cove just east of Drapers boasts a small but perfect white-sand beach, where the water is fed by a freshwater river that spits directly into the ocean. The area is owned by the Frenchman's Cove resort (p100). There's a snack bar serving jerk chicken and fish, alfresco showers, bathrooms, a secure parking lot and the option of taking boat tours (US$20) to the Blue Lagoon.

**San San Beach**                                 BEACH

(J$100; ⊙10am-5pm) San San is a gorgeous private beach used by residents of the villas on Alligator Head, and guests of the Goblin Hill, Fern Hill and Jamaica Palace hotels.

The bay is enclosed by a reef that's wonderful for snorkeling (US$15 per day) and kayaking (US$25 per hour). Undeveloped Monkey Island is a good snorkel spot, and you can swim there from the beach if you're in decent shape.

## 🏃 Activities

Good diving abounds: the shoreline east of Port Antonio boasts 13km of interconnected coral reefs and walls at an average of 100m to 300m offshore. Alligator Head is known for big sponge formations and black corals. Hammerhead sharks are common at Fairy Hill Bank.

For dive tours, instruction and equipment, contact Lady G'Diver (p96) at the Errol Flynn Marina in Port Antonio.

## 🛏 Sleeping

The stretch of coast between Port Antonio and Fairy Hill has some good accommodations options, and makes a good alternative to staying in Port Antonio itself. In 2016 plans were announced to develop a Sandals resort at Drago Bay.

**Drapers San Guest House**         GUESTHOUSE $

(☑993-7118; www.draperssan.com; Hwy A4, Drapers; r US$65-85; 🐾) Run by an Italian expat, activist and font of local knowledge, this cozy little house comprises two cottages with five doubles and one single room (two share a bathroom), all with fans, louvered windows and hot water. It's all very welcoming and family-oriented; there's a comfy lounge and communal kitchen and (excellent) dinners can be served by arrangement.

**Mikuzi Vacation Cottages**          COTTAGE $

(☑978-4859, 480-9827; www.mikuzijamaica.com; Hwy A4, Fairy Hill; r US$30-60; 🐾) Mizuki sits on top of the road leading down to Winnifred Beach. It's kind of funky and fun, but needs a bit of a clean-up. The property is divided between candy-bright cottages (the cheaper one lacks a kitchen), and one studio apartment. Meals available on request.

**Jamaica Palace**                           HOTEL $$

(☑993-7720; www.jamaica-palacehotel.com; Hwy A4; r US$170-190, ste from US$230; 🅿🍴🐾🏊) A white neoclassical wedding cake of a property overlooking Turtle Cove, Jamaica Palace almost feels more art gallery than hotel, perhaps like one of the original grande dames of the Jamaican Riviera. Cavernous, chintzy rooms and suites boast crystal chandeliers,

## East of Port Antonio

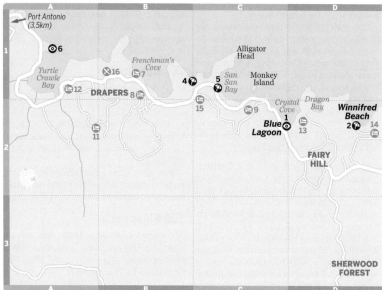

antiques and Georgian bay windows. In the landscaped grounds is a 35m-long pool shaped like the island of Jamaica.

**San San Tropez**    HOTEL **$$**
(☑ 993-7213; www.sansantropez.com; Hwy A4, San San Bay; s/d US$85/125; P ✳ 🛜 🏊) This friendly Italian-run hotel has gracious, well-lit rooms and suites and a European small-resort feel. The furnishings are modern and graced by bright tropical decor, there's a nice sun deck and the adjoining restaurant has splendid views and good food (meal plans are offered). Gives passes to San San Beach (p99).

**Frenchman's Cove**    RESORT **$$**
(☑ 933-7270; www.frenchmanscove.com; r/ste US$112/145, 2-/3-bedroom cottages US$260/360; P ✳ 🛜 🏊) This old great hotel frankly feels its age a little; some of the stone cottages and '70s modernist condos feel a bit dated. That said, lovely staff and ready access to one of Jamaica's prettiest beaches more than make amends.

★**Hotel Mocking Bird Hill**    HOTEL **$$$**
(☑ 993-7267; www.hotelmockingbirdhill.com; Mocking Bird Hill Rd; r US245-295; 🛜 🏊) 🌿 The Mocking Bird is one of the most vigorous proponents of ecotourism in Portland. The property is a lovely house at the end of a

winding dirt road; all rooms are lovingly appointed with well-chosen fabrics and art, ocean views and private balconies. Meals at the Mille Fleurs restaurant are sublime. Trails through the hillside gardens are fabulous for birdwatching.

★**Gee Jam**    HOTEL **$$$**
(☑ 993-7302, 993-7000; www.geejamhotel.com; off Hwy A4, San San Bay; r US$425-795, ste from US$1195; P ✳ 🛜 🏊) The hotel home of Gee Jam recording studios sets the standard for ultra-modern design, cuisine and exclusivity. There's a definite Manhattan in the tropics vibe, with cottages connected by jungle walkways with views of the coast. Owner Jon Baker is a music-industry veteran with a taste for hip-hop and reggae – guests who've stayed here form their own Grammy Award nominees list.

**Kanopi House**    HOTEL **$$$**
(☑ 632-3213; www.kanopihouse.com; Dragon Bay Rd, Drapers; cabins US$80, r from US$300; ✳ 🛜 🏊) 🌿 This Blue Lagoon ecoresort deserves the accolades given in honor of its luxury and comfort. Dark-wood chalets that seemingly grow from the jungle feel like a laid-back five-star hotel carved into a banyan tree. The property makes great efforts to leave a low ecological footprint and is

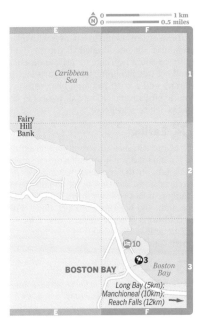

**OCHO RIOS, PORT ANTONIO & NORTH COAST** PORT ANTONIO TO FAIRY HILL

stuffed with elegant art. Fresh organic dinners are prepared on-site.

**Goblin Hill Villas**     RESORT $$$
(☑ 993-7443, 925-8108; www.goblinhillvillas.com; Goblin Hill Rd; 1-bedroom villas US$155-215, 2-bedroom villas US$235-295; P ❈ ☒) Popular with families, this 5-hectare hilltop estate above San San Beach has a cluster of two-bedroom and one-bedroom villas, fully equipped, frankly huge and surrounded by lawns, forest and amazing views; when the mists accompany the frequent rains, you can see why they call it 'Goblin Hill.' A meandering nature trail encircles the property. The villas come with their own private maid and butler (optional), two tennis courts and the fabulous Tree Bar, built around a massive fig tree.

## ✖ Eating

This stretch of road has many accommodations but few independent restaurants. Most folks eat at their hotels – which generally have restaurants open to nonguests – or are catered to by the staff of their villa.

**★ Woody's**     JAMAICAN $
(Hwy A4, Drapers; mains J$300-800; ⊙ noon-8pm) This truly brilliant spot – with an outdoor patio and an indoor counter that doubles as a local meeting place – prepares tremendous hot dogs and burgers, grilled cheese and Jamaican dinners to order. There's a great veggie burger heaped with stewed callaloo, and sublime homemade ginger beer. Service is anything but rushed, but the charming hosts always make this a winning experience.

**★ Mille Fleurs**     JAMAICAN $$$
(☑ 993-7267; Hotel Mocking Bird Hill, Mocking Bird Hill Rd; 3-course dinners US$55; ⊙ noon-2pm & 7-9pm; ✔) This restaurant offers some of the best haute Jamaican cuisine on the island, savored on a gorgeous terrace and served with a sense of elegance and intimacy. The locally sourced organic menu is influenced by what ingredients are seasonally available, includes vegetarian options, and ends with a cleansing trolley of regional liqueurs. Reservations required.

**Bush Bar**     FUSION $$$
(☑ 993-7000; Gee Jam; set meals US$60; ⊙ 8am-10pm) Set in a veranda that overlooks the jungle and the ocean and ensconced in multiple layers of hip, the restaurant at Gee Jam offers an immaculate Asian-Jamaican fusion experience, replete with cocktails as

neon-bright as Vegas, chilled background music and that ineffable sense of being part of life's winning team. Call ahead.

## ☆ Entertainment

Every Sunday evening in Drapers village, there's the free Vinyl Sundays street dance, playing oldies reggae and ska.

## ❶ Getting There & Away

Route taxis run throughout the day along this stretch of road between Port Antonio and Boston Bay – you'll pay J$150 for the full trip, or J$100 for a segment of it.

# Boston Bay

Boston Bay is a lick of a town with a cute pocket-size beach shelving into turquoise waters. High surf rolls into the bay, making it a popular place to catch some waves.

Boston is equally famous for its highly spiced jerk. Today, jerk has a worldwide fan base and is pretty much synonymous with Jamaican cuisine, but until the 1950s it was virtually unknown outside this area. The practice of marinating meat with jerk seasoning was first developed centuries ago not far from here by the Maroons, and the modest shacks at Boston Bay were among the first to invite attention – well worth making a detour for.

## ◉ Sights & Activities

**Boston Bay Beach** BEACH
(Boston Bay; J$200) Boston Bay's beach sits in a small pretty cove, and while its golden sand is draw enough, the shape of the bay and prevailing weather makes it a perfect surf spot. There are showers, changing rooms, a lifeguard and a small restaurant.

**Boston Bay Surfing** SURFING
(board hire US$20, 1hr surf lessons with board US$20) The cove at Boston Bay is a perfect place to learn to surf, or to hire a board for the day and hit the waves yourself. The instructors here will have you standing up on the board in no time – or at least enjoy the splash as you topple into the water.

## 🛏 Sleeping

★**Great Huts** RESORT $$
(☑353-3388; www.greathuts.com; Boston Beach Lane; huts per person US$55-80, tree houses US$163-255; 🐾) A green 'ecovillage' meets

sculpture park overlooking Boston Bay, this is a distinctive and imaginative collection of African-style huts and tree houses with open verandas, bamboo-walled bedrooms and alfresco showers. There's a private beach, a walking trail along the cliff, an Afro-centric library and a great restaurant-bar with live music on Saturday. If only all resorts in Jamaica felt this 'inclusive.'

## ✗ Eating

Near the entrance to Boston Bay beach on the main road you'll see half a dozen smoky jerk pits on the roadside. Vendors vie for your custom, but they're all equally good, serving up hot and sweet jerk with *festival*, plantain and breadfruit, washed down with a cold drink. They'll also sell jars of locally made jerk sauce (J$800) to take home – a great souvenir.

## ❶ Getting There & Away

Boston Bay is 15km east of Port Antonio. Route taxis ($J150) ply the route all day.

# Long Bay

Long Bay is well named; its creamy beach sweeps for 1.5km, with strong breezes pushing the waves forcefully ashore. While the burly easterlies bring good surf (and an undertow makes it bad for swimming), they also leave Long Bay exposed to extreme weather. Once a big draw for backpackers, the hamlet has a slightly forlorn hurricane-battered air today, and much of the beach has been eroded away.

## 🛏 Sleeping

**La Familia** GUESTHOUSE $
(☑892-2195; lafamiliajamaica@gmail.com; r US$35-45) Friendly Italian-run guesthouse just off the main road with a clutch of cheery rooms decorated with old ska and reggae vinyl records. There's an open-style kitchen-dining room, and your hosts can cook dinner on request.

**Pimento Lodge Resort** GUESTHOUSE $$
(☑882-5068; www.pimentolodge.com; r US$155-206; 🐾🌊) On the rise above Long Bay, and thus enjoying lovely views over the sea, Pimento Lodge has a clutch of large breezy rooms with bright tropical decor, a well-tended garden and pool to relax by and a circular bar for daytime and evening

drinks. Meals are on request, and the hosts can offer local excursions.

### Hotel Jamaican Colors — HOTEL $$

(☑893-5185, 407-4412; www.hoteljamaicancolors. com; Hwy A4; s/d/q/house US$80/90/130/136, air-con supplement US$20; P❋🗢🏊) This spiffy French-run hotel is located on the cliffs 2km south of Long Bay and has 12 comfortable cottages, all with plush double beds draped with mosquito netting (there's also a house for rent that can sleep five; rates are based on the number of guests). The open-air restaurant is great, and the owners dispense good travel information.

### Sea Cliff Resort & Spa — HOTEL $$$

(☑860-1395; www.facebook.com/Portland.seacliff; r US$200-235) A grand new venture for Portland, and one that's well-named, looming as it does over sheer cliffs. All rooms take advantage of the sea views and have balconies with hammocks. There's plenty of space to laze, and an excellent restaurant worth making a trip to in and of itself. A great addition to the local hotel scene.

In summer, rates are slashed by at least a third.

## ✗ Eating

Numerous rustic beachside shacks sell inexpensive Jamaican fare and double as nofrills 'rum shops' with music at night; find the busiest one with the best atmosphere.

### Fishermans Park — JAMAICAN $

(mains J$250; ⊙11am-10pm) On the main road in the center of Long Bay, Fishermans Park is a lively open-sided restaurant and sports bar, with a thatched seating area. Strong on fish (we also enjoyed the goat curry), with good-sized portions.

### Portland Cliff Hanger — JAMAICAN $$

(mains from US$8; ⊙noon-9pm Sun-Thu, to 10pm Fri-Sat) A thatched restaurant attached to Seacliff Resort & Spa, looking out over the cliffs near Long Bay. Refresh yourself with a juice mix while picking a selection of Jamaican dishes with a modern twist. Its signature dish is delicious Drunken Lion Fish – serving up the invasive species with a sauce of red wine, Red Stripe, hoisin and a secret ingredient.

## ❶ Getting There & Away

Minibuses and route taxis run between Port Antonio and Long Bay (J$250, 25 minutes).

# Manchioneal

The fishing village of Manchioneal (Man-kee-oh-neal) sits on a vividly blue bay where colorful pirogues are drawn up on the wide, shallow beach. It's a center for lobster fishing and the surf is killer – July is said to be the best month.

The main reason to head towards Manchioneal is the beautiful Reach Falls, 2km west of the village (and signed off the main road).

Three kilometers southeast of Manchioneal, Ennises Bay Beach is another great place to spend a lost afternoon. There's a refreshment stand and lovely views of the John Crow Mountains.

## ⦿ Sights

### ★ Reach Falls — WATERFALL

(adult/child US$10/5; ⊙8:30am-4:30pm Wed-Sun) Even in a country that abounds in waterfalls, Reach Falls stands out as one of the most beautiful places in Jamaica. The white rushing cascades are surrounded by a bowl of virgin rainforest; the water tumbles over limestone tiers from one hollowed, jade-colored pool into the next. It's possible to walk, wade and swim your way up to the edge of the falls, by an unmarked jungle path some way below the main entrance.

Once you enter the falls, guides will offer their services – crucial if you want to climb to the upper pools, which we highly recommend (there's a little underground, underwater tunnel a bit up the falls; plunging through is a treat). The Mandingo Cave, the crown jewel of the falls, can be accessed at the top of the cascades, but you need to bring climbing shoes and be prepared for a long climb.

Excellent local guides Leonard Welsh (☑849-6598) and Kenton Davy (☑438-3507) can take you and point out plants and wildlife along the way if you choose to hike to the falls.

The turnoff to Reach Falls is well-signed about 2km north of Manchioneal. Any Port Antonio–Manchioneal route taxi can drop you; it's a further 3km uphill to the falls.

## 🛏 Sleeping & Eating

### Zion Country — GUESTHOUSE $

(☑871-3623, 451-1737; www.zioncountry.com; s US$50, d without/with bathroom US$60/75) Four cute cottages built over the green cliffs overlooking Manchioneal bay and a chilled vibe lead to an excellent backpacker haven, with hammocks on the veranda and shared bathrooms. There's a small bar-restaurant with lovely views, and steep steps leading down to the beach.

**Bryan's Restaurant**  JAMAICAN $
(Main St; meals J$200-600; ☺noon-9pm) A rooftop eatery that offers simple but delicious Jamaican fare, served on a sunny veranda. Pay for your meal at the B&L Supermarket on the 1st floor before heading upstairs.

### ❶ Getting There & Away

Minibuses and route taxis run between Port Antonio and here (J$250, 40 minutes). Taxis can take you to Reach Falls for around J$1000. If you have your own vehicle, you can follow the coastal road south until it becomes the A2 heading to Kingston (beware of floods in the rainy season).

# WEST OF PORT ANTONIO

The coast west of Port Antonio takes in a variety of scenic bays, as well as inland attractions such as the Rio Grande Valley and Charles Town – one of Jamaica's original Maroon settlements.

### ◉ Sights

**Somerset Falls**  WATERFALL
(☎383-6970; www.somersetfallsjamaica.com; Hwy A4; J$1500; ☺9am-5pm) This dark waterfall is hidden in a deep gorge about 3km east of Hope Bay. The Daniels River cascades down through a lush garden of ferns, heliconias, lilies and crotons into glistening teardrop black pools. Visitors have to negotiate some steep, twisty steps to get here.

The entrance fee includes a guided tour through a grotto by boat to the Hidden Fall, which tumbles 10m into a jade-colored grotto. Bring a swimsuit to enjoy the large swimming area.

The site has a touristy restaurant, bar, ice-cream shop and small menagerie, but the falls themselves are unspoiled.

### 🛏 Sleeping

**Rio Vista Resort & Villas**  GUESTHOUSE $$
(☎993-5444; www.riovistajamaica.com; Rafter's Rest; r US$90-125, villas US$195-205; P❈☎🐾) This guesthouse sits atop a ridge above the Rio Grande near the turnoff for Rafter's Rest, 6km west of Port Antonio. The house,

built into the remains of an old plantation home, has enviable views across the river and mountains. The villas and rooms are breezy and clean, and the Buccaneer restaurant serves up decent meals.

### ❶ Getting There & Away

Minibuses and route taxis run between Port Antonio and Buff Bay (from where you can get transportation to Charles Town).

Both route taxis (J$150) and minibuses (J$100) pass Somerset Falls and Hope Bay between Annotto Bay and Port Antonio.

## Charles Town

A couple of miles inland from the modest town of Buff Bay is the Maroon settlement of Charles Town, home to the Asafu Culture Yard. You can also get a guide to take you on a three-hour hike to an 18th-century coffee plantation and Nanny's Look Out, a viewpoint over the coast.

### ◉ Sights

**Asafu Culture Yard**  CULTURAL CENTER
(☎445-2861; admission by donation) The Asafu Culture Yard is a sort of house complex with gardens and a museum operated by Maroon Colonel Lumsden, who's happy to clue visitors in to the nuances of his culture while leading them on a small walk past historical artifacts and plants and herbs used in traditional Maroon medicine.

### 🍴 Eating

There are no eating options in Charles Town, though there are a few Jamaican cheap eats in nearby Buff Bay.

**★Blueberry Hill Jerk Centre**  JERK $
(jerk meat J$300-750; ☺10am-9pm) Blueberry Hill Jerk Centre has developed a well-deserved reputation for its pork and chicken, drenched in a punishing sauce that will clear your sinuses (while filling them with a lovely smoky odor). A serious case is made by aficionados that this could be the best jerk in Portland parish, which is really saying something.

### ❶ Getting There & Away

Route taxis buzz between Charles Town and nearby Buff Bay all day. There are also one or two route taxis every day to Port Antonio (J$150, 30 minutes).

---

---

# Orange Bay

The road between Hope Bay and Orange Bay takes an inland route and is wonderfully scenic with dense jungle foliage, open forests of towering palms, and hillsides covered with tropical plants boasting leaves the size of elephant ears. You'll pass by huge stands of bamboo up on the ridge and expansive plantations of banana. Along the way there are simple roadside stands that sell produce and pepper shrimp.

At Orange Bay the road rejoins the coast. Keep an eye out for the old rail station that served the Kingston–Annotto Bay line until it ceased operation in 1983; it's sadly atmospheric, a relic of bygone days.

## 🛏 Sleeping

**Almond Lodge**     GUESTHOUSE **$**
(📞 385-4139; www.almondlodgeportantonio.com; d US$55; 🅿) Almond Lodge offers several simple, clean, fan-cooled, en-suite double rooms. There's a pebble and black-sand beach, which you are likely to have all to yourself – ask to borrow a snorkel – and a small restaurant and bar with pool table.

# Robin's Bay

A spur of highway crosses the Wag Water river east of Annotto Bay and ends at Robin's Bay (known as Strawberry Fields in the 1970s, when it was a hippie free-love haven). There are persistent rumors about pirates' treasure still hidden away in the area's sea caves. The area has some of the most rugged and undeveloped country on the north coast.

You can reach Robin's Bay from Port Maria by a hiking trail that leads along one of the few stretches of Jamaican coastline that remains pristine. Locals can lead you to remote Black Sand Beach, and the Kwaaman and Tacky Waterfalls (p105).

## ◉ Sights

**Kwaaman & Tacky Waterfalls**     WATERFALL
Kwaaman and Tacky Falls are so pristine and isolated that, if you stumbled across them wandering up the coast from Robin's Bay, you might be tempted to claim them as your own. Kwaaman Waterfall is a 32m cascade that tumbles into a clear pool you can swim in. It's a nearly one-hour hike from Robin's Bay.

Gazing up from the water at the contorted rock face behind the falls, you'll be able to make out what appears to be dreadlocks formed in the rock by the continual flow of water over centuries. Tacky Falls lacks the dreads but is equally worth the visit, particularly if the weather's calm and you can take a boat ride from Robin's Bay.

## 🛏 Sleeping

**River Lodge**     GUESTHOUSE **$**
(📞 863-4164; www.river-lodge.com; incl breakfast s US$35, d US$50-60, d cottages US$105-135; 🅿) This atmospheric option has sprouted from the ruins of an old Spanish fort. The rooms have white bleached-stone walls and are lit by skylights. The bathrooms (cold water only) are festooned with climbing ivy; the bathroom in the upstairs 'tower' room is alfresco. Meals (on request) are a social affair, served in a small thatched restaurant.

**Strawberry Fields Together**     RESORT **$$**
(📞 999-7169; www.strawberryfieldstogether.com; camping per person US$15, junior cottages US$70-90, deluxe cottages US$180-300; 🅿❄) This series of villas and cottages is ever popular. The cottages (which can sleep four to six) all have views to the hills and sea (there's a private beach), some come with whirlpool baths and all have eclectic wood decor – 'To Di World' and 'Bolt and Lightning' are our favorites. The surrounding land is lovely to trek through.

Meals are available at the Strawberry Patch restaurant, and budget travelers can pitch their own tents – a nod to the resort's origins as a 1970s backpacker haven.

## ℹ Getting There & Away

Route taxis are few and far between – a hire from Annotto Bay will cost around J$600. There's a daily bus from Robin's Bay to Kingston. The hotels can also arrange transfers.

# RIO GRANDE VALLEY

The Rio Grande river, fed by the frequent rains of wet Portland parish, rushes down from 900m in the Blue Mountains and has carved a huge gorge that forms a deep V-shaped wedge between the Blue Mountains to the west and the John Crow Mountains to the east. While not as remotely rugged as the Cockpit Country, the Rio Grande comes pretty close; if you need an escape from anything resembling a city, we recommend heading out here.

The Maroons, descendants of escaped slaves who have retained a strong sense of their African cultural heritage, have a strong presence here; to distinguish themselves from their cousins in the Cockpit Country, they are referred to as the Windward Maroons.

## Hiking

Popular hikes include those to White Valley, known for its large population of giant swallowtail butterflies; to Dry River Falls; and to Scatter Falls and Fox Caves.

Other hikes are demanding, with muddy, overgrown trails and small rivers that require fording. Don't attempt to hike off the beaten path without a guide. The Corn Puss Gap trail is particularly difficult, as is the wild path from Windsor to Nanny Town.

Various companies offer organized hikes. In Port Antonio, contact Valley Hikes (p96), which offers treks to Scatter Falls and Fox Caves as well as hikes to Moore Town, Nanny Falls and Nanny Town. Sun Venture Tours (p49), based in Kingston, offers hiking and cultural tours in the area. All of these outfits can organize homestays in the Rio Grande Valley, which is preferable to rocking up on your own or camping in an area you're unfamiliar with.

### Scatter Falls & Fox Caves

An excellent and easy hike takes you to Scatter Falls and Fox Caves, reached by crossing the Rio Grande on a bamboo raft at Berridale, then hiking for 30 minutes through a series of hamlets and banana groves. The falls tumble through a curtain of ferns into a pool where you can take a refreshing dip. There are changing rooms nearby as well as toilets, a campground, a bamboo-and-thatch bar, and a kitchen that serves a hot lunch – though this must be ordered in advance through Grand Valley Tours, based in Kingston.

A steep, 15-minute hike from the falls leads to the caves, which have some intriguing formations, some of which resemble Rasta dreads. The roof is pitted with hollows in which tiny bats dangle, and you can see where the falls emanate from the caves.

As the path is unsigned and you'll be passing through private property, it's imperative that you visit accompanied by a guide.

### Nanny Town

This former village stronghold belonging to the Windward Maroons is perched on the brink of a precipitous spur on the northeastern flank of Blue Mountain Peak, about 16km southwest of Moore Town as the crow flies. It is named for an 18th-century Ashanti warrior priestess and Maroon leader, now a national hero. In 1734 English troops brought swivel guns into the valley and blew up most of Nanny Town, but the local Maroons remained defiant. Essentially, they proved more trouble to subdue than they were worth, and Nanny Town was granted a sort of semi-autonomy that persists to this day.

It's a tough 16km hike from Windsor, 5km north of Moore Town. There are numerous side trails, and it's easy to get lost if you attempt to hike on your own.

**DON'T MISS**

### RAFTING THE RIO GRANDE

Errol Flynn supposedly initiated rafting on the Rio Grande during the 1940s, and moonlight raft trips were considered the ultimate activity among the fashionable.

Today paying passengers make the 11km journey of one to three hours (depending on water level) from Grant's Level (Rafter's Village), about 2km south of Berridale, to Rafter's Rest at St Margaret's Bay. When the moon is full, unforgettable night-time trips are offered. These are less regimented; your guide will be happy to pull over on a moon-drenched riverbank so that you can canoodle with your sweetie or just open the ice chests to release the beer.

Reserve at Rio Grande Experience (993-5778; per raft US$65) or at Rafter's Village at Grant's Level if you don't have reservations. This is a one-way trip, so if you're driving you need to hire a driver to bring your car from Berridale to St Margaret's Bay (Rio Grande Experience will help for US$15; the drivers are insured, but make clear to them that you expect them to drive slowly and safely).

A route taxi from Port Antonio to Grant's Level costs J$200; they depart from the corner of Bridge St and Summers Town Rd. Licensed taxis cost about US$20 roundtrip.

## UPPER RIO GRANDE VALLEY

Hiking is the only way to explore the Upper Rio Grande Valley. Arrange your trip via
**Ambassabeth Cabins** (☑ 462-8163; www.facebook.com/Ambassabeth; cabins US$50) ✈.
**Valley Hikes** (☑ 993-3881; Royal Mall) in Port Antonio also has guides that know the area.

The ranger station for Blue Mountains-John Crow National Park is at Millbank, 3km
before Bowden Pen, near the summit ridge of the John Crow Mountains, which parallels
the valley like a great castle wall. A trail leads to the **White River Falls**, a series of seven
cascades, while beyond you may find the ruins of abandoned Maroon villages. Be advised that this is a tough trek through some serious rainforest, so get a Maroon guide at
Ambassabeth or Millbank.

A short distance above Bowden Pen the track begins rising more precipitously and
the vegetation closes in. The trail (passable on foot only) continues over the **Corn Puss
Gap** and into St Thomas – a fabulous trek for the well prepared.

To get to the Upper Rio Grande, the road to the right of the Y-junction at Seaman's
Valley leads via Alligator Church to Bowden Pen, 16km or so up the river valley. The paved
road ends at Alligator Church. Beyond here, the dirt road is extremely rough and narrow
and you'll need a 4WD.

# Moore Town

This one-street village, 16km south of Port
Antonio, stretches uphill for several hundred meters along the Wildcane River. The
village was founded in 1739 following the
signing of a peace treaty granting the Maroons – rebel former slaves – their independence. Moore Town is still run semi-autonomously by a council of 24 elected members
headed by a 'colonel.' The locals attempt to
keep alive their lore and legends, and still
bring out their *abengs* (goat horns) and
talking drums on occasion, but many of the
youth are emigrating to the cities.

Visitors expressing interest in the fascinating history of the Windward Maroons
will be warmly welcomed. On arrival, it's
considered polite to pay respects to the local
colonel (Wallace Sterling during research;
just ask about and someone will take you
to him). If he's not about, you may be approached by one of his emissaries and asked
for a small donation.

## 🅞 Sights

Moore Town's main site of interest is **Bump
Grave**, at the southern, uppermost end of
town. Topped by a flagpole flying the Maroon and Jamaican flags, the oblong stone
and plaque mark the grave of Nanny, warrior
woman, freedom fighter and chieftain of the
Maroons. There's a gate protecting the grave,
but it can be opened for a small donation. Also
be on the lookout for the church of Mother
Roberts (the building is bedecked in flowers);
it's the AME Zionist Deliverance Center, and is
a major destination for faith healings.

Trails lead from Moore Town, including
one to a series of lovely pools at **Nanny
Falls**, about 45 minutes away.

## 🛈 Getting There & Away

Moore Town is unsigned and lies in a hollow to
the left of a Y-junction at Seaman's Valley; the
road to the right continues via Alligator Church
through the Upper Rio Grande Valley. Minibuses
and route taxis operate to Moore Town from Port
Antonio (J$150). A minibus from Port Antonio
runs in the early morning and again in the early
afternoon (J$100).

# Montego Bay & Northwest Coast

## Best Places to Eat

➡ Houseboat Grill (p122)

➡ Leroy's Beach Bar (p131)

➡ Marguerite's (p122)

➡ Water Square (p130)

➡ Far Out Fish Hut (p127)

## Best Places to Sleep

➡ Polkerris B&B (p119)

➡ Coach House (p134)

➡ Bird's Nest (p127)

➡ Windsor Great House (p135)

➡ Pura Vida (p130)

## Why Go?

Home to the nation's largest airport and a busy Caribbean cruise terminal, Montego Bay is many people's first view of Jamaica before they get whisked off to the surrounding beaches, golf courses and all-inclusive resorts. So it's ironic that, barring MoBay's excellent dining scene, most of the area's attractions are found outside Jamaica's second city. The north coast is replete with plantation-era history, from its well-preserved plantation houses to the historic core of Falmouth. Inland, adventure beckons, from hiking and spelunking in Cockpit Country – a roadless wilderness of hidden caves and eerily silent hills that is disorientating, even to hardened locals – to rafting and zip-lining through the jungle. Filling in the gaps is a dense network of small towns and tiny villages that pulsate with the rawness and romance of everyday Jamaican life.

## When to Go
### Montego Bay

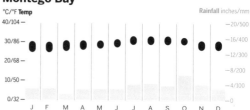

**Dec–Mar** High season means high rates, but generally sunny, clear weather.

**Jul** Montego Bay rocks out to the island's biggest reggae party, Reggae Sumfest.

**May–Jul** Low season and generally hotter, rainier weather means big accommodations savings.

# MONTEGO BAY

POP 110,115

Montego Bay has two distinct faces: there's the smooth tourist countenance that grins contentedly from the pages of a thousand glossy Caribbean brochures; and there's MoBay proper, a pretty gritty city, second only to Kingston in terms of status and chaos. Most of the big all-inclusive resorts are located well outside the urban core in the fancy suburb of Ironshore. Stay in the city, however, and you're faced with an entirely different proposition – a riot of cacophonous car horns and bustling humanity that offers an unscripted and uncensored slice of Jamaican life, warts and all.

The Hip Strip (aka Gloucester Ave), with its midrange hotels and ubiquitous souvenir shops flogging Bob Marley T-shirts, acts as a kind of decompression chamber between MoBay's two halves. You won't find many hipsters here, but in among the hustlers and smoky jerk restaurants there's a detectable Jamaican rhythm to the action on the street.

## Sights

### Hip Strip & the Beaches

**Doctor's Cave Beach** BEACH
(Map p118; 876-952-2566; www.doctors cavebathingclub.com; adult/child US$6/3; 8:30am-sunset) It may sound like a rocky hole inhabited by lab-coated troglodytes, but this is actually Montego Bay's most famous beach and the one with the most facilities. A pretty arc of sugary sand fronts a deep-blue gem studded with floating dive platforms and speckled with tourists sighing happily. Er, *lots* of tourists – and a fair few Jamaicans as well. The upside is an admission charge keeps out the beach hustlers, though it doesn't ensure that the beach is kept clean.

Founded as a bathing club in 1906, Doctor's Cave earned its name when English chiropractor Sir Herbert Barker claimed the waters here had healing properties. People flocked to Montego Bay, kick-starting a tourism evolution that would culminate in the appearance of *Homo Margaritavillus* decades later. There are lots of facilities on hand including a restaurant, a grill bar, an internet cafe and water sports, and lots of things to rent (beach chairs, towels, snorkeling gear).

**Dead End Beach** BEACH
(Map p112; Kent Ave) A meet-the-locals affair just north of Gloucester Ave, this narrow strip is also known as Buccaneer Beach. The lack of space promotes togetherness; at high tide it's pretty accurate to drop the 'beach' from 'dead end.' There are no facilities here, but the lack of crowds makes the sunsets over the bay all the more gorgeous.

**One Man Beach** BEACH
(Map p118; Gloucester Ave) With beachfront soccer and crowds of splashing locals, this crescent beach at the south boundary of Old Hospital Park is very popular but, sadly, rather litter-strewn.

**Walter Fletcher Beach & Aquasol Theme Park** BEACH
(Map p112; 979-9447; Gloucester Ave; adult/ child US$6/5; 10am-10pm; ) While the theme-park moniker is pushing it (the kid-orientated facilities consist of some blow-up water slides and a go-cart circuit), this place on Walter Fletcher Beach, with its food stalls and local crowds, offers a decent spot to relax in a chilled-out local environment.

The beach is sandy and relatively clean and the water is safe for swimming, with some limited snorkeling possibilities. Food and drink comes courtesy of the on-site deck-bar with things heating up at sunset especially at weekends. Look out for billboards advertising sporadic live-music events.

### Downtown

Church St is the most picturesque yet chaotic street in MoBay. Many of the most interesting buildings in town are clustered along it, from Jamaica's finest church to some grand 18th-century Georgian structures.

The highlight is **St James Parish Church** (Map p116; Rector 952-2775; Church St), regarded as the finest church on the island. It was built between 1775 and 1782 in the shape of a Greek cross, but was so damaged by the earthquake of March 1, 1957, that it had to be rebuilt.

The pretty **Town House** (Map p116; 16 Church St), fronted by a stately redbrick exterior, is buried under a cascade of bougainvillea and laburnum. The house dates from 1765, when it was the home of a wealthy merchant.

# Montego Bay & Northwest Coast Highlights

**1 Ironshore & Rose Hall**
(p126) Exploring plantation houses with a dark history.

**2 Cockpit Country** (p133)
Hiking, caving and birding in Jamaica's wild interior.

**3 Montego Bay** (p109)
Enjoying the varied dining scene of Jamaica's second city.

**4 Falmouth** (p128) Exploring the colonial architecture of this

well-preserved historic town on a heritage walking tour.

**5 Martha Brae Rafting**
(p129) Floating on a bamboo raft along a tranquil river.

**6 Lethe** (p132) Zip lining above the abundant greenery and rafting whitewater.

**7 Glistening Waters** (p130)
Watching sparks run down

your body as you swim in this bioluminescent lagoon.

**8 Rocklands Bird Feeding Station** (p114) Watching hummingbirds land on your fingers.

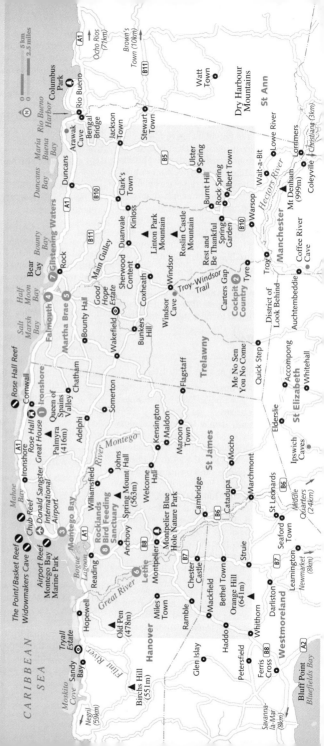

At the corner of Water Lane is a plantation-style octagonal structure that today houses a police station. About 50m west, at the corner of King St, is a redbrick Georgian building harboring the **Community & Workers of Jamaica Credit Union** (Map p116; 1 King St). A more impressive structure is the three-story Georgian building at 25 Church St – headquarters of Cable & Wireless Jamaica.

**Sam Sharpe Square**                    SQUARE
(Fort St) This bustling cobbled square is named for Samuel Sharpe (1801–32), national hero and leader of the 1831 Christmas Rebellion (see boxed text below); it is also where he was hanged in its aftermath. At the square's northwest corner is the **National Heroes' Monument**. Nearby is the **Cage**, a tiny brick building built in 1806 as a lockup for vagrants and other miscreants.

★**National Museum West**         MUSEUM
(Map p116; 940-6402; http://museums-ioj.org.jm/; Sam Sharpe Sq, Montego Bay Cultural Centre; J$400; 9am-5pm Tue-Sun) This well-curated, revamped museum, peppered with period objects, takes you through the history of Western Jamaica, from the Cohaba ceremonies of the indigenous Taínos and the arrival of the Spanish, followed by the English, to the trans-Atlantic slave trade, the advent of king sugar, Maroon rebellions, emancipation and the development of 20th-century Montego Bay as a tourist destination. A separate room introduces you to the rise of Rastafarianism, the alleged divinity of Haile Selassie and the back-to-Africa movement.

**Montego Bay**
**Cultural Centre**           CULTURAL CENTRE
(Map p116; 940-6402; Sam Sharpe Sq; 9am-5pm Tue-Sun) At the southwest corner of Sam Sharpe Sq you'll find the copper-domed Civic Centre, an elegant colonial-style, cut-stone building on the site of a ruined colonial courthouse where trials were held in the wake of the Christmas Rebellion of 1831 and where Sam Sharpe was sentenced to death. Inside there's a very good history museum, art gallery that hosts occasional exhibitions and a 200-seat theatre, used to host MoBay's cultural events.

**Burchell Memorial**
**Baptist Church**                    CHURCH
(Map p116; 952-6351; Market St) Two blocks east of Sam Sharpe Sq is one of the churches in which Sam Sharpe is said to have been a deacon. The building, which dates to 1835, is a slice of British countryside architecture smoldering handsomely away in the tropical heat. The original church was founded in 1824 by Reverand Thomas Burchell and was under renovation at research time. Sharpe's remains are buried in the vault.

**MONTEGO BAY & NORTHWEST COAST** MONTEGO BAY

## THE CHRISTMAS REBELLION

The weeklong Christmas Rebellion, which began on Kensington Estate on December 27, 1831, and engulfed much of the Montego Bay region, was the most serious slave revolt to rock colonial Jamaica. Its impact and the public outcry over the terrible retribution that followed were catalysts for the British parliament passing the Abolition Act in 1834.

The instigator of the revolt was Samuel Sharpe (1801–32), the slave of a Montego Bay solicitor. Sharpe acted as a deacon of Montego Bay's Burchell Baptist Church and became a 'Daddy' (leader) of the church. He used his pulpit as a forum to encourage passive rebellion.

In 1831 Sharpe counseled fellow slaves to refuse to work during the Christmas holidays. Word of the secret, passive rebellion spread throughout St James and neighboring parishes. Inevitably word leaked out, and warships and extra troops were sent to Montego Bay.

The rebellion turned into a violent conflict when the Kensington Estate was set on fire. Soon plantations and great houses throughout northwest Jamaica were ablaze, and Sharpe's noble plan was usurped by wholesale violence. Fourteen colonialists were murdered before authorities suppressed the revolt. Swift and cruel retribution followed.

As part of the colonialists' punishments, more than a thousand slaves were killed. Day after day for six weeks following the revolt's suppression, magistrates of the Montego Bay Courthouse handed down death sentences to scores of slaves, who were hanged two at a time on the Parade – among them 'Daddy' Sam Sharpe. He was later named a national hero and the Parade was renamed Sam Sharp Sq.

# Montego Bay

N
0 ———— 500 m
0 ———— 0.25 miles

Sandals Montego Bay (1.2km);
Evelyn's (1.3km)

Donald Sangster
International
Airport

Jamaica
Tourist
Board

The Queen's Dr

Kent Ave

Sunset Blvd

DeLisser Dr

Hart Blvd

Sheila Dr
Hall Dr
Fletcher Dr
Norwood Ave

Mango Walk
Paradise Cres

MANGO
WALK

PALM BEACH

A1

Gloucester Ave (Hip Strip)

Chatham
Beach

Cornwall
Beach

Doctor's
Cave Beach

Corniche Rd

Walter
Fletcher
Beach

Davis Ave
Park Ave

Leader
Ave

Leader Ave
Sewell Ave
Park Ave

Albion Rd

NEWMARKET

ALBION

Upper King St

BRANDON
HILL

MIRANDA
HILL

See Gloucester
Ave (Hip Strip)
Map (p118)

See Downtown Montego Bay
Map (p116)

Caribbean
Sea

1
2
3
4
5
6
7
8
10
11

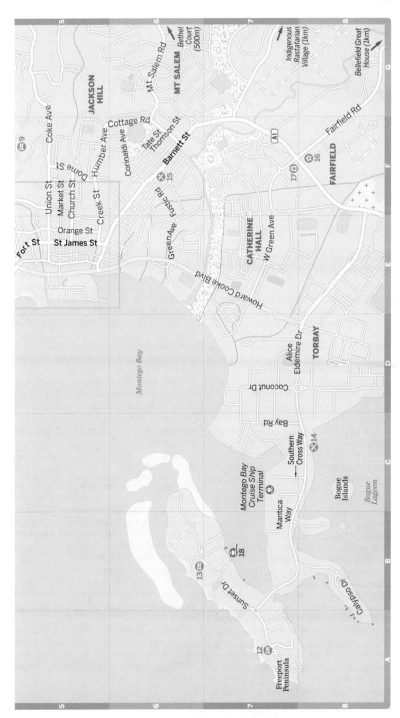

## Montego Bay

## ◎ Around Montego Bay

**Bellefield Great House**    HISTORIC BUILDING
(☑952-2382;    www.bellefieldgreathouse.com;
Farifield Rd; basic tour US$30, lunch tour adult
US$40; ⊙11am-4pm Mon-Fri by reservation) Built
in 1735, the restored Bellefield showcases
18th-century colonial living and Jamaican
culinary history. You get to see the local gardens with tremendous, centuries-old trees,
meander past an on-site jerk pit, get pleasantly tipsy on rum punch, wander the house,
and gorge yourself at a delicious lunch buffet (eight-person minimum).

The estate is southeast of central MoBay
along Fairfield Rd. Take the right turn at the
Y-fork marked for Day-O Plantation, then the
signed right turn at Granville Police Station.

Tours must be arranged at least 24 hours
in advance. There's a four-person minimum.

★**Rocklands Bird**
**Feeding Station**            BIRD SANCTUARY
(☑952-2009; off B8; US$20; ⊙9am-5pm) This
bird sanctuary is run by Fritz Beckford, a
passionate champion of birds who will pour
birdseed into your hand or provide you with
a sugar-water feeder. Guests sit agog as hummingbirds streak in to hover like tiny helicopters before finally perching on their outstretched fingers. To get here, drive or take a
bus or route taxi from Montego Bay towards
Anchovy/Montpelier/Cambridge on the B8.
Get dropped at the turnoff, from where it's
around 500m up a steep, rutted road.

Fritz estimates his feathered friends
devour nearly 900kg of seed each year (so
much for 'bird-sized' appetites). If you need
more avian action, Fritz leads tours from the
house into the bush (US$20 per person),
where you can also spot ground doves, orange- and bananaquits, Jamaican woodpeckers (flickers) and orioles. Birders have
flocked here since 1958 when it was founded
by noted ornithologist Lisa Salmon, who
tamed and trained more than 20 bird species to come and be fed by hand.

More than 140 bird species have been
recorded at this bird sanctuary, but the big
draw is the hummingbirds, including the
deep purple Jamaican mango hummingbird
and ever-popular 'doctorbird,' all best seen
around 4pm.

There's an on-site cottage (US$200) for
keen birders.

**Montego Bay Marine Park**
**& Bogue Lagoon**              NATURE RESERVE
(Map p112; ☑952-5619) The waters of Montego
Bay are gorgeous to behold both above and
below the surface, but they have long been
compromised by the effects of fishing, water sports and pollution. With the creation
in 1991 of the Montego Bay Marine Park,
environmental regulations at last began
to be strictly enforced to protect the area's
coral reefs, flora and fauna, and shoreline
mangroves.

The park extends from the eastern end of
the airport westward (almost 10km) to the
Great River, encompassing the mangroves
of Bogue Lagoon and the fishing waters
around Airport Point.

You can hire canoes or set out with a guide to spot herons, egrets, pelicans and waterfowl; swimming and crawling below are barracudas, tarpon, snapper, crabs and lobsters. Request a guide two days in advance; there's no charge but donations are gladly accepted.

### Indigenous

### Rastafarian Village
COMMUNITY

(☑ 285-4750; www.rastavillage.com; Fairfield Rd; 2hr/1-day tour US$25/100; ☺ tours by appointment) If you want to learn about the Rastafarian movement, come out to this... hmmm... 'theme park' is definitely not the right description. How about 'living interpretive exhibit?' There's not exactly a natural mystic floating in the air, but this 'village' is still a good introduction to Jamaica's most famous indigenous religion. If coming from downtown MoBay, head south on Barnett St and then drive east along Fairfield Rd for around 5km. Book your visit in advance

You'll be taken through a pretty, jungly settlement, shown medicinal plants (not what you're thinking) and given a coherent breakdown of what the Rasta faith traditionally believed in. As most travelers don't learn much about Rastafarians past the ramblings of dreadlocked hustlers, this is a pretty valuable experience, and the all-day tour includes some lovely treks into the surrounding countryside, complete with swimming in paradisiacal natural pools.

##  Activities

### Diving

MoBay offers a few good dive sites. For advanced divers, the Point/Basket Reef north of the airport has a good wall dive due to the fish, sharks, rays and dense coral that are fed by crystal-clear waters scoured by currents. The wall here starts at 20m and drops to at least 90m. Airport Reef, off the southwestern edge of the airport, is considered by some to be the best site on the island, with masses of coral canyons, caves and tunnels, and a DC-3 wreck that's become a multicolored mansion for masses of fish.

Besides boasting the sort of name you'd rightly expect in a *Pirates of the Caribbean* movie, Widowmakers Cave is an incredible tunnel filled with sponges, barracuda and

schools of smaller fish. This is a site for experienced divers, who can navigate through the 21.3m (70ft) passage and out the top of its chimney. Chub Reef, a 12.2m (40ft) dive site located just to the northeast of the city, is named for the preponderance of Bermuda chub, rather than any physical squatness. Rose Hall Reef, about 10km east of the city, is a shallow reef more suitable for less-experienced divers. The main attraction is the Fairy Castle, a pretty coral pillar as fantastic as its name suggests.

With all this said, don't dive here expecting top-rate macrodiving (ie lots of big fish). There are mantas, nurse sharks and the like in these waters, but most divers report seeing nothing larger than barracuda, reef fish and rock lobsters.

Most dive centers also offer snorkeling trips and provide multiple levels of PADI certification.

### ★ Dressel Divers
DIVING

(☑ in Spain 321-392-2338; www.dresseldivers.com; Iberostar Rose Hall Resort, Rose Hall; 1-/2-tank dive US$55/90) Acclaimed international diving outfit with a scuba centre in Iberostar Rose Hall Resort, 20km east of MoBay. Non-hotel guests are welcome on trips. For customized dive-package prices, use the online form on the website.

### Dive Seaworld
DIVING

(☑ 953-2180; www.diveseaworld.com; Ironshore; 1-/2-tank dive US$65/100) Located northeast of Montego Bay. Offers night dives and PADI certification courses as well as regular dives.

### Boat Trips

### Dreamer Catamaran Cruises
BOATING

(Map p118; ☑ 979-0102; www.dreamercatamarans. com; cruise incl transfer US$80; ☺ cruises 10am-1pm & 3-6pm Mon-Sat) An outfit that offers a catamaran adventure on three swift boats specially designed for partying, with an open bar and a snorkeling stop in the marine park. Cruises depart from Doctor's Cave Beach Club. A bus will pick you up at your hotel.

### Fishing

### Deep Drop Fishing Charters
FISHING

(Map p112; ☑ 572-0010; www.fishinginjamaica. com; Montego Bay Yacht Club; 4hr trip US$480) Runs recommended deep-sea fishing trips. Take up to four people.

# Downtown Montego Bay

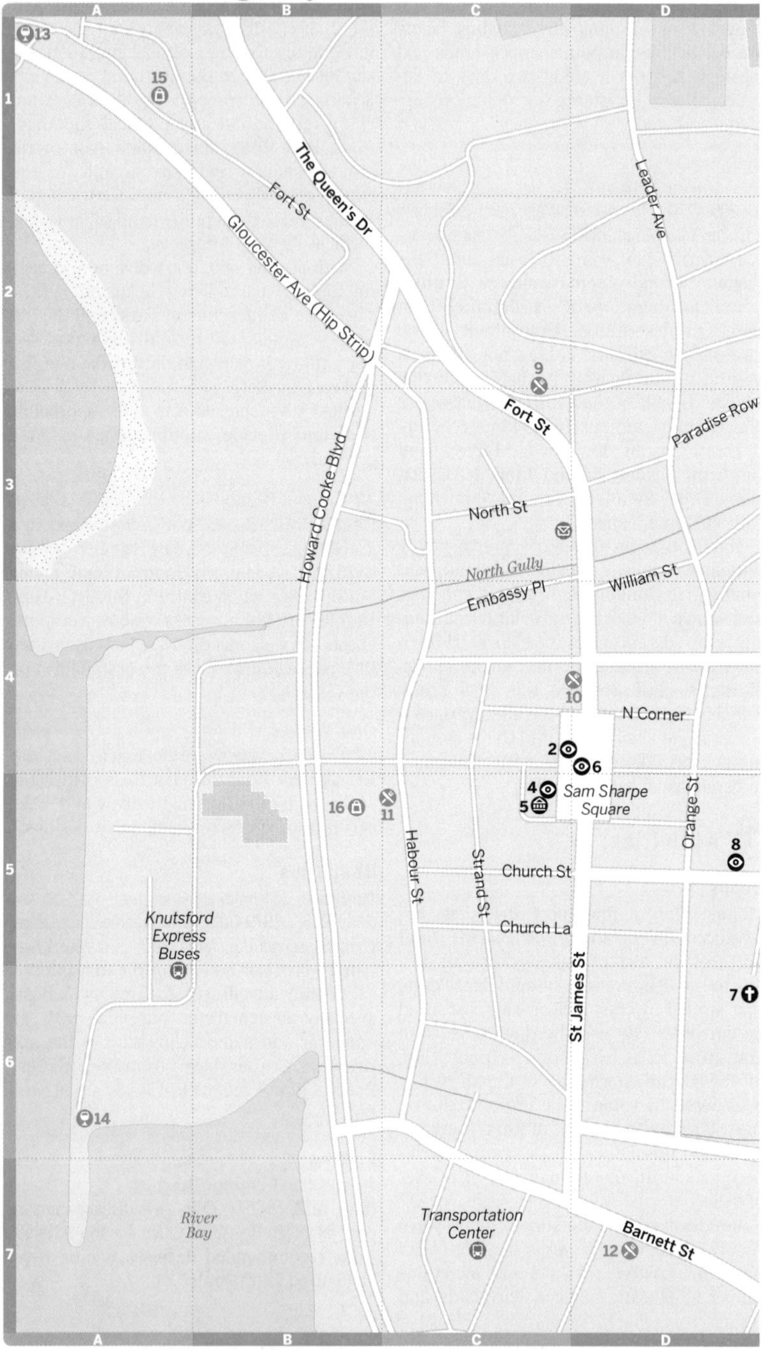

13

15

The Queen's Dr

Fort St

Gloucester Ave (Hip Strip)

Leader Ave

9

Fort St

Paradise Row

North St

Howard Cooke Blvd

North Gully

Embassy Pl

William St

10

N Corner

2 6

4 Sam Sharpe
5 Square

Orange St

8

16 11

Harbour St

Strand St

Church St

Church La

St James St

7

Knutsford
Express
Buses

14

River
Bay

Transportation
Center

Barnett St

12

## 🔗 Tours

To paraphrase Yakov Smirnoff, in Jamaica, the tour company finds YOU. Between your hotel or guesthouse and touts on the Hip Strip, someone's gonna approach you about a tour. There are always customization options available; trips to Negril, Dunn's River Falls (near Ocho Rios) and Nine Mile (the birthplace of Bob Marley, south of Ocho Rios) are de rigeuer. If you find a taxi driver you get along with who offers to give you a personalized tour, consider the option: your money may go directly to someone you like, rather than being split among commission-takers.

**Marzouca Tours**　　　SIGHTSEEING TOURS
(Map p118; ☑952-8784; 39 Gloucester Ave; ⊙9am-5pm Mon-Fri) Organizes a huge array of tours, from a historic tour of Kingston (US$150) and Montego Bay (US$50) to tours of the south coast. Also has a couple of cute apartments (p119) for rent right off Gloucester Ave (US$65).

**Island Routes**　　　OUTDOORS
(Map p118; ☑local or in USA 1-877-768-8370, outside USA 1-305-663-4364; www.islandroutes.com; 9 Queens Dr) A large professional outfit. Does good tours around the country, and has a

## Downtown Montego Bay

### ◎ Sights

### ⊗ Eating

### 🍸 Drinking & Nightlife

### 🛍 Shopping

# Gloucester Ave (Hip Strip)

N 0 ▬▬▬ 100 m

Cornwall Beach

Gloucester Ave (Hip Strip)

The Queen's Dr

Corniche Cres

MIRANDA HILL

Corniche Rd

Old Hospital Park

Gloucester Ave (Hip Strip)

Walter Fletcher Beach

nice spread of options in Montego Bay and Falmouth (including a horse-and-buggy ride for those so inclined to *really* feel like plantation owners).

**Barrett Adventures**     OUTDOORS
(Map p112; ☎ 382-6384; www.barrettadventures. com; Montego Bay Yacht Club) Barrett Adventures offers various tours along the north coast of Jamaica, from trips to Mayfield Falls and horseriding and river-boarding combos to Braco Stables, to snorkeling and Mountain Valley rafting.

**Tour Jamaica Today**     CULTURAL
(☎ 423-7522; www.tourjamaicatoday.com) Call Winston for a personalized, intimate tour in his own minibus (approved by Jamaica Union of Travelers, JUTA). He'll tailor schedules for individual itineraries, which provides a nice level of flexibility.

**Phillip Country Tours**     SIGHTSEEING TOURS
(☎ 447-0904; www.phillipcountrytours.com) Phillip provides personal (and personable) tours of his home island, catering for individual travelers. Destinations include Dunn's River Falls, Nine Mile and historical tours of MoBay.

## ⭐ Festivals & Events

Montego Bay hosts Jamaica's largest reggae festival.

★ **Red Stripe Reggae Sumfest**     MUSIC
(www.reggaesumfest.com; ⊙ mid-Jul) The largest reggae festival in Jamaica typically includes

more than 50 world-class reggae and dancehall artists. Held in July at the Catherine Hall Entertainment Center, it starts with a beach party on Walter Fletcher Beach, followed by a week of nonstop partying. Past performers have included Luciano, Beenie Man, Gregory Isaacs, Damien 'Jr Gong' Marley and Alicia Keys.

## 🛏 Sleeping

The top-end resorts and all-inclusives tend to cluster east of town in Ironshore, and there's a good concentration of guesthouses and hotels along the Hip Strip. Places further out require taxi rides. Note that all prices are high season (ie December to March) rates, which can be double or more during events like Reggae Sumfest.

### 🛏 Gloucester Ave (Hip Strip)

**Irie Inn**                                    APARTMENT **$**
(Map p118; ☎876-971-3859; 39 Gloucester Ave; apt US$65-115; ❋🌐) Two fully furnished, snug apartments. Great central location and a boon for self-caterers. Contact Marzouca Tours (p117).

**Hotel Gloriana**                                    HOTEL **$**
(Map p112; ☎876-970-0669; http://hotelgloriana.net; 1-2 Sunset Blvd; r US$45-68; P❋🌐🏊) The Gloriana, run by a local lady whose struggle against adversity has been immortalised in the film *Glory to Gloriana*, is excellent value for money, within suitcase-dragging distance of the airport and safe walking distance of the Hip Strip action. It's a mini-resort with a fountain-embellished pool, updated rooms and a restaurant where Jamaicans outnumber tourists. Wi-fi in lobby.

**Caribic House**                                    HOTEL **$**
(Map p118; ☎876-979-6073; 69 Gloucester Ave; d with/without seaview US$74/65; ❋🌐) This no-frills spot across the street from Doctor's Cave Beach is a favorite for the budget-minded. The rooms are basic, with cracked floor tiles, the hot water doesn't always work and there's no real communal area, but, what the hell – you're a backpacker, right?

**★ Polkerris B&B**                                    B&B **$$**
(Map p118; ☎877-7784; www.montegobayinn.com; 31 Corniche Rd; r incl breakfast US$194-202; P❋🌐🏊) The best B&B in Montego Bay? No question. Hanging above the Hip Strip, Polkerris, run by a British expat and his Jamaican wife, is sublime in every detail.

There's the trickling waterfall, the swimming pool, the view-embellished veranda, the stupendous breakfast and – most importantly – the one-of-the-family style of service that reminds you that you're in the real Jamaica.

**Knightwick House**                                    B&B **$$**
(Map p118; ☎952-2988; www.facebook.com/knightwickbedandbreakfast/; Corniche Rd; r incl breakfast from US$95; P❋🌐) Behind and above the Coral Cliff Hotel, this wonderful B&B is close to the action without being overwhelmed by it. Run by a charming couple, Jean and Stanley Magnus, the colonial structure – boasting terracotta floors, wrought-iron railings and abundant artwork – has three modest yet appealingly furnished bedrooms with one, two or three beds. All are airy and come with balconies.

**Toby's Resort**                                    HOTEL **$$**
(Map p118; ☎952-4370; www.tobysresorts.com; cnr Gloucester Ave & Sunset Blvd; r US$122-132; P❋🌐🏊) Located just off the 'top' of the Hip Strip, Toby's provides an admirable local vibe with amenities geared toward international travelers. Staff make Toby's feel like a gracious guesthouse, but with the benefits of large grounds, comfy rooms, a big pool and a smaller pool, and a good bar and restaurant (p122) serving a mix of Jamaican and international dishes.

**Wexford**                                    HOTEL **$$**
(Map p118; ☎952-2854; www.thewexfordhotel.com; 39 Gloucester Ave; r US$105-115; P❋🌐🏊) This spruced-up hotel offers rooms in the older wings that are efficient but comfortable, while the newer wing has more expensive digs decked out in minimalist boutique-style elegance. The Wexford is convenient for Aquasol theme park (p109) and its beach, to which guests have free access.

**Deja Resort**                                    RESORT **$$**
(Map p118; ☎876-940-4173; www.dejaresort.com; 92 Gloucester Ave; s/d incl full board $176/240; P❋🌐🏊) A recent refurb and management change has added some modern boutique touches to the hotel – the faux-grand facade wouldn't look out of place in a British seaside resort, circa 1973. Investigate closer and you'll find some welcome extras including a gym, a Jacuzzi, a swimming pool and a most elegant bar and restaurant. All meals and access to Doctor's Cave Beach included.

**Altamont West** HOTEL **$$**

(Map p118; 📞979-9378; www.altamontwest hotel.com; 33 Gloucester Ave; r US$110-210; 🅿❄🛜🏊) Bright Caribbean colors lure hotel window-shoppers into one of the Hip Strip's better accommodations options. A baby grand piano furnishes the front veranda (good sign!) and there are plenty of local Jamaican motifs dotted around to remind you this is the real deal. Rooms don't quite match the salubrious common areas, particularly the characterless cheapies facing the corridor.

## 🛏 Miranda Hill

**Big Apple** GUESTHOUSE **$**

(Map p112; 📞952-7240; www.facebook.com/pages/The-Big-Apple-Hotel-Montego-Bay-Jamaica/180794798654977; 18 Queen's Dr; d/ste US$65/95; 🅿❄🛜🏊) This pleasant hilltop inn is a good low-key option: simple and sweet. The property has a commanding view over MoBay, and tiled and air-con rooms with satellite TV. Rooms are all clean and well kept, but vary in size (most come with two double beds) and quality of views; ask about both if booking ahead and the pleasant staff will accommodate.

**El Greco** APARTMENT **$$**

(Map p118; 📞940-6116; www.elgrecojamaica.com; 34 Queens Dr; 1-/2-bedroom apt US$105/170; 🅿❄🛜🏊) More like a condo-rental than a hotel, El Greco is a nice choice for those who value their comfort and independence. The apartments have cable TV and kitchens, and private balconies that look out over a well-equipped complex that includes a pool, laundry service, tennis courts and kids' play area. Relax. This is an efficiently run operation.

## 🛏 Around Montego Bay

**Bethel Court** HOSTEL **$**

(Map p112; 📞476-7239; https://bethelcourt.word press.com/; Federal Ave; dm/r from US$20/40; 🅿❄🛜) Located in the peripheral, sometimes volatile, neighborhood of Mt Salem, Bethel Court is one of the few dedicated hostels in Jamaica. Run by the friendly Steve, who works hard to help set up tours and arrange transportation, it offers dorms and pretty basic private suites. The slightly out-of-the-way location necessitates route taxis to get in and out of town.

**Ridgeway Guest House** GUESTHOUSE **$**

(Map p112; 📞952-2709; www.ridgewayguesthouse.com; 34 Queens Dr; s/d US$60/70, without air-con US$45/55; ❄🛜) The rooms here surround a pretty garden and are as good a deal as any you'll find in MoBay. They're comparable to midrange digs: cozy beds, tiled floors, nice furnishings, all kept quite clean and presentable. The cheapest ones are fan-cooled. Located away from the beaches near the airport, but a free shuttle gets you to the sea and sand.

**Richmond Hill Inn** HOTEL **$$**

(Map p112; 📞952-3859; www.richmondhillinn-ja.com; Union St; s/d/ste US$130/153/228; 🅿❄🛜) Stay in a historic great house within Montego Bay's city limits. This spectacularly located gem atop a small hill once belonged to the Scotch Whiskey heirs and is bedizened with fine local art, antique furniture and the ghosts of prestigious former guests. Richard Nixon and James Bond in his third incarnation (Roger Moore) both stayed here. Good bar, too.

**Relax Resort** RESORT **$$**

(Map p112; 📞888-790-5264; www.relax-resort.com; 26 Hobbs Ave; r US$140, studio US$162, 1-/2-bedroom apt US$174/265; 🅿❄🛜🏊) This breeze-swept resort is often used as a layover for tourists whose flights have been delayed, which means it gets a bad rap in Tripadvisor reviews by people who have just sauntered out of a Sandals or a Hilton. Nonetheless, those without sky-high expectations will enjoy the ample grounds, large rooms adorned with floral prints and the ocean views.

## 🍴 Eating

Montego Bay is a good place to sample 'haute' Jamaican food – fancy takes on traditional Caribbean cuisine – particularly along the Hip Strip and in Freeport. Cheaper local eats are found in Central MoBay, and after-sunset jerk stands spring up along the Hip Strip.

### 🍴 Downtown

**Nyam 'n' Jam** JAMAICAN **$**

(Map p116; 📞952-1922; 17 Harbour St; mains J$500-1000; ⏰8am-11pm) On the cusp of the craft market, you can retreat to check out this truly authentic Jamaican dining experience. Settle down for snapper with a spicy sauce; jerk or brown stew chicken; curried goat; or oxtail with rice and peas. There's a round-the-clock branch at the City Centre Mall, too.

## MOBAY'S ALL-INCLUSIVE RESORTS

Many of Montego Bay's all-inclusive resorts are set apart from the city in the upper-crust districts of Ironshore and Rose Hall to the east, neighborhoods embellished by modern shopping malls and manicured golf courses, though there are several in MoBay proper. Cream of the crop is the Half Moon (📋 953-2211, in the USA 877-626-0592; www.halfmoon. com; Hwy A1; r/ste from US$422/711; P ✳ 🛜 🏊), the favored turf of queens and princes, which feels more like a utopian village than a resort. Also here is the Hilton Rose Hall (📋 953-2650, in the USA 800-445-8667; www.rosehallresort.com; all-inclusive r US$469-549; P ✳ 🛜 🏊), a humungous place with its own golf course, water park and 300m-long beachfront.

East of the airport and closer to Montego Bay are two of the popular Sandals hotels: Sandals Montego Bay (📋 952-5510; www.sandals.com/main/montego; N Kent Ave; all-inclusive r from US$479; P ✳ 🛜 🏊), one of the great-grand-daddies of all-inclusive resorts, and Sandals Royal Caribbean (📋 953-2231; www.sandals.com/main/royal/rj-home; Hwy A1; 3 nights all-inclusive r from US$1700, ste from US$2700; P ✳ 🛜 🏊), a couples-only outpost of the Sandals empire that lays on nostalgia for the British Empire. Sandals Inn (Map p112; 📋 952-4140; www.sandals.com/main/inn/in-home; Kent Ave; all-inclusive r from US$690; P ✳ 🛜 🏊) is just to the west of the airport.

Slightly closer to MoBay's city center on the Freeport Peninsula near the cruise ship terminal are two more all-inclusive resorts: the high-rise Sunset Splash Montego Bay (Map p112; 📋 in the USA 888-774-0040; www.sunsetmontegobay.com; Sunset Dr; all-inclusive r from $US360; P ✳ 🛜 🏊) and the closely guarded, couples-only Secrets St James (Map p112; 📋 953-6600; www.secretsresorts.com; Freeport; r from US$768, ste from US$1531; P ✳ 🛜 🏊).

If you want all the comforts of an all-inclusive resort, combined with easy access to the Hip Strip, then the the Sunscape Splash Montego Bay and the Royal Decameron Montego Beach Resort (Map p118; 📋 952-4340; www.decameron.com; 2 Gloucester Ave; all-inclusive r from US$260; P ✳ 🛜 🏊) are good choices.

MONTEGO BAY & NORTHWEST COAST MONTEGO BAY

### Adwa                                                    VEGETARIAN $
(Map p116; 📋 940-7618; City Centre Mall; mains J$500-750; ⊙ 8am-9pm; ✐) Tiny space in a health-food shop in a small shopping mall that mixes up decent if not hugely memorable vegetarian and I-tal fare, fruit juices and energy elixirs. The soy patties and veggie burgers can be boxed up and taken to the beach. Service without a smile.

### Pier One                                                AMERICAN $
(Map p116; 📋 286-7208; www.pieronejamaica.com; Howard Cooke Blvd; mains US$7-18; ⊙ 11am-11pm daily, till 2am Wed) Best known as a nightclub (p123), Pier One also has a restaurant with a good, clean, waterfront setting – all of which are as much of a draw as the very good Jamaican standards the place serves, as well as burgers and seafood. Usain Bolt sometimes 'bolts' in. Service can be disorganised.

### ✕ Gloucester Ave (Hip Strip)

### Pork Pit                                                     JERK $
(Map p118; 📋 952-1046; 27 Gloucester Ave; mains J$500-800; ⊙ 11am-11pm; 🛜) At this glorified food shack on the Hip Strip, a half-roasted chef slaves over a blackened barbecue fashioned from pimento wood sticks laid over smoking hot coals. His meat-cooking travails send a delicious aroma wafting down Gloucester Ave and provide a perfect advert for the Pork Pit's obligatory jerk pork (and jerk chicken). Eat it under the 300-year-old cotton tree.

### CC's Coffee & Cupcakes                                    CAFE $
(Map p118; 📋 633-7550; 36 Gloucester Ave; pastries from US$2.50; ⊙ 24hr; ✳ 🛜) Dive in off the hot Hip Strip for gulps of refreshing air-conditioned air, passable lattes and sweet cupcakes. There's also wi-fi and some savory snacks. It practically never closes.

### Berry College Restaurant                               JAMAICAN $
(Map p112; 📋 979-0045; 1 Sunset Blvd, Hotel Gloriana; mains US$8-10; ⊙ 7am-10pm) In the courtyard of the Gloriana Hotel, this home-style Jamaican eatery demands a long wait for good food made from scratch. The menu features time-honored favorites such as pepperpot soup, roast pumpkin and a unique, delectable snack that you'll want to take along for the ride: baked coconut chips. The breakfasts are equally robust.

### Golden Dynasty
CHINESE **$$**

(Map p118; ☑ 971-0459; 39 Gloucester Ave; mains J$800-1790; ⊙10:30am-10pm Mon-Sat, from noon Sun; ▣) Midpriced, midflavor and midsatisfying, Golden Dynasty represents MoBay's small Chinese population and serves a wide range of Cantonese-y dishes. Lunch specials (J$600 to J$975) mostly revolve around chow mein.

### Biggs BBQ Restaurant & Bar
AMERICAN **$$**

(Map p118; ☑ 952-9488; www.biggsbbqmobay.com; Gloucester Ave; mains US$15-29; ⊙noon-midnight; ▣) Perched on a terrace above a thin ribbon of accessible beach, this sports-bar-cum-diner lives up to its name – the portions are BIG in an unashamedly American way, and dishes range from pulled pork and ribs to steamed snapper. Choose between watching the big-screen TVs showing American football and sipping a Man Go Kill Yoself cocktail on the deck instead.

### Sands
AMERICAN **$$**

(Map p118; ☑ 952-3680; Doctor's Cave Beach; mains US$7-18; ⊙9am-1:30am) Trapped on Doctor's Cave Beach (you pay to enter), your only eating option is Sands, whose food – burgers, seafood and such – is average. Then again, you get to eat it with the sand between your toes and the salt water drying on your back, so who gives a toss?

### Toby's Good Eats
JAMAICAN **$$**

(Map p118; Tobys Resort, cnr Gloucester Ave & Sunset Blvd; mains J$600-1400; ⊙7:30am-10:30pm; 🛜) As casual eats go, Toby's is a good choice,

---

### QUICK EATS IN MOBAY

If you're in a rush or on the cheap or both, meat patties are always a good snack that could double as a meal. In MoBay, it's the usual toss-up between the ubiquitous **Juici Patties** (Map p116; 36 St James St; mains J$140-300; ⊙7am-10pm Mon-Sat) and the equally common **Tastee Patty** (Map p118; ☑ 979-5537; www.tasteejamaica.com; 13 Barnett St; patties from J$150; ⊙7am-10pm Mon-Sat; ▣). There's also a good alfresco vegetarian place with I-tal Rasta food called **Millennium Victory** (Map p112; ☑ 887-5545; www.millenniumvictory.weebly.com; 65 Barnett St; mains J$500-900; ⊙8:30am-6pm Mon-Sat, 8:30am-3pm Sun; ☑); look out for the colorful murals.

---

especially if you're staying on Sunset Dr and don't feel like venturing onto the actual Hip Strip. The menu features red snapper prepared the local way (steamed in foil with Jamaican veggies and spices), vegetable dishes and pasta. Stick around for some stick (ie pool) after dinner.

### Pelican
JAMAICAN **$$**

(Map p118; ☑ 952-3171; Gloucester Ave; mains J$1390-3850; ⊙7am-11pm; ▣🛜) Loved by upper-crust Jamaicans and tourists both, Pelican is good for goat curry and oxtail, and the seasonal lobster dishes aren't bad either. Opened the same year Jamaica gained independence (1962) and armed with the same chef since the early 1980s, this seminal Hip Strip restaurant has fully earned its right to be called a MoBay institution.

### ★ Marguerite's
FUSION **$$$**

(Map p118; ☑ 952-4777; Gloucester Ave; mains US$32-48; ⊙6-10:30pm) This celebrated restaurant provides a lovely setting from which to watch the sunset while drinking cocktails, followed by dinner on the elegant clifftop patio. The pricey (some would say overpriced) menu edges toward nouvelle Jamaican and fresh seafood, but also includes sirloin steak and inventive pasta. The chef displays his culinary chops at a central flambé grill.

## 🍴 Around Montego Bay

### Evelyn's
JAMAICAN **$**

(☑ 952-3280; Kent Ave, Whitehouse; mains J$500-1000; ⊙9am-9pm Mon-Sat, 10am-6pm Sun) Fantastic choice: a true local's spot, this rustic seafood shack (near Sandals Montego Bay) is also patronized by some very in-the-know tourists. Come here for the likes of curried conch with dhal or rice, and even filled rotis.

### ★ Houseboat Grill
JAMAICAN **$$**

(Map p112; ☑ 979-8845; http://thehouseboatgrill.com; Southern Cross Blvd; mains US$17-35; ⊙4-11pm Tue-Sun) Moored in Bogue Lagoon at Montego Bay Freeport, this converted houseboat is the best restaurant in the city. The changing menu offers eclectic Caribbean fusion cuisine: tiger shrimp in a fiery red curry, smoked marlin tartare, or beef medallions with goat's cheese and plantain-mashed potatoes. You can dine inside or reclusively out on the moondeck. Reservations strongly recommended.

# ♟ Drinking & Nightlife

The nightlife in Montego Bay consists of several visitor-friendly bars along the Hip Strip, where middle-class Jamaicans also come to party, and the Pier One nightclub; Negril is much livelier. Local bars outside of the Hip Strip can get raucous, but if you plan to venture beyond Fort St after dark, you may want to do so with some Jamaican friends.

### Blue Beat Jazz & Blues Bar          LOUNGE
(Map p118; www.facebook.com/pages/Blue-Beat-Jazz-Martini-Bar/172281429469422; Gloucester Ave; ☺6pm-5am Mon-Sat, to midnight Sun) Blue Beat kind of feels like a collection of clichés of what a classy cocktail bar should look like (smooth metal furnishing, dim lighting, dark curtains and a general sense of heavily cologned polish throughout); but as Montego Bay's first (and only) jazz and blues martini bar, it rocks its style with live music nightly, along with Asian-Caribbean fusion cuisine.

### ★Pier One          CLUB
(Map p116; ☑952-2452; www.pieronejamaica.com; Howard Cooke Blvd; ☺10pm-4am Wed-Sat) If you're into big nightclubs, Pier One is the place to go in Montego Bay. It attracts a largely local crowd, all dressed to impress and dancing as if their lives depended on it. The music is earsplitting, the dance floor is crowded (especially during Pier Pressure Fridays) and the locals can teach you the latest dancehall and soca moves.

### Jimmy Buffett's Margaritaville          BAR
(Map p118; ☑979-8041; www.margaritaville caribbean.com; Gloucester Ave; after 10pm cover US$10; ☺11am-midnight) Of the three Margaritavilles in Jamaica, this one actually offers something like a local nightlife experience. By day, yes, it's a tourist trap. A water slide carries revelers through the plumbing and flushes them ignominiously into the ocean, where their fellow booze cruisers await on a docked catarmaran. But as night falls, locals like to come here and, well, dance.

### MoBay Proper          BAR
(Map p116; ☑940-1233; www.facebook.com/mobaypropersportsbar/; Fort St; ☺noon-1am) Proper is often packed with locals and expats returned to the motherland. It's a friendly, occasionally raucous, spot and probably the easiest bar for tourists to access off the Hip Strip. Beneath a 'chandelier' of Heineken bottles, the pool table generates considerable heat, while dominoes are the rage with an older crowd out on the patio.

### Cafe Mocha          CAFE
(Map p118; ☑979-6692; www.facebook.com/CafeMochaJa/; Gloucester Ave; ☺8am-10pm) Sit in the air-conditioned hush of this cafe, the silence broken only by the click-clacking of fingers on laptop keyboards, or perch on the outdoor terrace with a Blue Mountain coffee. Skip the overpriced food.

# ☆ Entertainment

### Fairfield Theatre          THEATER
(Map p112; ☑952-0182; www.facebook.com/The-Fairfield-Theatre-176577332387951/; Fairfield Rd; ☺shows 8pm) The home stage of MoBay's innovative Little Theatre Company; check its Facebook page for info on upcoming shows.

# 🛍 Shopping

Aside from the Gallery of West Indian Art, MoBay's shopping scene is, frankly, underwhelming. Out of the typical souvenirs on offer, the items actually produced in Jamaica are: Blue Mountain coffee, rum, bamboo trinkets, woven baskets and lacquered wooden carvings of Rasta heads and animals. The rest is mass-produced in China and Indonesia; sellers lie about their items' origins.

### Harbour Street
### Craft Market          GIFTS & SOUVENIRS
(Map p116; Harbour St; ☺7am-7pm) The largest selection of typical Jamaican souvenirs in MoBay – coconut-palm baskets, woven hats, towels and clothing in Rasta colours, wood carvings and art – is found at this market which extends for three blocks between Barnett and Market Sts.

### Fort Montego
### Craft Market          GIFTS & SOUVENIRS
(Map p116; off Gloucester Ave; ☺8am-7pm) This crafts market behind the fort sells a good selection of Jamaica wood carvings, vibrant paintings ripped off from Haitian art, locally made items woven from coconut palm, and mass-produced Chinese tat. We like the friendly proprietresses of stalls 121, 132 and 97.

### ★Gallery of West Indian Art          ART
(Map p112; ☑952-4547; www.galleryofwest indianart.com; 11 Fairfield Rd; ☺10am-5pm Mon-Fri) In the suburb of Catherine Hall, this is the best quality gallery in town. It sells genuinely original arts and crafts from around the Caribbean including Cuban,

MONTEGO BAY & NORTHWEST COAST MONTEGO BAY

Haitian and Jamaican canvases, hand-painted wooden animals, masks and handmade jewelry. Most of the work here is for sale. Call ahead.

## ℹ️ Information

### DANGERS & ANNOYANCES

The well-policed Hip Strip (Gloucester Ave) is safe from criminals, but hustling may be an issue. There are aggressive hucksters in MoBay who will size you up and either try to charm or intimidate you out of a few bucks (or more) if they think you're green. Walk with purpose wherever you go; if you look lost or confused, you'll be an easier mark. That said, don't be afraid to ask for directions (shopkeepers are usually helpful, especially downtown).

Once you get downtown, the main drag (Fort St) is generally fine, but don't wander too far afield from it after dark; east of here, past Orange St, is a squatter neighborhood called Canterbury that's best avoided. You'll also want to steer clear of Flankers near the airport and parts of the Mt Salem neighborhood.

Just across from the KFC that sits between the Hip Strip and downtown MoBay is a sparsely vegetated field fronting a bit of sand known, pretty accurately, as Dump-Up Beach. It is best to avoid this area at night.

Only ever use official taxis, identifiable by their red number plates and prescribed route emblazoned on the side of the car.

### CONSULATES

**Canadian Honorary Consulate** (☎ 632-0371; 29 Gloucester Ave, Montego Bay)

**US Consulate** (☎ 953-0620; Hwy A1, Whitter Village, Ironshore; ⊙ 9am-12:30pm Mon-Fri)

### MEDICAL SERVICES

**Cornwall Regional Hospital** (☎ 952-5100; www.cornwallregionalhospital.com; Mt Salem Rd; ⊙ 24hr) Has a 24-hour emergency ward.

**Fairview Medical** (☎ 940-7063, 275-1119; www.themontegobaydoctor.com; Alice Eldermire Dr; ⊙ 7am-7pm Mon-Fri, 9am-5pm Sat, 10am-3pm Sun) Private clinic with emergency services.

**Fontana Pharmacy** (☎ 952-3860; Fairview Shopping Centre; ⊙ 9am-9pm Mon-Sat, 10am-9pm Sun) The best-stocked and largest pharmacy in town.

### MONEY

At **Donald Sangster International Airport** (MBJ; ☎ 952-3124; www.mbjairport.com) there's a 24-hour money-exchange bureau and a branch of National Commercial Bank in the arrivals hall, but it doesn't change at good rates.

You'll need local currency to take the bus into town, but taxis accept US dollars.

Better rates can be found on the main strip. Downtown, several bureaus can be found on St James St and Fort St; look for 'cambio' signs. Banks on Sam Sharpe Sq and in the Baywest Shopping Center all have 24-hour ATMs. Flanking the Doctor's Cave Beach Club are ATMs operated by National Commercial Bank and Scotiabank (Gloucester Ave). The cruise-ship terminal is served by a branch of National Commercial Bank in the Montego Freeport Shopping Centre.

**Cambio King** (☎ 971-5260; Gloucester Ave; ⊙ 9am-2pm Mon-Thu, 9am-4pm Fri) Currency exchange, northern end of the street.

**First Global Bank** (☎ 971-5260; 53 Gloucester Ave; ⊙ 9am-3pm Mon-Thu, 9am-4pm Fri)

**FX Trader** (☎ 952-3171; 37 Gloucester Ave; ⊙ 9am-5pm Mon-Sat) Currency exchange.

### POST

Post offices at **Fort St** (Map p116; ☎ 952-7016; Fort St; ⊙ 9am-5pm Mon-Fri) and **Miranda Hill** (Map p118; ☎ 979-5137; Gloucester Ave, White Sands Beach; ⊙ 9am-5pm Mon-Sat).

### TOURIST INFORMATION

**Jamaica Tourist Board** (Map p112; ☎ 952-3009; www.visitjamaica.com; Donald Sangster International Airport; ⊙ for flight arrivals) In the arrivals hall at Donald Sangster International Airport.

**Official Visitors Guide** (www.montego-bay-jamaica.com) The most extensive online resource for MoBay and environs.

**Visit Jamaica** (www.visitjamaica.com) Entertainment and culture listings.

## ℹ️ Getting There & Away

### AIR

**Intercaribbean Airways** (www.intercaribbean.com) operates a daily service between MoBay's Donald Sangster International Airport (p124) and Kingston's Norman Manley International Airport and Tinson Pen (US$61 each way).

**TimAir** (www.timair.net), an 'air taxi' service, offers charter flights to Negril (US$229), Ocho Rios (US$392), Port Antonio (US$619) and Kingston (US$515).

### BOAT

Cruise ships berth at the **Montego Bay Cruise Ship Terminal** (Map p112; Freeport) in the Montego Freeport, about 3km south of town. Taxis to downtown MoBay cost US$15. The savvy walk out of the port gates and flag cheaper route taxis.

**Montego Bay Yacht Club** (Map p112; ☎ 979-8038; www.mobayyachtclub.com; Montego Freeport) has hookups, gasoline and diesel, and will handle immigration and customs procedures.

## BUS & MINIBUS

Comfortable **Knutsford Express buses** (☏ 876-971-1822; www.knutsfordexpress.com; ⏱ 4am-9:30pm) run from their own bus terminal next to Pier One near downtown MoBay. Book tickets more than 24 hours in advance for a small discount. Be at the bus station 30 minutes before departure to register your ticket. Services include the following:

| DESTINATION | COST (J$) | TIME (HR) | FREQUENCY |
|---|---|---|---|
| Falmouth | 850 | 35min | 9 daily |
| Kingston | 2650 | 3¼–5½ | 10 daily |
| Mandeville | 2250 | 2¾ | daily at 1.30pm |
| Negril | 1600 | 1¾ | 2 daily |
| Ocho Rios | 1850 | 1¾ | 9 daily |
| Port Antonio | 3100 | 4½ | daily at 9am, 5pm |
| Savanna-La-Mar | 900 | 1½ | daily at 1.30pm |

Public buses other than Knutsford Express, minibuses and route taxis arrive and depart from the **transportation center** (Barnett St) at the south end of St James St. Destinations are written on the bus/van/taxi and people will direct you to the correct vehicle if you ask around.

Minibuses (ie vans) and shared taxis run directly to Ocho Rios (J$500, two hours; onward transfers to Port Antonio and Kingston), Lucea (J$225, one to 1½ hours; onward transfers to Negril), Negril (J$350, 1½ hours), Kingston (J$950, five hours), some inland villages and also Iron-shore and Rose Hall (J$150, 30 minutes).

Montego Bay Metro Line bus service links MoBay with the suburbs and outlying villages, such as Anchovy and Grange Hill.

You can almost always find a route taxi early in the morning or around 4pm to 5pm (ie commuting hours); there will likely be a wait at other times of the day, and long-distance taxi service slacks off after sunset. It's always easier to get a ride to towns on the coast compared to towns in the interior.

## CAR

Car-rental companies with offices at Donald Sangster International Airport:
**Avis** (☏ 952-0762; www.avis.com.jm)
**Budget** (☏ 952-3838; www.budgetjamaica.com)

**Hertz** (☏ 979-0438; www.hertz.com)
**Thrifty** (☏ 952-1126; www.thrifty.com)

Companies with offices in Montego Bay:
**Ace Rent-a-Car** (www.acerentacar.com; 34 Queens Dr)
**Dhana Car Rentals** (☏ 727-3798; www.mobay.com; 4 Holiday Village Shopping Centre)
**Efay** (☏ 952-8280; www.efay.com; 3 Churchill St)

## PRIVATE TAXI

**Jamaica Union of Travelers Association** (JUTA; ☏ 876-952-0813) has taxi stands on Gloucester Ave at the Gloucestershire and Coral Cliff hotels and at Doctor's Cave Beach Hotel, downtown at the junction of Market and Strand Sts, and by the bus station. Identify JUTA members by the red plates and JTB decal emblazoned on their vehicles.

A list of official JUTA fares from Montego Bay is posted at the airport. At last visit, certified fares from the airport for up to four passengers: Falmouth (US$60), Kingston (US$250), Negril (US$100), Ocho Rios (US$120) and Port Antonio (US$300).

## ❶ Getting Around

You can walk between any place along Gloucester Ave and downtown (it's about 2.5km from Kent Ave to Sam Sharpe Sq). You'll need transportation for anywhere further.

## TO/FROM THE AIRPORT

You'll find taxis waiting outside the arrivals lounge at the airport. There is an official taxi booth immediately outside customs. A tourist taxi to Gloucester Ave costs US$15. Alternatively, you can catch a minibus or route taxi from the gas station at the entrance to the airport (J$100).

## PUBLIC TRANSPORTATION

Route taxis ply set routes and charge set fares for set distances and are the cheapest way to get around Montego Bay. Assuming they have room, route drivers will pick up anyone standing along their route who waves the taxi down.

Route taxis can be recognized by the red license plates and the writing on the side of the driver's door, which indicates the taxi's route (in Montego, the routes are named for neighborhoods: Flankers, Mt Salem etc.)

The usual cost for a route is about J$100, perhaps double that if heading to the outer suburbs. There are no official pickup points, but taxis reliably congregate near Sam Sharpe Sq, the junction of Market and Strand Sts, and by the bus station. Rates go up by as much as 50% after dark, when route taxis become more difficult to find.

Although both route and JUTA drivers use red plates, it's safe to assume cars on the Hip Strip are JUTA vehicles, and those anywhere else are route taxis. Route taxi drivers will often offer to provide you with private transportation; if you like the driver, we say go for it.

### TAXI

Licensed JUTA taxis cruise Gloucester Ave; they charge a steep US$10 minimum. Published fares from Gloucester Ave are US$15 to the airport, US$30 to Greenwood, US$25 to Ironshore, US$20 to Montego Freeport and US$35 to Rose Hall.

# EAST OF MONTEGO BAY

## Ironshore & Rose Hall

As you head east of Montego Bay the coast becomes a long stretch of screensaver-worthy beach, speckled with golf courses, all-inclusive resorts, high-end condos and expensive malls. These are marketed to wealthy tourists and the Jamaican upper class, many of whom opt to live here instead of the ritzier suburbs of Kingston. Ironshore, about 8km east of Montego Bay, is the epicenter of this little window of luxury. Further east is Jamaica's most famous (and allegedly haunted) mansion, Rose Hall, while Greenwood, with its own great house, is further east again. Several restaurants are clustered around Half Moon Village, en route to Rose Hall from Montego Bay.

 **Sights**

★ **Greenwood Great House**          HOUSE
([✓] 953-1077; www.greenwoodgreathouse.com; adult/child US$20/10; ◷ 9am-6pm) This marvelous estate, sitting high on a hill, may not have Rose Hall's fame, but offers a far more intimate and interesting experience. Unique among local plantation houses, Greenwood survived unscathed during the slave rebellion of Christmas 1831. Most of the furnishings are authentic, and some of the rare objects are truly remarkable. Greenwood is 11km east of Ironshore and around 10km west of Falmouth, off Hwy A1; turn inland and follow the pitted road uphill.

Construction of the two-story, stone-and-timber structure was begun in 1780 by the Honorable Richard Barrett, whose family arrived in Jamaica in the 1660s and amassed a fortune from its sugar plantations. (Barrett was a cousin of the famous English poet Elizabeth Barrett Browning.) In an unusual move for his times, Barrett educated his slaves.

The original library is still intact, as are oil paintings, a 1626 map of Africa, and plentiful antiques, including a mantrap used for catching runaway slaves (one of the few direct references we found in any Jamaican historical home to the foundations of the plantation labor market, ie slavery). Among the highlights is the rare collection of musical instruments, including an exquisitely inlaid piano made for Edward VII by Thomas Broadwood (who made pianos for Beethoven), one of three working barrel organs in the world and two polyphones, one of which the guide is happy to bring to life. The resident ghost is decidedly low-key and you can drink in the view of the entire coast from the upstairs veranda.

★ **Rose Hall Great House**          HOUSE
([✓] 953-2323; www.rosehall.com; off Hwy A1; adult/child under 12yr US$20/10; ◷ 9am-5:15pm & 6:30-9pm) This 1770s mansion is the most famous great house in Jamaica. John Palmer, a wealthy plantation owner, and his wife, Rose (after whom the house was named), hosted some of the most elaborate social gatherings on the island. Much of the attraction is the legend of Annie Palmer, alleged to have murdered three husbands and whose ghost is said to haunt the house. Rose Hall is 3km east of Ironshore. Entry is by tour only.

Beyond the Palladian portico the house is a bastion of historical style, with a magnificent mahogany staircase and doors, and silk wall-fabric that is a reproduction of the original designed for Marie Antoinette during the reign of Louis XVI. Unfortunately, because the house was cleaned out by looters back in the 19th century, almost all of the period furnishings were brought in from elsewhere, and quite a few are from the wrong century. With that said, the exquisite imported antique furnishings are the genuine article, and many are the work of past leading English master carpenters.

Slaves destroyed the house in the Christmas Rebellion (p111) of 1831 and it was left in ruins for more than a century. In 1966 the three-story building was restored to its haughty grandeur.

Tours take in the rooms, including Annie Palmer's bedroom upstairs, which has been (re)decorated in crimson silk brocades because, y'know, red is the color of blood; the secret passage through which she was visited by her slave lover; her tomb; and the cellar with period objects and an English-style pub.

Day tours focus on the sumptuous furnishings, while evening tours are more theatrical and are not really suitable for under-12s.

## 🏃 Activities

Most all-inclusive resorts have scuba facilities and snorkeling gear for guests.

### Kiteboarding Jamaica
KITESURFING

(☑ 781-2190; www.kiteboardingjamaica.com; Ironshore; rental per day US$100, 1hr lesson US$80) Kiteboarding has been taking off in Jamaica for several years now and this German-run outpost along Ironshore is a great place to either get into the sport or hit the waves if you already know what you're doing. Lessons and board rentals are available, and there's private beach access with a pool deck for après-kiting chilling out.

### Half Moon
### Equestrian Centre
HORSE RIDING

(☑ 953-2286; www.horsebackridingjamaica.com; Hwy A1; beach ride US$120; ☺ beach ride 7am & 4pm, pony ride 9am-noon & 2-5pm; 🚸) The lovely grounds of this center, west of Half Moon Village, are a nice slice of the Kentucky blue grass in paradise with well-kept horses. The main draw is the classic bareback beach ride (US$120) during which you and your horse splash straight into the turquoise sea. For the kiddies there's also a beginners' ride (US$60).

These guys also do a great job of rehoming injured or abandoned horses, cats and dogs.

## 🛏 Sleeping

Ironshore is lined with all-inclusives.

### Dunn's Villa Resort Hotel
HOTEL $

(☑ 953-7459, in the USA 1-718-882-3917; www.dunnsvillaresort.com; Cornwall; s/d from US$58/65; ⓟ❄☎☀) You'll find this very friendly, family-run place in the village of Cornwall, in the hills 3km inland of Ironshore (follow the signs from the highway). This well-kept, homey spot has 11 frilly rooms with satellite TV, wide balconies and lots of pink-white color combinations. The spacious public areas are minimally but attractively furnished. There's a Jacuzzi on a raised sundeck.

The hosts rent mountain bikes and offer lunch, dinner and weekend brunch poolside.

### ⭐ Bird's Nest
HOSTEL $

(☑ 781-2190; www.thebirdsnestjamaica.com; 177 Patterson Dr, Ironshore; tent US$12, dm/d US$18/70; ❄☎☀) Sporty hostel run by an enthusiastic group of kitesurfers who catch some gusts (and waves) in nearby Bounty Bay on the other side of Falmouth. In the true tradition of Jamaican hostels, it's small (two private doubles and two dorm rooms, plus camping), but friendly. Pros: a pool, hammocks and a tranquil garden. Con: Ironshore location requires taxis or long walks.

### Royal Reef Hotel & Restaurant
HOTEL $$

(☑ 953-1700; Hwy A1, Greenwood; s/d US$95/110; ⓟ❄☎☀) On the A1 at Greenwood, this gracious, modern, Mediterranean-style hotel has 19 rooms. Its decor includes classical wrought-iron furnishings and exquisite tropical murals. An elevated amoeba-shaped pool is inset in the terracotta terrace, which has an outside grill overlooking a tiny beach overgrown by mangroves. The excellent continental cuisine is served both alfresco and in an intimate dining room.

## 🍴 Eating

### ⭐ Far Out Fish Hut
SEAFOOD $

(☑ 954-7155; Hwy A1, Greenwood; mains $J500-1000; ☺ noon-11pm) East of Greenwood Great House, look along the coast for a trailer painted to look like a sea-blue slice of the ocean. This place is one of the finest purveyors of seafood on the north coast. It's a locals' spot where you sit under thatch and order very fresh seafood for a very good price.

### Scotchies
JERK $

(☑ 953-8041; Hwy A1, Ironshore; half-lb portion J$770; ☺ 11am-11pm Mon-Sat, 11am-9pm Sun) Many Jamaicans will tell you that (a) Scotchies serves the best 'sit-down' jerk in the northwest and (b) the quality has slipped a bit with popularity. Savvy outsiders nod in agreement. 'Ya mon.' This is good-quality jerk, with a supporting cast of fried breadfruit, *festival, bammy* and other classic accompaniments.

### Prakash Restaurant
INDIAN, THAI $$

(☑ 953-8240; Half Moon Village; mains US$12-28; ☺ noon-10pm; 🚸) Two distinct kitchens serve one big dining room multiple variations of popular Indian or Thai cuisine. We will admit to being unprepared for how good the food was here; even discounting the fact there are barely any Indian or Thai restaurants in greater Montego Bay, this is very good stuff. Certainly the best bet for vegetarian food in the area.

### ℹ️ Getting There & Away

A great number of minibuses and route taxis ply the A1 road, traveling to and from Donald Sangster International Airport and Montego Bay. You'll pay about J$120 to travel from MoBay to Ironshore; J$150 to Rose Hall. Private taxis cost US$35.

## Falmouth

POP 8686

Built on riches amassed from sugar and slavery, and advanced enough by the early 19th century to have running water before even New York City, Falmouth feels like a sunken *Titanic* recently raised from the deep. Little altered architecturally since the 1840s when slave emancipation dramatically reversed its fortunes, the town retains one of the finest ensembles of Tropical-Georgian buildings in the Caribbean.

For anyone with even a passing interest in Jamaican history and architecture, Falmouth is an essential stopover. It is a bustling, proper Jamaican town, where old ladies in their Sunday best congregate outside the limestone-bricked, English-style church and market traders ply roasted yam and sugarcane under the pretty gingerbread verandas of commerce-packed Harbour Lane. This quintessential Jamaican-ness is under threat, as there is talk of banishing the produce market from the town centre and turning it into a sanitised version of Jamaican life for cruise-ship passengers.

### History

Falmouth was laid out in 1769 and named for the English birthplace of Sir William Trelawny, then the governor of the island. The streets were planned as a grid and patriotically named after members of the royal family and English heroes. Planters erected their townhouses using Georgian elements adapted to Jamaican conditions.

With its advantageous position, Falmouth became the busiest port on the north coast. Outbound trade consisted mainly of hogsheads (large casks) of wet sugar and puncheons (casks) of rum, while slaves were offloaded for sale in the slave market.

The town's fortunes degenerated when the sugar industry went into decline during the 19th century and it was dealt a further blow with the advent of steamships, which the harbor was incapable of handling. By 1890 the port was essentially dead. The city has struggled along ever since.

A cruise-ship dock was opened in Falmouth in March 2011 large enough to accommodate the world's second biggest cruise liner, the 6000-passenger *Oasis of the Seas*. Contrary to local expectations, the cruise-ship dock has done little to boost Falmouth's economy, since passengers are typically whisked off to tour to other parts of the island and not encouraged to spend time in the town.

### ◎ Sights

**Water Square** SQUARE
The best place to orient yourself is Water Sq, at the east end of Duke St. Named for an old circular stone reservoir dating from 1798, the square (actually a triangle) has a fountain topped by an old waterwheel. Back in the day this fountain pumped fresh water (before New York City had any such luxury). In the evening, the square really comes to life, with people limin' under the coconut trees, blaring reggae and delicious smells wafting from stalls.

Many of the wooden shopfronts in this area are attractively disheveled relics.

**William Knibb Memorial Church** CHURCH
(cnr King & George Sts; ⊘ hours vary) On July 31, 1838, slaves gathered outside William Knibb Memorial Church for an all-night vigil, awaiting midnight and then the dawn of full freedom (to quote Knibbs: 'The monster is dead'), when slave-shackles, a whip and an iron collar were symbolically buried in a coffin. Behind the church you can find Knibb's grave. A plaque inside the church displays the internment of these tools of slavery; to get in, ask at the Leaf of Life Hardware store on King St.

**Courthouse** NOTABLE BUILDING
(Seaboard St) One block east of Water Sq is Seaboard St and the grandiose Georgian courthouse in Palladian style, fronted by a double curling staircase and Doric columns, with cannons to the side. The current building, dating from 1926, is a replica of the original 1815 structure that was destroyed by fire. The town council presides here.

**Jewish Cemetery** CEMETERY
(Duke St) Established in the early 19th century, Falmouth's Jewish cemetery lay abandoned in recent decades before being restored.

## FALMOUTH HERITAGE WALKS

Listed as an endangered historical monument, Falmouth, founded in 1769, harbors one of the Caribbean's most beguiling and architecturally homogenous townscapes. Preserving it is no easy task, not that this has dulled the efforts of robust local organizations run by people who are passionate about the town and its history. To gain a fuller appreciation of the settlement's historical importance and why it's worth protecting, join one of three tours offered by Falmouth Heritage Walks (☑407-2245; www.falmouthheritagewalks. com; ⊙on cruise ship days and by reservation). The Heritage Walking Tour (adult/child US$25/15) is a two-hour ramble around Falmouth's small urban grid punctuated with handsome Tropical-Georgian architecture. The Food Tour (adult/child US$45/25) alternates cultural musings with tastings of street food, while the Jewish Cemetery Tour (adult/child US$15/10) visits a cemetery with gravestones etched in Hebrew. Walks usually take place on the days a cruise ship is in port, or else by appointment.

The gate is locked, but you can visit with Falmouth Heritage Walks (p129). It's three blocks west of the Anglican church.

### Police Station
HISTORIC BUILDING

(Rodney St) The oddly cute historic police station was constructed in 1814. The prison here once contained a treadmill: a huge wooden cylinder with steps on the outside. Shackled above the mill, slaves had to keep treading the steps as the cylinder turned. If they faltered, the revolving steps battered their bodies and legs. The ancient lockups are still in use and the station is not open to visitors.

### Barrett House
HISTORIC BUILDING

(2 Market St) At the top of Market St, opposite Scotiabank, is the ruin of Barrett House, missing its top floor. Built in 1799, it's hard to believe now that this used to be one of the finest merchant houses in Falmouth, belonging to the Barrett family who came to Jamaica in 1655 as part of Cromwell's army.

### Phoenix Foundry
HISTORIC BUILDING

(cnr Tharpe & Lower Harbour Sts) One of Falmouth's most distinctive buildings, Phoenix Foundry was built in 1810 and sports a strange-looking conical roof. Behind the foundry, guarded by locked gates, is the Central Wharf where slaves were brought ashore, to be replaced in the holds by sugar, rum and other victuals borne of their back-breaking labor.

### Albert George Market
MARKET

(Water Sq; ⊙dawn-dusk) The market structure on the east side of Water Sq, which dominates central Falmouth, was once the site of slave auctions. The current structure was built in 1894 and named in honor of two of Queen Victoria's grandsons: Albert and George.

### Tharp House
NOTABLE BUILDING

(Seaboard St) Tharp House sags from age yet is still one of the best examples of an elegant period townhouse. Today housing the tax office, it was formerly the residence of John Tharp, at one time the largest slaveholder in Jamaica.

### Baptist Manse
HISTORIC BUILDING

(cnr Market & Trelawny Sts) The restored Baptist Manse (not opened to visitors) was formerly the residence of nonconformist Baptist preacher William Knibb, who was instrumental in lobbying for passage of the Abolition Bill that ended slavery.

### St Peter's Anglican Church
CHURCH

(Duke St; ⊙hours vary) The oldest extant building in town is St Peter's Anglican Church, built in 1796 and enlarged in 1842. It lies four blocks west along Duke St.

## 🏃 Activities

### ⭐Martha Brae Rafting
RAFTING

(☑952-0889; www.jamaicarafting.com; Martha Brae Rd; per 2-person raft US$60; ⊙8:30am-4:30pm) A rafting trip down a 4.8km stretch of the Martha Brae River is a quiet thrill. The journey takes an hour on 9m-long bamboo rafts, each carrying one or two passengers, poled by a skilled guide. Trips begin from Rafters' Village, around 5km south of Falmouth. There you'll find a restaurant, swimming pool, bathrooms, changing rooms and a parking lot.

You'll head through a green tunnel of jungle, vines and cold mountain water; the whole experience can be quite romantic, depending on your tolerance of other people (the river gets crowded, as this is the most popular rafting spot in Jamaica). The upper reaches tumble at a good pace before slowing further downriver, where you stop at 'Tarzan's Corner' for a swing and swim in a calm pool. Your captain will pause on request if you want to take a dip or climb a tree. At the end, after being plied with rum punch, you'll be driven back to your car or tour bus. Most tour companies in Jamaica arrange outings to Martha Brae but the rafting is conducted by the single operator, Martha Brae Rafting.

## 🛏 Sleeping

**★ Pura Vida**                    GUESTHOUSE **$**
(☎ 438-2689; www.puravidajamaica.com; 25 Hague; r US$60; ❉ 🛜) In the tranquil Hague community a 10-minute drive east and across Hwy A1 from Falmouth, gregarious owner Richard welcomes guests to his cheerful yellow house. The three rooms are spacious and comfortable, and come with kitchenettes. But best of all, Falmouth-born-and-bred Richard can divulge local culinary secrets, advise on the best driving routes and even arrange trips to various attractions.

**Greenside Villa Inn**                    HOTEL **$**
(☎ 865-6894, 954-3127; www.greenside-villa.com; Hwy A1; studios US$55-65) This inn comes with simple, spacious studio apartments with private bathrooms and kitchenettes with small gas stoves. Meals are cooked on request. It lies about 3km west of Falmouth.

## 🍴 Eating

**Donna's**                    JAMAICAN **$**
(☎ 617-5175; Market St, cnr Duke St; mains J$600-1000; ☺ 7:30am-9:30pm) Divided into a casual, canteen-style dining area and a takeout section, this restaurant gets packed at lunchtimes as locals stop by for their fried chicken, curry goat and oxtail fix. Good for hearty Jamaican breakfasts involving callaloo and ackee.

**Tropical Bliss Oasis**                    CAFE **$**
(Albert George Market; snacks J$170-500; ☺ 9am-5pm Mon-Sat; 🛜) Enjoy a moment or two of bliss with a fruit smoothie and sandwich at this pleasant perch in Albert George Market.

**★ Water Square**                    STREET FOOD **$**
(Water Sq; mains from J$300; ☺ 6-9pm) Hands down the best place for local street food in the evenings. On one side, jerk chicken is cooked up in oil drums; there's also a good stall serving stewed chicken and other home-cooked food. An old guy cooks up the best jerk pork for miles around, while another specialises in *escoveich* fish (fried, with a spicy, pickled sauce) and *festival* (deep-fried dough dumpling).

## ❶ Information

**Police Station** (☎ 954-3222, 119; cnr Rodney & Water Sts)

**Post Office** (☎ 954-3050; cnr Cornwall & Market Sts; ☺ 8am-5pm Mon-Fri)

**Scotiabank** (☎ 954-3357; cnr Market & Lower Harbour Sts; ☺ 8:30am-2:30pm Mon-Thu, 8:30am-4pm Fri) Scotiabank also operates an ATM in the shopping center near the eastern edge of town.

## ❶ Getting There & Away

Buses, minibuses and route taxis arrive and depart on opposite sides of Water Sq for Martha Brae (J$120, 15 to 20 minutes), Montego Bay (J$200, 45 minutes), Albert Town (1½ hours, J$250) and Ocho Rios (J$350, 80 minutes). The **Knutsford Express** (☎ 971-1822; www.knutsfordexpress.com) stops in Glistening Waters 2km east of Falmouth from where you can flag down a route taxi (J$70) to bring you into town. If the planned prettification of the town centre goes ahead, all transportation will be moved way south along Market St.

# Glistening Waters

Just east of Falmouth is one of the most incredible natural wonders of Jamaica – a bioluminescent lagoon – along with clean beaches nearby. The 25,000-seat **Trelawny Greenfield Stadium** is located opposite the small village of Rock. Built in 2007 for the Cricket World Cup, it also hosts football and music concerts.

## ◉ Sights & Activities

**Glistening Waters**
**(Luminous Lagoon)**                    LAGOON
(30-min boat trip per person US$25; ☺ tours from 6:45pm) Glistening Waters, also known as 'Luminous Lagoon,' actually lives up to the hype. Located in an estuary near Rock, 1.6km east of Falmouth, the water here boasts a singular charm – it glows an eerie green when disturbed. The green glow is due to the presence of microorganisms that produce photochemical reactions when stirred; the concentrations are so thick that fish swimming by look like green torpedoes and when you swim, sparks run down your body.

Swimming through the luminous lagoon is semi-hallucinogenic, especially on starry nights, when it's hard to tell where the water ends and the sky begins. The experience is made all the more surreal thanks to the mixing of salt- and freshwater from the sea and the Martha Brae River; the freshwater 'floats' on the saltwater, so you not only swim through green clouds of phosphoresence, but alternating bands of cold and warm.

You have to take a boat out to reach the bioluminescent spots. Half-hour boat trips are offered from Glistening Waters Marina and two other locations next to it; the three boat companies are comparable. Any hotel from Ocho Rios to Montego Bay should be able to organize a trip out here.

**Burwood Beach** BEACH
(Hwy A1; J$500; ⊘9am-5pm) This upgraded public beach is popular with locals and cruise-ship passengers alike. It's a sugary-white crescent of sand with calm waters, 2km east of Glistening Waters.

### ℹ Getting There & Away

Minibuses and route taxis frequently travel the A1 road between Glistening Waters and Falmouth (J$80), the latter being about 38km east of Montego Bay and 40km west of Runaway Bay.

The Knutsford Express (p130) Falmouth station is actually situated at Glistening Waters Marina, 2km east of Falmouth. There are buses to Kingston (J$2700, 3½ hours, nine daily), Ocho Rios (J$1400, one hour, seven to nine daily), Port Antonio (J$2800, three hours, one to two daily), and Montego Bay (J$850, 35 minutes, nine to 10 daily), two of which carry onto Negril (J$1850, two hours).

## Duncans

This small town on a hillside 11km east of Falmouth is a pretty place to base yourself if you want to be removed from resort sprawl. It appears developers are buying up surrounding real estate at a fast pace, though, so this may not be the case for long. The village is centered on an old stone clock tower in the middle of a three-way junction.

Next to the Silver Sands Villa Resort is the turnoff for Jacob Taylor Beach, a fishermen's haunt where you'll find a rum shop, a mellow craft market and a celebrated local eatery.

**Kettering Baptist Church** CHURCH
(Main Rd; ⊘hours vary) Kettering Baptist Church, built in 1893, is a creamy-colored building that commemorates William

Knibb, a Baptist missionary and a leading abolitionist who founded an emancipation village for freed slaves here in 1840.

**Jacob Taylor Beach** BEACH
Right next to the Silver Sands Resort there's a turnoff for this small, flotsam- and jetsam-strewn fishermen's beach. The water's too dangerous for swimming, but you can rock out to the reggae blasting from the rum shop and indulge in fresh seafood at the seafront beach shack.

### 🛏 Sleeping & Eating

**Victoria's Villa B&B** B&B $$
(☑954-9353; www.villavictoriaja.com; r US$70-120; ℗❋) Delightful, lovingly run six-room B&B that's drowning in flowering bougainvillea on its quiet little patch of land on the outskirts of Duncans, near the Jacob Taylor Beach. Rates include half-board.

**Silver Sands Villa Resort** RESORT $$$
(☑888-745-7245, 954-7606; www.mysilversands.com; 1-/2-bed cottage from US$705/775, 4-bed villas per week from US$2380; ℗❋☀) This resort, 1km north of Duncans, has more than 100 upscale one- to five-bedroom villas and cottages along a gorgeous private beach. Each villa is privately owned and individually decorated, and has a cook, housekeeper and gardener – this sort of personal service is frankly way above what you get at most all-inclusives. Facilities include a bar-grill and a grocery store.

The cottages require a minimum stay of three nights, while villas require five. Most of the properties have TVs and their own pools. Weekly rates offer savings and include airport transfers. Nonguests may access the 300m-long, white-sand beach for a cool US$25.

**★ Leroy's Beach Bar** JAMAICAN $
(☑447-2896; Jacob Taylor Beach; mains J$800; ⊘6am-11pm) Awesome beachside shack that rocks out to reggae rhythms in the evenings and serves some of the freshest fish around by day. Try the jerk parrotfish.

### ℹ Getting There & Away

The highway diverts ongoing traffic around the town; keep watch for the turnoff from Hwy A1. Minibuses and route taxis dashing between Montego Bay and Ocho Rios pick up and drop off passengers to/from Duncans at the clock tower in the town center.

# SOUTH OF MONTEGO BAY

The hill country inland of MoBay is speckled with villages clinging to rocky outcrops, narrow roads and large fields of fruit, vegetables and, deeper in the interior, ganja. This is friendly country, where locals aren't as jaded with tourists as their counterparts on the coast. Be on the lookout for brightly painted shacks decorated with off-the-wall bric-a-brac (pottery, feathers, whatever) – these are often the homes of witchcraft-practicing bush doctors. There are a few scattered attractions in Jamaica's interior – from zip lining and whitewater rafting to a bird sanctuary, a working plantation and a village known for its German heritage. The southeast quarter of St James parish culminates in the wild Cockpit Country.

## Lethe

Lethe, in Greek mythology, was one of the rivers surrounding Hades, and to cross it caused you to lose memories of your previous life; it could happen to you in Lethe, Jamaica, too if you spend enough time in this hilltop village. Zip lining and rafting are Lethe's raisons d'etre, based at the Lethe Estate next to the village.

The graceful stone bridge spanning the Great River was built by slaves in 1820, and

**WORTH A TRIP**

### CROYDON IN THE MOUNTAINS PLANTATION

Located 34km south of Montego Bay, off the potholed B6 road, Croydon in the Mountains Plantation (☑979-8267; www.croydonplantation.com; ☺Mon-Fri) can feel more like an Indian or Balinese rural community than Jamaica, with its well-groomed, deep-green terraces sprouting fields and orchards of coffee, citrus and pineapples. A 'see, hear, touch and taste' tour is offered from 10:30am to 3pm weekdays (US$85 including lunch and transfers with a Montego Bay tour company). Advance reservations are required. If you're driving yourself, call ahead to confirm entry fee.

from its pastoral span you can see the overgrown remains of an old sugar mill rotting on the riverbank.

### ◎ Sights & Activities

**Animal Farm**                                    FARM
(☑899-0040; www.facebook.com/animalfarm jamaica; adult/child US$25/10; ☺tours by arrangement Mon-Fri, 10am-5pm Sat & Sun; 🐾) ✐ While disappointingly light on revolutionary pigs corrupted by the acquisition of power (if you haven't read your Orwell, never mind), this Animal Farm does happen to be a great place to take your kids. This pretty little homestead is powered by ecofriendly solar power and pig crap, and there are donkey rides and a petting zoo, as well as a menagerie of snakes and other critters. The farm is just outside Copse, 3km west of Lethe. Follow the signs.

Skilled guides take guests on birdwatching tours around the grounds (look for the funky-crested 'Rasta fowl'), and there's also access to swimming in the Great River and lovely views over Cockpit Country.

**Mountain Valley Rafting**                    RAFTING
(☑956-4920, 298-2866; incl transfer adult/children under 12yr US$65/32.50) Headquartered at Lethe Estate, this outfit offers tranquil one-hour river trips on the Great River from Lethe. You're piloted 3km downstream along the muddy river aboard long, narrow bamboo rafts poled by an expert rafter, who waxes poetic about the birds, flora and fauna as you glide along. For an extra US$15 per person you'll get lunch and a plantation tour. If you show up under your own steam, you'll pay US$50 for the raft trip alone.

**Jamaica Zipline Adventure Tours**                    ZIP LINING
(☑366-0124; www.ziplinejamaica.com; US$89; ☺9am-5pm) This Lethe Estate fixture is one of the longest zip lines in the Caribbean. The five lines add up to a total 'flying' distance of more than 1.3km, all of it through a lush jungley landscape. Pickup from Falmouth and Montego Bay are included in the price.

### ❶ Getting There & Away

Take Hwy A1 west out of Montego Bay for 4km, then take the B8 (Long Hill Rd) south at Reading towards Anchovy; the signed turnoff for Lethe is about 5km inland, and it's another 4km drive from the turnoff.

# NORTH COCKPIT COUNTRY

Look at a road map of Jamaica and you'll notice southwest Trelawny parish, inland of Falmouth is...blank. Just a big green eye of tantalizing mystery peeking at you from the tangle of towns, villages and roads that is the rest of Jamaica's face. So, what's that eye? Jamaica's most rugged quarter: a 1295-sq-km limestone plateau known as Cockpit Country. It's a vast network of eroded limestone studded with thousands of conical hummocks divided by precipitous ravines – a maze that gave runaway slaves shelter from their pursuers, and a landscape rich in hiking and spelunking opportunities.

## 🏃 Activities

Nowhere in Jamaica is more off the beaten track than the Cockpits, and hiking and caving here is a real-life adventure, compared to the artificial thrills of zip lining and other 'adventure activities' around the island. Cockpit Country also provides a vital habitat for Jamaica's birdlife, with Windsor being a prime destination for birding.

**Windsor Research Centre** BIRDWATCHING
(📞 997-3832; www.cockpitcountry.com; Windsor Great House, Windsor) A science-based operation at Windsor Great House is devoted to monitoring Cockpit Country's fragile environment. Susan, the resident biologist, can take you birding and bat-watching on request. The website, replete with information about regional ecology, is a joy for nature geeks.

### Hiking

Just over 30 crow-flying kilometers from the roasting sunbathers of Montego Bay glowers a foreboding wilderness that challenges popular images of Jamaica as tame, well trodden and bereft of backcountry. Cockpit Country is a broad, barely penetrable thicket of dense foliage and intricate karst topography scattered with caves, hollows and conical hills that, metaphorically speaking, resembles an upturned egg carton.

A few hunters' tracks and farmers' footpaths lead into and even across Cockpit Country. Most are faint paths, often overgrown, and hiking away from these trails can be dangerous going. The rocks are razor sharp and sinkholes are everywhere, often covered by decayed vegetation and ready to crumble underfoot. Never travel alone,

as there is no one to hear you call for help should you fall into a sinkhole. Take lots of water: there is none to be had locally.

It is imperative you take a trusted guide. The one company that regularly organises tours in the Cockpits is the **Southern Trelawny Environmental Agency** (STEA; 📞 393-6584; www.stea.net/ccat_main.htm; tours US$25-50), based in Rock Spring. STEA works with reputable local guides, simultaneously empowering local communities while giving visitors access to this little-explored corner of Jamaica. These locals are versed in ecotourism practices and know their way around these hills and caves.

You'll still need to bring stout walking shoes (or water shoes if caving), rain gear and a powerful flashlight in the event of a delay past sunset. Take warm clothing if you plan on staying overnight, as nights can get cold. Rates for guides vary based on hike length. STEA's most popular hike – and a great introduction to the Cockpits – is a 20km walk along the abandoned B10 road from Kinloss to Spring Garden that passes through Barbecue Bottom. Along the way, you get a real appreciation for the beautiful scenery – the honeycombed limestone cliffs and verdant valleys. It's a long hike, but with gentle inclines, so accessible to any moderately fit hiker, and with beautiful views – something you don't get hiking through the Cockpits' interior. Shorter hikes along that route are also possible.

Other trails through the Cockpits are little used and woefully overgrown. As locals drive more and walk less, the knowledge of the Cockpits' interior is becoming lost, which is great news for the ecosystem, but does mean that it's more and more difficult to find a guide who knows the longer routes. These include the arduous old military trail (p135) through the Cockpits connecting Windsor (in the north) with Troy (in the south), about 16km as the crow flies. It is a more difficult hike southbound, leading gradually uphill; an easier option is to begin in Troy and take the downhill route. A shorter loop hike is possible from Windsor, as is the Windsor–Quickstep trail.

### Caving

The Cockpits are laced with mostly uncharted caves that are a tempting draw for cavers. This is true adventure travel; guides lead trips into the better-known caverns, but past that, exploring is for experienced and properly outfitted cavers only. There is no rescue organization, and you enter caves at your own risk. The most accessible is the Windsor Cave at Windsor, though that's more interesting for its bats rather than rock formations. STEA (p133) organises an excellent two-hour caving excursion (US$50 per person) into the beautiful **Painted Circuit Cave** (Rock Spring; tours US$50 per person) with an underground river that requires wading through.

The Jamaican Caves Organisation (p178) provides resources for the exploration of Jamaican caves, sinkholes and underground rivers. In 2005 the group completed a project to formally classify and evaluate more than 70 caves within Cockpit Country. They lead the occasional trip to the Peterkin-Rota cave system near Maldon in St James, involving some swimming (US$100 per person; minimum US$250). Transportation is extra (US$100 depending on location).

# Good Hope Estate

Imagine a quaint Engish mansion plonked in the Caribbean, and you'll get a sense of what this honey-hued great house and working plantation looks like. The 2000-acre property, 13km south of Falmouth at the western end of Queen of Spains Valley, is set on the northern edge of Cockpit Country, and the views into that checkerboard of deep razor ridges and jungle domes has no rival.

The estate was owned by John Tharp (1744–1804), once the richest man in Jamaica, owner of more than 40 sq km and 3000 slaves in Trelawny and St James parishes. Built around 1755, the estate still houses a collection of 18th-century, Jamaican Georgian, cut-stone buildings, including a sugar works and waterwheel.

The estate is run by Chukka Caribbean Adventures, with several visitor day passes available.

David Pinto, an acclaimed ceramicist, operates a **pottery studio** (☑886-2868; www.jamaicapottery.com; ☺by appointment) open to the public on the grounds.

## 🏃 Activities

**Chukka Caribbean**
**Adventures**                    ADVENTURE SPORTS
(☑656-8026, in the USA 1-877-424-8552; www.chukka.com; Good Hope Estate; ☺9am-6pm) The Good Hope Estate branch of Chukka manages the Great Hope Great House and runs adventure activities such as zip lining, river tubing and ATV driving on the property. Three types of passes are available, with the Ultimate Thrill Seekers' Pass (US$149) granting access to all activities. All passes let you visit the old slave hospital turned exotic aviary.

Chukka mostly receives visits from all-inclusive hotels and cruise ships, but independent visitors are welcome. More attractions were being developed when we visited. If you're lucky, your tour of the great house will be led by Bonz, the general manager who's a keen historian.

## 🛌 Sleeping

**★ Coach House**                    VILLA $$$
(☑656-8026, in the USA 877-424-8552; www.chukka.com; 🛜 🏊 ) Just below the great house is the 1780s former coach house, which has been transformed into a luxurious six-room villa that is yet to open to the public. The high-beamed bedrooms, cooled by highland breezes, sport contemporary art, and the view from the infinity pool over the valley is something special. The villa comes with a chef and butler; seven-night minimum stay.

Pricing and date of opening were yet to be determined at research time.

# Windsor

You can get a taste of Cockpit Country by entering the narrow valley south of Falmouth. This passage, surrounded by towering cockpits, is accessed via Sherwood Content, a 20-minute drive south of Martha Brae. An unpaved single-track road leads from Sherwood Content to Windsor, near the head of the valley. It is technically possible to hike across the Cockpits from Windsor to Troy, but the trail is overgrown and reputable guides are essential. The charm of Windsor (population = 4 + dog) is its end-of-the-road remoteness, its verdant beauty and its importance as a natural habitat that lures birders and bat-lovers.

Sherwood Content is the birthplace of world-champion sprinter Usain Bolt, and you'll see signs honoring him and his searing speed dotted around. On the way to Windsor you'll pass the wall surrounding his parents' house and the cookshop run by his aunt Lilly in the hamlet of Coxheath.

## HIKING THE TROY–WINDSOR TRAIL

In the 1700s, Cockpit Country provided a savage refuge for runaway slaves – the Maroons – who waged an intermittent guerrilla war against the British colonizers. In an unsuccessful attempt to subjugate them, the British built a precarious military road across the Cockpits from Troy to Windsor that wound tortuously around hidden sink-holes and mosquito-infested jungle with paranoid place names including 'The Land of Look Behind' and 'Me No Sen You No Come.' Dicing with danger, many British soldiers disappeared into the Cockpits never to return, victims of ambush or sheer exhaustion.

Miraculously, the Troy–Windsor road still exists, though what remains of the route today consists of a vague, overgrown trail that should not, under any circumstances, be tackled without a guide; experienced backcountry hikers have almost died here. If you mean to hike it, hire a guide with a machete from the Jamaican Caves Organisation (p178), form a small group, and ensure that your party has a GPS, plenty of water (a minimum of 6L per person), mosquito repellent, high-energy snacks and a flashlight. Additionally, leave your name(s), contact information and estimated time of arrival with a reliable source. The trail measures 16km between the hamlet of Tyre and Windsor (although you need to add on an extra 3km at Tyre and 5km at Windsor to walk to the nearest reliable transport sources – Troy and Sherwood Content, respectively). It's very infrequently walked these days; sometimes not for years, so much of it is an arduous bush-whack, making it incredibly easy to get lost (not a good idea seeing as there are no settlements, no surface water and no chance of helicopter rescue.) Six hours is the minimum time required, eight hours is average, 10 hours isn't uncommon. Start early!

Difficulties aside, the hike is one of Jamaica's – nay, the Caribbean's – greatest challenges. Tree cover and steep-sided hills block any expansive views, and you have to walk in single file, meaning the most interesting aspect of the walk lies in studying the remarkable endemism of the karst ecology. The Cockpit's bloody history, as related by any good guide, is equally fascinating. Look out for the stone walls of the old road, which can be seen throughout much of the journey. The trail is easier done south to north starting from Troy. Beware, the mosquitoes are brutal!

For a guided hike with the JCO, you'll need a minimum of five people and your own transport. The cost is US$100 per person.

### ☉ Sights & Activities

**Windsor Cave**                                   CAVE
This cave may be off the beaten track to most people, but it's one of Jamaica's most important bat habitats, home to 12 species of around 100,000 bats. The cave was donated to the World Wildlife Fund in 1995 with the proviso that it never be developed. It's not terribly impressive inside, but you can either explore it with congenial guide Dango (p135) or, better yet, join a naturalist tour from Windsor Great House and watch the bats emerge at sunset.

The entrance is a 1km hike from the road, ending with a clamber up a narrow rocky path. Beyond the tight entrance you'll pass into a large gallery full of stalactites and a huge chamber with a dramatically arched ceiling; in rainy season you can hear the roar of the Martha Brae River flowing deep underground. Dango hangs out at the colorful Rasta shack at the bottom of the road to Windsor; negotiate a price with him, bearing in mind that he counts each separate chamber as a separate 'cave' (eg US$20 per person, per chamber).

**Dango**                                          CAVING
(www.jamaicancaves.org/dango-jamaica.htm) Friendly Rasta Franklyn 'Dango' Taylor is the self-appointed guardian of the Windsor Cave. He walks in from Coxheath every morning, and hangs out at the top of the Windsor road in case any visitors show up. Negotiate the tour price with him. He occasionally looks after a cabin that's available for overnight stays.

### 🛏 Sleeping & Eating

★**Windsor Great House**          GUESTHOUSE **$**
(☏ 997-3832; www.cockpitcountry.com; 1/2/3 people US$45/55/50) 🖉 How often do you get to sleep in a colonial mansion that happens to be a biological research station? Decked out with no-frills cut-stone rooms with shared bathroom, it's frequented by naturalists and

off-beat travellers. Resident naturalists Mike Schwartz and Susan Koenig occasionally stage 'Meet the biologist' dinners (US$40, minimum four people) with a pre-dinner bat-watching walk.

Built in 1795 by John Tharp, this colonial mansion was preceded in 1750 by a military outpost to guard against marauding Maroons (runaway slaves). Surrounded by lush jungle, it's lit up at night by peeny-wallies (fireflies) and the stars above. Its remoteness makes it ideal for spotting Jamaica's numerous endemic bird species, exploring the nearby cave and watching the bat vortex at dusk.

It's not about the creature comforts at this solar-powered outpost; the lure is the interesting company and the surrounding wilderness. And an exuberant Great Dane called Zella.

Rooms accommodate up to three people. Breakfast/lunch/dinner is US$7.50/7.50/15 per person.

It's not marked by a sign; to find it, take a left at the Rasta hut at the junction at the end of the road to Windsor. Email/call for directions.

Miss Lilly's                                        JAMAICAN $
(🔗 788-1022; www.jamaicancaves.org/lillys-jamaica. htm; Coxheath; meals J$600-1200; ⊘ 9am-8pm Mon-Sat) In the hamlet of Coxheath, 5km north of Windsor, you'll find this bar, restaurant, guesthouse and Usain Bolt gift shop all rolled into one, run by the welcoming and jovial aunt of Mr Bolt, Miss Lilly. There's good, home-cooked food on the menu, including curried goat and delicious yams, said to be the source of Usain's extreme speed.

This is a nice place to chill and meet locals, including some members of the direct and extended Bolt family who tend to congregate here for gossip, drinking and dominoes. The fast man himself throws a big shebang for his community around Christmas time.

## ❶ Getting There & Away

There are two ways of reaching Windsor: south from Falmouth via Martha Brae, or via the B5 road via Albert Town, Jackson Town, Clark's Town and Kinloss if coming from the south of the island.

Minibuses and route taxis (around J$120) operate between Falmouth and Sherwood Content. Coxheath is a 10-minute walk from Sherwood Content (taxis will drop you there if you ask). Windsor is another 5km down the paved but badly potholed single-track road (walk or pay a taxi driver an extra J$1500 for a lift).

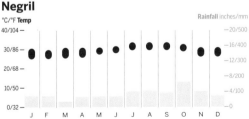

# Negril & West Coast

## Best Places to Eat

➡ Rockhouse Restaurant & Bar (p150)

➡ 3 Dives Jerk Centre (p149)

➡ Zimbali (p152)

➡ Sips & Bites (p150)

➡ Cosmo's (p147)

## Best Places to Sleep

➡ Caves (p147)

➡ Rockhouse (p147)

➡ Judy House Cottages & Rooms (p145)

➡ Moondance (p144)

➡ Mountambrin Villa & Gallery (p155)

➡ Kuyaba (p142)

## Why Go?

If you thought the north and east coasts of Jamaica were relaxed, head west to a land of long beaches and crimson sunsets where the pleasure-seeking resort of Negril shimmers like an independent republic of guilt-free sloth. Aside from producing sugarcane and surreptitiously growing Jamaica's best ganja, western Jamaica's raison d'être is almost exclusively touristic; elongated Negril and its hotel developments stretch for more than 10 miles along the entire western coast. In the quiet bucolic hinterland, little pockets of local life can still be glimpsed in places such as Lucea, a pretty coastal enclave bypassed by tourist traffic, wild and wet Mayfield Falls, and diminutive Little Bay, a nonresort that still feels like Negril, circa 1969. Few come to the west with a to-do list, electing instead to enjoy life in the true spirit of the hippies who founded Negril. Join them on a sun lounger and relax...*mon*.

## When to Go

### Negril

**Feb–Apr** Negril is at its most hedonistic during spring break.

**Apr–Jun** Accommodations prices halve during low season, yet it's less rainy here as the rest of Jamaica.

**Dec & Jan** Arguably the best weather – sunny, clear and dry – plus numerous music festivals.

# NEGRIL

POP 7832

Stuck out on the island's western tip and graced with its finest and longest natural beach, Negril was first colonized by hippies in the early 1970s. Unsurprisingly, 40 years of development has left its mark – not all of it good: Negril is renowned for its hustlers. But it's not all hassle. A strong local business community, fueled by a desire to safeguard Negril's precious ecology, has kept the area from becoming a full-on circus. Consequently Negril remains a laid-back place of impromptu reggae concerts and psychedelic sunsets.

In both geography and character, Negril can be split neatly in two. To the north is the erroneously named Seven Mile Beach (it's a little more than 4 miles long). Further south, the West End is the original Negril of hippy-era legend. Here precipitous cliffs, up to 50ft high in places, plunge into the azure ocean. Negril 'town' is sandwiched between the two, on the edge of the West End.

## History

Only in 1959 was a road cut to Negril, launching the development of what was then a tiny fishing village. Electricity and telephones came later. The sleepy beachfront village soon became a popular holiday spot for Jamaicans. About the same time, hippies and backpackers from abroad began to appear. They roomed with local families or slept on the beach, partook of ganja and magic mushrooms, and generally gave Negril its laid-back reputation. In 1977 the first major resort – Negril Beach Village (later renamed Hedonism II) – opened its doors to a relatively affluent crowd seeking an uninhibited Club Med–style vacation. By the mid-1980s Negril was in the throes of a full-scale tourism boom that continues today.

This let-it-all-hang-out tradition still overflows during the March to April spring break, when US college kids swarm for wet T-shirt contests, drinking competitions and general party time.

Nonetheless, the resort has developed an active and environmentally conscious spirit under the guidance of expat residents, resulting in the creation of the Negril Marine Park within the Negril Environmental Protection Area. The park encompasses the shoreline, mangroves, offshore waters and coral reefs, and is divided into eight recreational zones. Some hotels have taken admirable steps toward implementing green policies, and it is hoped that traveler preference for these resorts will lead to copying of environmentally friendly behavior across the beach.

## ⊙ Sights

### ★ Seven Mile Beach                                 BEACH

(Negril Beach, Long Beach; Map p146) Seven Mile Beach was initially touted on tourism posters as 'seven miles of nothing but you and the sea.' True, sunbathers still lie half submerged in the gentle surf, and the sweet smell of ganja smoke continues to perfume the breeze, but otherwise the beach has changed a great deal. Today it's cluttered with restaurants, bars and nightspots, and every conceivable water sport is on offer. It is still beautiful to behold, but if you're looking for solitude, look elsewhere.

It's worth noting that the Seven Mile Beach is actually only 4 miles long.

### Long Bay Beach Park                               BEACH

(Map p146; J$200; ⊙9:30am-5pm) Toward the north end of Seven Mile Beach, this beach is more peaceful and far less crowded than the sand further south. Here you'll find more sugary sand and picnic tables, plus changing rooms. But there's also coarse grass here, so it's not quite as picturesque.

### Bloody Bay Beach                                  BEACH

(Map p146) A splendid option in between two large all-inclusives, with no facilities and few people, save for a few savvy travelers and a smattering of locals enjoying some repose away from the hubbub. There's a jerk shack selling snacks and drinks if you need 'em.

### Kool Runnings
### Adventure Park                            AMUSEMENT PARK

(Map p146; ☑957-5400; www.koolrunnings.com; Norman Manley Blvd; ⊙11am-6pm Tue-Sun; ⋒) If you prefer your water fun doled out in a theme park, descend on this 2-hectare collection of different experiences, from riding on a bamboo raft and paintballing to canoeing, and even spinning in a human gyroscope. Separate entry fees for each experience.

## ⭱ Activities

There's plenty to keep you busy in Negril, from sunset boat cruises and glass-bottom-boat outings to getting in the water with a snorkeling mask or beneath the waves with a scuba tank. Fishing, parasailing and kayaking are other watery pursuits. Most lodgings can also arrange tours to Jamaican attractions further afield.

## Diving & Snorkeling

Negril has extensive offshore reefs and cliffs, including grottoes, shallow reefs perfect for novice divers and mid-depth reefs right off the sands of Seven Mile Beach. Clusters of dwarf tube sponges are a noteworthy feature. The West End offers caves and tunnels; its overhangs are popular for night dives. Hawksbill turtles are still quite common here.

Visibility often exceeds 30m and seas are dependably calm. Most dives are in 10m to 23m of water.

Several sites will be of interest to prospective divers. The **Throne** is a 15m-wide cave with massive sponges, plentiful soft corals, nurse sharks, octopuses, barracuda and stingrays. **Aweemaway** is a shallow reef area south of the Throne, and has tame stingrays. **Deep Plane** is the remains of a Cessna airplane lying 21m underwater. Corals and sponges have taken up residence in and around the plane, attracting an abundance of fish, and nurse sharks hang out at a nearby overhang. **Sands Club Reef**, sitting in 10m of water, lies offshore from the middle of Seven Mile Beach. From here, a drift dive to **Shark's Reef** leads through tunnels and overhangs with huge sponges and gorgonian corals.

Snorkeling is especially good off the **West End**. Expect to pay about US$5 an hour for masks and fins from concession stands on the beach. Most of the scuba-diving providers offer snorkeling tours (about US$25).

Most all-inclusive resorts have scuba facilities. Several companies offer PADI certification and introductory 'resort courses,' which are held in swimming pools.

★**Negril Adventure Diver**                    DIVING
(Map p144; ☑ 412-2502; www.negriladventure diver.com; Norman Manley Blvd, Coral Seas Beach Resort; 1-/2-tank dives US$60/100) This diving outfit gets particularly high marks for the patience and friendliness of its diving instructors. Particularly good for beginners, though they tend to get rave reviews from most customers.

★**Dream Team Divers**                    DIVING
(Map p148; ☑ 957-0054; www.dreamteamdivers jamaica.com; One Love Dr, Sunset on the Cliffs Resort; 1-/2-tank dives US$40/70) Highly recommended, professional diving outfit. A full range of PADI courses on offer, as well as discover scuba dives (US$80).

**Sundivers Negril**                    DIVING
(Map p144; ☑ 957-4503, 405 6872; www.sundivers negril.com; Travellers Beach Resort; 1-/2-tank dives US$55/90) Reliable, long-standing diving operator based at Travellers Beach Resort.

### Boat Trips

Several companies offer two- and three-hour excursions. Tours can be booked at most hotels. Most trips include snorkeling and plenty of booze, preferably done in that order. **Negril Cruises** (Map p146; ☑ 430-0596; www. negrilcruises.com; Hedonism II; US$40-60) operating out of the Hedonism II (p149), Couples Swept Away (p144) and Breezes resorts are a perennial favorite.

Glass-bottom boats (around US$40) depart both from Seven Mile Beach and West End.

### Fishing

The waters off Negril – teeming with tuna, blue marlin, wahoo and sailfish – provide some excellent action for sportfishing enthusiasts. **Stanley's Deep Sea Fishing** (Map p142; ☑ 957-6341, 818-6363; www.stanleysdeepseafishing.com; Negril Yacht Club; 1/2-day trips for up to 4 people US$500, additional passengers each US$50) offers custom fishing-trip charters. Three-quarter and full day trips are also available.

For a more offbeat experience, head out into the briny with a local fisher; ask around by the bridge over the South Negril River.

### Water Sports

The waters off Negril are usually mirror calm – ideal for all kinds of water sports. Numerous concessions along the beach rent sea kayaks, sailboards and Sunfish sailboats (about US$20 per hour). They also offer waterskiing (US$25 for 30 minutes), glass-bottom-boat rides (US$15) and banana-boat rides (US$15). Jet Skis are best avoided as they are eco-unfriendly.

**Ray's Water Sports**                    WATER SPORTS
(Map p146; ☑ 957-4349) Parasailing and other water sports are offered by Ray's Water Sports at the north end of Seven Mile Beach.

## ☞ Tours

Several tour operators offer a standard fare of excursions to the Black River Morass and Appleton Rum Estate, to the east in St Elizabeth parish (about US$85 to US$95); Mayfield Falls (US$70 to US$80); and YS Falls (US$85).

# Negril & West Coast Highlights

**1 Seven Mile Beach** (p138) Gazing into perfect sunsets that set fire to 4 miles of sugary-white sand.

**2 Mayfield Falls** (p154) Clambering, clawing and diving around the pristine whirlpools of some of Jamaica's loveliest waterfalls.

**3 Rick's Cafe** (p150) Watching cliff divers pluck up courage (or lose their nerve) while jumping off 10m cliffs.

**4 Mountambrin Villa & Gallery** (p155) Discovering art and music on the remote hill estate formerly belonging to Alex Haley, near Savanna-la-Mar.

**5 Half Moon Beach** (p153) Enjoying a tranquil slice of sand without the hustling and taking a boat out to a unique island restaurant.

**6 Negril** (p138) Exploring Jamaica's underwater topography with some of the island's best scuba outfits.

**7 Zimbali** (p152) Tasting some of Jamaica's finest food at this lofty organic farm and staying on for a day or three.

**8 Little Bay** (p155) Relaxing on deserted fishing beaches or diving at the local Blue Hole.

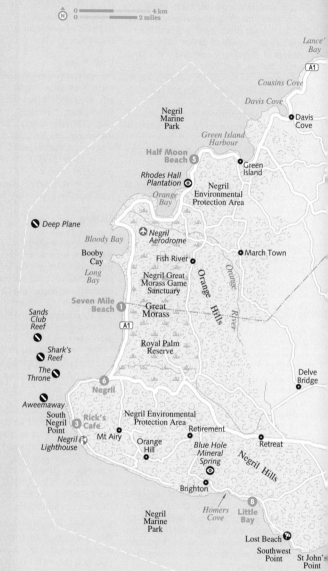

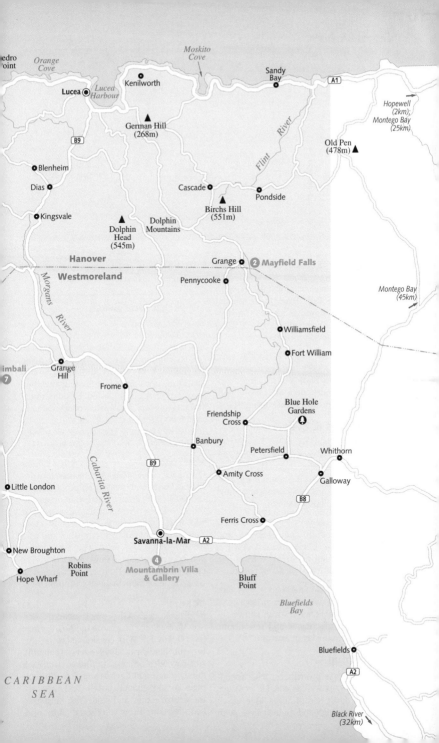

# Negril Village

**Clive's Transport Service**    SIGHTSEEING TOURS
(☑956-2615; www.clivestransportservicejamaica.
com) Offers reliable, comfortable tours to
Mayfield Falls, YS Falls, Black River, Martha
Brae and more, as well as airport transfers
(US$40 for one to two people) in a nine-
passenger minivan.

**Caribic Vacations**    SIGHTSEEING TOURS
(Map p144; ☑953-9895; www.caribicvacations.
com; Norman Manley Blvd) Negril's largest operator running tours to YS Falls, Rose Hall,
and other popular island-wide destinations.

## ⭐ Festivals & Events

**Rastafari Rootzfest**    CULTURAL
(www.rastafarirootzfest.com; ⊙Dec) Held for
three days in December in Negril, this new
festival celebrates the Rastafarian lifestyle,
from music and art to I-tal cuisine, ganja
cultivation and religious beliefs.

**Jamaica Beachfest**    CULTURAL
(⊙Feb-Apr) Starting in late February and
now spanning six weeks to early April is
Negril's famous spring break celebration,
featuring live music and plenty of booze.

**Negril Music & Food Festival**    MUSIC
(☑968-9356; www.facebook.com/Negrilmusic
foodfestival; ⊙Jan) This festival showcases
the best of Negril's reggae and restaurants
on the second Saturday in January.

## 🛏 Sleeping

The West End leans toward backpacker-friendly guesthouses, as well as cliffside boutique
hotels. The north end of Seven Mile Beach
is taken up by high-end all-inclusives, with

standard hotels and the odd cheapie scattered along the beach further south.

## 🛏 Seven Mile Beach

**Negril Yoga Centre**    RESORT $
(Map p144; ☑957-4397; www.negrilyoga.com; Norman Manley Blvd; r US$51-91; ❋🏠) A hearken-
ing back to hippie days of yore, these rustic
yet atmospheric rooms and cottages surround an open-air, wood-floored, thatched
yoga center set in a garden. Options range
from a two-story, Thai-style wooden cabin to
an adobe farmer's cottage; all are modestly
furnished. Naturally, yoga classes are offered
(US$10 for guests and US$20 for visitors).

**Roots Bamboo**    RESORT $
(Map p144; ☑957-4479; www.rootsbamboo.com;
Norman Manley Blvd; camping per person US$15, r
US$62-85; ❋🏠) Firstly, if you want peace and
quiet, look elsewhere. On the other hand, if
you need a party – well, stick around, *mon*.
This complex of cottages, campsites and chalets attracts a mixed crowd of the middle-aged
and backpackers who share a desire to get
crazy on the beach. There are regular reggae
concerts and a perpetual party atmosphere.

**⭐Kuyaba**    HOTEL $$
(Map p144; ☑957-4318; www.kuyaba.com; Nor-
man Manley Blvd; cottages/ste US$70/179, r from
US$139; ❋🏠) 🖉 With considerable style, this
tasteful, family-run hotel offers six quaint,
rustic wooden cabins with filigree trim, each
done up in bright Caribbean colors. The cot-
tages are nice enough, but the real draws are
the deluxe rooms and suite with king-sized
bed, upstairs in a handsome stone-and-

0 ——— 500 m
0 ——— 0.25 miles

Negril Great
Morass Game
Sanctuary

Sheffield Rd

Miss Brown's (300m);
Little Bay (20km);
Savanna-la-Mar (30km);
Bluefields/Belmont (48km)

Transportation
Center

Whitehall Rd

WHITEHALL

## Negril Village

timber house tastefully decorated with terra-cotta floors and modern design touches.

**Travellers Beach Resort**  HOTEL $$
(Map p144; ☑957-9308; www.travellersresorts.com; Norman Manley Blvd; r/ste from US$103/204; 🅿❄🛜🏊) Although overrun during spring break, Travellers is a real bargain the rest of the year. The family-owned resort is a lovely little midrange option, professionally run with clean, comfortable rooms that match the amenities of larger top-end resorts.

**Rondel Village**  RESORT $$
(Map p144; ☑957-4413; www.rondelvillage.com; Norman Manley Blvd; r from US$127, 2-bedroom villas US$302; ❄🛜🏊) 🏖 Rondel is a charmer. Rooms encased in beautiful white chalets are set off with sharp purple color accents and are surrounded by snaking swimming pools and verdant (largely edible) natural foliage. Eschewing big-resort ambitions, it is the epitome of Negrilian calm – relaxed, hassle-free and filled with all the ingredients for a week enjoyed doing absolutely nothing. Service is exemplary.

**White Sands**  HOTEL $$
(Map p144; ☑957-4291, in the USA 305-503-9074; www.whitesandsjamaica.com; Norman Manley Blvd; r US$95-120, studios/villas US$219/540; ❄🏊) This attractive property offers simple yet elegant one-bedroom octagonal units, and an excellent four-bedroom, four-bathroom villa that sleeps eight people and has its own pool. The latter is the real draw, as a group rental is a total steal. There's also a pleasant, well-maintained garden where you can relax while the resident parrot recites dub poetry.

**Beachcomber Club & Spa**  HOTEL $$
(Map p144; ☑957-4170; www.beachcomberclub.com; Norman Manley Blvd; r from US$170, 1-bedroom apt from US$280, 2-bedroom apt from US$380; 🅿❄🛜) Operating with crisp efficiency, this handsome multiroom hotel has an open-air beachside restaurant, Gambino's, that does great Italian, plus a nightly entertainment schedule, tennis and water sports. Yet for all this, it doesn't feel as corporate as an all-inclusive. All rooms are well furnished in a sort of standard high-midrange-hotel outlay of tans and beiges. Suites and apartments have kitchenettes.

**Charela Inn**  HOTEL $$
(Map p144; ☑957-4277; www.charela.com; Norman Manley Blvd; s/d/tr US$190/210/250; 🅿❄🛜🏊) Creating an individual style amid the ubiquitous beach resorts, Charela has the feel of a Spanish hacienda with large comfortable rooms (some with king beds) built around an attractive courtyard embellished with a perfectly round swimming pool. The whole establishment sits on a hassle-free, fern-shrouded slice of Negril beach and is championed for its Jamaican-French fusion restaurant Le Vendôme (p148).

**Mariposa Hideaway**  HOTEL $$
(Map p144; ☑957-4918; Norman Manley Blvd; r US$90-160, 2-bedroom apt US$170; 🅿❄🛜) A twee Italian-run hotel that feels like a nice marriage between the Mediterranean and the Caribbean. Rooms are all right, but the tiled studios with kitchenette and family-size apartment, all with cable TV and fridge, are the real standouts. Cleanliness

# Seven Mile Beach (South)

could be improved and the restaurant has gone downhill in recent times.

★ **Moondance** VILLA $$$
(Map p144; ☑ in the USA 800-213-0583; www.moondanceresorts.com; Norman Manley Blvd; villas US$750-2000; P❋🛜🌊) The ultimate in Seven Mile Beach luxury, the Moondance villas put even the best all-inclusives to shame. You have a choice of gorgeous one- to five-bedroom villas – the one-bedroom honeymoon villa is akin to a lovely tropical home, whereas the three-bedroom 'Dream Walk' home looks like a medieval Chinese

palace. For US$125 per adult per night you can get 24-hour all-inclusive service.

**Idle Awhile** HOTEL $$$
(Map p144; ☑ 957-9566, in the USA 877-243-5352; www.idleawhile.com; Norman Manley Blvd; r/ste from US$250/310; P❋🛜) Just what the therapist ordered! Idle Awhile is Negril in a nutshell: a simple but stylish 14-room beachside abode where a hearty breakfast, a hammock and a lucid sunset are all you need to make things right in your life. Bonuses come with the aptly named Chill Awhile restaurant and complimentary access to the

fantastic Couples Swept Away (p149) fitness complex.

**Nirvana on the Beach**  RESORT $$$
(Map p144; ☑957-4314, in the USA 716-789-5955; www.nirvananegril.com; Norman Manley Blvd; cottages US$175-350; ❈ ☎) The place to stay if you're seeking meditation and the sort of bohemian ambience you get when members of the counterculture decide to open up a tasteful boutique hotel. You can pick from one-, two- and three-bedroom cottages, all set in elegantly subdued yet still vibrantly colorful Zen-like tropical gardens.

## West End

★ **Judy House**
**Cottages & Rooms**  HOSTEL $
(Map p142; ☑957-0671, 424-5481; www.judy-housenegril.com; Westland Mountain Rd; s/d US$25/40, cottages US$90; ☎) This lush tropical garden on a hill above the West End guards two self-contained cottages with kitchen and five additional rooms (three singles and a couple of dorms, all with shared bathroom) aimed at backpackers. English owner Sue is a mine of candid info, the honesty bar and the friendly discourse are refreshing, and the hammocks in the garden are...zzzzzz.

The luxury here isn't in the gilded bath taps, it's in the unscripted extras.

**Seastar Inn**  HOTEL $
(Map p148; ☑957-0553; www.seastarinn.com; Seastar Rd; s/d incl breakfast US$59-79; P❈☎) This peaceful modern place is run by a charming Canadian-Jamaican couple. Pretty tiled rooms offset by tastefully frilly decor characterize the interior; outside the inn is fuzzed over with fecund trees and lush grounds. Hammocks are strung out over verandas, which is a bit of an issue, as you may never leave them. The Negril Jazz Festival is held here.

**Lighthouse Inn 2**  GUESTHOUSE $
(Map p148; ☑957-4052; www.lighthouseinn2.com; West End Rd; studios US$70-80, cottages US$95-160; ☎) A small, family resort that brings to mind the old-school charms of Negril's heyday, this is the sort of budget place with a gentle vibe that you kind of want to export to Seven Mile Beach, just to bring the madness there down a bit. Big efforts are made to accommodate guests with disabilities. Rooms and apartments are sparse but sweet.

**Blue Cave Castle**  HOTEL $$
(Map p148; ☑957-4845; www.bluecavecastle.com; West End Rd; s/d US$75/145; ❈☎) Winner of Negril's 'quirky hotel' prize is this mock castle that sits like a crenelated fortification warding off invaders on the cliffs of the West End. Fourteen fit-for-a-king rooms and a

WORTH A TRIP

## NEGRIL GREAT MORASS

This virtually impenetrable 3km-wide swamp of mangroves stretches 16km from the South Negril River to Orange Bay. The swamp is the island's second-largest freshwater wetland system and forms a refuge for endangered waterfowl. American crocodiles still cling to life here and are occasionally seen at the mouth of the Orange River.

The Great Morass acts like a giant sponge, filtering the waters flowing down to the ocean from the hills east of Negril, and is a source of much-needed fresh water. Drainage channels cut into the swamp have lowered the water levels, and sewage and other pollutants have seeped into the region's shallow water table, making their way to sea where they have poisoned the coral reefs and depleted fish stocks.

The easiest way to get a sense of the Great Morass is at the Royal Palm Reserve (Map p144; ☑364-7407; www.jpat-jm.net; informal fee US$10; ◷9am-6pm). Wooden boardwalks make a 1.5km loop around the reserve. Three distinct swamp forest types are present – royal palm forest, buttonwood forest and bull thatch forest. They're all home to butterflies galore as well as doctorbirds, herons, egrets, endangered black parakeets, Jamaican woodpeckers and countless other birds. Two observation towers provide views over the tangled mangroves.

If driving, take Sheffield Rd east of the roundabout for around 6km and turn left after the golf course.

At the time of research, the reserve had officially closed to the public due to lack of interest and government funds, but it should still sometimes be possible to get a guided tour with one of the staff who remain on-site.

# Seven Mile Beach (North)

itself as 'the meeting place of the gods.' Its clientele is decidedly human, but the setting is truly divine. You can choose from rooms, simple garden cottages and quaint octagonal seafront bungalows perched atop the cliff. Sun loungers are liberally scattered along the cliffs and steps lead down to the swimming area.

### Home Sweet Home
HOTEL **$$**

(Map p142; ☎ 957-4478, in the USA 800-925-7418; www.homesweethomeresort.com; West End Rd; r US$139, ste US$249-299; ❄ 🛜 🏊) A cliffhanger with a dozen rooms plus two suites, all with private balconies and fans. The rooms are, naturally, done up in anonymous tropical pastels. It features a clifftop bar and restaurant, a Jacuzzi and multitiered sundecks overhanging the teal-blue waters.

### Jackie's on the Reef
HOTEL **$$**

(☎ 957-4997, in the USA 718-469-2785; www.jackies onthereef.com; West End Rd; r & cottages per person US$150; 🛜 🏊) This tranquil option is 4km south of the lighthouse. Run by hospitable Jackie, it operates as a wellness haven focusing on spiritual renewal. A natural stone 'temple' is divided into four rooms, each with two handmade wooden beds and an outdoor shower and bathroom. We love the cottage with a vast circular window overlooking the sea. Yoga and half-board included.

### ★ Rockhouse
HOTEL **$$$**

(Map p148; ☎ 957-4373; www.rockhousehotel.com; West End Rd; r/studios/villa US$180/220/410; ❄ 🛜 🏊) One of the West End's most beautiful and well-run hotels, with luxury thatched

private grassy terrace create a less swashbuckling atmosphere inside. Repeat visitors testify to fine service and a blissful ambience. There's a swimming cave accessed via a slippery staircase.

### Catcha Falling Star
HOTEL **$$**

(Map p148; ☎ 957-0390; www.catchajamaica.com; West End Rd; r US$135,1-/2-bedroom cottages incl breakfast from US$110-350; 🅿 🛜) In inimitable West End style, these pleasant fan-cooled cottages – including several with two bedrooms – sit on the cliffs. Each is named for an astrological sign and the rooms do have the genuine variety of the zodiac; some peek into gardens abloom with tropical flowers, while others lip out on to the blue-on-blue vista of ocean. Breakfast is delivered to your veranda.

### Xtabi
HOTEL **$$**

(Map p148; ☎ 957-0120; www.xtabi-negril.com; West End Rd; r US$105-158, cottages US$271; 🅿 ❄ 🛜 🏊) This chic and casual hotel bills

rondavels (African huts) built of pine and stone, plus studio apartments that dramatically cling to the cliffside above a small cove. Decor is basic yet romantic, with net-draped poster beds and strong Caribbean colors. Catwalks lead over the rocks to an open-sided dining pavilion overhanging the ocean.

**Caves**                              BOUTIQUE HOTEL $$$
(Map p148; ☑ 957-0269, in the USA 800-688-7678; www.thecaveshotel.com; West End Rd; ste incl meals from US$723, all-incl cottages US$1090-1965; P ✹ 🛜 🛜) One of the finest boutique hotels in Jamaica, and one beloved of the Hollywood elite (some of whom are helicoptered in), the Caves offers handcrafted, individually styled, wood-and-thatch cottages set in lush gardens above cave-riddled cliffs. Rooms feature exquisite hand-carved furniture, batik fabrics and one-of-a-kind art; many have alfresco showers.

★**Spa Retreat**
**Boutique Hotel**                     BOUTIQUE HOTEL $$$
(Map p148; ☑ 399-3772; www.thespajamaica. com; West End Rd; cottages US$325; P ✹ 🛜 🛜) One of Jamaica's finest hotels comprises 18 wonderfully appealing, handcrafted stone cottages, nestled amid lush vegetation and overlooking the cliffside. They're fronted by liberally scattered sun loungers from which to admire the view and a clifftop pool. Service is exemplary, and much thought has gone into the handcrafted furniture. Perks include an excellent restaurant and a variety of pampering packages.

**Banana Shout**                       CABIN $$$
(Map p148; ☑ 957-0384; www.bananashoutresort.com; West End Rd; 2-/3-/4-person cabins US$150/200/250; P 🛜) Occupying a particularly choice bit of clifftop turf, these cheerful green and orange cabins are perched over the sea in offbeat and homey seclusion. Tastefully decorated with Jamaican and Haitian art, they're unique and charmingly idiosyncratic, even for the West End. Step outside to a dramatic stairway descending to a sea cave with sundeck and freshwater shower.

**Tensing Pen**                        RESORT $$$
(Map p148; ☑ 957-0387; www.tensingpen.com; West End Rd; r incl breakfast US$160-230, cottages US$370-720; ✹ 🛜 🛜) This tranquil option with thatched cottages has a stunning setting, with a narrow bridge above a cove. Most cottages are 'pillar houses' – an architectural style associated with the West End – perched above the coral cliffs and set in nat-

ural gardens. All have exquisite bamboo and hardwood details, but are completely glassed in – it's all air-con and no sea breezes.

## ✖ Eating

Negril restaurants run the gamut from sophisticated fusion cuisine (along the Seven Mile Beach and West End both) to seafood-focused eateries, local cookshops serving good Jamaican standards, and evening jerk stands along the southern part of Norman Manley Blvd and Negril village. Local delicacies include hallucinogenic mushroom 'tea' and ganja brownies. Small supermarkets are scattered along the West End Rd.

## ✖ Seven Mile Beach

**Cosmo's**                            SEAFOOD $
(Map p144; ☑ 957-4784; Norman Manley Blvd; mains J$600-1200; ⊙ 10am-11pm; 🛜) A tatty hippie outpost that sits like an island of good taste amid an ocean of insipid all-inclusive buffets. Cosmo's, in Negril-speak, is a synonym for 'fantastic seafood.' Eschew fine dining for burying your toes in the sand at a beachside picnic table – the plates of melt-in-your-mouth lobster, grilled fish and curried conch are deliciously spicy.

**Cafe Goa**                           BREAKFAST $
(Map p144; ☑ 454-6847; Norman Manley Blvd; mains US$6-16; ⊙ 8am-late) Replete with breakfasting locals and a few washed-up hippies who look as if they fell asleep in 1973 and have just woken up, Goa is top of the morning for French toast, eggs and pancakes, alongside callaloo omelets, and ackee and saltfish. Sundays see a jazz band that draws a mixed bag of locals and visitors.

**Kenny's Italian Cafe**               ITALIAN $
(Map p144; ☑ 957-4032; Norman Manley Blvd; mains US$10-15; ⊙ 11am-10pm Mon-Fri, 4-10pm Sat & Sun; 🛜) Winning the popular vote with lovely half-indoor, half-outdoor seating on padded stools, this cafe-/restaurant sticks local fish on Italian pasta, steams up cappuccinos (rare in Jamaica) and does a proper pizza. The decor is relaxed yet refined and the bar is a good place to swap your Red Stripe for a glass of wine.

**Pablo's Restaurant**                 JAMAICAN $
(Map p148; ☑ 407-9531; West End Rd; mains J$850-1800; ⊙ 7am-11pm) A friendly fist appears through the kitchen window promptly fol-

# West End

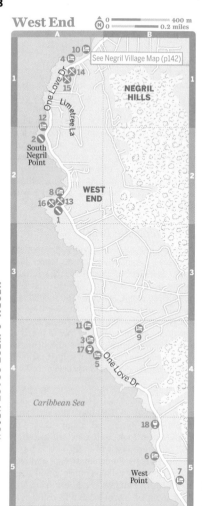

0 —— 400 m
0 —— 0.2 miles

See Negril Village Map (p142)

NEGRIL HILLS

One Love Dr

Limetree La

South Negril Point

WEST END

Caribbean Sea

One Love Dr

West Point

## West End

lowed by the words 'Respect, mon.' Return the greeting, take a seat and see what breakfast brings. Pablo's reinforces the view that, in Jamaica, the simpler the restaurant, the better the food and the friendlier the waitstaff. Talking of respect – this place has it in spades.

### Lobster House                    ITALIAN $$
(Map p144; ☑957-4293; Sunrise Club; mains US$10-27; ⏰7:30am-11pm) Renowned for its pink gnocchi in a Parmesan cream and its signature lobster dishes, this congenial outdoor spot has attained the status of best pizzeria in town, thanks to its brick oven. Many,

however, come for a cup of what is arguably the best espresso on the island, made using Blue Mountain coffee and the proprietor's vintage 1961 Faema espresso machine.

### Kuyaba on the Beach        INTERNATIONAL $$
(Map p144; ☑957-4318; www.kuyaba.com; Norman Manley Blvd; mains US$14-28; ⏰7am-11pm; 🛜) 'Kuyaba' means 'Celebrate!' in the Arawakan language, which is exactly what happens here each evening at sunset as guests tuck into the likes of shrimp rundown with papaya salsa, snapper with coconut callaloo and upscale Jamaican standards. The lunch menu is more laid-back: burgers, kebabs and gourmet sandwiches, plus superb pepper shrimp. Continents may drift before you get served, though.

### Le Vendôme                     FRENCH $$$
(Map p144; ☑957-4648; Norman Manley Blvd; mains US$30-48; ⏰7:30am-10pm; 🛜) Take your table on the terra-cotta terrace with garden view and choose from French classics such as duck à l'orange and escargots Burgundy-style, or regional creations like curried shrimp or red snapper in coconut milk. What sets everything apart is the Gallic attention to final execution and the use of locally grown vegetables and spices.

## West End

### ★ 3 Dives Jerk Centre
JERK $

(Map p148; ☑957-0845; West End Rd; quarter-/
half-chicken J$400/650; ☉3pm-midnight) This
colorful shack, which looks like it'll blow
away in the next category one hurricane,
serves up what may be the best jerk chicken
in Negril, plus other Jamaican classics. Let
your nose and taste buds be the judge. Feast
your eyes on those sizzling lobsters or that
smoking jerk and be prepared for a loooong,
totally worthwhile, wait.

### Just Natural
BREAKFAST $

(☑957-0235; Hilton Ave; mains J$500-1500;
☉8am-8pm Mon-Fri, to 9pm Sat & Sun; ☑)
Quintessentially Jamaican, Just Natural is
a jumble of tables, trees and foliage at the
southern end of the West End strip that
serves up a formidable breakfast of fruit, porridge, smoothies and eggs. It's quite incredible what delicacies emerge from its wooden
shack of a kitchen. Top of the morning!

### Sips & Bites
JAMAICAN $

(Map p148; ☑957-0188; West End Rd; mains
J$450-1600; ☉7am-10pm Sun-Fri) This casual,
welcoming restaurant serves classic Jamaican fare, and it serves it done right: rich, filling and more compellingly seasoned than in
many other Jamaican restaurants. The dishes include oxtail, curried goat, brown stew
lobster and conch steaks. This is the go-to
place for a slap-up ackee and saltfish breakfast and gingery sorrel drink (in season).

### Canoe Bar
JAMAICAN $

(Map p142; ☑878-5893; West End Rd; mains
J$550-1400; ☉7am-10pm) Simple wooden
shack. Right on the water. Live steel-drum
performances. Fresh fish plucked from the
nearby ocean. Thoroughly reasonable prices.
Big portions of Jamaican favorites. Gently
lapping waves. Bloody Mary sunsets. What
more do you want? Welcome to Canoe Bar –
or should that be paradise?

### Sweet Spice Restaurant
JAMAICAN $$

(Map p142; ☑957-4621; Sheffield Rd; mains
J$850-2450; ☉8:30am-11pm) This unassum-
ing bright-blue clapboard house is a favorite
among the several authentic Jamaican res-
taurants on Sheffield Rd. It's now frequent-
ed by as many visitors as locals. Portions are
heaped, prices are inexpensive and the food
is true blue Jamaican. The menu includes
curried goat and fish, conch steak and pep-
per steak. No alcohol, but plenty of fruit
juices.

### Miss Brown's
CAFE $$

(☑957-9217; Sheffield Rd; mains US$6-28;
☉7am-midnight) Miss Brown's (now run by
son Tedd) is one of Negril's most – ahem –
famous restaurants, with a short menu. It's
all just mushroom stuff, right? Mushroom
omelets, famous mushroom tea... *They're
hallucinogenic*. If you come here, make sure

NEGRIL & WEST COAST NEGRIL

---

### NEGRIL'S ALL-INCLUSIVE RESORTS

Although Negril's all-inclusives are low-rise (all buildings must be lower than the tallest
palm tree, ie three stories), they are not all low-key. The following are the pick of the bunch:

**Hedonism II** (Map p146; ☑957-5070; www.hedonism.com; Norman Manley Blvd; all-incl r per
person US$650-975; P✳☀☎) An adults-only resort that was inaugurated in 1982 and
soon gained notoriety for its risqué attitude, weekly lingerie parties and sheer tackiness.
Nudity rules here (although technically it's optional) and there are occasional swingers'
events.

**Couples Swept Away** (Map p146; ☑957-4061; www.couples.com; Norman Manley Blvd; all-incl
per person from US$770; P✳☀☎) A pleasure palace of fancy villas and botanical gardens
well known locally for its fantastic fitness complex, which nonguests can use for a fee.

**Sandals Negril Beach Resort & Spa** (Map p146; ☑957-5216; www.sandals.com; Norman
Manley Blvd; all-incl r per week from $US4788; P✳☀☎) A couples' resort popular with
honeymooners.

**Beaches Negril** (Map p146; ☑957-9270; www.beaches.com; Norman Manley Blvd; 3 nights
all-incl d US$2500-3700; P✳☀☎) Family-friendly resort loosely resembling a castle.

**Sunset at the Palms** (Map p146; ☑957-5350, in USA 877-734-3486; www.sunsetatthepalms.
com; Norman Manley Blvd; all-incl d/ste from US$625/993; ✳☀☎) ✿ Eco-conscious jungle
cabin–style rooms.

you have a trusted driver to get you back to your hotel (or a few hours to kill sitting around).

**Ivan's Restaurant & Bar** JAMAICAN $$
(Map p148; ☑ 957-0390; www.catchajamaica.com; West End Rd; mains US$6-35; ⊕ 5-11pm) There's West End clifftop romance at Catcha Falling Star (p146) hotel's affiliated restaurant. It's one of Negril's most lavish. The food is Caribbean with some creative fusion. The pineapple chicken is good, as is the lobster. Imaginative cocktails provide a good overture and generous desserts make an ideal coda. Service is glacial, so prepare for a leisurely dinner.

**Ciao Jamaica** ITALIAN $$
(Map p148; ☑ 393-1400; www.ciaojamaica.com; West End Rd; pastas US$12-20; ⊕ 2-10pm) It doesn't matter where you are in the world, it's always good to have a decent Italian to fall back on after seven straight nights of jerk chicken and curried goat. Ciao makes a night off Jamaican cooking feel guilt-free, with huge portions of crossover Jam-Italian pasta (including jerk!), Naples-worthy thin-crust pizzas and fantastic surprise desserts.

★**Rockhouse**
**Restaurant & Bar** FUSION $$$
(Map p148; ☑ 957-4373; www.rockhousehotel.com/eat; West End Rd; mains US$15-30; ⊕ 7:30am-10pm; 📶) Lamp-lit at night, this relaxed cliffside spot leads the pack when it comes to nouvelle Jamaican cuisine in the western parishes. Dine and gush over dishes such as vegetable tempura with lime and ginger, specialty pastas and daily specials such as watermelon spare ribs and blackened mahi-mahi with mango chutney. At the very least, stop by for a sinful bananas Foster.

 **Drinking & Nightlife**

Negril gives Kingston a run for its money when it comes to the after-hours pursuits. The booze starts flowing at sunset along Seven Mile Beach, when many bars offer happy-hour incentives to lure you in. West End bars are lively in the early evening before petering out as the beach bars take over. Some upscale resorts offer visitor passes.

 **Seven Mile Beach**

**Jimmy Buffett's Margaritaville** BAR
(Map p144; ☑ 957-4467; www.margaritaville caribbean.com/locations/negril; ⊕ 8am-late) The most ostentatious of the beach bars, Jimmy Buffett's sustains a spring-break vibe all year long, although it has a bit of a forlorn air on slow nights. There are big-screen TVs, trampolines in the sea, volleyball, swing hammocks and multiple bars waiting to get you trashed. It hosts wet T-shirt contests and the like, and has nightly specials.

**Sunrise Club** BAR
(Map p144; ☑ 957-4293; www.sunriseclub.com; Norman Manley Blvd; ⊕ 8am-11:30pm) At the hotel (s/d from US$90/100; 📶❄📶) of the same name, this is a relaxed bar for those looking to escape the beach mayhem. We particularly like the cocktails, though the Blue Mountain coffee is a great perk-me-up in the mornings.

 **West End**

★**Rick's Cafe** BAR
(Map p148; www.rickscafejamaica.com; West End Rd; ⊕ 3-10pm; 📶) You'll be joining the touristy throng at this ever-popular West End institution, but why not? Just for one evening. The drinks menu features empty-your-wallet cocktails and US$7 Red Stripes (skip

---

**NEGRIL PARTY PLANNER**

If you're serious about making the most of your party time in Negril, here's the breakdown of regular weekly jams:

**Monday** Live reggae night at Bourbon Beach

**Tuesday** Reggae beach party at Alfred's Ocean Palace

**Wednesday** Live Hurricane Band at Roots Bamboo

**Thursday** Live reggae night at Bourbon Beach; the Jungle hosts Ladies' Night

**Friday** Reggae beach party at Alfred's Ocean Palace

**Saturday** Live reggae night at Bourbon Beach; Party Night at the Jungle

**Sunday** Reggae beach party at Alfred's Ocean Palace; live jazz at Roots Bamboo

the food): you're paying for the ambience, pool access and the live band. While you sip your drink, local divers try to outdo each other from the 10m-tall cliffs.

### Mi Yard
BAR

(Map p142; ☑957-4442; West End Rd; ☺24hr) Popular with locals, this place draws a late-night crowd into the wee hours, when you can swig shots of white rum and slap down dominoes with the Rastas. Food served around the clock, too.

### Sir D's Firewater Love Nest
BAR

(Map p148; ☑521-0260; West End Rd; ☺4-10pm) If all you want is to watch the greatest show on earth – Negril's fiery sunset – with a Red Stripe in your hand, then this friendly little place that clings to the clifftop fits the bill perfectly.

## ☆ Entertainment

Negril's reggae concerts are legendary, with live performances every night in peak season. Several venues offer regular weekly jams, so they all get a piece of the action. You will also find sound-system jams where the DJs play shatteringly loud music – usually dancehall – on giant speakers. Most bars start the night playing reggae oldies and bust out the dancehall later.

### ★ Bourbon Beach
LIVE MUSIC

(Map p144; ☑957-4432; www.bourbonbeachnegril. com; Norman Manley Blvd; entry fee varies; ☺from 8pm Mon, Thu & Sat) The best spot for live reggae on Seven Mile Beach, Bourbon Beach has hosted such greats as John Holt and Gregory Isaacs; younger talent appears on Thursdays. Saturday is dancehall night. The lively bar is open daily and the jerk is excellent, too.

### Roots Bamboo
LIVE MUSIC

(Map p144; ☑957-4479; www.rootsbamboohotel. com; Norman Manley Blvd; ☺Wed & Sun) With a rotating roster of musicians anchored by a rock-solid 'riddim' section, the house Hurricane Band shows tourists a thing or two about roots music here each Wednesday. On selected nights, big dancehall shows rock the beach, while Sunday is jazz night.

### Alfred's Ocean Palace
LIVE MUSIC

(Map p144; ☑957-4669; www.alfreds.com; Norman Manley Blvd; US$5; ☺Tue, Fri & Sun) This Negril institution is one of the oldest beach bars. The Live Reggae Beach Parties feature local and occasional international acts, starting around 10pm and running deep into the night.

### Jungle
CLUB

(Map p144; ☑954-4005; www.junglenegril.com; Norman Manley Blvd; US$7-10; ☺10pm-4am Thu-Sat) The only bona fide nightclub outside the all-inclusives, Jungle, with its tacky decor, is not the most urbane place, but the DJs *definitely* know what they're doing; during high season guest talent from Miami and New York regularly takes command of the turntables. Thursday is Ladies' Night and Saturday is great for partying until dawn.

##  Shopping

Locals hawk carvings, woven caps, hammocks, jewelry, macramé bikinis and T-shirts on the beach and along West End Rd. Competition is fierce. Haggling is part of the fun. With the exception of some wooden carvings, bamboo items, rum and coffee, most handicrafts are mass-produced in China, Indonesia and India, but most sellers and shop owners will lie outright if asked.

### Negril Crafts Market
ARTS & CRAFTS

(Map p144; www.negrilcraftmarket.com; Norman Manley Blvd; ☺dawn-dusk) Just north of Plaza de Negril. Crafts that are locally made are the varnished wooden carvings (you'll see some guys carving), plus some woven hats, baskets and some 'jungle jewelry'. The rest is uninspiring: Chinese factory-made tat, and rip-offs of Haitian art.

### Kuyaba Arts & Crafts Boutique
ARTS & CRAFTS

(Map p144; Norman Manley Blvd; ☺9am-5pm) At the Kuyaba hotel (p142), with a nice craft selection, Caribbean art and assorted Africana.

### Top Spot
BOOKS

(Map p142; ☑957-4542; Sunshine Village, West End Rd; ☺9am-5pm Mon-Sat) Well stocked with international publications.

## ℹ Information

### DANGERS & ANNOYANCES
➡ Do not walk between Seven Mile Beach and the West End at night. Tourists have been, and continue to be, mugged while walking through this area. It's best to avoid dark patches of beach; the locals in Negril, police and civilian, are good about patrolling these areas, but sometimes a mugger slips through. At night you should definitely take taxis.

➡ Hustlers stalk Negril like nowhere else in Jamaica. You can expect to be endlessly offered everything from drugs to the hustlers themselves. Usually – but not always – you can shake them off with a firm 'no,' but Negril hustlers can be pretty in your face, and some will try to cop an attitude with you if they think it will intimidate you into giving them some money. Tourist police now patrol the beach but, by law, all Jamaican beaches must permit public access so the hustlers are free to roam, like it or not.

➡ Ganja is smoked in plain view in Negril, as it has been decriminalized in Jamaica; it is legal to have some on you for personal use only.

➡ Prostitution is an established part of the local scene and short-term holiday liaisons are a staple. Female visitors should expect to hear a constant litany of well-honed lines enticing you to sample some 'Jamaican steel.'

### EMERGENCY
**Police Station** (957-4268; Sheffield Rd)

### INTERNET ACCESS
Internet cafes are difficult to come by with the proliferation of (often free) wi-fi in hotels and restaurants.

**Blue Water Internet** (884-6030; West End Rd; per 20min/hr J$200/500; 8am-11pm) Very high-tech equipment; this cafe also serves delicious ice cream.

### MEDICAL SERVICES
For any major medical issues, you're best off heading to the private hospital in Montego Bay.

**Negril Health Centre** (957-4926; Sheffield Rd; 9am-8pm Mon-Fri)

**Negril Minor Emergency Clinic** (Norman Manley Blvd; 9am-5pm, doctor on call 24hr)

**Negril Pharmacy** (957-4076; Plaza de Negril; 9am-7pm Mon-Sat, 10am-2pm Sun)

### MONEY
While many hotels offer currency exchange, you'll get better rates at banks. It pays to come to Negril with both Jamaican dollars and US dollars, as places quoting prices in US dollars often use a poor exchange rate if you're paying in Jamaican dollars. Equally, if you pay in US dollars in places quoting their prices in Jamaican dollars, you'll get a poor exchange rate.

**National Commercial Bank** (NCB; West End Rd; 9am-5pm Mon-Sat)

**Scotiabank** (957-4236; Negril Sq; 9am-5pm Mon-Sat)

### POST
**Post Office** (Map p142; West End Rd; 8am-5pm Mon-Fri) Between A Fi Wi Plaza and King's Plaza.

## ⓘ Getting There & Away

### AIR
**Negril Aerodrome** (Map p146; 957-5016) At Bloody Bay, about 11km north of Negril Village, is served by the domestic charter company **TimAir** (957-2516; www.timair.net) An 'air taxi' service offering on-demand charter flights for small groups going to Montego Bay, Ocho Rios, Port Antonio and Kingston.

### BUS
From the **transportation center** (Map p142; Sheffield Rd), dozens of minibuses and route taxis run between Negril and Montego Bay. The 1½-hour journey costs between J$350 and J$500. Minibuses and route taxis also leave for Negril from Donald Sangster International Airport in Montego Bay (the price is negotiable, but expect to pay about US$15).

The handy and comfortable **Knutsford Express** (Map p144; 971-1822; www.knutsfordexpress.com; Norman Manley Blvd; 6:15am-8pm) runs one daily bus at 8am to Kingston (J$3100, five hours) via Savanna-la-Mar (J$600, 40 minutes) and Mandeville (J$2250, 3¼ hours), and two daily buses to Kingston (J$3100, 5¼ hours) that stop in Montego Bay (J$1600, 1½ hours), Falmouth (J$1850, two hours) and Ocho Rios (J$2500, 3½ hours) en route. Buses depart across the street from Times Square Plaza.

---

**DON'T MISS**

## ZIMBALI
............................................................................

In the hills above Little London, the wonderful organic farm Zimbali Retreat (485-2789; www.zimbaliretreats.com; Caanan Mountain, Little London; 4-course lunch/5-course dinner US$50/60; Mon-Sat; ) has become the go-to destination for some of Jamaica's most sophisticated meals (including imaginative vegetarian options), served in a strikingly stylish yet rustic bar. Book ahead for a morning or evening slot; the farm tour is included. Head north from Little London for 5km, or take a tour from Negril.

Better yet, you can stay in one of the seven snug rooms on the property (US$99 per person incl full board), swing in a hammock overlooking the lush hillside, and do numerous outings in the hills – hiking, swimming in the river and enjoying a cookout with a local Rasta over a wood fire. Pickups from Negril cost US$15.

TAXI

**TAXI**

→ A licensed **Jamaica Union of Travelers Association** (JUTA; ☑ 979-0778) taxi between Montego Bay and Negril will cost about US$100.

→ **Tropical Tours** (☑ 957-4110; www.tropical-toursja.com) offers shuttles between Montego Bay and Negril for around US$40.

## ❶ Getting Around

Negril stretches along more than 16km of shoreline, and it can be a withering walk. At some stage you'll likely need transportation. Upscale resorts at the north end of Seven Mile Beach have shuttles to the village, and several hotels on the West End run shuttles to the beach. Otherwise your options are route taxi or car/scooter/bicycle rental.

### BICYCLE & SCOOTER

More than a dozen places along Norman Manley Blvd and West End Rd rent motorcycles (US$40 to US$50 per day), scooters (US$45 to US$40) and bicycles (US$10 to US$15). For bicycle rentals, try **Wright's Bike Rental** (☑ 957-4908; Norman Manley Blvd). **Tyke's Bike Rental** (☑ 957-0388; West End Rd; ⊗ 8am-5pm), **Gas Bike Rental** (☑ 957-4835; West End Rd; per day US$10) and **Dependable Bike Rental** (☑ 957-4354; Norman Manley Blvd; ⊗ 9am-5pm) also rent scooters.

### CAR

Local car-rental companies include **Vernon's Car Rentals** (☑ 957-4354, 957-4522; Norman Manley Blvd) and **Jus Jeep** (☑ 957-0094; West End Rd). High-season rates start at around US$50 per day.

### ROUTE TAXI

Route taxis cruise the length of Seven Mile Beach and West End Rd all the time. You can flag them down anywhere. The fare between any two points was J$130 at research time during the day (they'll always take you as far as Negril Sq from either the West End or Seven Mile Beach). In the evenings, it can be up to J$200 per hop.

### TAXI

→ Tourist taxis display a red license plate.

→ Few drivers use meters. Negotiate your fare before stepping into the cab.

→ Do not get in a car if it doesn't have red plates and/or its route transfer displayed on the side.

→ Your hotel will call a cab for you, or you can order taxis from JUTA.

→ There are taxi stands at the Negril Crafts Market (p151) and in front of Coral Seas Plaza.

# NEGRIL TO MAYFIELD FALLS

## Green Island Harbour & Around

Immediately north of Negril, the A1 swings around a wide expanse of swampland – the Great Morass – and runs for 30km or so to Lucea on the north coast, ducking into half a dozen bays and coves on the way. Instead of dashing straight through, you can take it slow, visit a plantation, relax on a secluded beach, and perhaps stop for lunch in Green Island Harbour, where pirogues line the thin, gray-sand shore.

Numerous minibuses and route taxis ply the coastal highway between Negril and Montego Bay and can drop you off en route.

## ⊙ Sights

**Half Moon Beach**                        BEACH

(☑ 531-4508;     www.halfmoonbeachjamaica.com; US$5; ⊗ 9am-9pm) Around 12km north of Negril, Half Moon Beach is a beautiful, hassle-free stretch of sand beloved by locals and families, with calm, shallow water. On weekends there's sometimes live music, and a new island restaurant, Calico Jack's, has opened on a nearby island (US$5 round-trip by boat); serving tasty seafood, it's Negril's answer to the Pelican Bar. The beach is part of the Negril Marine Park; there are healthy reefs just offshore and no motorized watercraft. Topless sunbathing is permitted.

**Rhodes Hall Plantation**             PLANTATION

(☑ 957-6883; www.rhodesresort.com; Hwy A1; day pass US$15; ⊗ 9am-5pm) Around 10km northeast of Negril, this picturesque 220-hectare fruit-and-coconut plantation with several thatched bars and a restaurant backs a small, attractive beach where hot mineral springs bubble up. Numerous attractions are on offer here, from a walking tour through the coastal mangroves in search of crocodiles (US$30) and excursions to a nearby Arawak cave (US$40) to horseback rides through the lush, hilly countryside (US$70 for 1½ hours) and glass-bottom-boat outings to the offshore reef for snorkeling (US$40).

## Lucea

POP 7131

The halfway point between Negril and Montego Bay, 'Lucy' is a pretty harbor ringed by

NEGRIL & WEST COAST GREEN ISLAND HARBOUR & AROUND

hills on three sides, small enough for visitors to walk everywhere and charming enough to grab your attention for more than a quick blow through.

A bustling port during the sugarcane era, today it abounds in old limestone-and-timber structures in 'Caribbean vernacular' style, with gingerbread wood trim, clapboard frontages and wide verandas. The oldest dates to the mid-1700s, and although there is a general air of dishevelment, this is a well-preserved historic town. Lucea is atmospheric enough to have made an appearance in several films, including *Cool Runnings* and *Wide Sargasso Sea*.

There are no recommendable options in town. Most people press on to Negril or MoBay.

## ◉ Sights

### Sir Alexander
### Bustamante Square                    HISTORIC SITE
Bustamante Square is centered on a small fountain fronting the handsome former courthouse (now housing the Hanover Parish Council). Note the vintage 1932 fire engine beside the courthouse.

The courthouse has limestone balustrades and a clapboard upper story topped by a clock tower supported by Corinthian columns. The clock was sent to Lucea in 1817 by mistake – it was actually intended for the Caribbean island of St Lucia. It has supposedly worked without a hitch ever since.

On the east side of the square is Cleveland Stanhope market, which bustles on Saturdays.

### Hanover Museum                        MUSEUM
(☑ 956-2584; Watson Taylor Dr; J$400; ⊙ 8:30am-5pm Mon-Thu, to 4pm Fri) A side road beside the Catholic church leads to this interesting, refurbished museum inside the former Hanover workhouse, which has served as a prison and police station. It's an absorbing insight into the sugar-plantation era, with local slave records, a gibbet, stocks and manacles on display, as well as a hand-drawn map of Lucea Harbour by Captain William Bligh. Taíno articles found at nearby Moskito Cove are also displayed here alongside miscellaneous English lead weights and measures.

### Headland                             LANDMARK
(Watson Taylor Dr) On the headland beyond the parish church is Rusea High School, a venerable Georgian-style redbrick building constructed in 1843 as an army barracks. The overgrown remains of Fort Charlotte overlook the channel a short distance beyond Rusea High School. It's named after Queen Charlotte, wife of King George III of England. The octagonal fortress still boasts cannons in its embrasures.

Buses, minibuses and route taxis bound for MoBay (J$250, one hour) and Negril (J$300, one hour) arrive at and depart from the open ground opposite Lucea's market.

## Mayfield

Few of Jamaica's waterfall experiences match Mayfield Falls (☑ 792-2074; www.mayfieldfalls.com; Glenbrook; adult/under 9yr US$20/10; ⊙ 9am-5pm) for crowd-free natural beauty. Picture this: you climb into the cool river beneath giant thickets of bamboo and scramble upstream for around 40 minutes, swim through an underwater tunnel, jump into the deeper pools, then sit bubbling in the froth of a natural Jacuzzi and letting the 'washing machine' falls pound your shoulders. Arrive by potholed roads from Sav-la-Mar via Williamsfield and Grange, or via Cascade or Lucea Harbour from the A1.

The entrance area to the falls has been sensitively developed, with a changing area, lockers, water-shoe rental (US$7), a good restaurant (mains US$12 to US$18) and excellent guides who earn money from your tips and who are on hand to help you up the river and take photos of you.

Refrain from wearing sunscreen and bug repellent when swimming in the river.

None of the roads leading here are terribly well signposted, but the falls are not difficult to find. Some of the potholes are the size of Cleveland, but a regular car will get you there provided you take it slowly on some sections. Some tour companies run trips here from Montego Bay and Negril.

## SOUTH OF NEGRIL

Tourism has been slow to develop along the southern shore of Westmoreland, a parish dependent on the sugar industry. This is a picturesque part of the country – a flat, mountain-rimmed area, planted almost entirely in sugarcane and drained by the Cabarita River, which feeds swamplands at its lower reaches. There are several low-key attractions to explore as you're passing through, and more visitors now venture off the beaten track to the fishing village of Brighton (Little Bay) for some timeless sea-gazing.

# Little Bay & Around

Just 14km southeast of Negril, a narrow side road loops down to **Homers Cove** (locals call it 'Brighton Beach') and, immediately east, Little Bay, with deserted beaches and peaceful bathing. Little Bay is imbued with the kind of laid-back feel that pervaded Negril before the onset of commercialization. It's a great place to commune with Rastas and other Jamaicans who live a quiet life in ramshackle homes, dependent on fishing and their entrepreneurial wits. Little Bay is where Bob Marley once lived with one of his girlfriends, and locals can point out his former house. The main attraction around here is the Blue Hole, a sinkhole popular with jumping daredevils, and the clutch of leisure facilities that have sprung up around it, including a sound system that lures a local crowd from miles around.

## Sights

**Blue Hole Mineral Spring**    SPRING
(860-8805; Brighton; swimmers/nonswimmers US$10/5; ⊙9am-11pm) This popular sinkhole, an 8km drive southeast from the A2, has long been a feature on the landscape, and has recently become even more popular with the advent of an eight-room hotel on the property and a rocking sound system. The sinkhole requires a 20ft-plus plunge into refreshing mineral waters below, or you can descend via a ladder. There's an adjacent swimming pool and a bar-restaurant, which cooks jerk – tasty enough to persuade you to linger for an hour or three.

**Jurassic Park**    SCULPTURE
(entry by donation; ⊙10am-sunset) **FREE** Between Negril and Little Bay, a bumpy back road passes through the village of Orange Hill, (in)famous around the island as a major marijuana cultivation and distribution center. Jurassic Park is on the main road toward the Blue Hole turnoff; look for the giant iron pterodactyl on a plinth. Inside the small sculpture garden there are more pterodactyls (one with a human hand in its beak), giant centipedes, a cobra and smaller pieces, created by friendly local sculptor Daniel 'Iron Doctor' Woolcock.

## Sleeping & Eating

Little Bay has several low-key eateries that serve mostly seafood.

**OFF THE BEATEN TRACK**

If you want to get away from it all, try visiting **Mountambrin Villa & Gallery** (357-6363; canutegruhlke@yahoo.com; 120 Great George St; r US$96), up in the hills inland from Savanna-la-Mar, an otherwise undistinguished town. The former estate of Alex Haley, author of Roots, has been turned into a unique boutique guesthouse, surrounded by 800 acres of lush grounds, crisscrossed by hiking trails and ideal for birdwatching. There's a contemporary art gallery onsite, with a resident painter and sculptor, and bimonthly music evenings. Call for directions.

**Judy House Backpacker Hostel**    HOSTEL $
(424-5481; www.judyhousenegril.com; tent per person US$10) The Brighton offshoot of the excellent hostel in Negril is a bona fide backpacker haunt where you can camp out under the stars (tents provided), roam the beaches and check out the Blue Hole. Cooking facilities and shared bathrooms on-site. It's a 10-minute walk east of the Blue Hole.

**Richies on the Beach**    GUESTHOUSE $
(368-0376; www.richiesonthebeach.com; Little Bay; r from US$60; ❀✸) This delightful two-room guesthouse is right across the road from the beach in Little Bay. The home cooking is excellent and there's a breezy little terrace overlooking the lapping waves. It's on a badly potholed stretch of coastal road, around 10km southwest of the Little London turnoff.

**Little Bay Cabins**    CABIN $
(588-6700; www.littlebaycabins.com; Beach Rd; cottages US$50-75; ✸) If you want total detachment from Negril-esque clamor, track down the coast to this haven of blissfulness where you can convene with the local fishers. There are six rustic, fan-cooled cottages on the property, all with shaded verandas and meals provided on request. It's right on the water in Little Bay.

## Getting There & Away

You need your own wheels to get out to Little Bay. The Little Bay road from the signposted turnoff for Blue Hole, around 14km east of Negril, to Little London is mostly good but narrow and potholed, with a particularly bumpy stretch along the seafront.

# South Coast & Central Highlands

## Why Go?

Cut off from the clamorous north coast by the natural bulwark of Cockpit Country and protected from resort development by local communities that seriously value their near-virgin beaches, southwest Jamaica feels like a clandestine paradise for the trickle of off-island visitors who make it this far. Its biggest present is Treasure Beach, an antidote to pretty much everything else in Jamaica you will have encountered so far with its cow-filled pastures, a soporific pace of life and semi-deserted scimitars of sand.

Rural St Elizabeth parish is often called the breadbasket of Jamaica for the many crops that grow here, but fertile fields quickly give way to swamp around Black River and mountains around the lightly touristed, highland town of Mandeville. The region's most notable sights – the Black River, YS Falls and the Appleton Rum Estate – are usually visited by day-trippers on organized excursions from resorts in Negril and Montego Bay.

## Best Places to Eat

➡ Little Ochie (p165)

➡ Jack Sprat (p163)

➡ Jake's Country Cuisine (p164)

➡ Strikie-T (p163)

## Best Places to Sleep

➡ Katamah Beachfront Resort (p162)

➡ Jake's Hotel (p162)

➡ Luna Sea Inn (p171)

➡ Bluefields Villas (p171)

## When to Go

### Black River

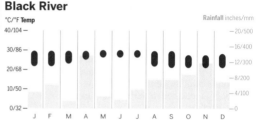

**Jan** The Accompong Maroon Festival is a compelling celebration of Afro-Caribbean culture.

**Dec–Apr** It's high season for a reason: little chance of hurricanes or rain, and calmer seas.

**Jun** Come to Treasure Beach for the biannual Calabash International Literary Festival.

# TREASURE BEACH & AROUND

The sun-kissed land southeast of Black River is sheltered from rain for most of the year by the Santa Cruz Mountains, so there is none of the lush greenery of the north coast. Instead, you'll find a thorny, surreally beautiful landscape almost East African in its scorched beauty. The region remains unsullied by resort-style tourism; bohemians and wealthy recluses alike come to Treasure Beach to slip into a lazy, no-frills tropical lifestyle almost impossible to achieve elsewhere on the island's coast.

Dividing the plains north to south is the aforementioned Santa Cruz range, a steep-faced chain that slopes to the sea and drops 520m at wonderfully scenic Lovers' Leap, while fishermen toil at Alligator Pond to feed diners with some of the freshest and tastiest catch in Jamaica.

## Treasure Beach

Welcome to a unique part of Jamaica that gets all the facets of the quintessential Caribbean experience exactly right. Winding country lanes, a dearth of hustlers, a local population of poets and artists, sublime deserted beaches, no gimmicky resorts, and – above all – a proud, foresighted local community that promotes sustainability and harbors a bonhomous but mellow culture. Too good to be true? Not at all.

Treasure Beach is the generic name for four coves – Billy's Bay, Frenchman's Bay, Calabash Bay and Great Bay. It's said Scottish sailors were shipwrecked near Treasure Beach in the 19th century, accounting for the presence of fair skin, green eyes and reddish hair among the local population. The area's residents are known for their strong community spirit. Collectives such as the Treasure Beach Women's Group and the Treasure Beach Foundation bring locals and expats together to work on projects relating to housing, education and local culture.

### ◉ Sights

**Fishermen's Beach**                           BEACH
(Frenchman's Bay) This is the most centrally located beach running east from the Treasure Beach Hotel as far as Jack Spratt Beach. It's watched over by a landmark buttonwood tree that has long attracted the attention of poets, painters and wood-carvers who ply their wares. It's a good place for sunning and swimming, and watching the sunset.

**Jack Sprat Beach**                            BEACH
(Frenchman's Cove) At the western edge of Jake's Hotel, brightly painted wooden fishing boats are pulled up on the sand, and there is invariably a fisher or two on hand tending the nets. Good for swimming, as it's somewhat sheltered.

**Calabash Bay Beach**                          BEACH
(Calabash Bay) The long, narrow arc of Calabash Bay Beach has a few beach shacks plying rum and – if you're lucky – some basic potluck cuisine (fish, mainly). Swimming is possible but can be choppy.

**Old Wharf Beach**                             BEACH
This pristine brown-sand beach is the least visited of the Treasure Beach bunch. It's just east of Taino Cove, and OK for swimming as long as the sea isn't too rough.

**Great Bay Beach**                             BEACH
(Great Bay) All the way down at the eastern 'bottom' of Treasure Beach, this is its least developed portion, where the main business remains a Fishermen's Co-op building. There are a couple of beachside shacks serving beer and cooking up fresh seafood. Swimming is possible.

### 🏃 Activities

With a long history (and a large population) of seafaring fishers, it's no wonder Treasure Beach is a great place from which to take to the sea, either for sightseeing or fishing. Cooking classes and yoga are organised at Jake's (p162), and spa treatments are available at Jake's and Lotus House (☑ 965-3820; Main Rd; massage US$70-90).

#### Boat Trips

From Frenchman's Beach, boat captains Dennis Abrahams (☑ 435-3779; dennisabrahams@yahoo.com) and Mr Nice Guy (☑ 433-0252; besutherland@yahoo.com) run combined trips to the Black River Great Morass (p168) and Pelican Bar (p164) and can organise fishing outings. Other recommended captains include Allan Daley (☑ 366-7394, 423-3673), Teddy Parchment (☑ 854-5442) and Joseph Brown (☑ 847-1951, 376-9944). Expect to pay around US$30 for a trip out to Pelican Bar and US$50 for a combo trip to Black River, although bear in mind the shifting cost of petrol makes prices subject to change.

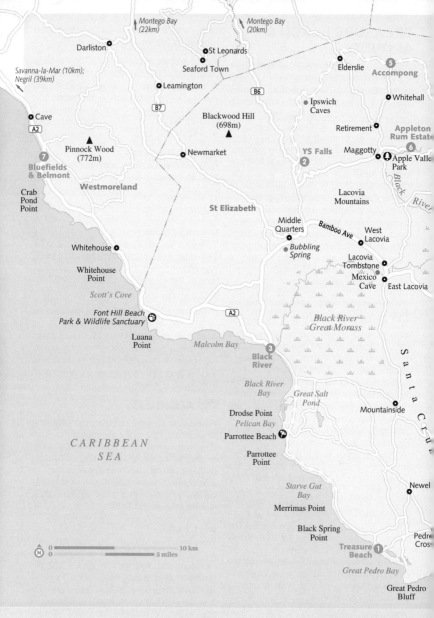

## South Coast & Central Highlands Highlights

**1 Treasure Beach** (p157)
Watching fisherfolk mending their nets and enjoying the slow pace of life in Jamaica's premier bohemian destination.

**2 YS Falls** (p179) Frolicking in the cool river pools or flying over the falls on a zip line.

**3 Black River** (p166) Croc-spotting in the mangroves fringing Jamaica's longest

river or touring the town's historic monuments.

**4 Little Ochie** (p165)
Watching your fish being caught, brought ashore and cooked at one of Jamaica's

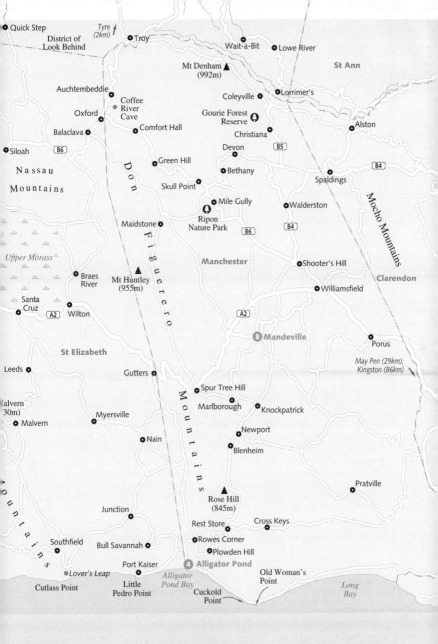

Quick Step

District of
Look Behind

Tyre
(2km)

Troy

Wait-a-Bit

Lowe River

St Ann

Mt Denham ▲
(992m)

Auchtembeddie

Coffee
River
Cave

Coleyville

Lorrimer's

Oxford

Gourie Forest
Reserve

Alston

Balaclava

Comfort Hall

Christiana

Siloah

B6

Devon

B5

Nassau

Green Hill

Bethany

Spaldings

B4

Mountains

Skull Point

Walderston

B4

Mile Gully

Ripon
Nature Park

B6

Manchester

Mocho Mountains

Maidstone

Upper Morass

Shooter's Hill

Braes
River

Mt Huntley ▲
(955m)

Williamsfield

Clarendon

Santa
Cruz

Wilton

A2

A2

Leeds

St Elizabeth

Mandeville

Porus

Gutters

May Pen (29km);
Kingston (86km)

Spur Tree Hill

Malvern
(30m)

Myersville

Marlborough

Knockpatrick

Malvern

Nain

Newport

Mountains

Blenheim

Pratville

Rose Hill ▲
(845m)

Junction

Rest Store

Cross Keys

Southfield

Bull Savannah

Rowes Corner

Plowden Hill

Port Kaiser

Alligator Pond

Lover's Leap

Alligator
Pond Bay

Old Woman's
Point

Cutlass Point

Little
Pedro Point

Cuckold
Point

Long
Bay

finest seafood restaurants in
Alligator Pond.

**5** **Accompong** (p176)
Heeding the call of the ancient
*abeng* (goat horn) at this well-
preserved Maroon village.

**6** **Appleton Rum Estate**
(p178) Delving into the island's
largest rum distillery before
sampling its wares.

**7** **Bluefields & Belmont**

(p170) Chilling with the Rastas
in the laid-back countryside.

**8** **Mandeville** (p172)
Exploring this wonderfully
untouristy highland town.

# Treasure Beach

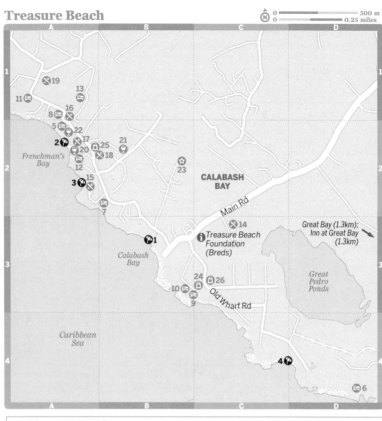

## Treasure Beach

The best time to book a trip is during the early morning or late afternoon; the winds tend to pick up during the middle of the day.

On bright moonlit evenings it's possible to take to the silvery waters for an enchanting tour of the coast.

Everyone with a boat in Treasure Beach is involved in some way with the pursuit of fishing, and it's easy to talk someone into taking you out to pull a trap or drop a line. Or you can book a fishing trip at Jake's Hotel (p162), which includes rods and bait. Fish frequently caught include grouper, kingfish and snapper; most restaurants are happy to prepare them for the night's dinner.

## 👉 Tours

**Treasure Tours** OUTDOORS
(📞 965-0126; www.treasuretoursjamaica.com; ⊕ 9:30am-5:30pm Mon-Fri) This excellent local outfit supports local communities around the south coast and arranges trips to YS Falls, Appleton Rum Estate, Black River, Negril and turtle-spotting in Treasure Beach. Airport transfers to Kingston and MoBay available.

**Dennis Abrahams** BOATING
(📞 435-3779; dennisabrahams@yahoo.com) A boat captain with more than two decades' experience, Dennis runs combo trips to Black River and Pelican Bar (US$50) as well as other boat outings.

## 🎊 Festivals & Events

**Calabash International
Literary Festival** LITERATURE
(📞 965-3000; www.calabashfestival.org; ⊕ late May/early Jun, even-numbered years) A daring, acclaimed literary festival at Jake's Hotel, drawing literary voices both domestically and internationally.

**New Year's Eve Bonfire Party** PARTY
At Fisherman's Beach, this boisterous party is an institution in these parts.

## 🛏 Sleeping

Accommodations range from backpacker-friendly, Rasta-run guesthouses scented with di holy 'erb to exclusive, secluded villas. Some provide bona fide luxury and considerable style, while others are more modest and practical, providing good value for groups or families. Details can be found at www.treasurebeach.net, www.jamaicaescapes.com and www.treasuretoursjamaica.com.

**★Welcoming Vibes** GUESTHOUSE $
(📞 538-8779; www.welcomingvibes.org; Church St; r $39; 🔊) The amazing open-air terrace of this house on the hill drinks in the full expanse of Frenchman's Bay while the common area fills with the aromatic smoke of di 'erb. The four spacious, en-suite, bug-netted

rooms are airy and cool and friendly owner Paul is happy to shoot the breeze. Park below and take the steep footpath up.

**Golden Sands Beach Hotel** HOTEL $
(📞 965-0167; www.goldensandstreasurebeach.com; 3-bedroom apt US$210-240; ❄🔊) This is one of the original Treasure Beach hotels, right on Frenchman's Beach. The rooms and apartments are tiled, plain and spacious, and tend to vary: the cheapies have ceiling fans, some of the pricier rooms boast sea views, while one- and three-bedroom cottages come with air-con, TV and kitchens. Location is everything, and service is friendly and helpful.

**Irie Rest Guesthouse** GUESTHOUSE $
(📞 965-0034; www.irierestguesthouse.com; Billy's Bay Way; r/q/whole house US$40/50/200; ❄🔊) An excellent budget choice, Irie consists of spacious rooms with tile floors outfitted in Rasta chic, arranged around open courtyards and lush gardens. The entire house can be rented out – a great deal if you're in a big group. Did we mention it's a five-minute walk to the beach? Find it around the corner from Strikie-T.

**Viking's Rasta Retreat** GUESTHOUSE $
(📞 457-4829; www.vikingsrastaretreats.com; Great Bay; s/d US$45/50; 🔊) Viking's is as rustic as it gets, with three slightly tatty rooms, two with kitchenettes and private bathrooms, located on a gravel track near Great Bay. The place has a lot of I-tal character; it's run by serious, religiously observant Rastafarians. As such, staying here can be an excellent means of learning about the deeper layers of Rasta belief. Viking's can also feel like being on a particularly Jamaican agricultural homestay, where guests chill out in (very) relaxed silence in Treasure Beach's version of the bush.

**Ital Rest** GUESTHOUSE $
(📞 421-8909, 473-6145; Great Bay; r US$50) In the right setting, a lack of electricity rockets a property right into the super-romantic category. Two exquisite all-wood thatched cabins are the deal here. Hang with the Rasta owners as the sun sets, then retire to a candlelit room with a loved one. All rooms have toilets and the upstairs room has a great sundeck. Kitchen facilities are shared.

**Waikiki Guest House** GUESTHOUSE $
(📞 965-3577; www.facebook.com/waikiki.house; Frenchman's Beach; r US$38-70; ❄🔊) Location, location, location: this solid budget option

## THE ENDANGERED TURTLES OF TREASURE BEACH

This stretch of Jamaica's south coast used to be a breeding ground for several species of turtles. All but 140 or so critically endangered hawksbill turtles are gone now, due to a combination of factors: illegal hunting, destruction of nesting habitat, and predators: dogs running loose, and mongooses digging up and eating the eggs. Under Jamaican law, the penalty for killing a turtle is US$100,000, but it is not enforced, and it's common knowledge that turtle hunting is practised west of Billy's Bay, where the road is poor, and education and job opportunities are low.

Some concerned locals have set up the worthwhile **Natural History Museum** (☑ 304-7778, 562-3855; admission J$400; ⏱ 9am-noon & 1-4pm Mon-Sat) near the nesting beaches to educate the public about the turtles' plight. Treasure Tours (p161) liaise with the turtle protection group, jointly running turtle-watching tours from June to September.

abuts Frenchman's Beach. The rooms, scattered across two cottages and a house, are clean and basic, with a minimum of features (no fridges). The 2nd-floor double in Waikiki's odd concrete tower (prettier than it sounds) is awesome; you can step out onto a little veranda and watch the sun set into the ocean.

### ★ Katamah
**Beachfront Resort**     BOUTIQUE HOTEL $$
(☑ 567-9562; www.katamah.com; ❄ 🖥) There's something for everyone at this adorable beachside place – from the three sensual, Moroccan-style rooms and the Berry Suite in the main house to the two breezy little cabins with hammocks under the trees. There are even three large glamping tents and thatched beachside gazebos for chilling. Owner Ricky can hook you up with a reliable local boat captain.

### Marblue Villa Suites
**Boutique Hotel**     BOUTIQUE HOTEL $$
(☑ 848-0001, 840-5772; Old Wharf Rd; junior ste US$125-145, ste from US$199; ❄ 🖥 🏊) One of Jamaica's most stylish boutique hotels, this well-run, welcoming property pampers its guests with thoughtful service and considerable, streamlined luxury. Five one-bedroom villa suites and one two-bedroom suite are appointed with furniture designed by the owners, Axel (architect) and Andrea Wichterich. Each veranda suite features living areas that open to spectacular views of the sea.

Two dramatic pools, superb meals arranged on request, and massage services in guest rooms round out the offerings. It's accessible for travelers with disabilities.

### Kudeyha Guesthouse     HOTEL $$
(☑ 870-7162; Old Wharf Rd; US$95-110; 🅿 🖥) 🐾 The only common link in Treasure Beach accommodations is they're all wonderful – but for different reasons. Kudeyha is a newish

offering within splashing distance of the waves that carries a Rastafarian theme in its three drop-dead gorgeous suites. One has a kitchenette, all have private bathrooms and coffee machines. I-tal meals can be arranged with ingredients plucked from the garden.

### Treasure Beach Hotel     HOTEL $$
(☑ 965-0110; www.jamaicatreasurebeachhotel. com; d garden/seaview US$116/125; ❄ 🖥 🏊) This rambling property, dotted with palms and nestled on a hillside overlooking the beach, has a good variety of midrange-quality rooms, including spacious, deluxe oceanfront suites that have king-size-four-poster beds and breezy patios. The Yabba Restaurant is on the premises, and the front desk can hook you up with a good range of tours and activities across the region.

### Southview Hotel     HOTEL $$
(☑ 965-0654; www.southviewhoteljamaica.com; r US$80-200; 🖥 🏊) 🐾 Southview is accessed via a winding lane that cuts through bucolic grassy pastures; it's around 4km inland from the beach and rather isolated. The main bonus here is the service – the convivial owners will go out of their way to help you, including picking you up from the beach after dinner. Set in fertile gardens with fruit trees and two swimming pools. The hotel is partly powered by its own wind turbine.

### ★ Jake's Hotel     BOUTIQUE HOTEL $$$
(☑ 965-3000, in the USA 800-688-7678; www.jakes hotel.com; r US$145-480; @ 🖥 🏊) 🐾 If you haven't been to Jake's, you haven't really been to Treasure Beach. This romance-drenched boutique hotel is the nexus of pretty much everything in the area – cooking courses, yoga classes and mosaic workshops all happen here. Individually crafted rooms spurn TVs but are big on style and atmosphere.

It's owned by Jason Henzell, son of film director Perry Henzell who conceived Jamaica's great seminal movie *The Harder They Come* in 1972.

### Minerva VILLA $$$

(⌂969-4828; www.minervahouse.com; per night for 1-8 people US$700; 🐾🏊) West of Billy's Bay, Minerva feels very much like a trendy Manhattan or Melbourne mansion with its cool white walls, polished-stone floors, monochromatic color scheme and furniture plucked from the drawing board of a painfully hip Scandinavian designer. The pool is lovely for lounging, as is the buttery-golden private beach.

## ✕🍴 Eating

Treasure Beach has an excellent dining scene, ranging from local eateries serving Jamaican standards to some of the best pizza on the island and fusion cuisine.

### Kim's Place BURGERS $

(⌂873-9148; Cassia Tree, Frenchman's Bay; mains J$800-1300; ⊙noon-10pm Sun-Fri) Shaded by the large cassia tree, this little cookshop serves excellent homemade burgers and freshly caught fried fish. If you've been missing your veggie, ask for an epic side salad. Locals play dominoes and shoot the breeze in the attached thatched bar in the evenings.

### Hold a Vibz Cafe CAFE $

(⌂540-7981; off Main Rd, Calabash Bay; smoothies J$450; ⊙8am-4pm; 🖊) This friendly little cafe has won local and visiting fans with its excellent fruit smoothies, revitalising veggie juices and tasty sandwiches and salads. Heading up Main Rd, turn into the little lane just before the gaudy, cake-like yellow-and-green building and walk for around 100m.

### Mellow Yellow ITALIAN, JAMAICAN $

(Frenchman's Bay; mains J$600-1200; ⊙noon-10pm Tue-Sun; 🐾🖊) Sway to the reggae from the speakers at this aptly named roadside

spot, with the few tables scattered about outside. The Italian-Jamaican team cooks up a good mix of Jamaican standards, pasta dishes and the likes of olive-oil-drizzled bruschetta. The muffins made with a certain special ingredient are very potent; heed the ladies' guidance regarding dosage.

### Smurf's Cafe JAMAICAN $

(⌂483-7523; mains J$300-650; ⊙6:30am-1pm) On the surface this is an all-hours bottle shop adorned with kitschy blue Smurf motifs. But out the back is a morning-only cafe that cooks up some of the best breakfasts in Jamaica (calalloo omelets, pancakes with bacon, porridge) and roasts and brews the most delicious and dangerously addictive coffee (J$100). Indulge in the breakfast of champions. Ask if you can purchase some of their micro-roasted coffee.

### ★Strikie-T JAMAICAN $$

(⌂869-8516; Billy's Bay; mains J$1200-2000; ⊙noon-10pm Mon-Sat Nov-Apr) A seasonal affair run by the energetic, ever-friendly Chris 'Strikie' Bennett, who has worked as a professional chef in the US and at Jake's. This understated food shack in Billy's Bay, festooned with fairy lights, is anchored by secret recipes and a hand-built jerk smoker. The food is great: Jamaican favorites, from jerk to lobster, home-cooked and mouth-watering.

### ★Jack Sprat FUSION $$

(⌂965-3583; mains J$700-2400; ⊙10am-11pm) Seafood and pizza aren't obvious bedfellows until you wander into Jack Sprat's, where they put fresh lobster on their thick Italian-style pies. For many it's enhanced by the dreamy location (candlelit tables under twinkle-lit trees) and bohemian interior (a mix of retro reggae and movie posters). The pizza is the best in Jamaica and the

### COMMUNITY CRICKET IN TREASURE BEACH

You'll hear it before you see it; the unmistakable thud of leather on willow, followed by a gentle ripple of appreciative applause. For a dedicated follower of cricket, this quintessential sporting scene needs no further explanation. For those of you who haven't got a clue about the LBW law or how to bowl a 'googly', welcome to an integral part of Jamaican culture.

Slow, unassuming Treasure Beach might have been designed with the rhythms of cricket in mind and cricket games, accompanied by wry commentaries and snippets of skanking reggae music, take place most Sunday afternoons year-round at Treasure Beach Sports Park (p164). Check at Jack Sprat cafe for upcoming schedules. The park's cute clapboard pavilion provides an ideal place to mingle with cricket-savvy locals over an icy Red Stripe as the game slowly unravels. Ply them gently and they might even get around to explaining the LBW law.

homemade crab cakes are ace. Plus there are open-air movie screenings some evenings.

⭐ **Jake's Country Cuisine** FUSION $$
(📞965-3000; www.jakeshotel.com; Calabash Bay; mains US$12-29; ⊙7am-11pm; 🖉) This atmospheric spot in the eponymous hotel serves excellent fare in an open-sided wooden restaurant with low lighting and hip music (you can also dine poolside). The menu shifts daily based on what's growing in the local gardens and what's fresh from the market. Typical dishes include roasted pumpkin soup, jerk lamb, lobster pasta and chocolate cake.

 **Drinking & Nightlife**

Treasure Beach appears to be a sleepy place, but local bars party late into the night until the last person leaves.

⭐**Pelican Bar** BAR
(Caribbean Sea; ⊙10:30am-sunset) A thatched hut on stilts, built on a submerged sandbar 1km out to sea after owner Floyd saw it in a dream, is still Jamaica's – and perhaps the planet's – most enjoyable spot for a drink. You can carve your name into the floorboards, play a game of dominoes, or just chill with a Red Stripe while wading in the shallows.

Getting there is half the fun: hire a local boat captain in Treasure Beach (around US$40) or Parottee (around US$20), who will call ahead to arrange things if you want to eat. This is essential for those who want to take a meal out here (mains are US$10 to US$20), which is novel but frankly not necessary – you'll get better food on land. It's best to come here for a cold Red Stripe (or rum, if such is your fancy). The bar's fame has spread far and wide, and the clientele is a mix of enchanted travelers and repeat-business fishers who while away the hours exchanging pleasantries with the owner.

**Frenchman's Reef** BAR
(📞965-3049; Frenchman's Bay; ⊙8am-11pm) Four words: draught Red Stripe beer (a rarity in Jamaica). Avoid the inexpertly mixed cocktails, but do sample the Jamaican standards and the decent strawberry milkshakes. There's often live music on weekends.

**Fisherman's Nightclub** BAR
(Frenchman's Bay; ⊙noon-late) Up a dirt road near Jake's Hotel, the Fisherman's has an open wooden bar where everyone plays dominoes and watches cricket, and an appealing reggae bar out the back with a rickety stage and powerful sound system where you can relive your Rude Bwai days.

**Eggy's Beach Bar** BAR
(Frenchman's Beach; ⊙9am-11pm) Sitting right on Frenchman's Beach, Eggy's is the place where locals and tourists alike gather to drink beer, watch the sunset and pass around torpedo-sized spliffs. The new and improved quarters mean that Eggy also churns out tasty seafood meals.

☆ **Entertainment**

Jack Sprat (p163) hosts small concerts, poetry readings and outdoor movies on Thursday nights.

**Treasure Beach Sports Park** SPECTATOR SPORT
(Calabash Bay) This badge of the local community was opened in 2012 and contains tennis courts, several football pitches and – pride of place – a cricket oval (p163). Look out for local posters for upcoming events or ask at Jack Sprat (p163) cafe.

🛍 **Shopping**

Due to the high concentration of artistically talented residents, Treasure Beach is an excellent place to shop for high-quality arts, crafts and even fashion – all locally made.

⭐**Africa Village** ARTS & CRAFTS
(Calabash Bay; ⊙11am-6pm) All the creations (bar the drums) inside this traditional mud hut were made by the prolific artist, and children's writer Sharon – half-Maroon and a citizen of the world. Each pendant, artwork, pillow, naturally dyed scarf and tambourine is individually made, fairly priced and has a story behind it, and Sharon is usually around for some impromptu drumming and a chat.

**Callaloo Gift Shop** ARTS & CRAFTS
(Frenchman's Bay; ⊙9am-6pm) Most items in this gift shop are Jamaican-made, including hand-sewn colorful dresses (designed by a former French fashion designer who lives in Treasure Beach) and cushions, hand-painted porcelain, beauty products made from local ingredients, and prints of Jamaican life by local artists. The compact, colorful scenes by Pierre-Henri Philippe are a bargain.

**Treasure Beach Women's Group** ARTS & CRAFTS
(📞965-0748; Old Wharf Rd; ⊙9am-3pm Mon-Fri, 9am-1pm Sat) A good range of locally made crafts is sold here, including batiks, crafts made from calabash shells, wood carvings and 'jungle jewelry' made from seeds.

# ❶ Information

**Dr Valerie M Elliott** (☑ 607-9074; ⊙ 7am-10pm Mon, Tue & Fri) Available on call.

**Police Station** (☑ 965-0163) Between Calabash Bay and Pedro Cross.

**Treasure Beach Foundation** ((Breds); ☑ 965-3000; www.breds.org; Kingfisher Plaza; ⊙ 9am-5pm) The Treasure Beach Foundation – or Breds (short for brethren) – is dedicated to fostering heritage pride, sports, health and education among the community, and represents a partnership between the Treasure Beach community, expats and stakeholders (Jamaican and foreign) in the local tourism industry. This little place also acts as the unofficial tourist office.

Work includes restoring decrepit housing, sponsorship of both a soccer team and a basketball team, the introduction of computer labs at local schools and education for the children of fishers lost at sea.

# ❶ Getting There & Away

There are no direct transport links to Treasure Beach from Montego Bay, Negril or Kingston.

Route taxis run to/from Black River (J$250 to J$350); from Mandeville, you'll need to get a route taxi to Junction or Santa Cruz and another taxi to Treasure Beach (J$200). From Pedro Cross, 7km north, route taxis run to Southfield (for Lovers' Leap) and Junction (transfers to Alligator Pond).

A private taxi will run around US$30 from Black River and US$50 from Mandeville. Most hotels and villas arrange transfers from Montego Bay or Kingston for US$120.

# ❶ Getting Around

A bicycle is a good means of getting around quiet Treasure Beach; some lodgings rent them out for a small fee. There are decent mountain bikes for rent for US$20 per day from **Pardy's** (☑ 326-9008; Frenchman's Bay; ⊙ 7am-3pm Mon-Sat).

It takes about 30 minutes to walk from Jake's Hotel to Billy's Bay and 30 minutes to get from Great Bay to Jake's Hotel. Beautiful walk too!

# Alligator Pond

Jamaica is a huge holiday destination for foreigners, but where do Jamaicans go when they want to chill out? Well, if you're from Kingston or Montego Bay, you may drive over to Alligator Pond, hidden at the foot of a valley between two steep spurs of the Santa Cruz and Don Figuerero mountains. This is about as far from packaged-for-foreigners tourism as you can get.

The busy fishing village is set behind a deep-blue bay backed by dunes. Each morning, locals gather on the dark-sand beach to haggle over the catch – delivered by fishers, whose colorful old pirogues line the long shore.

The main reason to come here is for quite possibly the best dining experience in Jamaica: Little Ochie.

# 🛏 Sleeping

**Sea-Riv Hotel**      HOTEL $
(☑ 463-1443; Main St; r US$30-45; 🅿 ☒) If you really need to stay over in Alligator Ponds, try this hotel on the black-sand beach next to a river mouth. There are 18 unspectacular, fan-cooled rooms, water sports and friendly management.

# 🍴 Eating

There is one legendary seafood joint which attracts Jamaicans from all over the island, as well as several other seafood restaurants.

**★ Little Ochie**      SEAFOOD $$
(☑ 852-6430, 353-2579; www.littleochie.com; mains per lb J$1135-2370; ⊙ 9am until last guest leaves) Little Ochie is a culinary phenomenon that, despite a cult following, refuses to sell out. Set on a slice of black-sand beach, it uses the same charcoal-blackened kitchen and scribbled chalkboard menu it has for eons. The secret? Fish and seafood straight out of the sea, served steamed, jerked, curried, or escoveitched in boats on stilts under thatched awnings.

You make your choice from what the fishers just brought in, pay by weight and then elect how you want it cooked. The jerk is always a good bet, though it can be HOT. Grilled lobster and steamed lionfish and snapper also have a dedicated following. And 'dedicated' is the word. Little Ochie is one of Jamaica's few bona fide destination restaurants and has established itself as the No 1 attraction in Alligator Pond. Jamaicans drive from Kingston just to eat here; when you find yourself happily covered in scales from the fish you've just eaten, like something out of *Lord of the Flies*, you'll know why.

**Oswald's**      SEAFOOD $$
(☑ 381-3535; www.facebook.com/Seafood restaurant26; mains from J$1200; ⊙ 10am until last customer leaves) Run by a former local fisherman, Oswald's is a worthy contender for Alligator Pond's best seafood crown. Set on the busy fishermen's beach, it serves such

classics as garlic conch, curried sea puss (octopus), jerk snapper and other tasties, done on a wood-fire grill over pimento wood.

### ❶ Getting There & Away

If coming via Mandeville or Santa Cruz, take the straight, mildly potholed road leading south from Gutters (19km) on the A2. From Treasure Beach, you have to go through Southfield and Junction.

Minibuses and route taxis operate between Alligator Pond and the Beckford St transportation center in Kingston (J$600), and from Mandeville via Gutters (about J$350). Coming from Treasure Beach (J$400), you have to change in Pedro Cross and Southfield.

It's also possible to hire a taxi in Treasure Beach to take you to and from Alligator Pond for around $40 round-trip.

## Lovers' Leap

The Santa Cruz Mountains don't tend to slope very gently into the coast even at their most gentle, but at myth-rich Lovers' Leap, 1.5km southeast of Southfield, they positively plunge over 500m into the ocean. This headland provides a very photogenic, end-of-the-world-esque view, and is overlooked by a solar-powered lighthouse.

Far below, waves crash on jagged rocks and wash onto Cutlass Beach, a stiff one-hour trek to the bottom.

### ☉ Sights

**Lovers' Leap**                                    VIEWPOINT
(☎965-6887; J$300; ☉9am-5pm) Lover's Leap, a headland 1.5km southeast of Southfield, is named for two young slaves who supposedly committed suicide here in 1747. Legend says the woman was lusted after by her owner, who arranged for her lover to be sold to another estate. When the couple heard of the plot, they fled and were eventually cornered at the cliffs, where they chose to plunge to their deaths. The viewpoint overlooks a stunning stretch of coastline.

### 🛏 Sleeping

**Ocean Breeze Hotel**                          HOTEL $
(☎418-4600, 594-4000; www.oceanbreeze-jamaica.com; Southfield; r garden/ocean view US$30/50; ❈☞❉) Just over 1.5km beyond Lovers' Leap (follow the signs), you'll find the spectacularly perched Ocean Breeze Hotel with 22 bright, tropical-themed rooms, a pool, garden and – well, behold the view! Excellent value for money.

### ❶ Getting There & Away

Route taxis from Pedro Cross (coming from Treasure Beach) stop in nearby Southfield, a 2km walk from Lovers' Leap. It's easiest to get here with your own wheels; there's a turnoff in Southfield and another along the Southfield–Junction road.

# BLACK RIVER TO BLUEFIELDS

## Black River

POP 5352

The capital of St Elizabeth, Black River is a busy little place that was the most prosperous port in Jamaica in the late 19th century. The namesake river is a slow-moving slick of moldering tannins patrolled by crocodiles and boats full of curious tourists. Most visitors opt to stay in nearby Treasure Beach, but Black River makes a good jumping-off point for visiting attractions like YS Falls and the Appleton Rum Estate, and there's a charm to its historic core that's well worth exploring. The town's Georgian buildings attest to its 19th-century prosperity, when Black River exported sugarcane and local logwood from which Prussian blue dye was extracted for textiles.

Locals proudly point out the Waterloo Guest House, which in 1893 became the first house in Jamaica to have electricity installed. The racetrack and spa that attracted the wealthy have sadly not survived the passage of time.

### ☉ Sights

It may be hard to reconcile the present-day image of this busy little administrative town with what once was the most prosperous place in Jamaica – not to mention the most technologically advanced (the first place to get electricity on the island). Still, there are numerous interesting historic buildings dotted around that hark back to Black River's bygone era, when the town was run by the powerful Leyden and Farquharson families.

Foremost among the historic structures worth checking out is the yellow-brick **Parish Church of St John the Evangelist** (Church St; ☉Mass 8am Sun), rebuilt in 1837 but dating back to the early 1700s. The breezy interior is graced by heavy mahogany porticoes and a stately balcony, while the 17th-century graves in the cemetery tell an interesting story of cross-racial love and acceptance. Heading east, High St, lined

# Black River

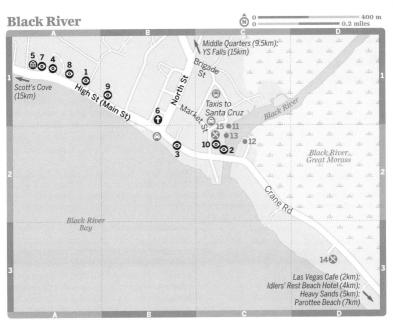

## Black River

with colonnaded Georgian merchant houses, leads to the 1913 **Hendricks Building** (2 High St) with a stop sign protruding from a small cannon next to it. Just beyond is the **Imperial bridge**, constructed with materials from all corners of the British Empire. It overlooks the river, with its remaining sugarcane warehouses; the slave market was held on the east bank.

On the corner of Market St and Main St, an upturned cannon sprouting a stop sign harks back to Black River's days as a British military garrison. North along Market St is the **Zong Massacre memorial**, commemorating the 1781 event in which 133 African slaves were thrown overboard by the crew of

the Zong slave ship, with the subsequent legal case contributing to the abolition of the trans-Atlantic slave trade.

Two blocks west of the parish church are the porticoed **courthouse** (58 High St) and the town hall, with lofty pillars, and beyond that, a simple **Roman Catholic church** (Main St). Also along this section of Main St are three houses that are splendid examples of the Jamaican vernacular style, with jalousies, decorative fretwork and shady verandas: stately 1890s **Magdala House** (Main St), which once belonged to Thomas Leyden, from the town's most powerful family at the time; the 1894 **Invercauld Great House** (High St), which belonged to the other powerful family, the Farquharsons; and **Waterloo Great House** (Main St), the first private house in Jamaica to get electricity.

##  Beaches

### Heavy Sands                                    BEACH
A few kilometers southeast of Black River, these long stretches of dark sand are still undiscovered by most international tourists. Just don't swim near the river mouth – crocodiles like to congregate here! You should be fine in the sea, but beware the tides as there will likely be no one around. Abutting it is Parottee Beach.

### Parottee Beach                                 BEACH
Several kilometers south of Black River, this is essentially a continuation of Heavy Sands beach – more dark sand studded with shells and loads of clean ocean. Excellent for swimming, but don't swim out too far as you'll likely be on your own out here.

## 🏃 Activities

### Captain Lando                                  FISHING
(📞 387-8008) Give friendly Captain Lando a call; he's happy to arrange fishing charters.

Expect to pay around US$70 for a half-day trip, although these rates may be higher if he gets a bigger boat.

##  Tours

### Guided Tours
A river trip is the main reason many tourists come to Black River and it has become a popular day out from the all-inclusives. Another excellent outing in Black River is a walking tour with local history enthusiast Allison Morris, who runs engaging **Way Back When Heritage Tours** (📞 965-2288; www.real-jamaica-vacations.com/way-back-when.html; per person US$25) that introduce visitors to the town's long and interesting history.

### Crocodile-Spotting
Picture this: you are propelled into the mangrove-rich interior of the Great Morass, and while nothing can be guaranteed when speaking of spotting wildlife, there's a good chance you'll see white marsh cranes and herons skimming the banks like pterodactyls, sword-beaked, fish-spearing anhinga and, of course, crocodiles. Thanks to all

---

### BLACK RIVER GREAT MORASS

An amoeba-ish clump of salt marsh, black waters, leaching tannins, wind-bent reed beds and spider mangroves rise like a mushroom from the mouth of Black River, pushing deep into the Jamaican interior. For its singular scenery and excellent wildlife-viewing opportunities, this 200-sq-km wetland – the Great Morass – is one of Jamaica's most fascinating (yet accessible) natural wonders (see www.jamaicablackriver.com for more information).

The best way to get a feel for the morass is to explore it by small watercraft or tour boat; quick excursions are easily arranged in Black River, but if you are heading on to Treasure Beach, lengthier forays up the river can be arranged there. Along the way, with the right guide, you can eat at delightful riverside shacks, discover hidden swimming holes and, of course, spot some grinning, sunning crocodiles. The morass forms Jamaica's most significant refuge for American crocodiles, and an estimated population of more than 300 live in the swamps. Several have made a habit of hanging out near the bridge in town, waiting for their next meal of raw chicken parts dispensed from tour operators who have a vested interest in keeping them around.

The crocodiles aren't the only animals to be spotted here, not by a long shot. The interplay of saltwater and freshwater, the generally dry climate of St Elizabeth and the parish's geologic composition all make for a complex ecosystem and a vital preserve for more than 100 bird species, including cinnamon-colored jacanas, egrets, whistling ducks, water hens and seven species of heron.

The culture of this region is unique as well. The impenetrability of the morass has made for an isolation that has preserved folkways lost in other parts of Jamaica. Locals go out in pirogues, tending funnel-shaped bamboo shrimp pots in the traditional manner of their West African forebears.

These interconnecting waterways are navigable for about 30km upriver. Along the way, the mangroves suck water through long tendrils drooping into the water. Beyond the confluence of the YS, Middle Quarters and Black Rivers, the mangroves broaden into marshy meadows of tall sedges and reeds. Feisty game fish are plentiful, including snook and tarpon. On rare occasions, endangered manatees may even be seen near the river estuary.

the visitors, these reptiles are tame around people now, and some operators let people go swimming in the river with them, which they insist is a safe endeavor (no one has been eaten yet!). If you do choose to swim, you do so at your own risk.

There are three main tour companies:

➡ **J Charles Swaby's Black River Safari** (☑ 965-2513, 962-0220; tour US$19; ⊘ tours 9am, 11am, 12:30pm, 2pm & 3:30pm) On the east side of the river just north of the bridge. Offers 60- to 75-minute journeys aboard the Safari Queen and is the oldest operator.

➡ **St Elizabeth River Safari** (☑ 965-2229, 965-2374; tour US$19; ⊘ tours 9am, 11am, 2pm & 3:30pm) Has the biggest boats and offers similar tours and prices. Located on the west side of the river, behind the Hendricks Building.

➡ **Irie Safaris** (☑ 965-2211; Riverside Dr; US$22; ⊘ tours every 90min 9am-4.30pm) Located a little further north of St Elizabeth River Safaris along the west side of the river; has smaller craft and offers a more intimate experience. Irie can also arrange kayaking trips, which come highly recommended.

For a less structured experience, you can easily hire a local fisherman to take you up-river by canoe or boat for about US$35–40 round-trip. Ask near the bridge in town. Several reliable boat captains in Treasure Beach run combo trips up Black River and on to Pelican Bar for around US$50 per person.

Midday tours are best for spotting croc-odiles; early and later tours are better for birding. Take a hat and some mosquito repellent. Large tour boats tend to stop at Sister Lou's River Stop, on the Salt Spring tributary, where delicious stuffed crab backs and pepper shrimp are served up, while smaller craft continue to a thatched bar and rope swing over the water a little further upstream.

## 🛏 Sleeping

### Waterloo Guest House          HOTEL $
(☑ 965-2278; 44 High St; r US$50-90; P ❄ 🌐 🏊) The only option in town proper, Waterloo Guest House is the refurbished motel-style building around the back of Waterloo Great House. Compact, clean rooms come with air-con, TV and pool access; look for the grave of the man who first brought electricity to Black River behind the building. Good restaurant and bar on-site looks like a Graham Greene haunt.

### Idlers' Rest Beach Hotel    BOUTIQUE HOTEL $$
(☑ 965-9000; www.idlersrest.com; Crane Rd; r from US$110; P ❄ 🌐) A worthwhile non-Treasure Beach option a little way out of town, Idlers' Rest redefines 'Irie.' The hotel is a tasteful boutique decorated in a comfy mix of modern chic, Caribbean color and pan-African art, with rooms cooled by gentle sea breezes. Our one quibble is maintenance: rooms could be cleaner and in better nick.

## 🍴 Eating

You can buy fresh produce at the open-air **produce market** (Market St; ⊘ sunrise-sunset) and there are several worthwhile eateries in and near Black River.

### Sister Lou's River Stop         SEAFOOD $
(☑ 386-6680; mains around J$700; ⊘ 11:30am-6pm) The fact that this is a popular tour-boat stop for croc-spotters hasn't impacted negatively on the taste of Sister Lou's stuffed crab backs and pepper shrimp at a shack that looks like it's been part of the landscape since the 1800s.

### Waterloo Great House           JAMAICAN $
(44 High St; mains J$600-1200; ⊘ 7am-10pm) There's a raffish quality to the colonial bar inside the Waterloo Great House that looks like it could have sprung from a Graham Greene novel. Good for a drink or big portions of typical Jamaican standards, as well as a few Chinese dishes.

### ★ Cloggy's on the Beach         SEAFOOD $$
(☑ 634-2424; www.facebook.com/pages/Cloggys-on-the-Beach/139402596166094; 22 Crane Rd; mains J$700-2400; ⊘ noon-10pm) This beach-side joint is your best culinary bet in Black River; it's an all-round pleaser with a relaxed vibe, great bar ambience and excellent seafood. Try a cup of conch soup for a revelation, and follow that up with some gorgeous curried lobster or conch on the breezy terrace. It occasionally throws well-attended beach sound-system parties, too.

## ℹ Information

**Black River Hospital** (☑ 965-2212; 45 Main St) A kilometer west of town.

**National Commercial Bank** (☑ 965-9027; 9 High St; ⊘ 9am-5pm Mon-Fri) Bank with ATM.

**Police Station** (☑ 965-2232; North St)

**Scotiabank** (☑ 965-2251; 6 High St; ⊘ 8:30am-2:30pm Mon-Thu, 8:30am-4pm Fri) Bank with ATM.

SOUTH COAST & CENTRAL HIGHLANDS BLACK RIVER

## ❶ Getting There & Away

Black River is a nexus for route taxis that shoot off in all directions. **Taxis** (High St) in front of the parish church run to Savanna-la-Mar (J$300) and Whitehouse (J$120); further east along High St there are taxis that depart for Treasure Beach (J$250), while others leave for Santa Cruz (Market St) from near the market. Minibuses go to Montego Bay (J$250 to J$300) and Sav-la-Mar (J$220) from the **transportation center** (Brigade St) behind the market.

# Whitehouse

The small fishing village of Whitehouse is short on attractions, but can be a tranquil stopover for those looking to sample provincial coastal life. It stretches for about 2km along the A2, parallel to a series of beaches where motorized boats and pirogues draw up and unload fish and conch taken on the Pedro Bank, a submerged, threatened reef mass, about 100km out to sea.

## ⏹ Sleeping

**South Sea View Guest House** GUESTHOUSE $$
(📞963-5172; r US$85-100; ❄ 🛜 ⛱) With a bit of imagination you could call this place Greek Island-ish in its aesthetics, all white-walled and open to the pale-blue sky and winds. Rooms are fresh and modern, with fluffy king-size beds, tropical murals and cable TV for those days when you need to veg. It sits by the waterfront towards the south end of Whitehouse.

## ✖ Eating

**Jimmyz Restaurant & Bar** SEAFOOD $
(📞390-3477; Main Rd; mains J$300-600; ⏱7am-7pm Mon-Sat) On Fisherman's Beach in central Whitehouse, next to a pavilion where local fishers sell their catch to wholesalers, this eatery is popular with old sea salts. The menu has fresh juices, including an exceedingly peppery ginger tonic, and dishes featuring steamed fish, ackee and saltfish breakfasts, 'sea puss' (octopus) and a particularly excellent spicy conch stew.

**Scott's Cove** SEAFOOD $
(A2; mains around J$700) About 4km southeast of Whitehouse, the A2 sweeps around this deep little inlet. Anyone with taste buds in western Jamaica will tell you that this is the best place on the island to buy fried snapper and *bammy* (fried cassava pancake), as well as conch soup. Sellers from the dozen or so scruffy food and beer stalls are very assertive.

## ❶ Getting There & Away

Whitehouse is located on the A2 halfway between Black River and Bluefields/Belmont. Route taxis and minibuses head in both directions and cost approximately J$150 to either destination.

# Bluefields & Belmont

Bluefields in southeastern Westmoreland parish is appropriately named: look out the door here and it's either big light-blue skies beyond the mountains or sea-blue harbors lapping the rocky beach. Today Bluefields and adjacent Belmont are populated by a quiet collection of fishers, tourists, escape artists, Rastas, regular artists, expats and returning Jamaicans, with rustic Rasta homestays and cerulean waters the big attraction. This is also the birthplace (and burial place) of reggae legend Peter Tosh.

In 1519 this was Oristan, one of the first Spanish settlements in Jamaica; Bluefields Bay provided safe anchorage for Spanish explorers, British naval squadrons and pirates. In 1670, long before he became a tacky rum mascot, infamous buccaneer Henry Morgan set out from Bluefields Bay to sack Panama City.

## ◉ Sights

**Bluefields Beach Park** BEACH
(Hwy A2; admission J$50; ⏱9am-5pm) Well signed from the Winston Jones Hwy (A2), this beach is a narrow stretch of pale sand, as beautiful as it is ignored by foreign tourists (although it's quite popular with locals on weekends). During the early evening and on weekends you'll find a nice collection of food stalls featuring locally caught fresh fish and plenty of Red Stripe.

**Belmont Beach** BEACH
(Hwy A2) There are actually two small Belmont Beaches, but one is too rocky to relax on and the other is a major mooring point for fishing boats. That said, if the day is clear the water will be as well, so you can swim out a little way and do some fine snorkeling or spear fishing. Most accommodations rent the required equipment.

**Peter Tosh Monument** MONUMENT
(Hwy A2; US$15; ⏱hours vary) Many monuments make a political statement, and the

memorial to reggae superstar Peter Tosh, just off the beach road in Belmont, is no exception. And the cause here is, as Tosh once sang, to 'legalize it.' This is a casual place with few visitors, run by the Tosh family and featuring a shockingly overpriced 'tour' of Tosh's mother's grave, Tosh's own tomb painted in Rasta colours, and a lacklustre garden. A tip is expected, too. For seriously hard-core fans only.

You can guess what 'it' is that Tosh wanted to legalize, but if not, just check all the murals, which depict a Rasta man with a huge joint, jumbo marijuana leaves, and, best of all, a red-eyed Lion of Zion on Tosh's actual tomb.

The chilled-out atmosphere is a stark contrast to the tourist maelstrom surrounding fellow Wailer Bob Marley's mausoleum in Nine Mile, but the principle of overcharging visitors for a paltry attraction is true in both cases. The caretaker won't tell you anything about Tosh that a fan wouldn't know already and the only time we recommend a visit is in mid-October when the annual Peter Tosh Birthday Bash, an informal local affair, features live roots reggae music played deep into the night.

## Tours

Travelers staying in the area can organize day trips and excursions to regional attractions including YS Falls, the Black River Great Morass and Alligator Pond.

**Natural Mystic Tours**  NATURE TOURS
(☑851-3962; www.naturalmystic-jamaica.com; per day per 2 people US$150) German expat Lydia leads offbeat tours (in English and German) all across the island. Delving into the Rasta way of life is particularly interesting.

**Nature Roots**  NATURE TOURS
(☑955-8162, 384-6610; www.natureroots.de) Go with Brian the Bush Doctor out on the sea and into the jungle; he's a terrific bird-watching guide.

## Sleeping

Accommodations are divided into roughly two categories: rustic rooms and cabins (plus a single midrange hotel) in Belmont and more upmarket digs, including exclusive villas, in Bluefields.

**Natural Mystic
Guesthouse**  GUESTHOUSE $
(☑851-3962; www.naturalmystic-jamaica.com; Belmont; cottage US$30-50; 🔊) Run by the friendly, German-speaking Lydia and perched on a hill in Belmont Village, these two pretty cottages (one with kitchenette) are set in a flower garden with a great view over the sea. The beach is a five-minute walk away. A cooking service and dominoes instruction are provided on request, and you may find yourselves at an impromptu music gig.

**Nature Roots**  HOMESTAY $
(☑384-6610, 955-8162; www.natureroots.de; Belmont; r US$30) Nature Roots, the home base for the tour outfit (p171) of the same name, consisting of the owner, 'Doc' Brian, offers chilled-out accommodations in a yard with good vibes, easy access to the beach, and a lovely, indolent air. It's the first right just west of Studio Black.

⭐**Luna Sea Inn**  BOUTIQUE HOTEL $$
(☑955-8099; www.lunaseainn.com; Hwy A2, Belmont; r US$140-190; 🅿❄🔊🏊) Overlooking cerulean waters right in the middle of Belmont, this sweet boutique hotel has named each of its nine individually styled rooms after a sea creature. Our favorite is the Anemone, with its ocean-view deck, but all rooms come with handmade furniture, four-poster beds, rain showers and modern amenities.

**Horizon Cottages**  COTTAGE $$
(☑955-8823; www.jamaicaescapes.com; Hwy A2, Bluefields Bay; cottage US$110-125; 🅿🔊🏊) One of the first accommodations in the area, this cozy spot right on the waterfront of Bluefields Bay features two sweet wooden cottages, the Sea Ranch and the Rasta Ranch, each tastefully appointed with local artwork and featuring small kitchenettes and shared hot-water shower in the garden. The beach is private, and kayaking, boating and fishing can be arranged.

⭐**Bluefields Villas**  VILLA $$$
(☑in the USA 1-877-955-8993; www.bluefieldsvillas.com; Hwy A2, Bluefields Bay; per week US$6685-10,828; 🅿❄🔊🏊) Exquisite is an understatement for these six private villas scattered around the Bluefields Bay waterfront that offer all-inclusive services (chef, cleaners, butlers etc) fit for Marie Antoinette. All have pools and luxury furnishings, and three of them even have their own tiny private islands. Villa sizes vary; some fit four, the largest caters for 13 people.

Throw in unique organized excursions, private nannies, and spectacular service that doesn't miss a single beat and you've got the holiday of a lifetime pretty much guaranteed.

##  Eating

**Prince's Bar and Restaurant** JAMAICAN $
(☑503-9501; Hwy A2, Belmont; mains from J$600; ⊗9am-midnight Mon-Sat, 2pm-midnight Sun) This colourful Rasta shack, right by the turnoff to the Peter Tosh memorial, is run by Tosh's nephew Kenial, who may well invite you to share some Red Stripes. Jamaican standards such as curried conch and fried chicken are also served.

**Cracked Conch** INTERNATIONAL $$
(☑383-6982; www.lunaseainn.com; Hwy A2, Belmont; mains J$700-2500; ⊗11am-9pm; 🔊) With the smart tables on its terrace overlooking the sea, this is Belmont's fanciest dining option. The menu is a happpy marriage of grilled lobster, fish and pasta dishes, with a supporting cast of salads. Some nice wines and cocktails, too.

## 🔒 Shopping

**Studio Black** ARTS & CRAFTS
(☑459-9918; Hwy A2, Belmont; ⊗9am-5pm) Warning: don't walk past this artistically attired Rasta shack that's been defying hurricanes, dodgy drivers and all else in Belmont since 1977; it's simply too good to miss. Run by amiable local artist, Jah Calo, it's replete with one-of-a-kind art and sculptures immersed in Rastafarian imagery. Calo's painted many murals in the area, including those at the Peter Tosh Memorial (p170).

The shop-shack is on the main beach road (A2) running through Belmont. With its colorful decoration, you can't miss it.

## ❶ Getting There & Away

The A2 is the only road that runs through Bluefields and Belmont, and minibuses and route taxis will drop you off wherever you ask in either village; otherwise they'll likely leave you in Bluefields' 'square,' a centrally located patch of open land with a small general-purpose shop.

Route taxis and minivans run frequently (hourly during the day) up the coastal road (A2) to Savanna-la-Mar (J$250, one hour), and from there to Montego Bay and Negril.

In the opposite direction (southeast), minibuses and route taxis run to Mandeville and Kingston, with some terminating at Black River (J$350, 1½ hours), from where you can get buses or taxis to Treasure Beach.

# MANDEVILLE & AROUND

In spite of the natural beauty of the mountainous Manchester parish, few visitors pause here on the way to the beaches of the west and the south. Yet Mandeville – the prosperous mountain town at the heart of the parish – is lingerworthy for its few sights, cooler climate and laid-back atmosphere that's absent in parts of Jamaica replete with tourists. Manchester seeks to establish itself as a community tourism hub and Mandeville makes a good jumping-off point for visiting a few outlying attractions in neighboring villages.

# Mandeville

POP 49,695

An antidote to Jamaica's busy, sometimes blemished, coast, Mandeville is a cool highland town, meaning you can traverse its busy streets without collapsing from heat exhaustion and enjoy a slice of everyday Jamaican life bereft of the camera-clicking tourists in evidence elsewhere. While the town center remains boisterously Jamaican, with uniformed schoolchildren playing cat and mouse with the speeding taxis, Mandeville's salubrious suburbs exhibit a more refined veneer. Mock Georgian mansions with manicured gardens provide second homes for Kingston entrepreneurs or returning expats who have made their money abroad. Devoid of major sights per se, Mandeville is best enjoyed as a pit stop for people who want to see the island from a different (Jamaican) perspective. Check out the historic monuments, visit an old great house, and enjoy the excellent dining scene and the pleasantly cool nights.

## History

Established only in 1816, Mandeville began life as a haven for colonial planters escaping the heat of the plains. In the 19th century, the city prospered as a holiday retreat for wealthy Kingstonians, and attracted soldiers and British retirees from other colonial quarters. Many early expats established the area as a center for dairy farming and citrus and pimento production. Jamaica's unique seedless citrus fruit, the *ortanique*, was first produced here in the 1920s and is grown in large quantities.

North American bauxite company Alcan opened operations here in 1940 (in 2000 it sold its operations to a Swiss company,

Glencore). Relatively high wage levels lured educated Jamaicans, bringing a middle-class savoir faire to the town.

## ◉ Sights

**Marshall's Pen**        HISTORIC BUILDING
(☏904-5454; www.annsuttonja.com; Mike Town Rd; house tour US$20; ⊙by appointment) One of the most impressive historical sights in the central highlands, the 18th-century Marshall's Pen great house has a story that manages to encapsulate the sweep of Jamaican history from Taíno times through colonialism to abolition, independence and the modern day. The private home of Jamaica's leading ornithologist and environmental scientist, Ann Haynes-Sutton, it's a great spot to watch birds. Visits are by prior appointment for groups of six. Take Oriole Close off Hwy A2, then the Mike Town/Somerset Rd.

Taíno people once inhabited nearby grounds, and archaeological digs still turn up their artifacts. The stone-and-timber great house itself, built in 1795, dates back to the Earl of Balcarres, the one-time Governor of Jamaica. Throughout its history the home has been a coffee plantation and cattle-breeding property (hence Marshall's 'Pen'). The present day owner of the 120-hectare grounds runs birding tours. More than 100 species have been recorded on the property itself, including 25 of the 30 species endemic to Jamaica, and it may be possible for birders to organise a stay here.

The exterior of the building, all cut-stone and louvred windows surrounded by landscaped gardens, is understated compared to the arresting interior – a honeycomb of wood-paneled rooms brimming with antiques, leather-bound books, Taíno artifacts, historical and original artwork and lots of other museum-quality pieces, many from Japan and China. Ann runs hour-long tours of the house with advance notice.

The estate entrance – an unmarked stone gateway painted red – is about 600m along the Mike Town/Somerset Rd. The unpaved drive is bumpy but passable.

**Cecil Charlton Park**        SQUARE
(Park Cres; ⊙9am-6pm Mon, Wed & Fri, 11am-7pm Sat & Sun) This tiny, attractive, English-style 'green', also known as Mandeville Sq, lends a slight Cotswoldian village feel to the town center. In the middle of the park, the three colored towers of the water-rockery feature represent the main industry of the parish: bauxite, alumina and aluminum production. The fountain is flanked by the busts

## Mandeville

### ◉ Sights
  1 Cecil Charlton Park...............................B4

### ⊗ Eating
  2 Little Ochie...............................................B3
  3 Oleeka's Garden Cafe..........................B3
  4 Red Rock Restaurant & Jerk
      Center...................................................A3

### ⊖ Drinking & Nightlife
  5 Manchester Arms Pub &
      Restaurant...........................................B4

### ⓐ Shopping
  6 Bookland................................................B1

of national hero Norman Manley and Cecil Charlton, Jamaica's longest-serving mayor. In the southeast corner of the park, a cenotaph commemorates Jamaican dead from the two world wars.

**Mrs Stephenson's Garden**  GARDENS
(☑ 962-2909; www.stephensonsflowersja.com; 25 New Green Rd; US$5; ⊙ by appointment) Elaine Stephenson is testament to the fact that any individual who cares enough to can carve out their own plot of Eden. Her award-winning garden has been planned and planted with much love and discipline. Keen amateur gardeners descend year-round to gasp at the collection that includes orchids and ortaniques. The family also runs a flower shop.

## ☞ Tours

**Countrystyle Community
Tourism Network**  CULTURAL
(☑ 507-6326; www.accesscommunitytourism.com) ✈ Led by the indomitable Diana McIntyre-Pike, this is a community initiative that aims to connect visitors in search of 'real' Jamaica with communities that have been left out of the coastal tourism boom. She can arrange homestays in the local area, as well as tours of Mandeville and authentic 'Taste of Jamaica' cooking experiences in the surrounding villages.

## 🛏 Sleeping

Mandeville's hotels are lackluster, but a couple of good guesthouses liven up the accommodations scene.

★ **Agapantha Cottage B&B**  B&B $
(☑ 586-3994; www.agapanthacottage.com; 2b DeCarteret Rd; r incl breakfast US$70-80; [P] [🏠]) Run by delightful hostess Lisa, this spacious house in a quiet Mandeville neighborhood comes with four spotless rooms and a generous Jamaican breakfast. Lisa is full of local tips and useful info and if you've been traveling for a while, you can even have your laundry done. Best for travelers with own wheels.

**Kariba Kariba Guest House**  GUESTHOUSE $
(☑ 321-8009; 1 McKinley Rd; r incl breakfast J$4000-5000; [🏠]) Northwest of the town center, Kariba is a beautiful fieldstone home run by a surpassingly friendly English-Jamaican couple. Admittedly, the exterior grounds and lobby are more attractive than the four rooms, which are a bit middling, but the owners are very accommodating and can lead customized excursions. It's the first house on the left, southwest of the A2/New Green Rd junction.

**Mandeview Flats**  HOTEL $
(☑ 961-8439; www.mandeviewhotel.com; 7 Hillview Dr, Balvenie Heights; s/d from US$64/78; [P] [🏠] [❄]) With deeply satisfying views over Mandeville's surrounding undulating hillsides, this gleaming small hotel offers 12 clean, fan-cooled rooms (a fan is all you need this high up). Simple, functional and hardly luxury; a quintessential Mandeville hotel.

## ✕ Eating

Mandeville has a varied and good dining scene, with excellent Jamaican and Chinese food and great Blue Mountain coffee, as well as a city offshoot of a seafood joint that's famous, island-wide, Little Ochie (p174).

**Red Rock Restaurant &
Jerk Center**  JAMAICAN $
(South Race Course Rd; jerk chicken from J$250; ⊙ 11am-9pm Mon-Thu, to 11pm Fri & Sat) In this smoky little local joint, papered with newspaper cuttings of Obama's 2008 election win, locals sway to the sound of Tom Jones and old-school country and western. The jerk chicken is among the best in town; you can also prop up the bar with a Red Stripe in hand, or grab an I-tal fruit juice by the entrance.

**Little Ochie**  SEAFOOD $
(☑ 367-6340; Leaders Plaza; mains from J$700; ⊙ 11am-11pm Mon-Thu, to 1am Fri & Sat, 2-7pm Sun) This satellite of the famous fish restaurant at Alligator Pond (p165) is very good. Not as good as its parent, but hey – we can't all approach perfection. The menu is seafood done in all the traditional Jamaican ways (jerk, steamed, curried...) served in a tranquil tropical bar setting. Pay for your shrimp/fish/crab/lobster/conch by weight and prepare for a leisurely meal.

**Oleeka's Garden Cafe**  JAMAICAN $$
(☑ 625-1491; 30 Hargreaves Ave; mains J$500-1200; ⊙ 7am-10pm Mon-Fri, 9am-midnight Sat; ✈) Managing to create a little oasis of tranquility just meters from the main street, Oleeka's is as Jamaican as the cow-skin soup with peanut that it serves. Other uber-Jamaican lunch specials may include fried chicken and curried tripe and beans, and there are also some fusion experiments, such as calalloo lasagna.

**Bamboo Garden Restaurant**  CHINESE $$
(☑ 962-4515; 35 Ward Ave; mains J$900-2200; ⊙ noon-10pm; ❊) Hidden at the back of a mini-mall, on the 1st floor, this is, hands down, Mandeville's best Chinese restaurant. The extensive menu of mostly Cantonese dishes is complemented by some of the most professional service in Jamaica.

##  Drinking & Nightlife

**Manchester Arms**
**Pub & Restaurant** PUB
(Hotel St, Mandeville Hotel; ⊙4:30-11pm) The Manchester Arms goes all out to give you that pub-in-the-midst-of-Jamaica feeling, an effort that's vaguely successful. The broad menu encapsulates fairly overpriced Jamaican and continental food, but the setting is pretty lovely, and you can sip your drink alongside visiting businessmen. The last Wednesday of every month is Jamaica Night, with a live mento band.

##  Shopping

**Bookland** BOOKS
(Manchester Shopping Plaza; ⊙8:30am-5pm Mon-Sat) You can struggle to find a decent bookshop in small-town Jamaica, so all hail to Bookland, notable for its encyclopedic and nicely laid-out Caribbean and Afrocentric fiction section, the odd travel guidebook, and tomes on Bob Marley and his legacy.

## ❶ Information

**Manchester Parish Library** (☑962-2972; 34 Hargreaves Ave; ⊙9am-5:30pm Mon-Fri, to 4pm Sat) Free internet access.

**Police Station** (☑962-2250; Park Cres)

**Post Office** (☑962-2339; South Racecourse Rd; ⊙8am-5pm Mon-Fri)

**Scotiabank** (☑962-1083; cnr Ward Ave & Caledonia Rd; ⊙8:30am-2:30pm Mon-Thu, 8:30am-4pm Fri) ATM.

## ❶ Getting There & Away

Mandeville is a big transportation hub. From the **Mandeville Transportation Center** (off Main St) minibuses and shared taxis depart for Kingston (J$450), Black River (J$350), Christiana (J$200), Santa Cruz (J$300) and Montego Bay.

The **St Elizabeth taxi stand** (Ward Ave) serves Santa Cruz (J$300), Mile Gully (J$150), Alligator Pond (J$200), and Junction (J$250); change at Junction for connections to Treasure Beach.

The island-wide **Knutsford Express** (☑971-1822; www.knutsfordexpress.com; 52 Caledonia Rd) buses connect daily to:

**Falmouth** (J$3200, 4¾ hours, two daily Monday to Saturday; via Kingston)

**Kingston** (J$1950, two hours, two to three daily)

**Montego Bay** (J$2250, 3¾ hours, two daily)

**Ocho Rios** (J$2700, four hours, one to two daily; via Kingston)

**Savanna-la-Mar** (J$1900, two hours, three to four daily)

# Mile Gully & Around

The village of Mile Gully sprawls along a valley that runs northwest from Mandeville in the lee of the forested north face of the Don Figuerero Mountains. The B6 leads northwest from Shooter's Hill, winding, dipping and rising past lime-green pastures dotted with guango and silk-cotton trees and crisscrossed with stone walls and hedgerows. There's little to detain you in Mile Gully itself, but there are several appealing churches nearby, as well as one of Jamaica's most haunted spots – all reachable via beautiful (if potholed) drives through the mountainous countryside.

## ◉ Sights

**Skull Point** AREA
(B6) About 1km west of Mile Gully, you'll find a venerable blue-and-white, 19th-century police station and courthouse at the junction for Bethany, plus the atmospheric remains of a defunct train station. The name has nothing to do with the police station, though; it comes from the local church – or at least the ruins of that church. It's a genuinely creepy place, all rotted and burnt out. The local consensus is the grounds are haunted by beheaded local slave James Knight.

**Bethany Moravian Church** CHURCH
(Bethany) The Bethany road climbs sharply and delivers you at the Bethany Moravian Church, 4km north of Mile Gully – a simple gray stone building dating to 1835, dramatically perched foursquare midway up the hill with fantastic valley views. The church is rather dour close up, but the simple interior boasts a resplendent organ.

**Nazareth Moravian Church** CHURCH
(Maidstone) South of the B6, perched atop the Don Figuerero Mountains, 7km from Mile Gully, is this humble church, which would look as comfortable on the American prairie as it does in the Jamaican bush. Founded in 1840, Maidstone is one of Jamaica's post-emancipation, pre-planned 'free villages,' an early experiment at the intersection of urban planning and social policy. The annual Emancipation Day Fair is celebrated at Maidstone on August 1, with mento bands, Jonkanoo celebrations, and maypole and quadrille dancing.

## 🛏 Sleeping

**Villa Isabel**                                    GUESTHOUSE **$**
(☑789-5829; www.villaisabelja.com; Mile Gully;
r US$35-45; ❄🛜) This friendly place with
three comfortable en-suite rooms makes
a good base for hiking and biking in the
picturesque countryside. Tours of the surrounding area can be arranged and meals
prepared on request.

## ❶ Getting There & Away

Frequent route taxis operate on the B6 between Mandeville and Maggotty via Mile Gully
(J$150). If you're driving from Mandeville, the
B6 continues west about 8km to Green Hill and
a T-junction. About 1.5km north (to the right)
of the junction, en route to Balaclava, is a very
dangerous spot: you'll climb a short hill that
tempts you to accelerate. Unfortunately there's
an unmarked railway crossing on the crest and a
hairpin bend immediately after. Drive slowly!

# SOUTH COCKPIT COUNTRY

South Cockpit Country is as beautiful, rugged and remote as its northern counterpart.
Few roads penetrate the hills, where the
sparse population is mostly involved in subsistence farming and, deeper in the valleys,
ganja plantations that it's best not to stum-
ble into without an invitation. St Elizabeth
is the driest parish in Jamaica thanks in part
to the rugged Cockpit Country, which joins
St Elizabeth to Trelawny parish in a rocky
fist-bump and blocks the south coast from
the rains whipping off the ocean. This inhos-
pitable land helped to preserve the culture
and liberty of the Maroons, with Accompong
being the best place to delve into this culture.

# Accompong

POP 3000

The Maroons (descendants of escaped slaves)
and their legacy make up a significant chap-
ter in the Jamaican national narrative, yet
there are only three actual Maroon communities in Jamaica. Accompong, named
for the brother of Maroon hero Cudjoe and
embedded in the outer edges of southwestern Cockpit Country, is the sole remaining
outpost in western Jamaica. This unique cultural lineage alone makes the town worth a
visit, but it is also a good base for exploring
the Cockpit Country, also known as 'Me No

Sen, You No Come,' a landscape that, by dint
of its ruggedness, is as responsible for Maroon
independence as Maroon battle prowess.

The village still enjoys aspects of
quasi-autonomy and is headed by a colonel
elected by secret ballot for a period of five
years. The colonel appoints and oversees a
council, and it is considered proper etiquette
to introduce yourself upon visiting (ask
around for Colonel Ferron Williams).

## ⊙ Sights

In many ways, the best sight in Accompong
is...well, Accompong. The village is more
than politically autonomous; despite the
fact the native Coromantee language has
vanished and knowledge of local rituals is
fading among the young, Accompong still
feels *different* from the rest of Jamaica. Locals will proudly tell you there is no crime,
police or taxes in Accompong, and while
they may be guilty of some exaggeration,
the town certainly feels tranquil compared
to settlements of similar size in other parts
of Jamaica.

If you arrive in Accompong under your
own steam, you'll be quickly greeted by locals offering to give you a tour of the spread-
out town; the going rate at time of writing
was US$20, which pays for a full tour of all
the sights around town, except the Peace
Cave (US$30).

Perhaps the best time to get a sense of
Accompong's uniqueness is during the traditional Accompong Maroon Festival, held
each January 6.

**Parade Ground**                                    SQUARE
Accompong is centered on the tiny Parade
Ground, where the Presbyterian church
looks over a small monument that honors
Cudjoe, the Maroon leader (the statue next
to it is that of Leonard Parkinson, another
Maroon freedom fighter).

**Accompong Community
Centre & Museum**                                    MUSEUM
(J$500; ⊘9am-5pm) Across from the Parade
Ground, this museum is a veritable peek
into the Afro-Caribbean world's cultural
attic: *goombay* drums, a blunderbuss allegedly used by Nanny (legendary Maroon
leader), and agricultural implements from
the Maroon era stacked alongside Ashanti
art and Taíno tools. There are also displays
on slavery, legendary Maroon leaders, medicinal herbs and the geology of the Cockpit
Country.

## ACCOMPONG MAROON FESTIVAL

The best time to get a sense of Accompong's uniqueness is during the traditional **Accompong Maroon Festival** (⊘ January 6). The festival celebrates Accompong's nominal independence and is a riot of traditional dancing, drumming, mento bands, street food, and local tonics and herbs. Between the storytellers, speeches, chanting, rhythmic drumbeats and appeals to pre-Christian spirits, this is an intense invocation of Afro-Caribbean heritage.

The festival culminates in a traditional march to the revered Kindah Tree, where a specially prepared Maroon dish of unsalted and unseasoned pork is consumed with yams; afterwards (because after all, this is still Jamaica) an all-night sound-system party rocks until daybreak. You'll never see Jamaica so quiet as Accompong sometime around 11am on January 7.

Because the festival is held in early January, a lot of Jamaicans call it 'Maroon New Year,' but it actually marks the signing of the 1739 peace treaty between Cudjoe of the Maroons and the British Empire. The provisions of that agreement guaranteed the Maroons significant personal freedom and 15,000 acres out of which to make their own community; a clerical error reduced said land to 1500 acres, still a source of some tension in these parts.

**Bickle Village** VILLAGE

Uphill from the Parade Ground is Bickle Village, studded with traditional thatch-roofed homes, with a Maroon burial ground nearby, a small herbal garden where local ladies can point out different medicinal herbs, and the Kindah Tree, an enormous sacred mango tree where the elders of the community congregate.

**Peace Cave** CAVE

One of Accompong's attractions is a one-hour trek down to the Peace Cave (guided hike about US$30), where Cudjoe signed the 1739 peace treaty with the British. The cave itself may be small and unimpressive, but the hike is beautiful.

### ✗ Eating

**Maroon Restaurant** JAMAICAN $

(mains J$500-700; ⊘9am-9pm) One of two restaurants in the Accompong community, which will enthusiastically rustle up traditional food with ingredients plucked from within a 100m radius of your plate. Ask locals for directions.

### 🛍 Shopping

**Craft Shop** ARTS & CRAFTS

(☑413-9940; Parade Ground; ⊘hours vary) *Goombay* drums, along with medicinal herbs, calabash shells and *abengs* (cow horns), are for sale in the tiny red-and-green craft shop as you enter town. The hand-carved *goombay* drum (around J$4000) is box-shaped and covered with goat skin,

while *abengs* (around J$3000), used by Maroons to signal rebellion, make a wonderfully deep and resonant racket. Call Steve if the shop is closed.

### ❶ Getting There & Away

Four kilometers north of Maggotty the road forks at Retirement; the right branch heads to Accompong (via Whitehall) and is narrow, winding and bumpy, with great mountain views.

Infrequent route taxis run from Shakespeare Plaza in Maggotty (J$250).

## Santa Cruz

Santa Cruz is a bustling market town and the most important commercial center in southwest Jamaica. Black River may be the capital of St Elizabeth parish, but Santa Cruz is arguably the more important settlement thanks to its economic clout. Back in the day, Santa Cruz was a market center for horses and mules bred locally for the British army. A livestock market is still held on Saturday, and the first Friday of every month a big produce market takes place, which means serious gridlock.

While there's little here to make you linger, it's a good place to stop for a bite to eat or to withdraw money. It's a major transportation hub as well. Santa Cruz can also make a convenient base from which to visit YS Falls, Black River, Accompong, Alligator Pond and Treasure Beach.

SOUTH COAST & CENTRAL HIGHLANDS SANTA CRUZ

## 🛏 Sleeping

**My Father's Works**  GUESTHOUSE **$$**
(📞852-7451; Lot 9, Gregory subdivision, off Coke Dr; r incl breakfast US$60; ❄🛜) Personable, friendly Nicole makes her guests feel very welcome in her chilled-out house down a quiet street. Comfortable beds, fresh fruit for breakfast and plenty of info on the area makes this a great stopover. From the Hwy A2/Coke Dr crossroads, head south for 600m along Coke Dr, and take the second right, past a prep school and Kingdom Hall.

## 🍴 Eating

**Hind's Restaurant & Bakery**  JAMAICAN **$**
(📞966-2234; Santa Cruz Plaza, Main St; mains J$400-650; ⊙7:30am-5pm Mon-Thu, to 7pm Fri & Sat) This is a clean, simple place to enjoy Jamaican fare such as brown stew and curried goat.

## ℹ Getting There & Away

Santa Cruz is a main stop for buses, minibuses and route taxis going to Kingston (J$400, 2½ hours), Mandeville (J$300, one hour), Black River (J$250, 45 minutes) and other destinations. They arrive and depart from the transportation center on the A2, at the east end of Santa Cruz. Knutsford Express coaches no longer stop in Santa Cruz.

## Troy & Around

The village of Troy, plunked in a valley bottom and surrounded by sugarcane fields, is the southeastern gateway to Cockpit Country and also a center for yam cultivation.

Auchtembeddie, 5km south of Troy, is a choice spot for cavers, it's the home of the **Coffee River Cave**, known for some magnificent rock formations and a whole lotta bats. The area is totally undeveloped for tourism, but you can get in touch in advance with the **Jamaican Caves Organisation** (JCO; 📞347-5184; www.jamaicancaves.org/main.htm; per person US$75-100) to see if they might be able to suggest someone who can take you spelunking.

A dirt road leads 3km north from Troy to Tyre, hamlet ruins on the edge of the Cockpits. An overgrown, largely disused trail leads all the way to Windsor (about 21km); contact STEA (p133) to see if they can recommend a reliable guide. Don't attempt this trek alone; it is easy to get lost and experienced backcountry hikers have almost died on this trail.

Three kilometers northeast of the tiny settlement of Balaclava, the B6 turns southeast for Mandeville; another road (the B10) leads north and climbs to Troy on the border with Trelawny parish. The latter is a beautiful drive as you climb through a series of dramatic gorges. It's difficult to reach Troy via public transport.

## Maggotty

Maggotty is a forgettable village with an unforgettable name, laid out on a bend of the Black River at the western end of the Siloah Valley. It's a tiny, sleepy regional center, but its proximity to YS Falls and the Appleton Rum Estate (which, incidentally, employs most of the residents here) makes it a passable overnighter, though you're better off heading to Santa Cruz or Black River. Maggotty's sole attraction is the sometimes-open Apple Valley Park (p179). The name, by the way, can be attributed to the missionary Rev John Hutch, who named Maggotty after his English birthplace.

## ⊙ Sights

**Appleton Rum Estate**  FACTORY
(📞963-9215; www.appletonrumtour.com; factory tour & rum tasting US$25; ⊙9am-3:30pm Mon-Sat, closed public holidays) You can smell the yeasty odor of molasses wafting from the Appleton Sugar Estate and Rum Factory well before you reach it, 1km northeast of Maggotty. The largest and oldest distillery in Jamaica has been blending rums since 1749. The tour explains how molasses is extracted from sugarcane, then fermented, distilled and aged to produce the Caribbean's own rocket fuel, which you can taste in the John Wray Tavern.

Around 17 varieties – including the lethal Overproof – are available for sampling. Unsurprisingly, the well-stocked gift shop does brisk business with visitors whose inhibitions have understandably been lowered over the course of the tour (and by the way, you get a complimentary bottle of the stuff at the end of the tour, so don't get too soused!).

Of all of Jamaica's rum factory tours, this is the best organised and most fairly priced. Every tour company in Jamaica can get you onto one of the busloads of tourists that truck to and from the Appleton estate (the 'from' part is pretty fun after 17 varieties of rum). Otherwise, it's easiest to get here from Mag-

## YS FALLS

YS Falls ([📞]997-6360; www.ysfalls.com; B6; adult/child US$19/10; [⊙]9:30am-5pm Tue-Sun, last entry at 3:30pm, closed public holidays), a series of eight cascades hemmed in by limestone cliffs and surrounded by lush jungle, are among the most beautiful in Jamaica. The cascades fall 36m from top to bottom, separated by cool pools perfect for swimming. Lifeguards assist you with the rope swing above one of the pools and a stone staircase follows the cascades to the main waterfall. There are no lockers, so watch your stuff.

The more adventurous can fly, screeching, over the falls along a canopy zip line for US$50/35 per adult/under-12. A tractor-drawn jitney takes all visitors to the cascades, where you'll find picnic grounds, changing rooms, a tree house and a shallow pool fed with river water.

Almost every tour operator in Jamaica (and many hotels) offer trips to YS Falls, but if you want to get here ahead of the crowds, drive yourself (or charter your own taxi) and arrive right when the grounds open.

The YS Falls entrance is just north of the junction of the B6 toward Maggotty. From the A2 (a much smoother road if you're driving) the turnoff is 1.5km east of Middle Quarters; from here you'll head 5.5km north to the falls. Public transport is not a reliable way of reaching the falls.

gotty; the factory is 1km east, and taxis will take you there and back for around J$600.

**Apple Valley Park** PARK
([📞]487-4521; adult/child J$450/350; [⊙]10am-5pm daily by reservation only) [🌿] Owned by Patrick Lee and his lovely Chinese-Jamaican family, this is a little triumph of green sensibility and community tourism. The park grounds consist of an 18th-century home, a manicured lake, an artificial pool and further on, a forest reserve that stretches past the waterfalls and swimming holes of the Black River Gorge. You can kayak and paddleboat in the park itself or hike into the woods or fish. The park was closed at research time for refurbishment.

The prettiness of the place is all the more remarkable when one considers this was once the scarred remains of a bauxite mine; Patrick Lee helped bring the area back to nature after hiring locals and subsequently boosting the surrounding economy, and for this reason we give some of the wear and tear evident on the grounds a pass. The 169-hectare family nature park is only open by appointment, so call ahead. The owners also operate a tractor-pulled jitney from the old train station in Maggotty.

### ❶ Getting There & Away

Public transportation vehicles infrequently arrive and depart from opposite Shakespeare Plaza at the north end of Maggotty, connecting to Mandeville (J$240) and Black River (J$210).

## Middle Quarters

This small village on the A2, 13km north of Black River, is a tiny vortex of good eats: it's renowned for women higglers (street vendors) who stand at the roadside selling delicious (spicy) pepper crayfish – pronounced 'swimp' in these parts – cooked at the **roadside grills** (Hwy A2; bag of shrimp J$500). The shrimp are caught in traps made in centuries-old West African tradition from split bamboo. Around J$500 will buy a spicy bagful. Middle Quarters' fame is also its link to Jamaica's most famous bamboo grove (p180).

### ❶ Getting There & Away

Middle Quarters is well connected to Santa Cruz, Black River and other destinations further afield, with frequent buses and route taxis passing through.

## Christiana

POP 8430
The harvesting heart of the central highland agricultural yam-basket, Christiana, some 16km north of Mandeville, is a pleasant market town set in a lovely backdrop of rippling hills and shallow valleys.

The area was settled by German farmers during the 18th and 19th centuries, which is a little bit evident in the complexion of some locals and the local Moravian church, located at the northern end of sinuous Main St. During the 19th century, Christiana became

**WORTH A TRIP**

## BAMBOO AVENUE

The soothing sound of a million leaves rustling in the wind is one of the quiet pleasures of **Bamboo Avenue** (Hwy A2), a photogenic tunnel of towering bamboo. The 4km-long stretch of the A2 between Middle Quarters and Lacovia is shaded by dense 100-year-old stands of *Bambusa vulgaris*, the largest species of bamboo in Jamaica. Cool and pretty, Bamboo Ave is the perfect place to stop for a coconut jelly, accompanied by a bag of pepper shrimp brought along from Middle Quarters.

a hill-town resort popular with European dignitaries and Kingstonians escaping the heat of the plains.

Around Christiana you'd be forgiven for imagining yourself in the Pyrenees or the Costa Rican highlands. The air is crisp, clouds drift through the vales and pine trees add to the alpine setting. There's some good hiking to be done here, and the change of pace from Jamaica's tourist centers can be refreshing.

### ◉ Sights

★ **Gourie Forest Reserve**          NATURE RESERVE
(☑924-2667; ⊙sunrise-sunset) FREE An unexpected bloom of pine trees, mahogany and mahoe grows atop the flinty heads of the Cockpits 3km northwest of Christiana, near Coleyville. This highland nature reserve is laced with picturesque hiking trails and has one of Jamaica's longest cave systems. Driving north up the B5 from Christiana, take the first left after Bryce United Church, then take the left at a Y-fork, then right at the next Y-fork and follow the road for around 500m to the park sign.

There are four main hiking trails through the park, ranging from 1.9km to 4.7km in length. They are not terribly well marked but are due to be developed further. There's also the rutted 4WD road through the park that leads to the community of Ticky Ticky; it's 11.9km in length, picturesque and easy to follow as a hiking trail.

If you want to explore the Gourie Cave, one of the park highlights, it's not a good idea to go alone. A warden lives just inside the park entrance, so it's best to consult him. A former hideout for runaway slaves, it has magnificent columns, and narrow fissures and follows the passage of an icy river with overhead air passages that barely clear 30cm in places; you'll be wading through water that's 3ft to 4ft deep. As such,

Gourie should only be attempted in dry weather, as flooding is a distinct possibility.

**Christiana Bottom**                WATERFALL
This beautiful riverside valley bottom, located below the town at the base of a shimmering waterfall, has two sinkholes, known collectively as Blue Hole. Full of crystal-clear water, they offer refreshing dips. If driving, turn right straight after NCB bank on the main street, then take the first left around a blind corner, then the first right. Park by the second left and take the path down to the river. It's a 3km hike from Christiana's main street; ask locals for directions.

### 🛏 Sleeping

**Hotel Villa Bella**                HOTEL **$**
(☑964-2243; www.hotelvillabella.com; Rte B4; r US$72-96; P🐾) A charming country inn perched on a hill at Sedburgh, at the south end of town, this villa is a former grande dame that retains her original mahogany floors and Victorian and deco furniture and trappings. The rooms don't entirely keep pace with the grandeur, but they're still lovely. A melange of Jamaican, Japanese and Chinese dishes can be prepared on request.

**Cabins**                CABIN
(☑924-2667) Out in the Gourie Forest Reserve, these two solar-powered cabins are an ideal base for hiking and were about to open to the public when we last visited. Sitting among the pine trees, each cabin sleeps six to eight people and comes with kitchen facilities. Call for rates.

### ⓘ Getting There & Away

Christiana is well served by route taxis and minibuses from both Kingston and Mandeville (J$150); from Mandeville you can access other major towns in the south coast and central highlands. To get to Montego Bay and Ocho Rios, head north in a route taxi to Albert Town (J$140) and change.

# Understand
# Jamaica

# Jamaica Today

Abroad, Jamaica sells itself to visitors as a destination where you're never troubled by anything more pressing than where your next rum cocktail is coming from. But paradise clichés will only get you so far. Look a little closer and the Jamaica of everyday reveals itself to be a far more interesting, exciting and complicated place than you could have imagined.

## Best on Film

**The Harder They Come** (1972) A classic rags-to-rude *bwai* (rude boy) story of a country boy turned Kingston criminal. One of the best soundtracks in film history.

**Marley** (2012) Exemplary documentary about the life and music of reggae superstar Bob Marley.

**I Am Bolt** (2016) Feature-length exploration of the Usain Bolt phenomenon, following him all the way to Rio 2016.

**Better Mus Come** (2013) Acclaimed feature about Jamaica's gang troubles of the 1970s.

## Best in Print

**A Brief History of Seven Killings** (Marlon James; 2014) An intricately woven, bloody tapestry of Jamaica in the 1970s.

**Here Comes the Sun** (Nicole Dennis-Benn; 2016) Debut novel exploring the underbelly of Jamaican resort life from one of Jamaica's newest literary stars.

**The Lunatic** (Anthony Winkler; 1987) Comic novel revolving around a village madman and his affair with a tourist.

**Lionheart Gal** (Sistren Collective; 1986) A lively short-story collection that reveals much about patois and the lives of women.

## Global Position

Modern Jamaica looks less and less to Britain, its old imperial ruler, and has turned its head more toward the USA. Far from just being that slice of tropical paradise sold through the brochures of all-inclusive resorts, Jamaica is a developing country negotiating its way through the 21st century, with all the challenges – and opportunities – that presents. In recent decades an increasing number of Jamaicans (and the majority of those with a post–high school education) are emigrating. Remittances from the Jamaican diaspora made up nearly 17% of the economy in 2013.

Jamaica carries an enormous external debt, and much political and economic work goes toward managing it. It's no easy job when the economy is dominated by imports and only a handful of industries generate hard currency of any volume. Tourism is the most important player here, and Jamaica certainly isn't the only Caribbean nation currently looking nervously at developments in Cuba to see how they'll be affected by the new exciting tourism kid on the block.

The island's economy has stabilized recently, however, and once cripplingly high interest rates are now at the lowest they've been for years. For all this good news, in 2016 the Jamaican people kicked out the incumbent People's National Party and prime minister Portia Simpson-Miller in favor of the Jamaica Labour Party, led by Andrew Holness.

## Talking Reparations

One complicated area where politics and economics meet – along with Jamaica's troubled colonial history – is the issue of slavery reparations. In 2015 Jamaica followed the lead of the Caricom Reparations Committee to request nonconfrontational discussions with the British government over the issue. Rather than simply ask Britain for money, the Committee proposed that Britain acknowledge how it had benefited from slavery to the detriment of Jamaica and its people, and that it contribute to a joint program of rehabilitation and renewal. When the then British prime minister David Cameron visited Jamaica in 2015, he was quick to dodge the issue, instead concentrating on Britain's development aid to Jamaica and the prospects for future trade. But with Caricom pursuing the issue as an active goal, the question of reparations seems unlikely to go away any time soon.

## Cultural Pride

In 2016 Jamaica left the athletics track at the Rio Olympic Games with yet another armful of medals. Usain Bolt completed his 'triple triple' – his third Olympics with gold medals in the 100m, 200m and 4x100m relay. For the women, Elaine Thompson established herself as the name to beat, taking gold in the 100m and 200m, and the crown from Shelly-Ann Fraser Pryce.

While Bolt continued his bid to make his country as famous for its runners as its reggae, Jamaica also made its presence felt on another international stage. In 2015 author Marlon James won the Man Booker Prize for *A Brief History of Seven Killings*, his epic novel spun out from the attempted assassination of Bob Marley ('The Singer') in 1976. James' success is now opening doors for the new generation of local writers, including Kei Miller and Nicole Dennis-Benn – yet another avenue for Jamaica to tell its story to the world.

## Jamaican Conversations

Jamaicans tend to be passionate people. Their full-bore approach to life is what often attracts (and occasionally intimidates) visitors to their island. The easiest way to hear lively patois is to talk politics with a Jamaican; most, including deceptively laid-back Rastas, have well-crafted and informed opinions on current affairs in Jamaica, and even the optimistic ones have their gripes.

On this island there are as many opinions on how to fix things as there are Jamaicans. Travelers, however, remain well regarded by the average Jamaican. Tourism – an industry where Jamaica was an early pioneer of globalization – is the country's largest foreign-currency earner, and remains a testament to the fact that, despite the challenges, Jamaicans are determined to share their island with the world.

POPULATION: **2.68 MILLION**

GDP: **US$14.01 BILLION**

GDP PER CAPITA: **US$4998**

INFLATION: **1.6%**

UNEMPLOYMENT: **13.7%**

### if Jamaica were 100 people

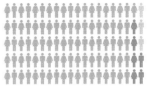

91 would be black
6 would be mixed
3 would be other

### belief systems
(% of population)

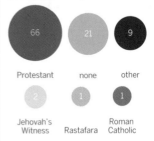

| Protestant | none | other |

66 — Protestant
21 — none
9 — other
2 — Jehovah's Witness
1 — Rastafara
1 — Roman Catholic

### population per sq km

JAMAICA    UK    USA

🧍 = 35 people

# History

Jamaica's story was forged at the sharp edge of Western imperialism. Conquest, sugar and slavery led to the island becoming Britain's wealthiest colony, yet internal resistance helped create a national identity that led to reform and the path to independence. It's a history that has left its mark on the island, but the passion and the perseverance of its people, which have made the island and its culture so vital, still leads Jamaicans to work toward a stronger future.

## Xaymaca

*The Story of the Jamaican People by Philip Sherlock and Hazel Bennett offers a new interpretation of Jamaica's history centering on Afro-Caribbean culture rather than European colonialism.*

The Caribbean was inhabited long before Christopher Columbus sailed into view, colonized by a successive wave of island-hopping incomers originally from South America. Most notable were the Arawaks, and then the Taínos who first settled 'Xaymaca' ('land of wood and water') around AD 700–800.

The Taínos were both farmers and seafarers, living in large chiefdoms called *caciques*, and honing their skills as potters, carvers, weavers and boat builders. They worshipped a variety of gods believed to control rain, sun, wind and hurricanes, and who were represented by *zemes* (idols of humans or animals).

Clothing was made of cotton or pounded bark fibers, along with jewelry of bone, shell, and gold panned from rivers. While Taíno artifacts remain relatively few, the crops they bequeathed to the world were revolutionary, from tobacco and yams to cassava and pineapples.

## Columbus & Spanish Settlement

Christopher Columbus landed on the island in 1494 on his second voyage to the New World, landing at Bahía Santa Gloria (modern St Ann's Bay) and making first contact with the Taínos along the coast at Discovery Bay. Although he didn't linger, he claimed the island for Spain and christened it Santa Jago.

Columbus returned disastrously in 1503, when his poorly maintained ships sank beneath him. He and his crew spent almost a year marooned,

| TIMELINE | AD 700–800 | 1494 | 1517 |
|---|---|---|---|
| | Taínos settle on the island, calling it 'Xaymaca,' meaning 'land of wood and water.' | Christopher Columbus first lands on Jamaica, which he names Santa Jago; it later becomes his personal property. | The Spanish bring enslaved Africans to do their bidding on the island in place of the Taínos, whose population has been decimated by European violence and disease. |

and suffered from disease and malnutrition. Finally, two officers paddled a canoe 240km to Hispaniola to raise a rescue expedition.

Jamaica became Columbus' personal property and when he died in 1506 it passed to his son Diego, who appointed a governor to establish a capital called Nueva Sevilla, near present-day Ocho Rios.

Within three decades of their first meeting with Europeans, the Taínos were quickly reduced to a shadow of their previous numbers, stricken by European illnesses and the forced labor required to dig for gold. In response, the Spaniards began importing enslaved Africans.

In 1534 a new settlement was founded on the south coast, Villa de la Vega (Spanish Town). However, Spain had become distracted by the immense riches coming from its new possessions in Mexico and Peru, and Jamaica languished as a post for provisioning ships sailing between Spain and Central America.

Put Jamaican history into context with Carrie Gibson's superb *Empire's Crossroads: A History of the Caribbean from Columbus to the Present Day*.

## The English Invasion

On May 10, 1655, an expeditionary force of 38 ships landed 8000 troops on weakly defended Jamaica as part of Oliver Cromwell's 'Grand Western Design' to destroy the Spanish trade monopoly and amass English holdings in the Caribbean.

The British had to fight both Spanish loyalists and the *cimarrones* (runaways) – freed slaves left in the Spaniards' wake. The guerrilla warfare lasted several years until the last Spanish forces were finally routed at the Battle of Rio Bueno (outside Ocho Rios) in 1660.

By 1662 there were 4000 colonists on the island, including exiled felons as well as impoverished Scots and Welsh who arrived as indentured laborers. Port Royal, across the bay from Spanish Town, became the island's capital, and a viable trading economy slowly began to evolve.

## The Age of Buccaneers

Throughout the 17th century, Britain was constantly at war with France, Spain or Holland. The English sponsored privateers to capture enemy vessels, raid their settlements and contribute their plunder to the Crown's coffers. These buccaneers became the Brethren of the Coast, committed to a life of piracy, and grew into a powerful and ruthless force, feared throughout the Antilles.

In 1664 the Jamaican governor Sir Thomas Modyford invited the Brethren to defend Jamaica, with Port Royal as their base. Their numbers swelled astronomically, and within a decade Port Royal was Jamaica's largest city – a den of iniquity and prosperity.

When England and Spain finally made peace, the pirates' days became numbered. Mother Nature lent a hand in their suppression when

Before it was swallowed up by the earthquake of 1692, booming and licentious Port Royal was dubbed 'the richest and wickedest city in the world.'

| 1643 | 1655 | 1692 | 1700 |
|---|---|---|---|
| Jamaica is sacked by English pirate William Jackson, raising doubt about the security of the Spanish colony. | The English capture Jamaica from the Spanish, who retreat to Cuba. | Port Royal slides into the harbor after an earthquake, killing more than 2000 people. Kingston is founded the following year as a replacement to the port. | There are more than five slaves for every English settler on Jamaica. The practice of slavery creates enormous economic bounty for the English, at terrible cost to the enslaved. |

## THE ATLANTIC SLAVE TRADE

The Atlantic slave trade was dubbed 'the triangular trade.' European merchants sailed to West Africa with goods to exchange for slaves. Although domestic slavery had long been an established part of many African societies, European demand (and trade goods such as firearms) turned African states into asset-strippers, sucking in captives in insatiable numbers, often from tribes living hundreds of miles from African slave ports.

Traders packed shackled captives into the bowels of their ships. Around one in eight died during the voyage, which lasted two to three months. The slaves were sold for sugar, which was then exported back to Europe – the third profitable leg of the trade.

During the lifetime of the trade, around 12 million slaves were brought to the Americas, of whom around 1.5 million ended up in Jamaica.

a massive earthquake struck Port Royal on June 7, 1692, toppling it into the sea. More than 2000 people – one-third of the city's population – perished, and survivors fled to newly founded Kingston, believing the earthquake to be punishment from God.

## Sugar & Slavery

Europe's sweet tooth had been growing for years, and sugar – cultivated by enslaved Africans – helped turn Jamaica into Britain's wealthiest colony and provide the capital that fueled the Industrial Revolution.

Planters built 'great houses' in Georgian fashion high above their cane fields, and lived a life of indolence, while others were absentee landlords, forming the powerful sugar lobby back in London. Many overindulged in drink and had sexual relations with slaves – some of the mixed-race offspring were freed; known as 'free coloreds,' they were accorded limited rights and often sent to study in England.

Plantations were both farm and factory, growing the cane and refining the sugar. The by-product molasses was turned into cheap rum for export. Sugar production was backbreaking work, and plantation owners used extreme violence to terrorize their slaves into obedience. Plantation society was firmly wedded to the rule of the whip.

Most slaves worked on plantations; others were domestic servants. During their few free hours, the slaves cultivated their own tiny plots, and could sell produce at market. In rare instances they might save enough money to buy their freedom, which masters could also grant as they wished. By 1800, however, the slave population of 300,000 outnumbered the free population 20 to one.

Matthew Parker's *The Sugar Barons* is a gripping account of the founding of Britain's Caribbean slave empire, with Jamaica taking center stage.

| 1760 | 1814 | 1831 | 1845 |
|---|---|---|---|
| Tacky, a runaway slave, starts an uprising in St Mary that is brutally suppressed with the aid of the local Maroons. | Jamaican sugar production peaks at £34 million. During the first half of the 19th century, the island is the world's largest producer of sugar. | Sam Sharpe launches Jamaica's largest slave rebellion. Harsh reprisals contribute to moves to abolish slavery in the British empire, which takes place the following year. | To fill the labor gap left by the abolition of slavery, 30,000 Indians are brought to Jamaica as indentured laborers. |

# Maroon Resistance

Colonial life was paranoid over the possibility of slave rebellion. The first major revolt occurred in 1690 in Clarendon parish, when escaped slaves joined the descendants of slaves who had been freed by the Spanish, coalescing into two powerful bands called Maroons. The Windward Maroons lived in the remote Blue Mountains, while the Leeward Maroons colonized the almost impenetrable Cockpit Country. Both groups raided plantations and attracted runaway slaves.

Colonial troops fought several prolonged campaigns against the Maroons, who were led by Nanny in the Blue Mountains and Cudjoe in Cockpit Country. The thickly forested mountains, however, were ill-suited to traditional British military tactics and perfect for the Maroons' ambush-style guerrilla warfare. Nonetheless, after a decade of costly campaigning, the English gained the upper hand.

In March 1739 the English signed a peace treaty with Cudjoe, granting the Maroons autonomy and 1500 acres of land. In return, the Maroons agreed to chase down runaway slaves and return them to the plantations and to assist the English in quelling rebellions. The Maroons of the Blue Mountains, now led by Quao, signed a similar treaty one year later. To this day, the Maroons still practice a semiautonomous form of government.

Visit the ruins of the first Spanish settlement on the island at the Seville Great House near St Ann's Bay.

# Revolt & Reform

After a prolonged campaign by abolitionist campaigners such as Thomas Clarkson and William Wilberforce, Britain abolished the slave trade in 1807, although the institution of slavery itself was left untouched.

Jamaica's 1831 Christmas Rebellion lent particular focus to the debate. Inspired by 'Daddy' Sam Sharpe, an educated slave and lay preacher, up to 20,000 slaves razed plantations and killed their masters. The rebellion was violently suppressed, and 400 slaves were hanged as a result. The brutality of the response lent weight to British abolitionist debates. In 1834 the British Parliament finally passed antislavery legislation, emancipating the empire's slaves.

The resulting transition from a slave economy to one based on paid labor caused economic chaos; most slaves rejected the starvation wages offered on the estates, choosing to fend for themselves. Desperation over conditions and injustice finally boiled over in the 1865 Morant Bay Rebellion (p189).

Get inside the lives of the enslaved on Jamaica's sugar plantations with Marlon James' devastating novel *The Book of Night Women*.

| 1865 | 1907 | 1930 | 1938 |
|---|---|---|---|
| The Morant Bay Rebellion, led by Paul Bogle, is brutally suppressed by the British authorities. | A great earthquake topples much of Kingston on January 14, causing widespread destruction and killing more than 800 people. | Haile Selassie is crowned emperor of Ethiopia, encouraging the rise of Rastafari in Jamaica. | Jamaica's first political party, the People's National Party (PNP), is formed by Norman Manley, who works with the Bustamante Trade Union to make working-class issues a main focus of Jamaican politics. |

## JAMAICA'S NATIONAL HEROES

After independence, Jamaica honored seven heroes for their special roles in forging the national identity. Memorialized at National Heroes Park in Kingston, they're also depicted on the currency and school walls everywhere.

➡ Paul Bogle (c 1820–65) staged the 1865 protests that became the Morant Bay Rebellion (p189).

➡ Alexander Bustamante (1884–1977) was a firebrand trade unionist and founder of the Jamaica Labor Party, who became independent Jamaica's first prime minister.

➡ Marcus Garvey (1887–1940) was a key proponent of Pan-Africanism and father of the 'black power' movement (p190).

➡ George William Gordon (1820–65), a lawyer, assemblyman and post-emancipation nationalist, was a powerful advocate of the rights of the poor.

➡ Norman Manley (1893–1969) founded the People's National Party and became the self-governing island's first prime minister, prior to independence.

➡ Nanny of the Maroons (c 1686–c 1733) was a leader of the Windward Maroons in the 18th century. Folklore attributes her with magical powers.

➡ Samuel Sharpe (1801–32), a slave and Baptist deacon, was hanged for his leadership of the Christmas Rebellion of 1831.

## Banana Island

In 1866 a Yankee skipper, George Busch, arrived in Jamaica and loaded several hundred stems of bananas, which he transported to Boston and sold at a handsome profit. He quickly returned to Port Antonio, where he encouraged production and soon had himself a thriving export business. Captain Lorenzo Dow Baker followed suit in the west, forming the United Fruit Company. Within a decade the banana trade was booming. Production peaked in 1927, when 21 million stems were exported.

To help pay the passage south to Jamaica, banana traders promoted the island's virtues and took on passengers. Thus, the banana-export trade gave rise to the tourism industry, which continues to grow and flourish.

## Birth of a Nation

During the Depression of the 1930s, sugar and banana sales plummeted, causing widespread economic hardships. Strikes and riots erupted in 1938, but out of the clamor stepped the charismatic labor leader Alexander Bustamante and his Bustamante Industrial Trade Union. That

| 1941 | 1943 | 1944 | 1962 |
| --- | --- | --- | --- |
| Thousands of Jamaican servicepeople volunteer to fight for Britain during WWII. | The Jamaica Labour Party (JLP) is formed by Alexander Bustamante. | A new constitution introduces universal suffrage and the first elections are held for a locally based government. | On August 6, Jamaica becomes an independent nation within the British Commonwealth. |

same year, his cousin Norman Manley formed the People's National Party (PNP), Jamaica's first political party.

Separately they campaigned for economic and political reforms, putting the working class into political life and securing constitutional changes. Not content with trade-union activism, Bustamante formed the Jamaica Labour Party (JLP) in 1943.

A year later, a new constitution granted universal suffrage and Jamaica's first elections, which were won by Bustamante's JLP. There was a brief flirtation with the fledgling West Indies Federation of British colonies, but on August 6, 1962, Jamaica finally gained full independence. The Union Jack was replaced by Jamaica's new flag, in glorious black (for the people), green (for the land) and gold (for the sun).

Mavis Campbell's *The Maroons of Jamaica* is a serious study of the origins of the Maroons and their evolution as a culture through to the late 19th century.

## The Manley-Seaga Era

The legacies of Bustamante and Manley have dominated post-independence politics. Manley's son Michael led the PNP toward democratic socialism in the mid-'70s. His policy of taxation to fund social services deterred foreign investment and caused widespread capital flight, and bitterly opposed factions engaged in open urban warfare before the 1976 election. Amid a controversial state of emergency, the PNP won the election by a wide margin.

The US government was hostile to Jamaica's socialist turn, withdrew aid and purportedly planned to topple the Jamaican government. The economy (tourism in particular) went into sharp decline. JLP–PNP violence escalated until a cease-fire was finally brokered, celebrated by the famed 'One Love' concert in April 1978, when Bob Marley got Manley and the JLP's Edward Seaga to hold hands in a symbol of unity.

### THE MORANT BAY REBELLION

In the 1860s Paul Bogle, a black Baptist deacon in St Thomas parish, preached resistance against the post-emancipation injustices of the local authorities. He was supported by George William Gordon, a mixed-race planter and assemblyman.

On October 11, 1865, Bogle and his supporters marched to the Morant Bay courthouse to protest the trial of a vagrant for trespassing. A riot ensued and the courthouse and town center were razed. As the countryside erupted, Bogle fled with a bounty on his head, but was captured by Maroons and hanged from the burned-out courthouse. Gordon was arrested in Kingston, condemned by a kangaroo court and also hanged.

Governor Edward Eyre ordered vicious reprisals. Martial law was declared and some 439 people killed in arbitrary executions and more than 1000 homes burned down. Such was the subsequent outrage in Britain that Eyre was stripped of his post along with the powers of the Jamaican House of Assembly, turning the island into a Crown colony.

| 1963 | 1966 | 1972 | 1976 |
|---|---|---|---|
| At the height of the ska era in Jamaican music, Clement Dodd begins recording Bob Marley and the Wailers. | On the second stop of his Caribbean trip, HIM Haile Selassie I is greeted by nearly 100,000 chanting Rastafaris at the airport. | Michael Manley launches socialist reforms, and tries to promote Jamaica's self-sufficiency by rejecting close ties with the US and allying Jamaica with Cuba. | In the lead-up to the election, tensions between Jamaica's two political parties erupt into open warfare in the streets between politically aligned gangs. A state of emergency is declared. |

## UP YOU MIGHTY RACE!

Marcus Garvey was born of working-class parents in St Ann's Bay on August 17, 1887. After traveling to Costa Rica, Panama and England, he returned a firm believer in self-improvement and he founded the Universal Negro Improvement Association (UNIA) in 1914 to unite 'all the Negro peoples of the world to establish a state exclusively their own.' When Jamaica's middle classes proved largely unreceptive to his message, he moved in 1916 to the US, where he received a rapturous welcome and formed a branch of the UNIA in New York. The UNIA is credited for giving birth to the Black Panther movement, which in turn paved the way for the civil rights movement. Garvey, a gifted orator, established a weekly newspaper, the *Negro World*, and built an enormous following under the slogan 'One God! One Aim! One Destiny!'

Garvey set up the Black Star Line, a steamship company, with the aim of eventually repatriating blacks to Africa, though it ultimately failed due to poor management. Garvey's greatest achievement was to instill the postcolonial black community with a sense of self-worth and pride: 'Up you mighty race, you can accomplish what you will.'

Considering Garvey a dangerous agitator, the American and British governments conspired against him, and in 1922 they arrested him on dubious mail-fraud charges. He served two years in Atlanta Federal Prison before being deported to Jamaica, where he founded the reformist People's Political Party. Universal franchise did not then exist in Jamaica, and he failed to gather enough support at the polls. In 1935 he departed for England, where he died in poverty in 1940.

His remains were repatriated to Jamaica in 1964 and interred with state honors in National Heroes Park in Kingston. The advent of reggae music in the 1970s gave rise to a new wave of Garveyism.

Nevertheless, almost 800 people were killed in the lead-up to the 1980 elections, which were won by Seaga. Seaga opened the door to the free market and International Monetary Fund, and became a staunch ally of the Reagan administration.

Relatively peaceful elections in 1989 returned a reinvented 'mainstream realist' Manley to power; when he retired in 1992, he handed the reins to his deputy, Percival James Patterson, who became Jamaica's first black prime minister.

Tony Sewall's *Garvey's Children: The Legacy of Marcus Garvey* looks at the rise of black nationalism inspired by national hero Marcus Garvey.

## The PNP Years

The Patterson-led PNP triumphed in the 1993 and 1997 elections. In spring 1999 the country erupted in nationwide riots after the government announced a 30% increase in the tax on gasoline. Kingston and Montego Bay, where sugarcane fields were set ablaze, were particularly badly hit. After three days of arson and looting, the government rescinded the tax.

| 1978 | 1980 | 1988 | 2004 |
|---|---|---|---|
| The One Love peace concert is held in Kingston, following Bob Marley's homecoming; 100,000 people attend. The PNP and JLP declare a cease-fire in its honor. | The JLP's Edward Seaga is elected to power and begins transforming Jamaica's foreign engagement, cutting ties with Cuba and positioning himself as a friend of the Reagan administration. | Hurricane Gilbert slams Jamaica, killing 45 people and causing damage estimated at up to US$1 billion. | At least 15 people are killed by Hurricane Ivan, with Negril being particularly hard hit. The banana trees are ravaged, and the following year banana exports drop by 68%. |

In the lead-up to the 2002 elections, violence in West Kingston soared to new heights as criminal posses battled to control electoral turf and profit from the largesse that victory at the polls in Jamaica brings. Rival political gangs turned the area into a war zone, forcing residents to flee, and schools, businesses and even Kingston Public Hospital to close.

In 2004 Hurricane Ivan bounced off Jamaica en route to the Cayman Islands, causing widespread damage, and Edward Seaga – still representing the JLP as opposition leader – retired after more than three decades in politics. Two years later Prime Minister Patterson resigned, making way to Portia Simpson-Miller, Jamaica's first female prime minister and Michael Manley's protégé. 'Mama P' was initially popular with the masses, but 18 years of PNP rule bred voter disillusionment with the party. In the 2007 elections, Bruce Golding of the JLP carried the day, inheriting high rates of crime and illiteracy as well as threats to the environment through deforestation and overdevelopment.

## From Dudus to the Present

Politics and gang crime came to a head in 2009, when the US called for the extradition of Christopher 'Dudus' Coke, the don of the pro-PNP Tivoli Gardens ghetto and one of the most powerful men in Jamaica, on alleged gun- and drug-running charges. In May 2010 a joint police-military force undertook the deeply controversial Tivoli Incursion, which left some 74 dead – including many bystanders – with others the victims of alleged extra-judicial executions. Dudus himself remained on the run for a month before being apprehended, and is now serving a 23-year sentence in the US.

In 2011 Portia Simpson-Miller was returned as prime minister. Her government looked to China as much as America, using Jamaica's long-standing Chinese community to leverage increased investment from Beijing. In 2013 the government had to go cap in hand to the IMF for restructured loans. Although the economy began to stabilize, in 2016 the voters deemed it was time for a change, voting out the PNP and returning the JLP to power, with Andrew Holness becoming prime minister just in time for another Jamaican golden sweep of the athletics track at the Rio Olympics.

Jamaica has long struggled under enormous foreign debts. *Life & Debt*, a documentary film by Stephanie Black, takes a provocative look into the island's burden.

HISTORY FROM DUDUS TO THE PRESENT

| 2006 | 2008 | 2010 | 2016 |
|---|---|---|---|
| Portia Simpson-Miller, of the PNP, becomes Jamaica's first female prime minister. | Usain Bolt explodes onto the world stage at the Beijing Olympic Games, breaking world records in 100m and 200m and announcing Jamaica's arrival as an athletics powerhouse. | Christopher 'Dudus' Coke, don of the Tivoli Gardens ghetto, is extradited to the US after an armed standoff between gang members and the Jamaican police and military. | The JLP returns to power in national elections, with Andrew Holness becoming prime minister. |

# Jamaican Way of Life

**Spliff-puffing Rastas, violent rude boys from the Kingston ghettoes, deep reggae vibes and slack dancehall lyrics – people sure can arrive in Jamaica with a basketful of clichés. However, the reality is a lot more interesting and complex, and the island is home to a culture as diverse as the island's geography is varied. It's a country as smooth as a cup of Blue Mountain coffee, and as buzzing as a shot of white overproof rum.**

## 'Out of Many, One People'

When Jamaicans speak patois, often they drop their 'h's (thus, *ouse* instead of 'house') and add them in unexpected places (eg *hemphasize*). Jamaicans usually drop the 'h' from 'th' as well: hence, *t'anks* for 'thanks.' 'The' is usually pronounced as *de* and 'them' as *dem*. They also sometimes drop the 'w,' as in *ooman* (woman).

The nation's motto reflects the diverse heritage of Jamaica. Along with the many West Africans imported as slaves, the population was salted with English, Scots, Irish, Welsh and Germans, along with Hispanic and Portuguese Jews and 'Syrians' (a term for all those of Levantine extraction), as well as Chinese and Indians, who arrived as indentured workers following emancipation.

Jamaica proclaims itself a melting pot of racial harmony. Still, insecurities of identity have been carried down from the plantation era. The issue of class lines drawn during the colonial era has left profound societal divisions and is closely tied to color: lighter-skinned Jamaicans are far more likely to hold better-paid jobs, and skin bleaching is a common phenomenon. The middle classes have always sought to distance themselves from the inhabitants of shanty towns. There is some lingering resentment against whites, particularly among the poorer segment of society, and disillusionment with postindependence Jamaica.

Jamaicans can be the most gracious people you'll ever meet: hardworking, helpful, courteous, genteel and full of humility. However, charged memories of slavery and racism have continued to bring out the spirit of anarchy latent in a society divided into rich and poor. Jamaicans struggling hard against poverty are disdainful of talk about a 'tropical paradise.'

Jamaicans love to debate, or 'reason.' They tend to express themselves forcefully, turning differences of opinion into voluble arguments with some confounding elliptical twists and stream-of-consciousness associations.

Jamaicans' sarcasm and sardonic wit is legendary. The deprecating humor has evolved as an escape valve that hides their true feelings. In a country in which it's hard to make a living, the saying that 'everyt'ing irie' – no problems – can mark black humor indeed.

## Economic Life

Originally from West Africa, the spider Anansi is Jamaica's celebrated trickster folk hero. Check out the patois folktales of Louise Bennett for the best of his fables.

Jamaica is classed as a middle-income country, and it has a small but significant middle class – well educated, entrepreneurial and frequently with close ties to the UK and America.

Despite this, many Jamaicans live in pockets of extreme poverty, either in the countryside, eking out lives as farmers, fishers or plantation laborers, or scraping by in Kingston's ghettoes and shanties. Job opportunities are difficult to come by without a proper education, which doesn't come cheap, so many low-income Jamaicans hustle, waiting for an opportunity to present itself. The average per capita income is less than US$5000 a year and many Jamaicans are reliant on remittances sent by family members living abroad.

# Religion & Spirituality

Jamaica professes to have the greatest number of churches per square kilometer in the world. Although most foreigners associate the island with Rastafari, around 70% of Jamaicans identify themselves as Christian and the Church remains a powerful political lobby group in the country.

## Christianity

On weekends, it's common to see adults and children walking along country roads holding Bibles and dressed in their finest outfits. Every church in the country seems to overflow with the righteous, and the old fire-and-brimstone school of sermonizing is still the preferred mode. It's hard to over-emphasize the social and cultural influence of the Church in Jamaica.

The most popular denomination is the Anglican Church of Jamaica, followed by Seventh-Day Adventists, Pentecostals, Baptists, Methodists and Catholics.

## Rastafari

Dreadlocked Rastas are as synonymous with Jamaica as reggae. Developed in the 1930s, the Rastafari creed evolved as an expression of poor, black Jamaicans seeking fulfillment, boosted by Marcus Garvey's 'back to Africa' zeal.

Central to Rastafari is the concept that the Africans are one of the displaced Twelve Tribes of Israel. Jamaica is Babylon, and their lot is in exile in a land that cannot be reformed. The crowning of Ras Tafari (Haile Selassie) as emperor of Abyssinia in 1930 fulfilled the prophecy of an African king and redeemer who would lead them from exile to the promised land of Zion, the black race's spiritual home.

Ganja smoking is a sacrament for many (if not all) Rastas, allowing them to gain wisdom and inner divinity through the ability to 'reason' more clearly. The parsing of Bible verses is an essential tradition, helping to see through the corrupting influences of Babylon. The growing of dreadlocks is an allegory for the mane of the Lion of Judah.

Despite its militant consciousness, the religion preaches love and nonviolence, and adherents live by strict biblical codes advocating a way of life in harmony with Old Testament traditions. Some Rastas are teetotalers who shun tobacco and keep to a strict diet of vegetarian I-tal food, prepared without salt; others, like the 12 Tribes Rastafari, eat meat and drink beer.

Barry Chevannes' *Rastafari: Roots and Ideology* and *Rasta Heart: A Journey into One Love* by Robert Roskind are noteworthy books on Jamaica's most-talked-about creed.

JAMAICAN WAY OF LIFE RELIGION & SPIRITUALITY

### THE RASTAFARI LEXICON

One of the 21 tenets of Rastafari is the belief that God exists in each person, and that the two are the same. Thus the creed unifies divinity and individuality through the use of personal pronouns that reflect the 'I and I'.' 'I' becomes the id or true measure of inner divinity, which places everyone on the same plane. Thus 'I and I' can mean 'we,' 'him and her,' 'you and them.' (The personal pronoun 'me' is seen as a sign of subservience, of acceptance of the self as an 'object.')

Rastafari reasoning sees the English language as a tool in the service of Babylon, designed to 'downpress' the black people. The belief that language itself is biased has led to a whole lexicon laced with cryptic intent and meaning, which has profoundly influenced 'Jamaica talk.'

## Revivalism

Jamaica has several sects that are generically named Revivalist cults after the post-emancipation Great Revival, during which many blacks converted to Christianity. The most important Revivalist branches are Zionism and Pocomania (Pukkumina), the former being more Bible-centered, and the latter involving ancestor worship.

A core Revivalist belief is that spirits live independently of the body and can inhabit inanimate objects and communicate themselves to humans.

Revivalist ceremonies are characterized by the flowing robes of the congregation, chanting, drumming, speaking in tongues and spirit possession. They are held in designated poco yards, led by a 'shepherd' or 'mother', who interprets the messages of the spirits.

Rarer these days, Kumina is the most African of the Revivalist cults, combining evocation of ancestral spirits with call-and-response chanting and intricate drumming rhythms and dancing.

Follow the cricketing progress of the Jamaican Tallawahs in the Caribbean Premier League at www.cplt20.com.

# Women in Jamaica

While Jamaican society can appear oppressively macho to outsiders accustomed to dancehall lyrics, women tend to be strong, independent and economically active. This spirit often translates into the kind of self-assurance so apparent in Portia Simpson-Miller, the former prime minister. Jamaican women attain far higher grades in school and have higher literacy rates than Jamaican men, and middle-class women have attained levels of respect and career performance that are commensurate with their counterparts in North America and Europe.

The darker side of a Jamaican woman's life is the proliferation of sexual violence. According to statistics, one in four women is subject to a forced sexual encounter during the course of her life. While Jamaica has one of the highest rates of teenage pregnancy in the region (18% of all births are to teenage mothers), abortion remains illegal except on medical grounds.

## HOMOPHOBIA IN JAMAICA

Ever since Buju Banton's 1990s dancehall hit 'Boom Bye Bye' made international headlines for its apparent celebration of the murder of gay men, Jamaica has gained an unfortunate reputation as a deeply homophobic country.

Dancehall homophobia is merely a reflection of deeper currents within Jamaican society. This is a deeply devout Christian country, where homosexuality is preached against as a biblical sin, and often seen as a Western colonial import – a threat to the fabric of society itself.

Homophobic violence is common, from verbal and physical abuse to 'corrective rape' against lesbians (in a country where sexual violence against women is sadly all too commonplace). Pejorative terms like 'batty man' and 'fish' are still thrown about despite attempts to strip dancehall of its homophobic elements. Homelessness is a particular problem for young gay men, who are often ostracized by their families. Jamaica has the highest rate of prostate cancer in the world, with anecdotal evidence suggesting a link to a perceived homosexual stigma attached to getting a rectal checkup.

Despite this, Jamaica's LGBT community is increasingly visible and assertive, from organizations such as J-Flag (Jamaica Forum for Lesbians, All-Sexuals and Gays; www.jflag.org) and Quality of Citizenship Jamaica (www.qcjm.org), to the continued campaign to repeal the 1864 Buggery Law, which criminalizes all anal sex. Despite pushback from Christian organizations, societal attitudes remain in flux, from the wild popularity of the outrageously camp comedy actor Keith 'Shebada' Ramsey and the celebration of openly gay Booker Prize–winning author Marlon James, to the influence that gay fashion has had on the hyper-masculine dancehall world. Since 2015 Jamaica has successfully held gay pride events, with public support from government ministers. Like many things in the country, homophobia is a lot more complicated than it first appears.

## OBEAH & MYAL

Jamaica has its own folk magic system, based on practices derived from West Africa, and similar to Haiti's Vodou or Cuba's Santería. Myal is essentially 'white magic' to obeah's 'black magic.' Largely a rural practice, it involves invoking the services of a practitioner who can cast or dispel a curse, bring you luck, or force your partner to be faithful, using an arsenal of herbs, powders (including grave dust), specially shaped candles and power rings to achieve their objective.

The summoning of duppies (spirits) is central to the practice. Jamaicans believe that your spirit roams the earth for nine days after you die, and in that time it can be summoned to do good or evil. Many Jamaicans still observe Nine Night, a 'wake' held for nine nights after someone's death to ensure that the spirit of the deceased (duppy) departs to heaven – these can be pretty big parties complete with sound systems.

Invoking duppies involves a ritual circle comprised of bottles topped with candles. The entrance or 'gateway' to the circle is barred with a cutlass or machete and the circle may contain food offerings to the spirits, as well as chalked symbols.

Nonbelievers dismiss obeah as superstitious nonsense, but everyone knows where the nearest obeah shop is, and local newspapers often feature hilarious 'duppy' stories in their news roundups. Judging by the charms you find in many Jamaican homes, obeah still has a powerful grip on the nation's psyche.

# Sporting Jamaica

If anyone can wrest away Bob Marley's mantle as the world's most recognizable Jamaican, it's the ultra-charismatic Usain Bolt, currently the fastest man on the planet and 'triple-triple' Olympic gold medalist, winning gold in the 100m, 200m and 400m relay at the Beijing, London and Rio games. He's part of Jamaica's astonishing home-grown crop of athletics champions, along with Shelly-Ann Fraser-Pryce and Elaine Thompson (both Olympic 100m and 200m gold-medal holders).

Jamaica is cricket mad, and cricketers such as fast bowler Courtney Walsh and batsman Chris Gayle are revered. Jamaica plays nationally as part of the West Indies team, who were quarter-finalists in the 2011 and 2015 World Cups, and champions in the 2012 and 2016 World Twenty20. Jamaican cricket's home is Sabina Park in Kingston, which hosts national and international test matches as well as the Caribbean Premier League (CPL) – of which the Jamaican Tallawahs are the 2016 champions.

Football is also madly popular. The Reggae Boyz – Jamaica's national soccer team – took part in the 1998 World Cup, though they haven't qualified since. Spirited international matches are played at Kingston's National Stadium.

Get the scoop on how Jamaica became an athletics powerhouse with Richard Moore's *The Bolt Supremacy: Inside Jamaica's Sprint Factory*.

# Jamaican Arts

**The rest of the region might not agree, but for many visitors Jamaican culture is synonymous with Caribbean culture as a whole. There's more to the island than just an endless Bob Marley mixtape, however: from dancehall vibes and a rich visual arts tradition to a literary scene that's currently enjoying international acclaim, Jamaicans prove time and again the strength and depth of their cultural scene.**

## Music

Few places are as defined by their music as Jamaica. Thanks to Bob Marley, reggae is the island soundtrack that went on to conquer the world, helping permanently brand the country and bestow on it a global cultural influence well out of proportion to the island's tiny size. In fact, there's a lot more to Jamaican music than just reggae, as Jamaica's relentlessly busy studios attest. Per capita, Jamaica is the world's most prolific creator of recorded music. Or as the patois proverbs put it, 'We likkle but we talawah' (We're small, but we're powerful.)

### Routes & Roots

Modern Jamaican music starts with the acoustic folk music of mento. In the early 1960s this blended with calypso, jazz and R&B to form ska, the country's first popular music form. This evolved, via the intermediate step of rocksteady, into the bass-heavy reggae of the 1970s, the genre that ultimately swept all before it. Dancehall, a faster and more clubby sound than its predecessors, followed thereafter, and continues to dominate the contemporary music scene today. For all that these styles are distinct, they constantly blend and feed off each other – this syncretism is the true magic of Jamaican music.

Timothy White's *Catch a Fire* remains the go-to Bob Marley biography. Pair it with a screening of Kevin Macdonald's superb 2012 feature documentary, *Marley*.

### Reggae Rhythms

In his song 'Trench Town,' Bob Marley asked if anything good could ever come from Jamaica's ghettoes. In doing so, he challenged the class-based assumptions of Jamaican society, with the minority elite ruling over the

---

### TOP REGGAE PLAYLISTS

**007 (Shanty Town)** Desmond Decker & the Aces

**Picture of Selassie I** Khari Kill

**Legalize It** Peter Tosh

**One Love** Bob Marley and the Wailers

**Cool Rasta** The Heptones

**The Harder They Come** Jimmy Cliff

**Rivers of Babylon** The Melodians

**Pass the Koutchie** The Mighty Diamonds

**Funky Kingston** Toots & the Maytals

**Is This Love** Bob Marley and the Wailers

## TOP DANCEHALL PLAYLIST

**Who Am I** Beenie Man

**Murder She Wrote** Chaka Demus and Pliers

**Sycamore Tree** Lady Saw

**Get Busy** Sean Paul

**Ting-a-Ling** Shabba Ranks

**Under Me Sleng Teng** Wayne Smith

**It's a Pity** Tanya Stephens

**Ring the Alarm** Tenor Saw

**Clarks** Vybz Kartel ft. Popcaan and Gaza Slim

**Zungguzungguzeng** Yellowman

The gorgeous coffee-table book, *Reggae Explosion: The Story of Jamaican Music,* by Chris Salewcz and Adrian Boot, traces the evolution of Jamaican music in words and (amazing) photographs.

disenfranchised masses. Of course, the answer came in the message of pride and spiritual redemption contained in the music itself, as reggae left the yard to conquer the world, in the process turning Bob Marley into a true global icon.

Bob Marley's band, The Wailers, sprang from the ska and rocksteady era of the 1960s. Producers Lee 'Scratch' Perry, Clement 'Sir Coxsone' Dodd and King Tubby played a key role in evolving the more spacious new reggae sound, while the resurgence of Rastafarianism that followed Haile Selassie's 1966 visit to Jamaica inspired the music's soul. Through his signing of The Wailers, the Jamaican-born founder of Island Records, Chris Blackwell, helped introduce reggae to an international audience.

Reggae is more than just Marley. His original bandmates Peter Tosh and Bunny Wailer both became major stars, joining a pantheon that runs from Desmond Dekker and Dennis Brown to Burning Spear and Gregory Isaacs. While dancehall has since taken over as Jamaica's most popular domestic music, in recent years there has been something of a roots reggae revival, with artists such as Chronixx, Proteje and Jah9 bringing back some rasta consciousness to rejuvenate the genre for the new century.

### Dancehall Culture

The modern sound of Jamaica is definitely dancehall: rapid-fire chanting over bass-heavy beats. It's simplistic to just call dancehall Jamaican rap, because the formation of the beats, their structure and the nuances of the lyrics all have deep roots in Jamaica's musical past.

The new sound sprang up at the close of the 1970s with DJs such as Yellowman, Lone Ranger and Josey Wales, who grabbed the mic, and powered the high-energy rhythms through the advent of faster, more digital beats. This was a period of turmoil in Jamaica, and the music reacted by moving away from political consciousness towards a more hedonistic vibe. The scene centered on the sound systems and 'sound clashes' between DJs, dueling with custom records to win the crowd's favor and boost their reputation.

By the 1990s the success of artists such as Shabba Ranks turned dancehall global, but stars including Buju Banton, Beenie Man, Bounty Killer and Sizzla continue to be criticized for lyrics celebrating violence and homophobia. This came to a peak in 2014 with the conviction for murder of 'World Boss' Vybz Kartel, dancehall's biggest and most innovative star. Curiously, his prison sentence has barely slowed his music release schedule. Criticism of dancehall's more outlandish facets is a staple of the Jamaican press, but for all this, dancehall remains in rude health – Sean Paul and Konshens have long ascended into international stardom, while acts such as Cham and Tommy Lee ride the riddims at home.

Dancehall's iconic dance move is the (female only) dutty wine. Wining involves bending over and gymnastically rotating posterior and head. The male equivalent is 'daggering' – rough dry sex on the dance floor. Prudes need not apply.

### Experiencing Jamaican Music

It's a surprise to some, but the live music scene in Jamaica is relatively small. The sound system rules supreme here; many working musicians often head to the resort hotels to earn a crust playing reggae for package tourists, although in recent years the roots revival has seen more club nights in Kingston featuring live acts. There are also some excellent reggae festivals, most notably Montego Bay's SumFest every July, and Rebel Salute held every January in St Ann. February is designated 'Reggae Month' in Jamaica (in part to honor Bob Marley's birthday on the 6th), when there's lots of live music to be had, especially in Kingston.

If you want to hear dancehall, there are plenty of clubs, but the street parties in Kingston are by far the most vibrant. For the sound systems, the toasting, the street fashion and the dancing, they're hard to beat. Ask locals, especially those working in your hotel or guesthouse, where you'll find the best parties and promoted events. On the whole they're well-run, community-policed events. Parties run late though – don't even think of arriving before midnight.

> Carolyn Cooper's *Sound Clash: Jamaican Dancehall Culture at Large* is a key text for exploring contemporary Jamaica's dominant music form.

## Literature

The current star on Jamaica's literary scene is undoubtedly Marlon James, author of *A Brief History of Seven Killings* and *The Book of Night Women*, but other hot names to look out for include Kei Miller *(The Last Warner Woman, August Town)*, Olive Senior *(Dancing Lessons)*, Garfield Ellis *(For Nothing At All)* and Diana McCaulay *(Huracan)*. Nicole Dennis-Benn's debut novel *Here Comes the Sun* announced the arrival of another great Jamaican writer in 2016.

The novels of Anthony Winkler are celebrated for the wry eye they cast over Jamaican life, most notably in *The Lunatic*, *The Duppy* and *The Family Mansion*.

> One of the most electrifying voices of Jamaican dub poetry today is that of Mutabaruka. Learn about his work and read his poems at www.mutabaruka.com.

Through the years, Jamaican literature has been haunted by the ghosts of slave history and the ambiguities of Jamaica's relationship to Mother England. Best known is Herbert de Lisser's classic Gothic horror, *White Witch of Rose Hall*.

The streets of Kingston are the setting for the gritty novels of Roger Mais, notably *The Hills Were Joyful Together* and *Brother Man*. Orlando Patterson's *The Children of Sisyphus* mines the same tough terrain from a Rastafari perspective.

Jamaica has produced a fine crop of female writers. They include Christine Craig *(Mint Tea)*, Patricia Powell *(Me Dying Trial)*, Michelle Cliff *(Abeng, Land of Look Behind)* and Vanessa Spence *(Roads Are Down)*.

### A BRIEF HISTORY OF MARLON JAMES

Jamaica is used to punching well above its weight in the cultural sphere, from reggae and dancehall to the athletics track. To its crown it can now add literature, thanks in no small part to Marlon James, who won the Man Booker Prize in 2015 for his rolling, cacophonous novel *A Brief History of Seven Killings*.

James, who grew up in Kingston, nearly didn't become a writer. His first novel, *John Crow's Devil* was rejected 78 times before an agent at the Calabash literature festival in Treasure Beach finally signed him up (resigned to rejection, he had already tried to destroy every copy of the manuscript). *The Book of Night Women*, a harrowing account of the life of an enslaved woman in colonial Jamaica, followed, and then his prize-winning epic *A Brief History*, centered on the 1976 assassination attempt on Bob Marley.

As well as being a poster boy for the current crop of Jamaican writers, James has also become an unwitting figurehead after coming out as gay in the searing *From Jamaica to Minnesota to Myself* in 2015. James' current project is a much-anticipated fantasy trilogy, loosely titled the *Dark Star* sequence, inspired by ancient African mythology.

Bridging the gap between literature and performance is the patois-rich genre of dub poetry. Louise Bennett *(Selected Poems)* and Linton Kwesi Johnson *(My Revolutionary Fren)* are essential texts.

# Film

For many, Jamaican cinema begins with cult classic *The Harder They Come* (1973), starring Jimmy Cliff as a 'rude bwai' in Kingston's ghettoes. *Smile Orange* (1974) tells the story of Ringo, a hustling waiter at a resort – a theme not irrelevant today. *Rockers* (1978), another music-propelled, socially poignant fable, is a Jamaican reworking of *The Bicycle Thief* featuring a cast of reggae all-stars.

*The Lunatic* (1991), based on the Anthony Winkler novel, is a humorous exploration of the island's sexual taboos.

Rick Elgood's 1997 film *Dancehall Queen* found an international audience for its tale of redemption for a struggling street vendor, who escapes the mean streets of Kingston through dancehall music. Jamaica's highest-grossing film is Chris Browne's 2000 crime drama *Third World Cop,* in which old friends straddling both sides of the law must come to terms with each other. *Shottas* (2002) follows in its footsteps, featuring two Kingston criminals trying their luck in the US. *One Love* (2003) explores Jamaica's social divides against the backdrop of a controversial romance between a Rasta musician and a pastor's daughter.

Currently making waves on the Jamaican movie scene is director Storm Saulter, whose communal approach to film-making has brought many admirers, most notably for his 2013 movie *Better Mus Come,* about Kingston's gang troubles in the 1970s, one of the most critically acclaimed films to come out of the Caribbean in the last 10 years.

# Visual Arts

British trends and colonial tastes traditionally shaped Jamaican art, but in the 1920s the Jamaican School of local artists began to develop its own style, shaped by realities of Jamaican life. There were two main groups: the painters who were schooled abroad, and island-themed 'intuitives.'

Jamaican Independence leader Norman Manley's wife, Edna, an inspired sculptor and advocate for indigenous Jamaican art, became a leading catalyst for change. Through the example of seminal works such as *Negro Aroused* (1935) and *Pocomania* (1936), which synthesized African and Jamaican archetypes within a deeply personal vision of the national psyche, Manley provided an electrifying example of the potential of Jamaican art. At a grassroots level, Manley organized free art classes and training courses to energize and organize rising talent.

This fertile ground gave birth to three of Jamaica's great painters. Self-taught artist John Dunkley was 'discovered' by Manley in his brilliantly decorated Kingston barbershop. His brooding landscapes of sinister tropical foliage, never-ending roads and furtive reptiles and rodents spoke of a vision that resonated with the historical traumas of the nation. In contrast, Albert Huie produced intricately detailed and beautifully composed works depicting an idyllic dreamscape of rural scenes far removed from the urban strife of his native Kingston. More rooted in his immediate surroundings, David Pottinger's primary interest is in the urban landscape. His portrayals of downtown life reveal the melancholy of poverty while also suggesting the indomitable spirit of life.

Leading lights of the contemporary Jamaican visual arts scene currently include the painter Ebony Patterson and the photographer Marvin Bartley. Both have strong links to Kingston's Edna Manley College of Visual and Performing Arts, which remains an important crucible for the country's artistic scene. Good annual events for taking the temperature of Jamaica's visual arts are the Kingston on the Edge festival and the National Gallery of Jamaica's Biennial Art Exhibition.

Jamaica's most celebrated theater company is the National Dance Theatre Company, which performs at the Little Theatre in Kingston and incorporates Kumina movements into routines.

*Jamaica Art* by Kim Robinson and Petrine Archer Straw is a well-illustrated treatise on the evolution of the island's art scene.

# Landscapes & Wildlife

Jamaica is the third-largest island in the Caribbean, and one of its greenest. The original Taíno inhabitants gave it its name, Xaymaca, meaning 'land of wood and water', and it certainly lives up to its billing as an immensely fertile garden of a country. It's rich in plant and animal life – especially birds – but like other countries in the region faces a host of delicate environmental challenges.

## The Island

At 10,991 sq km (roughly equal to the US state of Connecticut, or half the size of Wales), Jamaica is the largest of the English-speaking Caribbean islands. It is one of the Greater Antilles, which make up the westernmost Caribbean islands, and is a near neighbor to Cuba and Haiti.

'Mainland' Jamaica is rimmed by a narrow coastal plain, except for the southern broad flatlands. Mountains form the island's spine, rising gradually from the west and culminating in the Blue Mountains in the east, which are capped by Blue Mountain Peak at 2256m. The island is cut by about 120 rivers, many of which are bone dry for much of the year but spring to life after heavy rains, causing great flooding and damage to roads. Coastal mangroves, wetland preserves and montane cloud forests form small specialized ecosystems that contain a wide variety of the island's wildlife. Offshore, small islands called cays offer further habitats for marine life.

### Caves

Two-thirds of the island's surface is composed of soft, porous limestone (the compressed skeletons of coral, clams and other sea life), in places several miles thick and covered by red-clay soils rich in bauxite (the principal source of aluminum). The constant interplay of water and soft rock makes Jamaica an especially good destination for spelunkers (p33).

## Animals

### Birds

If you're into caving, burrow into the website of the Jamaican Caves Organisation (www.jamaican caves.org).

When it comes to sheer variety of color and song, birds are Jamaica's main animal attraction. More than 255 bird species call Jamaica home, 26 of which are endemic, while others are passing through on migration routes to and from North America, making Jamaica a particularly rewarding destination for birdwatching (p32).

Jamaica's national bird is the 'doctor bird' or red-billed streamertail – an indigenous hummingbird with shimmering emerald feathers, a velvety black crown with purple crest, a long bill and curved tail feathers. It's image is reproduced everywhere. In total, four of the 16 Caribbean species of hummingbird are represented in Jamaica.

Stilt-legged, snowy-white cattle egrets are ubiquitous, as are 'John crows,' or turkey vultures, who are the subject of many proverbs. The patoo is the Jamaican name for the owl, which many islanders regard as a harbinger of death. Jamaica has two species: the screech owl and the endemic brown owl. There are also four endemic species of flycatcher, a woodpecker and many rare species of dove.

In the extensive swamps, birdwatchers can spot herons, gallinules and countless other waterfowl. Pelicans can be seen diving for fish, while magnificent frigate birds soar high above the coast.

Birdwatchers should turn to *Birds of Jamaica: A Photographic Field Guide* by Audrey Downer and Robert Sutton and the classic *Peterson Field Guide to Birds of the West Indies*.

## Mammals

Jamaica has few mammal species. Small numbers of wild hogs and feral goats still roam isolated wilderness areas, but the only native land mammal is the endangered Jamaican coney *(hutia)*, a large brown rodent akin to a guinea pig. Habitat loss now restricts the highly social, nocturnal animal to remote areas of eastern Jamaica.

The mongoose is the one you're most likely to see, usually scurrying across the road. It was imported from India in 1872 to rid sugarcane fields of rats. Unfortunately, they proved more interested in feeding on snakes, a natural predator of the rat, and are now considered a destructive pest.

## Amphibians & Reptiles

Jamaica harbors plenty of both amphibians and reptiles. The largest are American crocodiles (called 'alligators' in Jamaica), found along the south coast, but also in and around Negril's Great Morass and adjacent rivers. Abundant until big-game hunters appeared around the turn of the century, crocs are now protected. Crocodile river-safaris are big business in Black River.

Jamaica has 24 species of lizard, including the Jamaican iguana, which hangs on to survival in the remote backwaters of the Hellshire Hills. Geckos can often be seen hanging on ceilings by their sticky feet. Local superstition shuns geckos, but their presence in your hotel room means fewer bugs.

### TIPS FOR TRAVELERS

➡ Never take 'souvenirs' such as shells, plants or artifacts from historical sites or natural areas.

➡ Keep to the footpaths. When hiking, always follow designated trails. Natural habitats are often quickly eroded, and animals and plants are disturbed by walkers who stray from the beaten path.

➡ Don't touch or stand on coral. Coral is extremely sensitive and is easily killed by snorkelers and divers who make contact. Likewise, boaters should never anchor on coral – use mooring buoys.

➡ Try to patronize hotels, tour companies and merchants that act in an environmentally sound manner, based on their waste generation, noise levels, energy consumption and the local culture.

➡ Many local communities derive little benefit from Jamaica's huge tourism revenues. Educate yourself on community tourism and ways you can participate. Use local tour guides wherever possible.

➡ Respect the community. Learn about the customs of the region and support local efforts to preserve the environment and traditional culture.

LANDSCAPES & WILDLIFE ANIMALS

Jamaica has five snake species, none venomous and all endangered thanks mostly to the ravages of the mongoose, which has entirely disposed of a sixth species – the black snake. The largest is the Jamaican boa, or yellow snake – a constrictor (called *nanka* locally) that can grow 2.5m in length.

There are 17 frog and one toad species. Uniquely, none of Jamaica's 14 endemic frog species undergoes a tadpole stage; instead, tiny frogs emerge in adult form directly from eggs. All over Jamaica you'll hear the whistle frog living up to its name. While it makes a big racket, the frog itself is smaller than a grape.

## Insects

Jamaica has mosquitoes, bees and wasps, but most bugs are harmless. A brown scarab beetle called the 'newsbug' flies seemingly without control and, when it flies into people, locals consider it a sign of important news to come. Diamond-shaped 'stinky bugs' are exactly that, advertising themselves with an offensive smell. Fireflies (called 'blinkies' and 'peeny-wallies') are also common.

Jamaica has 120 butterfly species and countless moth species, of which 21 are endemic. The most spectacular butterfly is the giant swallowtail, *Papilio homerus*, with a 15cm wingspan. It lives only at higher altitudes in the John Crow Mountains and the eastern extent of the Blue Mountains (and in Cockpit Country in smaller numbers).

### Marine Life

Coral reefs lie along the north shore, where the reef is almost continuous and much of it is within a few hundred meters of shore.

More than 700 species of fish zip in and out of the reefs: wrasses, parrot fish, snappers, bonito, kingfish, jewel fish and scores of others. Smaller fry are preyed upon by barracuda, giant groupers and tarpon. Sharks are frequently seen, though most of these are harmless nurse sharks. Further out, the deep water is run by sailfish, marlin and manta rays.

Three species of endangered marine turtle – the green, hawksbill and loggerhead – lay eggs at the few remaining undeveloped sandy beaches.

About 100 endangered West Indian manatee – a shy, gentle creature once common around the island – survive in Jamaican waters, most numerously in the swamps of Long Bay on the south coast.

# Plants

Jamaica is a veritable garden, with some 3582 plant species (including 237 orchids and 550 species of fern), of which at least 912 are endemic. Although much of the island has been cultivated for agriculture, there are large stretches, especially in the interior, where the flora has largely been undisturbed since human settlement. Probably the most famous indigenous plant species is pimento (allspice), the base of many Jamaican seasonings.

Introduced exotics include bougainvillea, brought from South America via London's Kew Gardens in 1858; ackee, the staple of Jamaican breakfasts, brought from West Africa in 1778; and mangoes, which arrived in 1782 from Mauritius. Breadfruit was introduced in 1793 by Captain Bligh (of 'Mutiny on the Bounty' fame), as a food crop for the slave population. Closer cousins to local plants are cocoa, cashew and cassava, native to Central America and the West Indies. A native pineapple from Jamaica

## MARVELOUS MANGROVES

The spidery mangrove, which grows along the Jamaican coast, is crucially important to coastal preservation, besides functioning as a nursery for countless marine and amphibian species. By acting as a shield between the ocean and the mainland, mangroves maintain the integrity of the Jamaican coast; it is estimated their destruction, due to agriculture, resort development, timber cutting, human settlement and pollution, has resulted in the erosion of up to 80 million tons of topsoil per year. This habitat destruction obviously sets off an ecological chain reaction of disaster; as mangroves die, so too do the nurseries of important fisheries. As a result, the National Environment & Planning Agency (www.nepa.gov.jm), in concert with local community organizations, has identified more than a dozen areas for mangrove rehabilitation across the country; check the agency's website for more information.

was the progenitor of Hawaii's pineapples (the fruit even appears on the Jamaican coat of arms).

Needless to say, ganja (marijuana) is grown in remote areas to evade the eyes of law enforcement, although the hope is that legalization may soon turn the herb into an important cash crop. The harvest season runs from late August through October. Ganja was originally imported to the island by laborers from India, although the Rastafari will tell you the plant was first cultivated off the grave of King Solomon in Ethiopia.

### Tree Species

The national flower is the dark-blue bloom of the lignum vitae tree, whose timber is much in demand by carvers. The national tree is blue mahoe, which derives its name from the blue-green streaks in its beautiful wood. You'll also want to keep your eyes peeled for the dramatic flowering of the vermilion 'flame of the forest' (also called the 'African tulip tree').

Logwood, introduced to the island in 1715, grows wild in dry areas and produces a dark-blue dye. Native species include rosewood, palmetto, mahogany, silk-cotton – said to be a habitat for duppies (ghosts) – cedar and ebony; the latter two have been logged to decimation during the past two centuries. Over the last decade, deforestation has also led to the deterioration of more than a third of Jamaica's watersheds.

## National Parks

Jamaica's park system comprises four parks: Blue Mountains-John Crow National Park, Montego Bay Marine Park, Port Antonio Marine Park and Negril Marine Park. There is also a fistful of other wilderness areas with varying degrees of protection, such as the Portland Bight Protected Area.

The 780-sq-km Blue Mountains-John Crow National Park (Jamaica's largest) includes the biologically diverse forest reserves of the Blue and John Crow mountain ranges. All marine parks are situated around resort areas and were developed to preserve and manage coral reefs, mangroves and offshore marine resources.

Proposals to turn Cockpit Country into a national park have been met with stiff resistance from the Maroons who live there and fear increased governmental authority will infringe on their hard-won autonomy.

The pimento tree provides the wood whose smoke gives Jamaican jerk its distinct flavor. The leaves are crushed to produce intoxicating allspice.

## Environmental Issues

Like many Caribbean nations, Jamaica faces significant environmental issues.

In the mid-1990s Jamaica had the highest rate of deforestation (5% per year) of any country in the world and, although there is now greater awareness of the problem, it is still a threat. Many of Jamaica's endemic wildlife species are endangered, largely due to habitat loss, including the American crocodile, Jamaican boa, Jamaican iguana, coney, green parrot and giant swallowtail butterfly.

Bauxite mining – the island's second-most lucrative industry after tourism – is considered to be the single largest cause of deforestation in Jamaica. Bauxite can only be extracted by opencast mining, which requires the wholesale destruction of forests and topsoil. The access roads cut by mining concerns are then used by loggers, coal burners and yam-stick traders to get to trees in and around designated mining areas, extending the deforestation. Local pressure has blocked periodic attempts to open Cockpit Country to bauxite (and limestone) mining. Deforestation has also damaged parts of the Blue Mountains, where farmers felled trees to clear land to grow lucrative coffee plants.

The National Environmental & Planning Agency (NEPA) is entrusted with responsibility for promoting ecological consciousness among Jamaicans and management of the national parks and protected areas under the Protected Areas Resource Conservation Project (PARC).

The Jamaica Conservation & Development Trust (www.jcdt.org.jm) and the Jamaica Environment Trust (www.jamentrust.org) are at the forefront of environmental issues in Jamaica.

# Survival
# Guide

# Directory A–Z

## Accommodations

Low season (summer) is usually mid-April to early December; the high season (winter) is the remainder of the year, when hotel prices increase by 40% or more. All-inclusive packages are usually based on three-day minimum stays.

### All-Inclusive Resorts

Rates for all-inclusive resorts in our listings are guidelines based on unpublicized 'rack' or 'standard' rates. (Note: reviews for all-inclusive options will include a mention of 'all-incl' in the practicalities details where costs are shown.) You will likely spend considerably less depending on the source of booking, the season and current specials, which are perpetually publicized.

### Camping

Jamaica is not particularly developed for campers, and it's unsafe to camp in much of the wild. Many budget properties will let you pitch a tent on their lawns for a small fee. Some even rent tents and have shower, toilet and laundry facilities.

### Guesthouses

Most guesthouses are inexpensive and good places to mix with the locals. Breakfast is often included. Some are homely houses, others are indistinguishable from hotels.

### Villa Rentals

Jamaica boasts hundreds of private villas for rent. Rates start as low as US$150 per week for budget units with minimal facilities. More upscale villas begin at about US$750 weekly and can run to US$10,000. Rates fall as much as 30% in summer. A large deposit (usually 25% or more) is required.

**Villas in Jamaica** (JAVA; ☑in USA 800-845-5276; www.villasinjamaica.com) is a useful booking site for villa rentals.

## Electricity

**Type A**
**110V/50Hz**

**Type B**
**110V/50Hz**

## Embassies & Consulates

If your country isn't represented in this list, check 'Embassies & High Commissions' in the Yellow Pages of the Greater Kingston telephone directory.

**Canadian High Commission** (☑926-1500; www.canadainternational.gc.ca/jamaica-jamaique; 3 West Kings House Rd, Kingston)

**Dutch Embassy** (☑926-2026; Victoria Mutual Bldg, 53 Knutsford Blvd, Kingston 5)

**French Embassy** (☑946-4000; www.ambafrance-jm-bm.org; 13 Hillcrest Ave, Kingston 6)

**German Embassy** (☏631-7935; www.kingston.diplo.de; 10 Waterloo Rd, Kingston 10)

**Italian Embassy** (☏968-8464; 10 Surbiton Rd, Kingston 10)

**Japanese Embassy** (☏929-7534; www.jamaica.eab-japan.go.jp; NCB Tower 6th fl, 2 Oxford Rd, Kingston 5)

**UK High Commission** (☏936-0700; www.gov.uk; 28 Trafalgar Rd, Kingston)

**US Embassy** (☏702-6000, after hours 702-6055; http://kingston.usembassy.gov; 142 Old Hope Rd, Kingston)

# LGBTI Travelers

There is a gay scene in Kingston, but it is an underground affair as Jamaica is a largely homophobic society (p194). Sexual acts between men are prohibited by law and punishable by up to 10 years in prison. Many reggae dancehall lyrics by big-name stars could be classified as antigay hate speech. Gay-bashing incidents are almost never prosecuted, with law enforcement, in most cases, looking the other way.

Nonetheless, you shouldn't be put off from visiting the island. In the more heavily touristed areas you'll find more tolerant attitudes, and hotels that welcome gay travelers, including all-inclusives. Publicly, though, discretion is important and open displays of affection should be avoided.

Useful websites:

**Gay Jamaica Watch** (http://gay-jamaicawatch.blogspot.com)

**J-FLAG** (www.jflag.org)

**Quality of Citizenship Jamaica** (www.qcjm.org)

# Health

## Before You Go

### HEALTH INSURANCE

Health insurance is essential for all travelers to Jamaica. If you develop a life-threatening medical problem, you'll probably want to be evacuated to a country with state-of-the-art medical care. Since this may cost tens of thousands of dollars, be sure you have insurance to cover this before you depart.

*ABC of Healthy Travel* by E Walker et al, and *Medicine for the Outdoors* by Paul S Auerbach, are other valuable resources.

### INTERNET RESOURCES

**MD Travel Health** (www.mdtravelhealth.com) Provides complete travel health recommendations for every country, updated daily, at no cost.

**World Health Organization** (www.who.int/ith) Publishes a superb book called *International Travel and Health*, which is revised annually and is available for free online.

## In Jamaica

### AVAILABILITY & COST OF HEALTH CARE

Acceptable health care is available in most major cities and larger towns throughout Jamaica, but may be hard to locate in rural areas. To find a good local doctor, your best bet is to ask the management of the hotel where you are staying or contact your embassy in Kingston or Montego Bay. Note that many doctors and hospitals expect payment on the spot, regardless of whether you have travel health insurance.

Many pharmacies are well supplied, but important medications may not be consistently available. Be sure to bring along adequate supplies of all prescription drugs.

### NO SEE UMS

No see ums, also known as midges, are tiny biting insects that live near water. Females are blood suckers, and while their bites are not painful, they are awfully itchy. No see ums congregate in large swarms near bodies of water, puddles etc; to avoid them, wear insect repellent and skirt around their swarm areas, as the bugs will not fly too far from their 'home' body of water.

### TRAVELER'S DIARRHEA

Throughout most of Jamaica tap water has been treated and is safe to drink, but in some far-flung rural areas it is safest to avoid it unless it has been boiled, filtered or chemically disinfected (with iodine tablets). Eat fresh fruits or vegetables only if cooked or peeled; be wary of dairy products that might contain unpasteurized milk; and be highly selective when eating food from street vendors. If you develop diarrhea, be sure to drink plenty of fluid, preferably an oral rehydration solution containing lots of salt and sugar.

**TAP WATER**

Water is generally safe to drink from faucets throughout the island except in the most far-flung rural regions. It is safest, however, to stick with bottled water, which is widely available. It's a good idea to avoid ice, particularly that sold at street stands as 'bellywash,' 'snocones' or 'skyjuice' – shaved-ice cones sweetened with fruit juice. Unless you're certain that the local water is not contaminated, you shouldn't drink it. In Jamaica's backwaters, clean your teeth with purified water rather than tap water.

# Internet Access

➡ Wi-fi is available in Jamaican hotels, but internet access is still restricted in rural areas. Data services are available throughout the country, although 3G reception can be patchy.

➡ Most town libraries offer internet access (US$1 for 30 minutes), and there's usually at least one commercial entity where you can get online.

# Legal Matters

➡ Jamaica's drug and drink-driving laws are strictly enforced.

➡ Don't expect leniency just because you're a foreigner. Jamaican jails are distinctly unpleasant.

➡ Ganja has been decriminalized, and possession of up to 2oz attracts a fine, rather than arrest.

➡ If arrested, insist on your right to call your embassy in Kingston to request assistance.

# Money

➡ The unit of currency is the Jamaican dollar, the 'jay,' which uses the same symbol as the US dollar ($). Jamaican currency is issued in bank notes of J$50, J$100, J$500, J$1000 and (rarely) J$5000. Prices for hotels and valuable items are usually quoted in US dollars, which are widely accepted.

➡ Commercial banks have branches throughout the island. Those in major towns maintain a foreign-exchange booth.

➡ Most towns have 24-hour ATMs linked to international networks such as Cirrus or Plus. In more remote areas,

look for ATMs at gas stations. In tourist areas, some ATMs also dispense US dollars.

➡ Traveler's checks are little used and attract fees for cashing.

➡ Major credit cards are accepted throughout the island, although local groceries and the like will not be able to process them, even in Kingston.

## Tipping

A 10% tip is normal in hotels and restaurants. Check your bill carefully – some restaurants automatically add a 10% to 15% service charge. Some all-inclusive resorts have a strictly enforced no-tipping policy. Outside Kingston, tourist taxi drivers often ask for tips but it is not necessary; JUTA (Jamaica Union of Travelers Association) route taxis do not expect tips.

# Opening Hours

The following are standard hours for Jamaica; exceptions are noted in reviews. Note that the country virtually shuts down on Sunday.

**Banks** 9:30am to 4pm Monday to Friday.

**Bars** Usually open around noon, with many staying open until the last customer stumbles out.

**Businesses** 8:30am to 4:30pm Monday to Friday.

**Restaurants** Breakfast dawn to 11am; lunch noon to 2pm; dinner 5:30pm to 11pm.

**Shops** 8am or 9am to 5pm Monday to Friday, to noon or 5pm Saturday, late-night shopping to 9pm Thursday and Friday.

# Post

➡ Offices of Jamaica Post (http://jamaicapost.gov.jm/) are found in every town. The postal system is reliable, if not terribly fast – expect 10 days to a fortnight for a postcard to reach North America or Europe.

## PRACTICALITIES

➡ **Newspapers** The *Jamaica Gleaner* (www.jamaica-gleaner.com) is the high-standard newspaper. Its rival is the *Jamaica Observer*, followed by the gossipy tabloid *Jamaica Star*.

➡ **Radio** Of the 30 radio stations, Irie FM (105.1FM; www.iriefm.net) is the most popular.

➡ **TV** There are seven channels; most hotels have satellite TV with US channels.

➡ **Smoking** Banned in public places (including bars and restaurants).

Metric and imperial measurements are both used. Distances are measured in meters and kilometers, and gas in liters, but coffee (and ganja) is often sold by the pound.

## GANJA

Ganja is an integral part of life for large sections of Jamaica's population – whether as a recreational toke or Rastafari sacrament – though it has long been illegal. In 2015, however, the Jamaican parliament decriminalized possession. Possession of up to 2oz (56g) is now treatable in the same manner as a parking offense, garnering a fine of up to US$100 but no criminal record. Full legalization is on the cards, if not immediately imminent. For now, the only way to buy ganja legally is with a permit from the Health Ministry if you have a prescription for medical marijuana.

While some travelers are keen to seek it out, even those wanting to avoid it are unlikely to get through their trip without at least a whiff of secondhand smoke. You'll undoubtedly be approached by people offering to sell you ganja, whether a 'nudge wink' hustler, or a vendor at a dancehall street party openly selling it alongside candies and rum. If you want to smoke, we still recommend doing so discreetly, at your hotel. Some local strains are particularly strong, and tourists have reported suffering harmful side effects from ganja, especially from ganja cakes and cookies.

Jamaica's tourism board already sponsors the Rastafari Rootz Fest, which hosts the Ganjamaica Cup for growers, and come legalization, ganja tourism will undoubtedly become a big thing. But while we hear of winery-style 'tasting' tours to ganja plantations, if you're hiking in the Jamaican backcountry and come across a field of ganja, it's best to give it a wide berth for now unless you're with a trusted local companion – Jamaicans are fiercely protective of these secret spots and there's a good chance they will loudly (and perhaps aggressively) demand you leave the area.

➡ The major international couriers all operate in the country. Jamaica Post offers a DHL package service.

## Public Holidays

**New Year's Day** January 1

**Ash Wednesday**, **Good Friday** & **Easter Monday** Dates vary

**Labour Day** May 23

**Emancipation Day** August 1

**Independence Day** First Monday in August

**National Heroes Day** Third Monday in October

**Christmas Day** December 25

**Boxing Day** December 26

## Safe Travel

Jamaica is probably more plagued by bad media about safety than it is by violent crime that affects tourists. Many travelers fear the worst and avoid the country; those who do make it here are far more likely to come away with positive impressions than horror stories. Petty crime is the most serious issue, although some travelers may be more concerned with the increasingly fluid legality of ganja.

### Crime

While areas including Spanish Town and some parts of Kingston are best avoided due to gang trouble, crimes against tourists have also dropped greatly, and the overwhelming majority of visitors enjoy their vacations without incident.

Travel advice is common sense: keep hotel doors and windows locked at night, and lock car doors from the inside while driving. Don't open your hotel door to anyone who can't prove their identity. If you're renting an out-of-the-way private villa or cottage, check in advance to establish whether security is provided.

Carry as little cash as you need when away from your hotel. Keep the rest in a hotel safe, and don't flash your valuables (particularly smartphones).

### Drugs

Ganja (marijuana) is everywhere in Jamaica and you're almost certain to be approached by hustlers selling drugs. Cocaine is also widely available (Jamaica is a major trans-shipment point for the Colombia–US route), along with hallucinogenic wild mushrooms. The globalization of the drugs trade has undoubtedly helped fuel gang violence in Jamaica.

While ganja has been decriminalized, other drugs are strictly illegal and penalties are severe. Roadblocks and random searches of cars are common, undertaken by well-armed police in combat gear. Professionalism is never guaranteed, and 'dash' – extortion – is often extracted to boost wages. Drug checks at airports can be particularly strict.

### Harassment

Usually the traveler's biggest problem is the vast army of hustlers (mostly male) who harass visitors, notably in and around major tourist centers – Montego Bay, Negril and to a lesser extent Ocho Rios.

Be polite but firm with unwanted advances; never ignore them, which is taken as an insult. Aggressive persistence is the key to their success and trying to shake them off can be a wearying process.

Hustlers often persist in the hope that you'll pay just to be rid of them. If harassment continues, seek the assistance of a tourist police officer or the local constabulary.

## Telephone

Jamaica's country code is ☑876. To call Jamaica from the US, dial ☑1-876 + the seven-digit local number. From elsewhere, dial your country's international dialing code, then ☑876 and the local number.

For calls within the same parish in Jamaica, just dial the local number. Between parishes, dial ☑1 + the local number. We have included only the seven-digit local number in Jamaica listings.

### Cell Phones

You can bring your own cell phone into Jamaica (GSM or CDMA). Be aware of hefty roaming charges or you can buy a local SIM card.

If your phone is unlocked, buy a SIM card from one of the two local cell-phone operators, Digicel (www.digiceljamaica.com) or Flow (www.discoverflow/jamaica), or you can buy a cheap handset. You'll need to bring ID to buy either. SIM cards are free – ask for the best current offers, usually from around J$500 for calls plus data. Prepaid top-up cards are sold in denominations from JS$50 to J$1000, and you'll find them at many gas stations and grocery stores.

## Time

Jamaica runs on Eastern Standard Time (GMT minus five hours), but does not operate daylight saving. Hence, from April to October, it is six hours behind London and one hour behind New York.

## Toilets

➡ There are few public toilets, and those that

do exist are mostly best avoided, except in major tourist areas.

➡ Most restaurants have restrooms, but many require you to make a purchase before you can use them.

## Tourist Information

The Jamaica Tourist Board (JTB; www.visitjamaica.com) has offices in key cities around the world. You can request maps and literature, including hotel brochures, but they do not serve as reservation agencies.

## Travelers with Disabilities

Very few allowances have been made in Jamaica for travelers with disabilities, although larger hotels and all-inclusives (especially those owned by international brands) tend to be more accessible, with ramps and elevators.

## Visas

For stays of six months or less, no visas are required for citizens of the EU, the US, Commonwealth countries, Mexico, Japan and Israel. Nationals of Argentina, Brazil, Chile, Costa Rica, Ecuador, Greece and Japan don't need a visa for stays of up to 90 days.

All other nationals require visas (nationals of most countries can obtain a visa on arrival, provided they are holding valid onward or return tickets and evidence of sufficient funds).

## Volunteering

Always ask demanding questions of volunteer programs – many are short-term projects designed to suit the needs of volunteers rather than beneficiaries.

The following local environmental organizations sometimes take foreign volunteers:

**Environmental Foundation of Jamaica** (Map p50;☑960-6744; www.efj.org.jm; 1b Norwood Ave, Kingston 5)

**Jamaica Environment Trust** (www.jamentrust.org)

## Women Travelers

Many Jamaican men display behavior and attitudes that might shock visiting women, often expressing disdain for the notion of female equality or women's rights. Despite this, women play pivotal roles in Jamaican society.

If you're single, it may be assumed you're on the island seeking a 'likkle love beneat' de palms.' Protests to the contrary will likely be met with wearying attempts to get you to change your mind. If you go along with the flirting, your innocent acceptance will be taken as a sign of acquiescence. Never beat about the bush out of fear of hurting the man's feelings.

Rape is not uncommon in Jamaica and occasionally involves female tourists. Women traveling alone may reduce unwanted attention by dressing modestly when away from the beach. Women should avoid walking alone at night and otherwise traveling alone in remote areas.

## Work

Visitors are admitted to Jamaica on the condition that they 'not engage in any form of employment on the island.' Professionals can obtain work permits if sponsored by a Jamaican company, but casual work is very difficult to obtain. For more information on work permits, visit the **Ministry of Labour & Social Security** (☑922-9500; www.mlss.gov.jm; 14 National Heroes Circle; ☎).

# Transportation

## GETTING THERE & AWAY

### Entering the Country

Expect a wait in the immigration halls at the airports in Kingston and Montego Bay. There are often only two or three immigration officers on hand to process the planeloads of passengers, and often multiple flights land within minutes of each other, increasing the burden on officials.

## Air

### Airports & Airlines

Jamaica has two international airports:

**Norman Manley International Airport** (KIN; Map p44;☑924-8452; www.nmia.aero), Kingston

**Donald Sangster International Airport** (MBJ;☑952-3124; www.mbjairport.com), Montego Bay

Jamaica is well served by international carriers from cities across North America and Europe.

Useful regional airlines include the following:

**Caribbean Airlines** (☑744-2225; www.caribbean-airlines.com)

**Cayman Airways** (www.cayman airways.com)

**COPA Airlines** (www.copaair.com)

**Fly Jamaica** (☑656-9832; www.fly-jamaica.com)

## Sea

Jamaica is a popular destination on the cruise roster, mainly for passenger liners but also for private yachts.

For maps and charts of the Caribbean, contact **Bluewater Books & Charts** (☑800-942-2583; www.bluewaterweb.com). The **National Oceanic & Atmospheric Administration** (☑888-990-6622; www.nauticalcharts.noaa.gov) sells US government charts.

### Cruise Ship

More than a million cruise-ship passengers sail to Jamaica annually, making it one of the world's biggest cruise-ship destinations. Most ships hit four or five ports, sometimes spending a night, other times only a few hours. Port visits are usually one-day stopovers at either Ocho Rios, Montego Bay or Falmouth.

### Yacht

Many yachties make the trip to Jamaica from North America. Upon arrival in Jamaica, you *must* clear customs and immigration at Montego Bay, Kingston, Ocho Rios or Port Antonio. In addition, you'll need to clear customs at *each* port of call. The main ports for yachts:

**Errol Flynn Marina** (Map p94; ☑715-6044, 993-3209; www.errolflynnmarina.com; Port Antonio, GPS N 18.168889°, W -76.450556°)

**Montego Bay Yacht Club** (☑979-8038; www.mobay yachtclub.com; Montego Bay

---

**CLIMATE CHANGE & TRAVEL**

Every form of transportation that relies on carbon-based fuel generates $CO_2$, the main cause of human-induced climate change. Modern travel is dependent on aeroplanes, which might use less fuel per kilometre per person than most cars but travel much greater distances. The altitude at which aircraft emit gases (including $CO_2$) and particles also contributes to their climate change impact. Many websites offer 'carbon calculators' that allow people to estimate the carbon emissions generated by their journey and, for those who wish to do so, to offset the impact of the greenhouse gases emitted with contributions to portfolios of climate-friendly initiatives throughout the world. Lonely Planet offsets the carbon footprint of all staff and author travel.

## COSTS

Taking public transportation is terrifically inexpensive. Buses and minibuses charge in the neighborhood of J$100 per 50km, and route taxis charge about J$150 to J$250 per 50km, with short rides of around 10 minutes costing J$100. As an example of longer routes, at the time of writing a coaster from Kingston to Port Antonio (two hours) cost J$600.

Freeport, GPS N 18.462452°, W -77.943267°; ⏰10am-10pm)

**Royal Jamaican Yacht Club** (Map p44; ☎924-8685; www. rjyc.org.jm; Palisadoes Park, Norman Manley International Airport, Kingston, GPS N 17.940939°, W -76.764939°)

# GETTING AROUND

## Air

In Kingston, most domestic flights use **Tinson Pen** (Map p44; Marcus Garvey Dr), 3km west of downtown; it's a 40-minute ride to the domestic airstrip from **Norman Manley International Airport** (KIN; Map p44; ☎924-8452; www.nmia.aero). Ian Fleming Aerodrome near Ocho Rios handles private charters.

### Airlines in Jamaica

Jamaica's small size makes domestic flights largely redundant, but (ridiculously expensive) charter flights are available with TimAir (www. timair.net) between its hub in Montego Bay and Kingston, Negril, Ocho Rios and Port Antonio. Rates start at around US$320 for two passengers; fares go up or down for fewer or more passengers.

## Bicycle

Mountain bikes and 'beach cruisers' (bikes with fat tires, suitable for riding on sand) can be rented at most major resorts (US$10 to US$30 per

day). Road conditions can be poor when off the main highways, and Jamaican drivers are not considerate of cyclists. For serious touring, bring your own mountain or multipurpose bike.

## Boat

Tourists may use boats for day trips, but there are currently no organized boat services for getting from A to B in Jamaica. Paradise Ferry (www.paradiseferry.com) has a planned ferry service between Ocho Rios, Montego Bay and Negril.

## Bus & Public Transportation

An extensive transportation network links virtually every village and comprises several options that range from standard public buses to private taxis, with minibuses and route taxis in between.

There is usually no set timetable – buses leave when the driver considers them full – and passengers are crammed in with little regard for comfort. Taxis and buses tend to fill quickly early in the morning (before 8am) and around 5pm as people depart for work or home. There are fewer public transportation options on Sunday.

Public buses, minibuses and route taxis depart from and arrive at each town's transportation station, which is usually near the main market. Locals can direct you to the appropriate vehicle, which should have its des-

tination marked above the front window (for buses) or on its side.

## Buses

Large buses are few and far between in Jamaica due to the narrow twisting roads. Throughout the island there are bus stops at most road intersections along routes, but you can usually flag down a bus anywhere except in major cities. If the bus doesn't have a bell to indicate when you want to get off, shout out 'let down' or 'one stop' to the driver.

**Knutsford Express** (Map p50; ☎971-1822; www.knutsford express.com; 18 Dominica Dr, New Kingston Shopping Center parking lot) operates big comfortable, air-conditioned coaches and covers most destinations. Sample fares/times are Kingston–Ocho Rios (J$1850, two hours), Kingston–Montego Bay (J$2950, four hours). Online booking is available, along with student, senior and child fares.

## Minibuses

Private minibuses, also known as 'coasters,' have traditionally been the work-horses of Jamaica's regional public transportation system. All major towns and virtually every village in the country are served.

Licensed minibuses display red license plates with the initials PPV (public passenger vehicle) or have a JUTA (Jamaica Union of Travelers Association) insignia. JUTA buses are exclusively for tourists. Public coasters don't run to set timetables, but depart their point of origin when they're full. They're often overflowing, and the drivers seem to have death wishes.

## Route Taxis

Communal route taxis are the most universal mode of public transportation, reaching every part of the country. They run on set routes, picking up as many people as they can along the way. They're very convenient and are a cheap way of getting around the island. Simply pick them up at their terminal in town (they go when full), or flag them down on the road and tell the driver where you want to get off. If you get in an empty taxi – particularly at the taxi station – be clear if you just want to pay the regular fare instead of a charter.

Most route taxis are white station wagons marked by their red license plates. They should have 'Route Taxi' marked on the front door, and they are not to be confused with similar licensed taxis, which charge more. Avoid any taxi that lacks the red license plate.

# Car & Motorcycle

## Automobile Associations

There is no national roadside organization to phone when you have car trouble. Most car-rental agencies have a 24-hour service number in case of breakdowns and other emergencies. If you do break down, use a local mechanic for minor work only; otherwise the car-rental company may balk at reimbursing you for work it hasn't authorized. If you can't find a phone or repair service, seek police assistance. *Never* give your keys to strangers.

## Driving Licences

To drive in Jamaica, you must have a valid International Driver's License (IDL) or a current license for your home country or state, valid for at least six months, and be at least 21 years of age.

## Fuel

➡ Many gas stations close at 7pm or so. In rural areas, stations are usually closed on Sunday.

➡ At the time of writing, gasoline/diesel cost about J$120/112 per liter.

➡ Most gas stations only accept cash payment, although a growing number of modern gas stations in larger towns accept credit cards.

## Car Hire

Most major international car-rental companies operate in Jamaica, including **Avis** (www.avis.com.jm) and **Hertz** (www.hertz.com).

Local car-hire firms can be a lot cheaper than the international brands. Recommended firms include the following:

**Beaumont Car Rentals** (☏926-0311; www.beaumontcarrental ja.com)

**Island Car Rentals** (☏929-5875; www.islandcarrentals.com)

You can reserve a car upon arrival, but in the high season be sure to make your reservation in advance. Reconfirm before your arrive.

Before signing, go over the vehicle with a fine-tooth comb to identify any dents and scratches. Make a note of each one before you drive away. You're likely to be charged for the slightest mark that wasn't noted before. Don't forget to check the cigarette lighter and

interior switches, which are often missing.

### WHAT KIND OF CAR

Most of the companies rent out modern Japanese sedans. A big car can be a liability on Jamaica's narrow, winding roads. Some companies also rent 4WD vehicles, which are highly recommended if you intend to do *any* driving away from main roads.

Stick shift is preferable because frequent and sudden gear changes are required when potholes and kamikaze chickens appear out of nowhere. Remember that you'll be changing gears with your *left* hand. If this is new to you, you'll soon get the hang of it.

### COSTS

High-season rates begin at about US$40 per day and can run as high as US$100 or more, depending on the vehicle. Cheaper rates apply in the low season. Some companies include unlimited distance, while others set a limit and charge a fee for excess kilometers driven. Most firms require a credit-card imprint as a deposit. Keep copies of all your paperwork.

---

### OFF THE BOAT

While cruise lines' optional land tours are conveniently packaged to take in many of the island's sightseeing highlights, they also move quickly and tend to shield visitors from interaction with locals. In addition, a fair percentage of the money paid for these tours stays with the organizers rather than going into the local economy. If you venture out on your own, you're likely to enjoy a richer cultural experience. If you want to tour the island, consider hiring a local taxi driver, who will likely shed light on local issues and give you a more colorful tour. Wander the streets of the main town, poke into little shops, eat at local restaurants and buy mementos from street vendors, or veer off the beaten track. Visit small businesses and chat with the owners, buy local rums and other souvenirs in small shops instead of onboard – you'll help fuel the local economy (and save money in the process).

## Insurance

Check in advance whether your current insurance or credit card covers you for driving while abroad. All rental companies will recommend damage-waiver insurance, which limits your liability in the event of an accident or damage.

## Motorcycles & Scooter Hire

Dozens of companies hire motorcycles and scooters; they're available at any resort town. These companies are far more lax than the car-rental companies; you may not even have to show your driver's license. If you are not an experienced motorcycle driver, it might be better to rent a scooter, which is far easier to handle. Scooters cost about US$35 to US$50 per day and motorcycles about US$45 to US$60 per day; note that deposits can be high.

Road conditions in Jamaica are hazardous. Always wear a helmet.

## Road Conditions

Jamaica's roads run from modern multilane highways to barely passable tracks.

Jamaica's best road is the new highway between Kingston and Ocho Rios, which has dramatically cut transit times to the north coast. It's a toll road – cars pay around J$1000.

You can expect any road with the designation 'A' to

be in fairly good condition. 'B' roads are generally much narrower and often badly potholed, but still passable in the average rental car. Minor roads, particularly those in the Blue Mountains and Cockpit Country, can be hellish. If you plan to drive off the major routes, it's essential to have a stalwart 4WD.

Signage on main roads is good, but directional signs are few and far between as soon as you leave them. Many B roads are not shown on maps. And what may appear on a map to be a 30-minute journey may take several hours. More often than not there are no signs to indicate sharp curves, steep ascents or work in progress. Road are often poorly lit at night, if at all.

## Road Hazards

Laid-back Jamaica has some of the world's rudest and most dangerously aggressive drivers. Cars race through towns and play chicken with one another with daredevil folly. Use extreme caution and drive defensively, especially at night when you should be prepared to meet oncoming cars that are either without lights or blinding you with high beams. Use your horn liberally, especially when approaching blind corners, and watch for pedestrians.

## Road Rules

➤ Always drive on the left.

➤ Jamaica has a compulsory seat-belt law.

➤ Speed limits range from 50km/h to 80km/h and vary from place to place across the island.

➤ Carry ID and all relevant car-rental paperwork at all times.

## Hitchhiking

Hitchhiking is common enough among Jamaicans but, because public transportation is absurdly cheap, few tourists stick out their thumbs.

Hitchhiking is never entirely safe in any country in the world and we don't recommend it, especially in Jamaica where there are a lot of people looking to take advantage of naive tourists. Travelers who decide to hitchhike should understand that they are taking a small but potentially serious risk. If you choose to take that risk, you will be safer if you travel in pairs and let someone know where you are planning to go.

## Local Transportation

### Taxi

Licensed taxis – called 'contract carriages' – have red PPV license plates (those without such plates are unlicensed). They're expensive, but affordable if you share the cost with other passengers.
**Jamaica Union of Travelers Association** (JUTA; ☑952-0813; http://jutatoursltd.com/) operates island-wide and is geared almost exclusively to the tourist business. Kingston has a number of private radio taxi firms.

The Transport Authority has established fixed rates according to distance (different rates apply for locals than for tourists, who pay more). Licensed cabs should have these posted inside. Taxis are also supposed to have meters, but many don't use them.

## TAXI FARES

The following are typical fares, based on up to four people per taxi:

| ROUTE | FARE |
| --- | --- |
| Kingston–Montego Bay | US$220 |
| Kingston–Ocho Rios | US$110 |
| Kingston–Port Antonio | US$120 |
| Montego Bay–Ocho Rios or Negril | US$100 |
| Norman Manley International Airport–Kingston (Uptown) | US$35 |
| Donald Sangster International Airport–Montego Bay | US$20 |

# Behind the Scenes

## SEND US YOUR FEEDBACK

We love to hear from travelers – your comments keep us on our toes and help make our books better. Our well-traveled team reads every word on what you loved or loathed about this book. Although we cannot reply individually to your submissions, we always guarantee that your feedback goes straight to the appropriate authors, in time for the next edition. Each person who sends us information is thanked in the next edition – the most useful submissions are rewarded with a selection of digital PDF chapters.

Visit **lonelyplanet.com/contact** to submit your updates and suggestions or to ask for help. Our award-winning website also features inspirational travel stories, news and discussions.

Note: We may edit, reproduce and incorporate your comments in Lonely Planet products such as guidebooks, websites and digital products, so let us know if you don't want your comments reproduced or your name acknowledged. For a copy of our privacy policy visit lonelyplanet.com/privacy.

## OUR READERS

**Many thanks to the travelers who used the last edition and wrote to us with helpful hints, useful advice and interesting anecdotes:**

Angie Hook, Anne Jahan, Carl Simpson, David Ingleman, Heinz Helbling, Jane Winfield, Kair Keller, Kate Doran, Luanne Wielichowski, Peter Davies, Simon Mercier.

## WRITER THANKS
### Paul Clammer

In Kingston, big thanks to Matthew Smith and Ishtar Govia, to David Scott, Joshua Chamberlain, Annie Paul, everyone at LifeYard, and to staff at the National Library of Jamaica. In Ocho Rios, thanks to Shelly Ann Johnson. In Port Antonio, thanks to Charlene Bryden and Jim Sibthorpe. Grazie to Carla Gullotta in Drapers. At home, thanks and love as always to Robyn, especially for Monkey-wrangling while I was on the road.

### Anna Kaminski

A big thank you to Bailey for entrusting me with half of Jamaica, to fellow scribe Paul and to everyone who helped me along the way. In particular: Richard and Nicole in Falmouth/Santa Cruz/Accompong, Valerie and Leroy in MoBay, Ann and Lisa in Mandeville, Susan in Windsor, Allison in Black River, Captain Dennis in Treasure Beach, the brownie lady in Negril, Nancy and Lindsey in Kingston, and Elise and Darryl for the most memorable meal in Ochi.

## ACKNOWLEDGEMENTS

Climate map data adapted from Peel MC, Finlayson BL & McMahon TA (2007) 'Updated World Map of the Köppen-Geiger Climate Classification', Hydrology and Earth System Sciences, 11, 163344.

Cover photograph: Seven Mile Beach, Negril; Sladja Kisic/4Corners ©

# THIS BOOK

This 8th edition of Lonely Planet's *Jamaica* guidebook was researched and written by Paul Clammer and Anna Kaminski. The previous edition was written by Paul Clammer and Brendan Sainsbury. The 6th edition was written by Anna Kaminski, Adam Karlin and Richard Kloss. This guidebook was produced by the following:

**Destination Editor** Bailey Freeman

**Product Editor** Kate Kiely

**Senior Cartographer** Corey Hutchison

**Book Designer** Nicholas Colicchia

**Assisting Editors** Imogen Bannister, Helen Koehne, Fionnuala Twomey

**Assisting Cartographer** Hunor Csutoros

**Cover Researcher** Naomi Parker

**Thanks to** Kate Mathews, Tony Wheeler, Amanda Williamson

# Index

# Map Legend

## Sights
- Beach
- Bird Sanctuary
- Buddhist
- Castle/Palace
- Christian
- Confucian
- Hindu
- Islamic
- Jain
- Jewish
- Monument
- Museum/Gallery/Historic Building
- Ruin
- Shinto
- Sikh
- Taoist
- Winery/Vineyard
- Zoo/Wildlife Sanctuary
- Other Sight

## Activities, Courses & Tours
- Bodysurfing
- Diving
- Canoeing/Kayaking
- Course/Tour
- Sento Hot Baths/Onsen
- Skiing
- Snorkeling
- Surfing
- Swimming/Pool
- Walking
- Windsurfing
- Other Activity

## Sleeping
- Sleeping
- Camping

## Eating
- Eating

## Drinking & Nightlife
- Drinking & Nightlife
- Cafe

## Entertainment
- Entertainment

## Shopping
- Shopping

## Information
- Bank
- Embassy/Consulate
- Hospital/Medical
- Internet
- Police
- Post Office
- Telephone
- Toilet
- Tourist Information
- Other Information

## Geographic
- Beach
- Gate
- Hut/Shelter
- Lighthouse
- Lookout
- Mountain/Volcano
- Oasis
- Park
- Pass
- Picnic Area
- Waterfall

## Population
- Capital (National)
- Capital (State/Province)
- City/Large Town
- Town/Village

## Transport
- Airport
- Border crossing
- Bus
- Cable car/Funicular
- Cycling
- Ferry
- Metro station
- Monorail
- Parking
- Petrol station
- Subway/Subte station
- Taxi
- Train station/Railway
- Tram
- Underground station
- Other Transport

*Note: Not all symbols displayed above appear on the maps in this book*

## Routes
- Tollway
- Freeway
- Primary
- Secondary
- Tertiary
- Lane
- Unsealed road
- Road under construction
- Plaza/Mall
- Steps
- Tunnel
- Pedestrian overpass
- Walking Tour
- Walking Tour detour
- Path/Walking Trail

## Boundaries
- International
- State/Province
- Disputed
- Regional/Suburb
- Marine Park
- Cliff
- Wall

## Hydrography
- River, Creek
- Intermittent River
- Canal
- Water
- Dry/Salt/Intermittent Lake
- Reef

## Areas
- Airport/Runway
- Beach/Desert
- Cemetery (Christian)
- Cemetery (Other)
- Glacier
- Mudflat
- Park/Forest
- Sight (Building)
- Sportsground
- Swamp/Mangrove

# OUR STORY

A beat-up old car, a few dollars in the pocket and a sense of adventure. In 1972 that's all Tony and Maureen Wheeler needed for the trip of a lifetime – across Europe and Asia overland to Australia. It took several months, and at the end – broke but inspired – they sat at their kitchen table writing and stapling together their first travel guide, *Across Asia on the Cheap*. Within a week they'd sold 1500 copies. Lonely Planet was born.

Today, Lonely Planet has offices in Franklin, London, Melbourne, Oakland, Dublin, Beijing and Delhi, with more than 600 staff and writers. We share Tony's belief that 'a great guidebook should do three things: inform, educate and amuse'.

# OUR WRITERS

### Paul Clammer

Kingston, Blue Mountains & Southeast Coast; Ocho Rios, Port Antonio & North Coast Paul Clammer has worked as a molecular biologist, tour leader and travel writer. Since 2003 he has worked as a guidebook author for Lonely Planet, contributing to over 25 Lonely Planet titles, covering swathes of South and Central Asia, West and North Africa and the Caribbean. In recent years he's lived in Morocco, Jordan, Haiti and Fiji, as well as his native England. Find him online at paulclammer.com or on Twitter as @paulclammer. Paul also researched and wrote the Plan, Understand and Survival Guide chapters.

### Anna Kaminski

Montego Bay & Northwest Coast; South Coast & Central Highlands; Negril & West Coast Having majored in Caribbean and Latin American history at university and having lived in Kingston and worked in Jamaica's prisons and ghettos in 2006, Anna was thrilled to research Jamaica for Lonely Planet a second time. On this occasion, she drove the scenic and often gnarly back roads of west Jamaica, visited numerous plantation houses, hiked through rugged Cockpit Country, attended the Maroon Festival, attended the country's second-largest reggae gig and went to Boston Bay in search of Jamaica's best jerk pork. When not on the road for Lonely Planet, Anna calls London home.

**Published by Lonely Planet Global Limited**
CRN 554153
8th edition – Oct 2017
ISBN 978 1 78657 141 0
© Lonely Planet 2017    Photographs © as indicated 2017
10 9 8 7 6 5 4 3 2 1
Printed in China